Ross Winans

One Religion: many Creeds

Ross Winans

One Religion: many Creeds

ISBN/EAN: 9783337130541

Printed in Europe, USA, Canada, Australia, Japan

Cover: Foto ©ninafisch / pixelio.de

More available books at **www.hansebooks.com**

ONE RELIGION: MANY CREEDS.

BY

ROSS WINANS.

"*I believe in God the Father Almighty, Maker of Heaven and Earth, and of all Things Visible and Invisible.*"
BOOK OF COMMON PRAYER.

SECOND EDITION.

BALTIMORE:
JOHN P. DES FORGES,
3 ST. PAUL STREET.
1870.

ENTERED, according to Act of Congress, in the year 1870, by

ROSS WINANS,

In the Clerk's Office of the District Court of Maryland.

alike benevolently intended; that the latter, though never vindictive, are never relaxed, and that both are designed by God for the sole purpose of training man to the destiny marked out for him. This training, which begins on this side of the grave, continues beyond it, and during eternity, to the end that every human being shall become more and more god-like, and capable of appreciating God's glory and rendering Him higher praise and worship.

From these remarks it will be seen that while we accept every portion of the Bible that is in accordance with the Bible written in men's hearts—or in other words, with natural religion—we repudiate all that professes to be based upon its supernatural or special inspiration.

We object to what the Church demands, an unbounded and unjustifiable confidence in the infallibility of the writings of Moses and the Prophets, and the Evangelists, and the Apostles. We dissent from a sentimental attachment to an impossible compound of God and man. We protest that Christian theology, as we have it, is not taught by God Himself, nor by Christ himself, nor is it consistent with established facts, nor is it comprehensible by our reason. We would show you that Christianity, as taught among us, is no better than other systems taught in other than Christian countries, and in some respects not so good.

These are the objects of this publication. If in the course of presenting our views, any thing should be said which may be deemed offensive or disrespectful to those who hold contrary opinions, certainly no such offence or disrespect is intended. We write under an honest conviction of the truth, and yield nothing to preconceived views. Truth is truth, and will find its way to the surface. Shrieks and lamentations over the scepticism and free-thinking of the nineteenth century will not serve the purpose of concealing it. Nor is it desirable that it should be concealed. We must believe, not what it is convenient, or comfortable, or customary to believe; but what is most in accordance with truth. Truth, and not what is called orthodoxy, should be our prime object. It is not enough, to maintain what we believe; we must believe what we maintain. Any one may bring himself to give blind assent to that which he is inclined to believe, or thinks it becoming or expedient to believe, but this is not genuine belief. It is one thing to wish to have truth on our side; and another to wish, in all sincerity, to be on the side of truth. If the conclusions, at which we arrive, have the weight of evidence in their favor, we have no alternative but to accept them and bide the results. Neither is there occasion to contemplate with uneasiness the admission of truth, or the result of being governed by it, in any matters whatsoever, and more particularly in those pertaining to religion. God did not endow us with perceptive and reasoning faculties, in order that they might be employed upon all other subjects, and remain torpid in relation to that one subject only. We hold to it, therefore, that the truth must be accepted at all hazards, even if it lead to a denial of the supernatural inspiration of Scripture and all dogmas connected therewith, which we are fully persuaded it will do.

Nor, we repeat it, need the prospect of this alarm the most timid. God, the Father, who alone governed the world from the first, governs it now, and will ever govern it. No broader foundation for the faith of all men in their eternal welfare is possible, than that laid by

God Himself when He established his never changing laws; and when He so constituted and endowed man, that under the influence and effect of such unvarying laws, he should be conducted to the happy destiny designed for him from the first. The only fear in these matters, becoming to man, is a fear lest he fail in watchfulness to guard against violations of God's laws pertaining to his being; lest he fail in any portion of his duty to God and to his fellow-creatures. All else may be implicitly left to his Maker and benefactor.

In all countries, whether civilized or uncivilized, the popular system of theology has invariably been claimed to be based on some supernatural revelation from God.

The founders or acknowledged heads of these systems have claimed, or it has been claimed for them by their followers, that they were supernaturally inspired, and miraculously and specially endowed and commissioned of God to make His will and word known to mankind. Among the persons claiming or who have been claimed, to have been so inspired and commissioned, and who have gained extensive credence in such claim, are the following: Moses, the great leader, historian, and Prophet of the Jews, fourteen or fifteen hundred years before Christ; Zoroaster, who founded the theology that prevails among the Parsees, certainly not less than twelve hundred years before Christ, Confucius, born five hundred and fifty-one years before Christ, the most eminent teacher of natural religion in the great Chinese nation; Buddha, who founded a system of worship in India, called Buddhism, five hundred years before Christ; Godama, who, also about five hundred years before Christ, founded the system of worship which now prevails in the Burmese Empire, Christ, the claimed basis of the Christian theology; and Mohammed, the founder of the Mohammedan creed.

Among the so-called sacred books embodying systems of theology and said to be derived from supernatural inspiration are the following. The Old Testament of the Jews; the Zend-Avesta of the Parsees; the Great Learning of the Chinese; the Rig Veda of the Hindoos; the Vini Pidimot of the Burmese Empire; the Christian Bible; and the Koran.

All or most of the church dogmas, legends, fables, and traditions, in relation to the miraculous conception, birth, miracles, and other pretended supernatural circumstances connected with the history of Jesus, are borrowed from— or find their counterpart in—the several systems of worship founded and practised from four to twelve centuries before his birth.

The historic part of the Bible, in relation to the creation of the world, has its counterpart also in the several systems of theology here mentioned. They all had their cosmologies based on equally good authority and equally wide of the truth, as that recorded in the Bible. This will appear hereafter, when we come to look into the history of the Ancient creeds just mentioned. The time and manner of the creation, no man has ever known, or ever will know, in this life; nor is such knowledge of importance in preparing ourselves for the life to come.

ONE RELIGION: MANY CREEDS.

I.

MAN needs no teaching to be convinced that there is a God, the creator, the sustainer, the preserver, and the governor of the universe. The idea is innate, imperative, and essential, and declares itself in the mind and conscience so soon as the human being begins to observe, to compare, and to reason. There is no one, however rude or ignorant—unless he be idiotic, or otherwise incapable of consecutive thought—who has not some notion, however vague, of this great and almighty Being. There is no one in the exercise of his intellectual faculties, who would not recognize the existence of a God as an absolute and necessary truth, even if there had been no other book to teach it, than the great book of Nature. The earth, the sea, the sun, the moon, and all the hosts of Heaven, spread out before him in their infinite beauty and majesty, each silently but eloquently and irresistibly proclaims that they have had a divine, omnipotent, eternal, and infinite cause and maker. Man has, moreover, not alone an intuitive conviction of the existence of an overruling Spirit, he is conscious that he has within himself a soul, in affinity—in a limited sense—with that great overruling Spirit.

But while all men are thus conscious not only that God is, but that God must be, and that the spirit of man bears a certain relation to Him, some men, pretending to be preternaturally and directly inspired by God to declare His will and to explain His nature and His attributes, have made assertions and propounded doctrines, at various times and among various nations, that have greatly bewildered the minds of their fellow-men. These artificial teachings and vain imaginings—whether they be called mythologies, theologies, religions, faiths, or systems of belief—contradict each other on the most vital and fundamental points. Some of them assert that there is but one God, and that He is not only spiritual, but physicial and material, having a body and organs like a man. Some have exalted human attributes, clothing humanity in beautiful or majestic forms, and have deified their own production. Some have adopted a precisely opposite course, and have invented fantastic and hideous divinities. Some deny God's personality, and teach that all Nature is the body, of which he is the animating soul. Some say that there are two Gods, one the God of good, the other the God of evil—and that the two are constantly at war with each other. Others maintain that there are three Gods, co-eternal and co-equal in power, in wisdom, and in glory, and that these three are one, and must be worshipped as one. The second person—say they—in this triune divinity stands toward the first in the relation of the Son to the Father; while the third also is a person, and proceeds from the Father and the Son. The earliest nations appear to have been taught, either that the sun—the most glorious luminary visible to the unassisted human eye—was God, or that the number of the Gods was as infinite as the manifestations of Nature. Even Abraham and Moses, who believed and taught the unity of God, attributed to this all-wise, all-just, all-good, all-knowing, and all-mighty being, the form of a man. Moses pretended to have talked with him face to face "as a man talketh with his friend," and declared that he had been permitted to see His "back parts." In the Pentateuch, and indeed throughout both the Old and New Testaments, God is described as being ignorant and short-sighted, and possessing many of the passions of the human creatures whom He Himself has made.

Creeds and modes of worship have been many and various; but there is not one of them now accepted in the world, which has not, however pure and lofty some may be in their moral teachings, promulgated and endeavored to palm upon popular credence the most astounding scientific and historical errors and untruths. Thus they have acted, to some extent, as a drag upon the intellect, and an impediment to the progress of mankind. They were written for the most part by priests of the various theologies and forms of faith which they were designed to uphold, and often with the too palpable purpose of keeping the people in ignorance and of maintaining the priesthood as a privileged class. All of them of Asiatic origin and authorship, and declared in their several countries to be the direct, infallible, unerring utterances of God, they have given currency to the most vulgar and debasing fictions, and represented God as something like an Oriental Caliph or Sultan, subject to lusts and vices and fits of cruel anger, and constantly liable to be thwarted in His designs by powers of evil whom He desired, but was not able, to destroy.

All these myths and dreams have varied in different ages and countries, according to the character of the nations which adopted and nominally believed them, and they have come down to us from an antiquity so remote, as to be impenetrable. They are partly to be traced to the most ancient civilization, the record of which has been preserved by tradition and sepulchral monuments—and notably to India, Assyria, Phœnicia, and Egypt. In their original forms these mythologies have perished—except in India and non-Mahommedan Asia, where they are still accepted by the unreasoning multitudes of half the human race.

A portion, however, of these fables, greatly modified in form and detail, was borrowed from the Egyptians, first by the Jews under Moses, and secondly by the Arabians under Mahomet. So far as the books attributed to Moses and other priests and prophets of the Hebrews, are concerned, these fables are held forth to this day as grounds for belief and guides for conduct to all the so-called Christian nations of the world. We, as Christians—according to the common acceptation of the term—and sharers in the advancing civilization of the nineteenth century, are mainly interested in the theology and doctrines of Moses and Jesus. All other systems of belief, except natural religion, which is universal, being accepted of all men in all places, modern civilization has agreed to condemn. Even the most devout Christian laughs at the grotesque stories, and speaks with contemptuous pity of the superstitious absurdities of all mythologies except his own. But let his own rules of criticism be applied to the Old and New Testament, and it will immediately be condemned as heretical; and the critic himself will be accused of impiety and infidelity. This very state of things prevails in Asia, where the teachings of Moses and Christ receive as little respect from the priests of Oriental theologies, as Christians bestow upon the myths of the Hindoos, or the nihilism improperly attributed to the Buddhists.

Up to the birth of Jesus, the Jews had their cosmogony and theology entirely to themselves. The outer world knew nothing of their sacred books; and, indeed, only knew the Jews themselves as a small and peculiar people, in whom there was nothing to esteem or imitate. No one challenged their doctrine, for the reason that no one understood or cared anything about it. Whatever schism or difference of opinion may have existed among them, in their own little country, was on minor matters, and Moses and the Prophets seemingly reigned supreme. But a different state of things was about to prevail. Jesus, known during his life as the son of a carpenter, and claiming direct royal descent from David and Solomon, challenged the truth of this ancient system, and became a most conspicuous reformer. He protested chiefly against the superstitious ceremonies of the Mosaic ritual. His protest was indeed partial, though, as far as it went, strong and decided. It was a very important movement towards separating that which was claimed to be religion, from that which was and is really religion—between that which causes contention, and that which all agree upon.

But very little progress had been made amongst the Jews in the arts and sciences—indeed very little was made for a long time after the introduction of Christianity. The printing press, that grand medium for the dissemination of knowledge, is comparatively a modern invention, not having been introduced until the middle of the fifteenth century. There were no microscopes to reveal to the delighted intellect of man the wonders that lie concealed in apparent nothingness—no telescopes to unveil to him the countless worlds and planetary systems which, but for it, never would have been discovered. The law of gravitation—that universal, infinite, governing power, by which the whole universe is sustained—was unsuspected. Electricity, known probably to some extent, was employed only in tricks and artifices to startle and surprise those who were ignorant of its effects. The science of Geology was very imperfect. Astrology was far more esteemed than Astronomy. The earth was thought by all nations to be the centre of the universe. The sun was looked upon as nothing more than a lamp hung in the heavens to give light to this superior orb. Indeed it was not even known to be an orb; the idea prevailed, that it was a vast extended plane without visible limits.

Under these circumstances, Jesus could make no protest against the Mosaic history or tradition. He was necessarily compelled to accept these as he found them. Rejecting the Mosaic notion of the character and attributes of God, he earnestly protested against the doctrine that the Deity, whose gospel he preached, was a God of hatred or anger, or subject to the passions or imperfections of humanity. He loudly proclaimed in the highways and the byways, and to all descriptions of people—but chiefly to the poor and the unhappy—that God is a God of Love, a Spirit to be worshipped in spirit and in truth, a God who demands of His creatures no vain observances, no heavy burdens of ceremonials, but a cheerful, happy enjoyment of life, provided they keep within the limits of the divine laws, which are neither galling nor heavy, but easy, light, and good. He adopted so much of the ten commandments as accords with natural religion. He very wisely rejected all that does not teach the two great duties, love to God and love to man. "If thou wilt enter into life," said he to one who already professed to be performing this part of his duty, "keep the commandments: Thou shalt do no murder; thou shalt not commit adultery; thou shalt not steal; thou shalt not bear false witness; honor thy father and thy mother; and, thou shalt love thy neighbor as thyself." To the lawyer also who asked him a question, tempting him, and saying, "Master, which is the great commandment in the law?" Jesus replied, "Thou shalt love the Lord thy God with all thy heart, and with all thy soul, and with all thy mind. This is the first and great commandment. And the second is like unto it. Thou shalt love thy neighbor as thyself." He thus reduced the detail of the code, leaving in it all that he considered essential, and summing it up in the two general duties pertaining to God and man. It may be noticed in passing, that he struck out altogether the commandment that pertains to the Sabbath day, the violation of which Moses, with a bloodthirstiness peculiar to the early Jews, considered more of a crime against God than any other. In fact, he considered it the great crime of all others, and visited upon him who should dare to break it, the penalty of death. In this matter, the Christian Church of our day sets Moses above Christ, since notwithstanding the abrogation of the law by Jesus, his professed disciples still adhere to it, and look upon the breach of it as one of the most heinous sins that can be committed.

The result of the enlightened protestantism of Jesus was his death upon the cross. He became a martyr to divine truth. But he left a noble legacy to his Apostles, and to the world, in his advocacy of the sublime teachings of natural religion. In discarding all theology and all dogmas, he cleared away much of the mist and fog that enshrouded religion, and made himself a benefactor to his race. But, unfortunately, his disciples were not only Jews, they were prejudiced in favor of Jewish observances. The leaven of their original faith fermented in their minds, and was too strongly at work to permit them to follow their Master in the divine simplicity of his early teaching. They accepted the historic and scientific record of Moses, erroneous as it was, because nothing in disproof had been brought to bear against it—whereas the Church of our day maintains its dogmas, in the face of scientifically established truths. The ancient religion was miraculous; so also should that be which was advocated by Jesus. And therefore, by degrees, they and their successors engrafted a mythology upon the religion which Jesus advocated, having no warrant whatever, in the words or deeds of their Master. We cannot tell at what exact period after his death were concocted the many marvellous stories related of him, such as that of his supernatural birth; of the visit of the wise men from the East, led to his cradle by a star; of his having been begotten by the Holy Ghost, and of the consequent abandonment of the pretension set up as to his royal descent from David and Solomon; of his miracles; and of his resurrection on the third day after his crucifixion. It is, we say, difficult, and all but impossible, to discover when these fables were intermingled with the ordinary human portion of the narrative of his life and teachings. As to their being found in the four Gospels now held to be canonical, that is no warrant of their authenticity. These four Gospels form but a small portion of the "Gospels" that were in possession of the Christians of the third and fourth centuries; nor is there any absolute and satisfactory proof that they were ever written by the persons whose names they bear, and that they passed, unaltered, from generation to generation through the hands of honest custodians and faithful transcribers. Indeed it appears that at the Council of Laodicea, A. D. 363, there were two hundred varied versions of the adopted Evangelists, and fifty-four several Gospels, all differing essentially from each other, and each purporting to be a true account of Jesus. From these our four Gospels were selected. But it must be borne in mind, that the present Gospels are not originals, but taken from copies of the sixth century, which in turn were taken from some other unknown copies. There are no copies in existence, bearing a date nearer than five hundred years to the time of Jesus.

And this question of the origin and authenticity of the Scriptures appears to have been a grave matter of doubt in the Christian Church. Nearly twelve hundred years after the meeting of the Council at Laodicea, that is A. D. 1545, another Council assembled at Trent and decided and ordered what was and what was not genuine. It is not pretended, we believe, that the prelates who composed this Council were themselves inspired by the Holy Ghost. Nevertheless, being fallible men, they dealt in summary fashion with spiritual affairs, and declared that their own infallibility was beyond doubt. The first named conclave having made its selection of the four Gospels, this one picked out a special version of the Bible, termed the Vulgate, and pronounced it the only true one; made the Apocrypha an integral part of it; proclaimed that the Church alone was at liberty to interpret whatever might be doubtful; and added the extraordinary edict, that tradition was to be, equally with the Bible, a rule of faith. Under this rule was comprised that incomprehensible and much-disputed doctrine of the Trinity, which is now held to be essential to man's salvation, although no warrant for it can be found in the Christian's text book, the Bible. Its reception as an indispensable part of the creed had been disputed with the acrimony that distinguishes all combatants for faith of man's invention, as the records of other famous ecclesiastical Councils show—notably that of Nice, A. D. 325. Its worth, however, and its binding character, ought not to be much enhanced, even in the view of Christians themselves, by remembrance of the fact, that at least three centuries elapsed after Jesus' death, before the Trinity obtained a hold upon the worshippers of his name. But Councils were omnipotent—as witness the second one at Nice, A. D. 787, that declared the worship of images and of the cross to be sanctioned by the Holy Scriptures.

These astounding assumptions of irresponsible and infallible power, by men pretending to deal with divine things, would be deemed impious and disgusting, if time and habit and the artful management of the priesthood had not tended to make men impervious to historical truth and logical argument. We ask then with reference to the Scriptures, whether, if a similar claim of divine origin and unquestionable authenticity were put forward on behalf of the sacred books of any other sect which Christians agree in condemning they would be accepted as aught else than fiction. Take, for example, Matthew's story of the great convulsion of nature at the crucifixion, when the earth is said to have been shaken and many bodies of the Saints to have risen from their graves and appeared unto many. Such a story could scarcely have been told in the hearing of any one whether Jew or Roman, who had been a contemporary of Jesus; and it has no place in Roman or Jewish history. Again, as to the slaughter of all the male infants of Judea, in order that the youthful Christ might be destroyed, commonly called the Massacre of the Innocents, what corroborative evidence have we of any such act of atrocity having been committed by Herod? If Herod was chargeable with such an act of barbarity, it cannot be doubted that Josephus would have made some mention of it. But his very silence is the best evidence we could have to the contrary. He fills thirty-seven chapters with the history of Herod, and has treated minutely of all the principal cruelties for which he is responsible; but of this special massacre he makes no mention. Philo, also, who lived at the time, and the Rabbins who were assiduous to blacken Herod's memory, give not the slightest hint of so monstrous a decree. Indeed we find that the three Evangelists, Mark, Luke, and John, agree with the historians of those times, in their total silence on this subject. It is, however, a curious and most noteworthy coincidence, that in the sacred writings of the Hindoos there is a similar story related of the tyrant Kanga, in connection with the birth of the Hindoo god, Crishna. Sir William Jones bears testimony to the remarkable similarity that exists between Crishna's life and actions and the life and actions of Jesus, declaring expressly that it is impossible to deny it. He says that Crishna's name and the general traditions concerning him were extant long anterior to the birth of Jesus, and probably anterior also to the time of Homer. The celebrated poem *Bhagavat*, which contains an account of Crishna's life, is filled with a narrative of the most extraordinary kind. The incarnate Deity was cradled among herdsmen or shepherds. A tyrant, at the time of his birth, ordered all new-born males to be slain; and yet this new-born babe was preserved in the most wonderful manner. He performed amazing miracles in his infancy, and at the age of seven years held up a mountain on the tip of his finger; he saved multitudes by his miraculous powers; and he raised the dead. But he was the meekest and mildest of created beings; he washed the feet of the Brahmins, and preached very nobly and sublimely. He was pure, and chaste, and benevolent, and tender.

Again, to show how prone the popular imagination of the ancients was to fictions of this kind, we borrow some illustrations from the pages of Strauss. He points out that the life of a child destined for great objects, who is endangered and miraculously preserved, is one of the fundamental themes of all heroic legends, and found recurring in those of the Hebrews, the Persians, and the Romans. To say nothing of the dangers which threatened the life of Zeus, or of Hercules, and of the mode in which they were averted, something similar occurs in the histories of the infancy of Moses, in the Pentateuch—of Isaac, in a later Jewish legend—of Cyrus, in Herodotus—of Romulus, in Livy—of the childhood of the first Roman Emperor, according to Suetonius, himself living in the century that saw the birth and death of Jesus—and then in that of the Christian Messiah, in the Gospel of Matthew. The idea is carried out in all these instances in a manner so similar, that it is impossible to doubt the influence of one legend upon the other, or to overlook the common psychological source of all. This

PSYCHOLOGICAL SOURCE OF THESE LEGENDS. 13

source is that peculiar propensity, which leads men to make the value of a good or great man the more sensibly felt, by setting forth on one side the near approach of his possible loss, and on the other the care of Providence for his preservation. The combined influence of the two—that is to say, the inherent desire to enhance the value of what was esteemed, and the multiplicity of the examples around—may well account for these fables of imminent danger and supernatural protection, as introduced into the life of Jesus.

In the record of the infancy of Jesus, the mode in which the danger is brought about is also peculiar. The cause of it is a Star, which appears in Heaven and guides certain Eastern Magi to Jerusalem, where their enquiries after the new born King of the Jews attract the attention of Herod the Great. Thus the Star appears as the means of the endangerment of Jesus' life. Still, this portion of the legend had an object of its own. There is a belief reaching from remote antiquity even to our own times, that new appearances of stars, particularly comets, coming unexpectedly and vanishing again, prognosticate revolutions in human affairs, and the birth and death of great men. Men start from the supposition, that so striking a phenomenon in the Heavens must have, corresponding to it, a similar one on earth, affecting mankind. Thus, when an historical event happens, which it is wished particularly to distinguish, some extraordinary natural phenomenon, that never took place, is invented to chime in with it. Thus we read in Rubeni, a rabbinical author, that at the moment of Abraham's birth, a star stood in the East, which swallowed up four other stars, each appearing in one of the four quarters of the Heavens. Justin also tells another of these fictitious tales about Mithridates, to the effect that in the year in which he was born, and in that of his accession, a comet appeared, and continued visible on each occasion for four hours during every day, and for seventy successive days. It was of so large a size, and so bright, that it occupied a quarter of the sky, and outshone the brightness of the sun. Before the birth of Augustus, it was said to have been prognosticated at Rome, by a prodigy, that Nature was pregnant of a King for the Roman people. According to Jewish writings, the account of the peril which threatened the life of the Lawgiver, had its parallel also in the history of the Patriarch of the nation. In this case Pharoah is Nimrod. In one account, Nimrod sees a star in a dream; this star, according to the other account, actually appears in the sky, and his sages explain it to him to mean that a son is at that moment born to Tharah, from whom shall come a mighty nation destined to inherit the present and the future world. Observe also that when, at length, the same embellishment had been introduced into the history of the infancy of Jesus, it was introduced into the history of the infancy of John the Baptist, who, having been endangered by the massacre at Bethlehem, was also said to have been preserved by a miracle.

Now, in the legends of Cyrus, Romulus and Abraham, the tyrants give special orders for murdering only the children who are pointed out as dangerous to them. The narratives concerning Moses, Augustus, and Jesus, resemble each other in this—that the potentates seek to catch the destined infant, who is unknown to them personally, in a wide net, together with others. The story, then, in relation to the wholesale massacre by Herod, is totally unworthy of credence or historical consideration, as before

INCREDIBLE STATEMENTS OF OLD TESTAMENT. 15

remarked. Neither will it stand the test of criticism, when considered in relation to the justice and omniscience of the Almighty: for if God specially interposed to blind the mind of Herod by suggesting to the Magi that they should not return to Jerusalem to notify him of the circumstances, why did He not inspire them to proceed, in the first instance, direct to Bethlehem? Herod would thus have been in ignorance of the child's existence, and this cruel and unnecessary massacre would have been entirely avoided—that is, if it ever occurred.

The date, when these fables were introduced into the New Testament, is not of much importance, even if it were possible to discover it. We know, however, that the early Christians not only accepted the mythology of Moses, but that they superadded a mythology of their own, of which these extraordinary stories form a part, and that the result of the union was a system of theology or belief, in which the teachings of Moses and the Apostles and Jesus were blended, and for upwards of fourteen hundred years—not improperly called the "Dark Ages,"—were taught and accepted as a part and parcel of Christianity. No one, during these dark ages, was allowed to separate the history and the mythology from the doctrine. They were denied the liberty of rejecting the one and accepting the other, under the severest penalties in this world, and the threat of eternal damnation in the next. He who accepted the doctrines of Christianity was compelled also to accept, or pretend so to do, the most senseless fables and theories that were presented to him, or be anathematized. He was required to believe the most incredible statements; among them, that this earth, together with the planetary system of which it is a member, was created only about four thousand years before the birth of Jesus. Even as late as toward the end of the fifteenth century Columbus, the discoverer of this continent, was excommunicated and branded as a heretic, by one of the boasted successors of St. Peter, for advancing the theory that the earth is spherical, in opposition to the idea that it is a mere extended plane.

It was also incumbent that he should believe a thousand other absurdities; that the Sun revolved round the Earth; that God dwells in a local habitation, a place called Heaven, and the Devil in a place called Hell; that God made a man and a woman, and placed them in a garden, intending that they and their progeny should live forever in this world—happy, innocent, naked, and having nothing to do; that in this purpose, however, God was thwarted by Satan, or the Devil, who, in the form of a serpent, persuaded the woman to eat of the fruit of a tree called the Tree of Knowledge, of which God had forbidden them to eat, under penalty of death; that they did eat, and that they fell from their state of innocence, happiness and nudity; that God, offended at their disobedience, drove them out of the garden, imposed labor upon them as a curse, and taught them the use of clothes; that the first two men, born of this original pair, quarrelled because God was better pleased to accept a sacrifice of fat cattle roasted with fire upon an altar, from Abel, than a bloodless offering of herbs and fruits from Cain, and that Cain, therefore, slew his brother in a fit of anger; that the race of men, born of Adam and Eve, becoming utterly corrupt and wicked, God repented that he had made such ungrateful and abominable creatures, and resolved to drown the whole race of men, as well as the beasts of the field and the fowls of the air, which had not offended Him; that He spared but one man and his family saved in an ark, together with a single pair of all created animals and birds; that the progeny of these miraculously preserved men and women afterwards divided the earth among themselves, but were in no degree better than the progeny of Adam and Eve, and continually vexed the Almighty, and stirred Him to fierce wrath by their fearful wickedness; that a man named Nimrod, a great king and hunter, conceived the idea that Heaven, the abode of God was just above or in the clouds, and not more difficult of access than the tops of the highest mountains, and that he could build a tower to reach to God's throne; that God, apprehensive that he might succeed in the attempt, defeated his sacrilegious purpose by confounding the language of the men who wrought upon it, so that they could not understand each other, and had to desist from their labors—whereas all that was necessary to be done was to leave Nimrod and the ignorant work-people alone, until their means and patience were exhausted; that God chose the Jews for his peculiar people out of His mere grace and favor, and for no good that they had ever done; but that Moses never could make the Jews understand who God was, or in what respect He was wiser than, or superior to, the pretended gods of neighboring nations; that this people was enslaved by the Egyptians, remained in slavery for several hundred years, and were miraculously freed from bondage after God had caused the death of all the first born male children of Egypt, and afflicted the land and the people with innumerable plagues—not on account of the sins of the Egyptians, but solely on account of the stubbornness of Pharaoh, their king, who as often as he relented had his heart hardened by God, Himself, in order that he might be further plagued and punished; that the Jews, when they had established themselves in Canaan, by the massacre of the original possessors of the land, grew weary of a priestly government, and demanded to have a king, like their neighbors; that God endeavored, but in vain, to dissuade them from their purpose, and, yielding at last to their importunity, chose a king for them in the person of Saul, for no other recorded reason, than that he was taller, by the head and shoulders, than any of his people; that Saul reigned indifferently well over the Jews, but offended God past all hope of forgiveness, because he was more merciful than his Maker, and would not, after he had conquered and overthrown his enemies in fair battle, rip up the bellies of women with child, put all the children, male and female, to the sword, and destroy all their horses, oxen, sheep, and other cattle; that Joshua made the sun to stand still at his bidding—an event which, if it could have occurred, would have reduced the solar system to chaos. All these and many other stories, which it is needless to recapitulate—evidently mythological, and many of them allegorical—Christianity now, as then, requires to be literally accepted as positively and divinely true, under penalty of all the plethora of curses, temporal and eternal, that angry priestcraft can pronounce.

And the mythology of the New Testament is imposed as ruthlessly upon the believer as that of the Old. Indeed the former was engrafted upon the latter; and both must be accepted, without question or hesitation, as equally true. As man had fallen under Adam, he was to be lifted up under Jesus; but as God required a sacrifice before He could forgive the human race for the transgression of Adam and Eve, Jesus—being himself God— offered himself a sacrifice to his Father, who was also

God—though there was but one God—and the sacrifice was accepted. As an evidence of this, it is asserted that when he died upon the cross all nature was convulsed by the event; the earth upheaved, and the dead rose out of their graves and walked through the streets, in sight of the awe-stricken multitudes. This was a marvel and a mystery, which no human being could understand; but it was to be received as a dogma and an article of faith—without believing in which, no one could enjoy the benefit of the transcendent sacrifice, or live in the next world, except in fire and brimstone and eternal torment. For the purpose of teaching the new theology and of performing this sacrifice, God, in the person of the man Jesus, came into the world and wrought many miracles to convince the people of the divinity alike of his character and mission. But so also was it claimed by and for Godama, who founded the theological system which now prevails in the Burmese Empire. "I, a God," said he, "having departed out of this world will preserve my laws and my disciples in it for the space of five thousand years." Again, the people of Judea believed that the diseases of the human body were to a great extent due to the agency of devils—the number of the devils being infinite—and that they entered corporeally into the blood, the bones, the brain, and the intestines, of epileptics, cataleptics, apoplectics, lepers, lunatics, maniacs, and other unhappy persons afflicted with bodily or mental disorders. As Jesus was represented in the new mythology as casting out devils by an effort of his volition, and sometimes as speaking to them while in the bodies of tormented persons, and ordering them to come out, the Christians of the Dark Ages were of necessity taught to believe that such devils really existed, and that diseases were the results of their agency, rather than of natural or hereditary causes, or of the contravention of the laws of health by the afflicted persons themselves. The early Christians were also taught to believe that the arch-devil—the lord and king of all these minor devils, the Satan and Beelzebub of the Jews, the Ahrimanes of the Persians, the Lucifer of the poets—ignorant of the fact that Jesus was God, and believing that he was only an able and ambitious man, took him up into a high mountain and showed him all the kingdoms of the world—which he could not have done from the top of any mountain, however lofty—and promised him dominion over them, on the sole condition that he, who was God, should kneel down and worship him, who was Devil; that Jesus, without making himself known to him, refused the offer, saying, "Get thee behind me Satan, thou art an offense unto me." Moreover, they were required to believe that Jesus raised the dead from the grave; walked upon the waters of the sea; stilled the raging of the tempest, by a motion of his hand or word of his mouth; fed thousands of people, once with five, and once with seven loaves of bread and a few small fishes—the unconsumed remnants of both, after the multitude had freely partaken, being immensely greater than the original bulk of the articles provided; and that he performed other miracles, all of which were of a beneficent, but more or less startling character, according to the circumstances. But the most remarkable thing is that, notwithstanding he is said to have performed such wonderful things as we have enumerated, he never succeeded in persuading either the Romans or the Jewish people, or the many thousands who witnessed them, or even his own immediate followers and disciples, that his mission was to introduce a new and spiritual religion, or that he was indeed God, or the son of God, in any other sense than that in which all men are God's children. This is a most significant fact; and a fact it must be acknowledged by the Christian Church, inasmuch as it is borne out by the Scriptures themselves. The indifference of the Romans is shown in Pilate's washing his hands of Christ's blood, and in the temperate dealings of Festus and Agrippa with Paul. How Christ impressed the leading Jews is proved by the manner in which they persecuted him and put him to death. What the multitudes thought of him may be gathered from the reiterated testimony of the Evangelists, to the effect that the people "understood not his sayings," that they "marvelled greatly," that they were "astonished at his doctrine," that they were "very attentive to hear him," and that the fullest extent of their conviction went no farther than this: "they rejoiced at all the glorious things that were done by him." It is nowhere recorded that they looked upon him as the veritable son of God, co-equal with God, and voluntarily sacrificing himself as an expiation for Adam's original sin—nor did he claim this himself. As to the immediate contemporaries, followers, and intimate attendants upon Christ, it is only needful to remind the reader of what happened, when all his personal influence and all the effect of his whole career culminated, in his final interview with the eleven disciples, after his resurrection. St. Mark says, that he upbraided them for their unbelief and hardness of heart. Yet St. Matthew says, with a candor that is absolutely killing—in reference also to Jesus' last intercourse with those favored individuals— "but some doubted!" The disciples, therefore, in the presence of their risen Master, were very far from exhibiting an implicit and unreserved faith, at the moment of all others when they should have experienced it to the innermost core. What, we ask, has the Church done, to make belief in all these stories acceptable to us in these days, when we find them less and less able to bear the test of calm and critical examination?

It was only after Christ's death that Christianity, under a new phase, began to develop itself and to dispossess the previously existing paganism of the Roman Empire. Then it was that the Priests and the Popes, who had charge of the new doctrine, arrogated to themselves and to their "Saints," both living and dead, the miraculous and supernatural powers which they at first claimed only for their divine Master. A new series of wonders was invented suitable for the credulous and ignorant multitudes. These found ready credence in an age when Kings and Emperors could not even read or write; indeed, when there were no books, and but very few accessible manuscripts; and when the mass of mankind were sunk in the deepest mental darkness—impenetrable even to such rays of light as gleamed and flashed from the lustrous learning and eloquence of the Greek and Roman philosophers. Knowledge was trodden down by the furious wars that followed the fall of the Roman Empire. What little remained of it the priests possessed, and used—as priests invariably do—to enslave the intellect of the people. And thus, in process of time, a third mythology was superadded to the mythology of the Pentateuch and the Four Gospels, fully as marvellous and as contrary to the laws of Nature and to all human experience, as its predecessors. In this mythology, Mary,—"the Mother of God"—is raised to the divine rank of Queen of Heaven, and plays a most conspicuous part in the Church which bears the name of her Son. In fact, it is said that she enacts wonders more wonderful than any attributed to him. She condescends to enter into images and statues carved in her honor; and, as an incontrovertible evidence of her presence therein, she makes them wink their eyes, and shed real tears over the agonies of those penitents who supplicate her mercy and her mediation with her blessed Son. Her pictures, too, worked miraculous cures on the deaf, the dumb, and the blind, provided they were touched in a properly reverential and confiding spirit. She appears visibly to the eyes of men and women, and promises her intercession with her Son in Heaven, for the forgiveness of all who truly believe in herself and in him. Nor this alone; the relics of real or supposed saints and martyrs are also endowed with virtue to heal diseases. Nay, even pieces of the wood of the cross on which Jesus had suffered— that was supposed to have been discovered in a heap of ancient and indistinguishable rubbish in the Golgotha of Jerusalem, through the pious agencies of the Empress Helena, more than three hundred years after the crucifixion—were also endowed with similar powers and attributes of divinity. Mr. Charles Mackay, in his *Memoirs of Extraordinary Popular Delusions*, says that it is among "the traditions of the Romish Church that the Empress Helen, the mother of Constantine the Great, first discovered the veritable 'true Cross,' in her pilgrimage to Jerusalem. The Emperor Theodosius made a present of the greater part of it to St. Ambrose, Bishop of Milan, by whom it was studded with precious stones, and deposited in the principal church of that city. It was carried away by the Huns, by whom it was burnt after they had extracted the valuable jewels it contained. Fragments purporting to have been cut from it were, in the eleventh and twelfth centuries, to be found in almost every church in Europe, and would, if collected together in one place, have been almost sufficient to have built a cathedral. Happy was the sinner who could get a sight of one of them; happier he who possessed one. To obtain them, the greatest dangers were cheerfully braved. They were thought to preserve from all evils, and to cure the most inveterate diseases. Annual pilgrimages were made to the shrines that contained them, and considerable revenues were collected from the devotees." Tears of Jesus, of the Virgin Mary, of John the beloved disciple, and even of Peter, who denied his Master when he fell into trouble and suspicion, were also discovered in Judea, where they had been divinely and miraculously preserved for centuries, and brought to Europe at the time of the Crusades. They were kept in churches and cathedrals—to be exhibited on great occasions, and when there was any chance of making money by the exhibition or sale of them to the faithful. For, be it observed, the laws of evaporation and absorption must, ever since they were shed, have been miraculously suspended. These tears work supernatural cures, too, when enshrined in little glass beads and worn on the bosom, or even if the beads that contain them are held in the hand or pressed to the lips of the devout Christian. But to continue. The nails with which the hands and feet of Jesus were pierced to fasten him on the cross, and even the thorns of the crown with which he was mockingly arrayed by his persecutors, found their way to Europe in large quantities. It has been alleged by historians that there was iron enough in all these nails, if collected and thrown into the furnace, to have made a thousand ploughshares. And yet each nail was supposed to be divinely endowed with the power of working miracles, to prove the truth of the Christian doctrine !

But while this new mythology was growing and expanding and exercising its pernicious sway over the intellect of men—and especially of women, who are always the greatest upholders of the churches, in all parts of the world and in all ages—the printing press came into operation. By its influence in stimulating men to increased mental and physical activity, and facilitating the operation of many minds one upon another for the good of the whole, it aimed a heavy blow at superstition and priestcraft. From that era and from that invention went forth an impetus in the affairs of mankind, a rapidity of advancement in the arts, sciences, and civilization, unprecedented in the history of the world, ensuring a far more splendid inheritance to those who come after us, than that to which we have ourselves succeeded. One of its first results was the multiplication of copies of the Old and New Testaments, which were translated into the English, German, French, and other European languages, and placed for the first time in the hands of other people than the clergy. A second result was the growth of a conviction that the new mythology of the Romish priesthood, that had grown up in the Dark Ages, was an excrescence upon Christianity, formed no part of its spirit or teaching, and was not to be believed or accepted as truth. Many men came to the conclusion that the first two mythologies—those of Moses and the Gospels—were quite sufficient for belief, and were to be accepted on account of their venerable antiquity. They rejected the Third mythology, and made up their minds that its miracles—performed by winking Virgins, pieces of the True Cross, and toe-nails of the Saints, were no miracles at all, but cheats, shams, and impostures, only invented to prop up an ecclesiastical system which had degenerated into a trade—to impose and prey upon the less gifted and cultivated—and to perpetuate the physical power and intellectual domination of the priesthood. The prevalence of free thought increased in an advancing ratio; and about this time, what is termed the Reformation took place. The protest on this occasion was strong as far as it went; but it was partial and incomplete. It protested again the truth of the modern,—not of the ancient miracles; against the Pope—not against the historical and scientific falsehoods and errors, inherited by him and his predecessors from the original Christians, or by the original Christians from the so-called sacred Books ascribed to Moses and the Evangelists. The Protestantism of that dawning day protested against all doctrine but that contained in the BOOK, and built up a new idol, a new divinity, a new God, in the shape of the BIBLE, which they set on high in the face of men, to be worshipped by all who would escape eternal perdition. It rejected one-third of a false system, and took the other two-thirds to its heart, and enshrined them there as infallible, unerring, perpetual, and divine. Yet this partial protest was of inestimable value to future generations. It was the thin end of the wedge introduced into the hard block of superstition. He who protests a little to-day may protest a great deal to-morrow. The very fact of a protest amounts to a declaration of independence in thought; and Protestantism—as soon as it had begun to protest—deprived itself of the power of saying to any clearer-sighted, better informed, and more courageous protestant than itself: "Thus far shalt thou protest, and no farther!" This was a mighty advantage; and the Romish Church, with the keen instinct of self-preservation, felt and knew it to be so, and waged war to the death against the bold, democratic, and innovating movement that threatened to hurl it from its throne.

The disciples of the reformed faith, as cheerfully as the earlier Christians of the days of St. Paul and St. Peter, went to the block and the stake, to seal with blood their belief in the conscientious protest which they had made. Meanwhile the great printing press was busily at work. Every succeeding year gave it new power for good and an increased momentum in well-doing. The priests were no longer the sole depositories of learning. The outer world penetrated into all the pretended holy mysteries of the clergy. The intellect of mankind was liberated; and no longer confining itself to questions of Theology, as in the Dark Ages, grappled bravely with Mechanics, Physics, Optics, Astronomy, Chemistry—all the Arts and Sciences —and became, under this active exercise, too vigorous and penetrating to be longer held under the domination of priestcraft. The cheat was detected; spurious teaching and doctrines began to be thrown overboard as useless lumber, or clogs to that true religion which is founded on the real Bible, or Book of God, the true revelation of the Creator, to be read in His works, terrestrial and celestial, and in His impress upon man—and not in the writings of ignorant and erring, though possibly well-meaning, men. The law of Gravitation suspected by Dante, and Shakespeare, and perhaps others, but only reduced to a formula and a proof positive by Newton—the earlier invention of the Telescope, and the later invention of the Microscope— the discovery of the eternal and sublime forces sometimes called Galvanism, Magnetism, and Electricity—all these things worked together for the exposition to mankind of a thousand unsuspected truths of the divine government of the world, whereof the theologies and mythologies had never dreamed. All of these were consistent with each other, but inconsistent with the truth of the theologies and mythologies, however seemingly sacred in the estimation of mankind the latter might be.

These discoveries, these teachings, these expositions, these promulgations, continued during the seventeenth, eighteenth, and nineteenth centuries, without producing any very obvious effect upon the mythological Christianity, based upon the fables of the Old and New Testaments. The mass of professing Protestants accepted the new facts, but gave themselves no trouble to reconcile them with the old traditions. Nevertheless, the spirit of enquiry which was so busily at work had, and could not but have, its effect upon the intellect of the generations that were growing up in the light of these discoveries; and a spirit of what is called "Infidelity" pervaded the upper and educated classes. Infidelity is an easy word. To the Mahommedans, all Christians are infidels. To Christians, all Mahommedans, Jews, Buddhists, Parsees, and believers in Mumbo Jumbo, are equally "infidels." Infidelity is no reproach. The various theologies, intermingled with what is true in worship, in different quarters of the world, are the creatures of circumstance, rather than of pure, unmitigated, and conscientious belief. If Martin Luther had been born in China or Japan, he would not have been a champion of Protestant Christianity. If Mahommed had been born in Scandinavia where Odin was worshipped, he might have established a new and peculiar theology; but it would not have been such a one as that which now goes under his name. In this sense, the stigma of "Infidelity," affixed by one class who think for themselves in religious matters, upon others who think with quite as much if not more learning and earnestness to back them, is but an idle word. It is more despicable than an idle word, when applied to those who worship God after the dictates of their own hearts and consciences, believing that love to God and good works constitute the whole duty of man. The Church may vent its anathemas ever so vehemently, now as heretofore; yet let it not close its eyes to the fact, that this religion has so deep a root in men's natures, that it will ere long disperse the cloud of theology with which the Church has endeavored to overshadow it. In fact it has already done so to a much larger extent than appears on the surface, among the learned, scientific, thinking, and reasoning men of our country. Nor will it long be confined to the learned and scientific; while,.as for the thinking and reasoning classes—with the avenues of knowledge now opening to them, they will soon become the majority, and will then not hesitate to declare themselves openly in favor of the first and only religion.

Indeed its influence has spread even to the clergy themselves. Even their minds, usurped as they are in most instances by the prejudices of education and the emoluments of their profession, are very much expanded by the developments of scientific investigation, acting upon and co-operating with their own innate consciousness of truth. The effect is, that while they do not preach with the enthusiasm of olden times on such subjects as eternal punishment, the personality, power, and influence of the devil, man's total degeneracy, the vengeance of the Almighty, and so forth—those of them, who do not drawl out their common-place sermons as if they neither themselves believed them nor intended others to believe them, are a little more rational in their course.

If they are not bold enough to enunciate principles directly in accordance with natural truths, they tread lightly on the subject, and confine themselves to such themes as will enable them to make a compromise with scientific developments. The reign of terror, which the pulpit once exercised, has departed—Ichabod is written upon it. It has a rival in the press, which now occupies the intellectual throne, and has things to say, whereto the pulpit must succumb. And whenever the two come in conflict, it is not the pulpit that is finally appealed to, as it once was. It is the judgment of public opinion through this potent medium, the press, that obtains the mastery.

Internal dissensions, too, are vastly weakening to the cause of dogmatic Christianity. Sects are everywhere multiplied, and are multiplying; but theology is neither strengthened nor increased thereby. In fact, it loses ground every time there is a split made in it. This is as though another blow were struck upon the wedge introduced into the block of error. It is an addition to the force that is destined to rive theology asunder and beat it into fragments, so that it may be ground into powder and scattered to the four winds. It is its own destruction—not the destruction merely of one of its parts, because every sect, however much it may differ from or denounce its rival, derives its authority from Moses or the Gospels. Even Mormonism, the last gasping effort of modern civilization to establish a religion upon the Bible, finds a sufficient justification for polygamy in the practice of Abraham and the Jewish patriarchs, who—therein declared to be not only the true servants of God, but most favored by Him—are the very men that most indulged in it. The great majority of those, who accept

Christianity, consists of the poor. They go to church and hear it announced that it is to them that the Gospel is preached, and that it is easier for a camel to go through the eye of a needle than for a rich man to enter into the kingdom of Heaven. They are told that Heaven is a place where the poor of this world are recompensed for their poverty and misery—a place wherein they themselves will be rich and powerful, wherein they will wear white robes and golden crowns, and whence they will be graciously permitted to look down with the greatest complacency—not altogether unmixed with human or even with inhuman satisfaction—upon the misery of those Dives in Hell, who did not give them all they had in this world, now in vain asking them for a drop of water to cool their burning tongues. Of this class we say the Church is largely made up, because of the encouragement and consolation they derive or imagine they derive from the above description of teaching. Others go to church for fashion's sake, recreation, excitement, and novelty—in short, more to see than to hear, and to be amused by the priest flaunting before their eyes his embroidered garments, the frippery of stole and vestment, and all the paraphernalia of ecclesiastical millinery. In Roman Catholic countries the churches are left almost wholly to the women; in Protestant countries a minority of men still attend, but mostly as a duty enforced by custom and fashion, or with the hope of being entertained if the preacher be what is called a popular one. If not, and they think it adds to their respectability, they go and listen with what insomnolency they can to an uninteresting discourse, which tells them nothing they did not know before, and too much that flatly contradicts the pure truths of science and common-sense facts. But this state of things must soon fall into decay. Indeed we find that even those, who are in high places and receiving large emoluments from the ecclesiastical system to which they are attached, are dropping off, one by one, from the decaying old tree that has supplied them with shelter and support, and are coming out boldly in defence of the right. Their reason becomes too strong for that dead faith which was instilled into them, and which they have been trying to instill into others, until their better sense and better judgment, aided by other minds and genuine truths, have compelled them to abandon it.

In the first place, they have removed out of the way that greatest of all stumbling blocks, "The Pentateuch," which, when tested by the truths of geological discovery, is shown to be a mass of crude absurdities.

And now, in the next place, not only is the rest of the Old Testament to be submitted to the same and similar tests, but the New Testament also must submit to go through the crucible of investigation, and stand or fall by the ordeal. Everywhere there is fermentation of thought. Science, we admit, has not yet overthrown theology and mythology *vi et armis*, by battering at their ancient walls; but she has been and is still—quietly and slowly, yet perceptibly—sapping and mining them to the very foundation. She is proving her own truths, as well as that great and divine principle, that no one truth, great or small, can ever be hostile to, contradict, or disprove another. She is showing, by an examination of everything in Nature, that God is infinite in goodness, infinite in wisdom, and infinite in truth. That He cannot be what the Pentateuch proclaims him to be—a God who has fits of anger, who errs and repents of it, who can be at one time what he is not at another. Geology has demonstrated that the earth must be more than six thousand years old. It may be six hundred thousand, or six hundred millions, or as much longer as the imagination can stretch, for all that we know. But one thing is certain—it is proved as conclusively as by a mathematical demonstration, that there is no semblance of truth in the Jewish computation, that it was called into existence so recently as the Scriptures assert. Astronomy, too, has proved that, so far from the earth being the most important body in our solar system, it is one of the three least; that our solar system itself—the majestic sun and all the orbs that circle around him—is but a comparative speck in the infinite immensity of the sidereal universe; and that the faint light of the great Nebula in Orion, seen in the summer sky, takes sixty-seven thousand years to travel from that remote portion of the universe to our little globe, and become visible to the eyes of men. In fact the world has come, or is fast coming, to that advanced state of progress, when the men, who really think for themselves in spiritual matters as independently as they compare and judge in the actual business of their lives, will subject all the so-called sacred books of all creeds to thorough examination, and relegate them to the same pedestals as are occupied by the Iliad and the Odyssey, or the early histories of ancient nations. They will believe all that is credible, and reject all that is manifestly, mathematically and positively false. To those—and they include many of the leading minds of our time—who are too timid, and to some who are not too timid to declare themselves, as well as to vast numbers who show their new faith, or rather the rejection of their old faith, by the negative process of refusing to lend any public countenance to it, the conviction has become too strong to be avoided, that God has revealed Himself to mankind only through His works as exhibited by the eternal world, and through the inherent intuitions, faculties and perceptions, placed in the soul and mind of each individual. He holds no one accountable for a belief in the written or spoken words of any man or any set of men. Men are to be relied upon, only so far as they describe the physical, moral and intellectual laws of God, in accordance with other natural truths.

In view of this advancement of the human race, and of the numerous discoveries of modern science, each one of which is consistent with the other, and with the beneficent nature and unchanging and unchangeable laws and purposes of the Creator—in view of the hollowness of the religious systems, through which endeavors have been made for many ages back to impose upon mankind a belief in stories and traditions that it is impossible to accept—in view of the attempted disparagement of the religion of nature and conscience, which these efforts have produced, as well as the vast amount of hypocrisy which they have caused amongst the multitude of ordinary men, who pretend to believe for fashion's sake, or to save themselves the trouble and inconvenience of standing out against any established system—in view of all this, the time seems to have arrived for protesting against all false cosmogonies, theologies, and mythologies, through which the designing have held more or less pernicious sway over the mind and means of the many for so long a period. As long as these attempts are permitted to trammel the minds and influence the conduct of men and debase true religion, they act as fetters upon the intellect and impede the progress of mankind. A Protest, to be in accordance with the intelligence of the day, must be one against the idea that death is a new comer, or that the inhabitants of the earth, from man downwards to the lowest animalcule, were not intended for death from the beginning. It must protest against the idea that death is an evil, or anything but a blessing, and a step of the soul in its infinite progression from good to better. It must protest against the idea that there is any evil, except that which is caused by man's ignorant or wilful breach of divine laws, inasmuch as all else which seems to be evil appears so only on account of our imperfect knowledge, and must be good in the ulterior purposes of a God who is all perfection. It must protest against the idea that labor is a curse imposed upon man in consequence of transgression, and assert, on the contrary, that it is a prime and chief blessing, the educator of the body, the elevator of the mind, the sweetener and enhancer of the multifarious enjoyments of life. It must protest against the idea inculcated in the Old Testament of the Jews, and thence conveyed into the New Testament of the Christians, that God's purpose was ever changed by man's transgression, or by man's intercession, or by any other agency whatsoever. It must protest as Christ protested, and reject the barbarous and blood-thirsty creed of the Jews, and specially those portions of that creed which have corrupted that which Jesus taught, and which were introduced into it after his crucifixion by his ignorant disciples, and form no portion of the divine doctrine that God is infinite in goodness and wisdom, and that it is the duty of men to love God and one another. It must protest against the idea that it is any part of God's purpose—out of revenge, or from any other motive—to punish man in everlasting fire, or by any other torment beyond the grave, for the deeds done in the body, such a doctrine being totally inconsistent with God's goodness. It must protest against the idea that God, out of His mere grace or favor, has elected a remnant of mankind to be saved, to the exclusion of the majority, as being inconsistent with his even-handed justice. It must protest against the idea that man can commit any sin for which God has not provided adequate punishment, that is inflicted on the offender, not vicariously or vindictively, but to the end that God had in view, at the creation—and this end was that, under the training provided for the purpose, all men should, eventually, be brought to understand and do His will. It must protest that God is never moved to anger, nor can He be surprised or disappointed by anything that man may do, for He observes with perfect complacency all His works, all His creatures, and all their doings, knowing that by the gradual fulfilment of His original purposes, all things will work together in a manner entirely consistent therewith. It must protest against the idea that any man's fate is altered by the prayers of the Church, either before or after his decease—this being inconsistent with God's foreknowledge, and His ability to provide for all possible contingencies from the first. It must protest against all teaching which is contrary to this view. It must protest against receiving the facts recorded by either Moses or the Apostles, as other than mere statements resting upon human testimony, to be judged of as evidence is judged of in a court of justice, and to be credited only when consistent with each other, with Nature, with probability, and with the goodness of God. In fine, it must protest against everything which is not in accordance with the substance of these following propositions, derived from natural teaching, and confirmed by an innate consciousness of their truth: that it is no

GOD ALL POWERFUL. 37

part of religion to entertain any other faith or belief, than that there is but one God—that this one God is omnipotent, and that His perfections are infinite—that He rules all things by laws, which, like Himself, are unchangeable—that all men are alike amenable to His laws in person—and that He requires that we should exercise ourselves in good offices one toward another, and toward all sentient beings. All faiths and beliefs, which are inconsistent with these broad axioms, are more or less pernicious. And most undoubtedly all faiths and beliefs respecting God, which are propounded for the entertainment of men, and which are not consistent with His infinite power, knowledge, goodness, and impartial justice, are untrue and to be deprecated.

God's perfections are the touchstone by which to test the genuineness of our faith. In working out His plans and designs, He needs not, nor did He contemplate, the assistance of any such persons as Christ and the Holy Ghost, who are called divine; or of the Virgin Mary, who is said to be immaculate and the mother of God. There is no personal, nor imaginary Devil; nor is it possible that there can be any. Man is as God originally created him, and as God originally intended and provided he should be, to the end that all shall in good time adore Him from a sense of His goodness to each and all. God's perfections are proof positive that the laws which He established for the government of all things are absolute and incapable of amendment, and therefore must endure perpetually. They can neither be changed nor made better. Hence, neither Jesus nor His disciples, nor any other creature ever had, by any special providence, the power either inherent or granted for the working of miracles. Any pretended occurrence or phenomenon, not in accordance with the ordinary course of nature, is fallacious. There is much in the Bible, in relation to God and His attributes, which is inconsistent with His perfections and therefore must be untrue; hence the Bible cannot be said to be infallible.

In speaking of the Church, we use the word, in every instance, in its broad sense, not as applying to any particular denomination or sect, but to all alike who make any part of their doctrine or creed to consist of any one or more of the things here cited as being inconsistent with God's perfect attributes. Any one of the many sects may denounce the doctrines of the others, with whom they do not agree. We claim the same privilege, and shall address ourselves against any and all, who hold to dogmas and theologies which we conceive to be not in accordance with the nature, and perfections, and omnipotence of God.

The new protest must avoid the short-comings and errors of its predecessors. It is not enough, in our day, to protest against that which is false in theology; it is essentially necessary to affirm that which is true. In addition to what is done spontaneously by the heart and conscience, it has hitherto been the office of poets, rather than of preachers, to "vindicate the ways of God to man;" but science has now stepped into the arena, and has become a more powerful vindicator of God's goodness and wisdom than either priest or poet. Science and theology may be antagonistic powers; but science and the religion of the heart march together, side by side, and together they will achieve a signal victory over the errors and false teachings that have trammelled the minds of men from the earliest ages. The intelligent and unshackled enquirer studies the so-called sacred books of the Jews and Christians, and finds what of divine truth there is in them so over-ridden and contradicted by, and so subordinated to, human dogmas—repugnant alike to intuitive religion, conscience, and common sense—that no consolation or healing for the soul, or satisfaction for the intellect, can be extracted therefrom. He who hungers and thirsts for the true bread and water of life, which leads man heavenward, will hunger and thirst in vain, if he expects to find it in the Bible or the doctrines of the Church. But when the truly religious man studies the great open volume of Nature, he discovers nothing to weaken or contradict; everything in it tends to strengthen and confirm the great and fundamental idea—the only possible basis of a true and living religion—that God is infinite, eternal, unchangeable, and all-wise. Nothing can eradicate the impression which it makes upon us, to the effect that He is good and kind to all His creatures, and that He cannot have created man in order to make him miserable either here or hereafter. The diligent student of this sublime book—whether he gathers instruction from the little globe of which man is the noblest inhabitant, or whether he seeks it with a devout and reverential spirit from the gorgeous host of suns and planetary systems that fill the remotest regions of space and by their number and magnitude reduce this globe of ours comparatively to the dimensions of a grain of sand on the sea shore of creation—will observe in it, throughout, the universality of law and the most perfect mathematical consistency. Every newly discovered truth will be found to be in perfect harmony with the whole. He will recognize as a principle and as a fact, that the laws of God, which are perfect and invariable now, must have been perfect and invariable from the first, and that in this world—as in the countless worlds of all the galaxies of space—they accomplish everlastingly the exact original purpose of their divine author. He will also recognize that God's intention in creating the universe, and placing man upon the earth—and, for all we know, in millions of other worlds even more glorious than this—cannot have been thwarted by any agency, mortal or immortal. It has been carried out from the beginning; and it will be carried out in exact conformity with His will and foreknowledge throughout all eternity. Every atom of matter, and the faintest flickering of mind that ever existed, was made subservient to the accomplishment of a definite purpose, and was endowed, from the creation, with all the properties, qualities, forces, and faculties necessary to fulfil that purpose, without any further supervision.

Among the agencies which perform important offices in the production of the various phenomena of Nature are light and darkness, heat and cold, negative and positive electricity, magnetism, the centripetal and centrifugal forces, chemical affinities and repulsions, gravitation, attraction, and probably other instrumentalities of which science has not yet discovered the secret. These agencies are only perceptible to man, through their action on visible and tangible matter. It required the accumulated experience of centuries, and a high state of mental culture in succeeding generations, before Philosophy could either discover or comprehend them even to the present limited extent.

Man has never had any true conception of God or His attributes, except through the medium of His creation. By means of the phenomena presented to man through the material world, through the action of infinite mind upon inorganic matter, through life as exhibited in animals and plants, and through the emotions and aspirations of the human soul, God has revealed Himself to man—and thus only. By these means, the revelation is abundantly sufficient to enable all men to fulfil God's will and purpose. By these means, to the full extent of their intelligence and their needs, will they be enabled to perform the duties that are required of them so long as they remain in this world; and, by analogy, it may be concluded that, after they have quitted it, they will be similarly aided, through some means not revealed to us. With this great and glorious revelation open before him— the divine instruction written on the soul of man—how can he fail to keep within the bounds of duty and love to God?

Three words, which theologians employ in a sense at variance with truth, and with God's wisdom in creating the world, and by which the minds of men have been enthralled to their damage, are Labor, Pain, and Death. They have been represented as evils, and as forming no part of God's original purpose in placing man upon the earth. A great portion of the human race has been taught for thousands of years, that for man's disobedience to a supposed command—which God never can have given, with the threatened penalties for a breach of it, and under all the circumstances claimed by the Church— labor was imposed upon him as a curse; that pain was introduced as a punishment instigated by God's anger; and that death—no part of God's first intention—was made the doom of every living thing. And this ancient fable still exercises a pernicious influence, although men are gradually beginning to understand as regards labor and pain, that they are by no means evils, but a part of the economy of God's will toward man in this world.

Instead of being a curse, labor, to a legitimate extent, is found to be a blessing; and this law refers not alone to man and the earth, but to the whole Universe. We admit that excess of labor is an evil; but so, also, is excess in anything. It is beneficial to eat and to drink; but prejudicial to eat and drink too much. It is delightful to labor; but disagreeable to exhaust one's self in doing in one day the work of two or three days. It is labor, labor alone, that raises man to his true position. It is imposed upon him for no angry or revengeful purpose—if such were possible to God—but with the kindest intention. It was instituted to promote his happiness, in order that he might be induced to improve his faculties, physical, moral and intellectual. He is born naked; out of his necessities come mental and physical cultivation, civilization, and all the ennobling arts and graces that follow in its train. In the gratification of man's wants consists the enjoyment of life; for, if he had no wants in this life, he would have no pleasures. Were he to draw his food out of the atmosphere by the act of breathing, had he no call to cultivate the earth or to labor for shelter or covering, he would be without that stimulant and that incentive to do and be doing—without that prompting to activity of body and spirit—which is indispensable to buoyancy, and health, and the giving zest to life. Action is the order of nature. The air sweeps over hill and dale. It dallies wantonly with the foliage, and on the surface of the waters. It rustles in the trees, plays with the grass and the flowers of the fields, and fans the waving grain that sways gracefully before its breath. The clouds move majestically about from one part of the heavens to another. The sea uplifts its waves for joy, and embraces again and again the rock-bound shore, leaving its impress and its bounds in circles on the sands, as it daily ebbs and flows. The animals participate in this general law of existence. They are ever busy, providing for and protecting themselves in every emergency. And thus we see that all nature is alive with activity.

> Stop the wheels of Nature,
> And Nature will cease to be.

Let stagnation lay her hand upon the earth, and this fair and lovely Paradise, now instinct with movement and health, will become the dreary seat of sterility and death.

In like manner, pain, thought to be a curse secondary only to death, is not only useful, but necessary and beneficent. It is a special warning to us that something has gone wrong, and may go further wrong, in this our curious and mysterious physical constitution, if we do not see to it to set the wrong right.

> Pain is the friend and guardian of the wise.
> Would'st place thy hand
> In the consuming and destroying fire,
> And ask it not to burn? Would'st fall from heights
> Upon the strong bosom of the earth,
> And ask it not to bruise? Would'st break the laws
> That govern and uphold the universe,
> The modulation of harmonious Heaven,
> And, without knowledge of thy sacrifice,
> Destroy thy being? Wise, and good, and just
> Are all the laws and purposes of God.

Death is naturally the dread of all, to the end that all may cling to life while they may; yet death is no more an evil, than pain or labor. The world was constituted and prepared for death from the beginning. Millions of years ago, as geology has discovered, there were life and death on this globe ; life and death in the waters, and on the dry land. A square inch of the chalky cliffs of Dover or the Isle of Wight contains the shells of myriads of minute sea-fish, that must have lived and died hundreds of thousands of centuries ago—even before the world was ready for the habitation of man, and consequently before man's transgression could have involved this supposed penalty.

> Death is no evil. Cease, O, foolish man,
> Thy querulous moaning, and consider death
> No longer as thy foe. A ministering saint,
> Her hand shall lead thee step by step to God.
> Be worthy of her ; and so learn to live,
> That every incarnation of thy soul
> In other worlds, and spheres, and firmaments,
> Shall be more perfect. God's eternity
> Is thine to live in.

This we hold to be man's destiny hereafter ; and it is his high privilege to participate in working out the supreme happiness in store for him. Discarding therefore all these obsolete and unworthy ideas of labor, pain, and death—products of the early want of knowledge by man, and the erroneous teaching of theologians—and investigating fairly and candidly the capabilities of man, and the purposes of God in creating him, it will be found by the study of natural laws that man is especially charged, within certain limits, with the guardianship of himself. God intended that man should participate in taking care of both his soul and his body ; that he should look to the preservation and perpetuation of his kind ; and both morally and physically so perform the duties imposed upon him as to conduce to his own well-being, and the well-being of his fellow men, both in time and in eternity. The numerous instincts, appetites, senses, and other faculties with which he is endowed, God has given him as guides for this purpose. Without these guides, he might fail in the great duty of self-preservation, and the procreation of his kind, so as to endanger the continuance of his race. Without the cravings of appetite and the pleasure which its gratification affords, he might fail to supply himself with the food and drink requisite to preserve life. But for the suffering, which is the penalty of neglect, he might not be sufficiently vigilant in protecting himself from injury. But for the pain and discomfort which are the necessary and wholesome monitors of excess, he might habitually indulge in eating and drinking too much. But God's goodness and care do not stop here. Besides these checks and admonitions given to him for his improvement, there are offices to be performed on his behalf, over which he has little or no control, and some over which he has no supervision whatever. There are chemical and mechanical processes continually in operation within him, about which he knows very little, and of which God has altogether taken charge. These are so completely provided for in his organization, that they go on while he is unmindful of them. Such are, the circulation of the blood, the drawing of the breath, the generation of vital heat, the digestion of food, and the distribution of the nourishment thus obtained, to all parts of the body, to promote growth and serve for the repair of the system. To subserve these ends, and to give rest to the body and spirit, in order to prevent the too rapid expenditure of vital energy, and the consequent premature decay of the beautiful and complex human machine, it is indispensable that the active brain and intellect should, at certain periods, not too far apart, be brought to that state of quiet and repose which sleep alone can superinduce. Hence it is put out of man's power to resist sleep to any considerable extent, without injury or death. And thus God's laws are constantly operating for man's benefit, though man is unconscious or unmindful of the kindly despotism by which, for his own good, those laws are imposed upon him.

How beautiful and full of goodness, not only to man, but to all living creatures, are what are called the instincts! The new-born babe is taught by this divine prompting, the moment it comes into the world, to seek its nourishment at the mother's breast. All living things—the bees, the ants, the beavers, the birds, the wild animals of whatever description, the flocks and herds belonging to men, even the flowers and herbs—are governed and govern themselves by the instincts which God has given them, and are preserved to life and enjoyment by their obedience thereto. This is in accordance with logic of the highest order; and yet these happy creatures do not reason on the subject, any more than the infant at the breast. Instinct is as divine a gift as reason itself. It is the gift of God to every living thing. It is implanted upon each according to its kind, at creation, and transmitted without alteration to the feeble and the strong alike. God's superior intelligence, thus made manifest and available in all created beings, is necessary to the divine purpose. Without it, no living creature on the earth could exist. All those beings that people the air, the earth, or the waters—various as they may be in their forms and organization—have each their own set of laws, instincts, and intuitions, which are especially adapted to them, and harmonize in the most minute particular with their structure and mode of life, the kind and variety of their food, the means of supply, the perpetuation and nourishment of their kind, their self-protection, and whatever is necessary to their existence and enjoyment. Eagles, vultures, hawks, owls, and other birds which feed upon flesh, have beaks and claws especially adapted for capturing and killing their prey and for dividing asunder their food into convenient quantities to be readily devoured. They are led by their appetites to crave such food as is appropriate to their nature; and under the influence of their instincts they exercise wondrous perseverance and adroitness in the pursuit of it. Birds that feed upon carrion have the power of scenting it from all but incredible distances. The hare, rabbit, and many other animals, which from their structure and propensities are not well fitted for self-defence, fly from danger, and employ sometimes speed, and sometimes stratagem for the purpose. The deprivation of one quality is compensated for, by the gift of another that is equally available for the intended object. There are many species of insects that would become extinct, if instinct had not taught them to shield themselves from the frost of winter by burrowing in the earth. The means are present; but to make burrowing sufficient to the end in view, it must be done at proper times, and in anticipation of the frost. This is insured, by inherent instructions from God.— Wolves and various other carnivorous animals pursue a prey which leaves a scent or trail upon the earth, with a marvellous acuteness of smell, while animals that labor under no similar need, are gifted with no such capacity. The dog is enabled to scent his master along the paved streets of populous cities, and to distinguish his trail from that of others crossing or intermingled with it, even though hours may have elapsed between the tread of his master's foot and the pursuit. The instinct of self-preservation sometimes assumes the form of cunning. Some animals feign death, in the presence of their foe. Many insects do the same. The skunk, when alarmed for its safety, emits a disagreeable odor, that repels or disgusts its pursuer. The cuttle-fish when in peril discharges a black liquid, that discolors the water for a considerable distance around it, and prevents, by obscuration, the eye of its enemy from tracing the course, upwards or downwards or lateral, by which it effects its escape. The hare, in the long winters of far Northern latitudes, changes the summer color of its skin to that of the snow amid which it lives, and is thus enabled to elude the keen glance of the bird of prey high up in the air, which otherwise would be better able to single out, pounce upon, and destroy it. The feathers of the grouse that feed upon the moor are of the color of the moor and the heather; while the plumage of the ptarmigan, that dwells among the granite peaks of the highest mountains of Scotland and Norway, resembles granite even when seen from a short distance. The pheasant, the better to shield her young and helpless brood from approaching danger, feigns to be crippled, and flutters away from her chicks—that hide themselves—in such a way as to draw off the intruder from her charge by pretending to be, herself, an easy prey. The domestic hen gathers her chickens under her wings, when the hawk or falcon soars above, a mere speck in the sky. She does this by a peculiar call, which the young birds understand and obey instinctively. The lamb knows the bleat of its mother among all the sheep of a flock, however numerous; and the mother in like manner distinguishes the cry of her own progeny, though scores of lambs may be bleating simultaneously. Thus, manifestly do the wisdom and goodness of God support and train every living creature that he has made, throughout the whole range of creation.

But all these wonderful provisions in Nature, which harmonize so beautifully with the peculiar constitution, appetites, means of support and protection of life, that we observe in animals, are a most emphatic contradiction to the Christian theory, that, before the Fall, these creatures were not antagonistic to each other, and that God did not contemplate death in His original plan at the creation.

Neither the physical nor the spiritual eye of man can penetrate any department of Nature, without discovering objects to excite wonder, admiration, and worship. Even the members of the vegetable world have been endowed with something analogous to the instincts of the animal creation. The roots of trees and plants are attracted from considerable distances to the spot where the nourishment that best suits them is found in greatest abundance, and can be made available for their growth and development. Trees that grow on the plains, unsheltered by other trees or objects, have wider and deeper-spreading roots and a firmer hold on the earth, in order to meet their greater needs, and put out their strongest roots in the direction whence come the prevailing winds and rudest blasts. Trees in the dense forest vie with each other, as men do in crowded communities, each striving to tower above its neighbor in quest of that abundance of sunlight and fresh air, so essential to its existence and growth. The ivy and the vine which depend on their sturdier and more earth-fast neighbors for support, when they rear their delicate foliage to the light, and put forth their tendrils as though they were fingers, seem to discern and choose the friends on whom to lean, and straightway incline their stems and train their course thitherward. And if God has given instincts to the trees, the grass, and the flowers, by which they preserve their existence and conform to the laws of their well-being, it is difficult not to believe that to them also, in one sense, is given a certain amount of enjoyment. The sunshine and the rain must give them pleasure; and the rose, the lily, and the violet may know that they are beautiful, and take pleasure in the fact, not as sensitively perhaps, as the beautiful of our own species, yet in a degree. It may not be altogether a fancy of the poet, but an unsuspected truth, that the trees, which quiver to the summer wind or bend or moan in the wintry blast,

     * * * * * * * to men unknown
       Have pleasures of their own,
And feel sweet sympathies with all dear Nature's moods.

   We deem that all the leaves,
    In morns, or noons, or eves,
  Or in the starry stillness of the night,
   May point to Heaven in prayer,
    Or bend to earth and share
  Some joy of sense, some natural delight;
   That root, and branch, and stem,
    Partake the joy with them,
And feel through all their sap, God's goodness infinite.

God's laws provide not only for the incessant reproduction or recomposition of vegetable and animal-life, so as to compensate for the decay which time has been commissioned to operate on all that lives—thus keeping the face of nature forever fresh and beautiful—but He has provided that the earth itself, however venerably old, shall always be young, always fruitful, always bountiful, always lovely. The same recuperative power, that exists in man and animals, exists through all Nature. The waving fields of corn and grass, when too rudely pressed by the gale or storm, or disfigured by the trail of man or beast, are in a brief space, under the genial influence of the sun, the breezes, and the inscrutable laws of Nature—which train plants heavenward—put to rights, if such a phrase may be used, and restored to their original beauty. The majestic oak, shattered by the lightning, and deprived of vitality, does not forever stand a gloomy object in the landscape. The ivy, "friend and adorner of decay," as if in sympathy with its fate, binds up, as it were, its wounds, its nakedness, its seared old trunk and limbs, and renders it beautiful with its own life, turning its helplessness to cheerful purposes. Even at the fall of the leaf, and in the old age of the year, when the landscape is disrobed of its verdure, Nature does not cease to be lovely. She bestows upon each season its own compensations in the present, for what it may have lost in the past. The howling winds—the drifting snow forming into graceful undulations, slopes and curves, and mantling the landscape with their beauty—the icy gems that attach themselves to every tree, and bush, and herb, and sparkle in the sunlight like precious stones—these do not impress the soul with gloom, but with a never wearied sense of the grandeur, the goodness, and the beauty of all God's works and ways.

And while God is thus careful for His creatures, He is equally careful in preserving and beautifying the earth for their enjoyment. For is not the earth itself as much the object of His goodness and divine government, as the living things that He has placed upon it? There are laws pertaining to its affairs, of which if any one became inoperative, the destruction of all animal and vegetable life would speedily ensue. Among these may be named evaporation and condensation, cohesive attraction, friction, gravitation, and the centrifugal and centripetal forces. If there were no such laws as evaporation and condensation at work, the watery vapor that floats in the atmosphere would not be liquified, and consequently we should have no rain to water the earth; it would become parched for want of moisture, and the streams and rivers would cease to flow. If the effect of cohesion and friction were wanting, the particles of matter of which the hills and mountains are composed would descend into the valleys, and under the same law by which the waters of the rivers now flow into the sea—the whole surface of the globe would assume a perfectly spherical shape, be covered with water, and become uninhabitable for men, beasts, birds, or any other creatures except fishes and sea reptiles. Without the law of gravitation, the whole material of our globe would fly asunder, and be scattered in space. Without centrifugal force, the earth would gravitate to the sun and be destroyed. Without centripetal force, or gravity, the earth would leave its orbit, wander from the planetary system, be deprived of the heat and light of the sun, and be rendered unfit for either animal or vegetable life.

The next great point to be considered is of even more importance than any that we have yet touched upon. If the study of Nature in all its varied moods and manifestations, proves that God's goodness extends in this world to all that He has placed within it, and even to the world itself which He governs and sustains, shall not the divine goodness be extended to the soul of man through all eternity? God may be continually employed in creating new worlds and new systems; but never, if the foregoing arguments be sound, can He be employed in correcting such mistakes as are implied in the Bible history of the fall of man, and the Church doctrine of his consequent damnation, if he do not believe the incredible. The laws which He laid down at the beginning, for the preservation and government of the physical universe, must be equally beneficent, wise and unchangeable, when applied to our spiritual life, not alone in time, but in eternity. Their application to tangible matter may be more apparent; but the spirit feels internal evidence that God's goodness and care are ever shielding the immortal as well as the mortal part of man. It would be past the comprehension of the wisest, if this were not the case, and inconsistent with God's character, as exhibited throughout the universe, so far as man has been enabled to study it. It would be irrational, to believe that God did not take care at the creation, to ordain, establish, and put in operation—to be transmitted unimpaired to all mankind—instincts, intuitions, inspirations, and whatever properties may be essential to the soul's need in time and eternity, equal at least to His care in provision made for the body!

None will deny that the provision pertaining to man's physical nature was as full and effectual at first, as now. Yet those who uphold the doctrine of the fall of man, and that of Christ's divinity and mission, must be held to say that God omitted at the beginning to make provision for conducting the soul of man through time, with sufficient definiteness to answer the purposes of His creation; and that, upon afterthought suggested and necessitated by man's unexpected perverseness, He had to make further provision to meet the emergency.

This idea of afterthought, though not palpable at first view, is nevertheless inseparable from church teaching, and no sophistry can rescue it from the charge of being irreligious, absurd, and inconsistent with God's infinite perfections. It pre-supposes that all mankind who lived and died before the advent of Jesus, and all those who have not heard or shall not hear of salvation through his crucifixion, were and are without the benefit of that love which it is claimed, was only vouchsafed to man through his divinity. According to such a doctrine as this, if a man lives a life of purity and charity and benevolence— in fine, just such a life as Jesus recommended in his early teachings—it will avail him nothing. He must have faith in a dogma which reason cannot understand, and which contradicts the idea of both God's wisdom and goodness. To reconcile this belief with a belief in God's goodness, it is claimed that, for those who have never heard or never will hear of redemption through Christ, God has a mode of salvation which the church fails to specify, but which answers all practical purposes. If this be so, it is difficult to see in what, as regards the soul of man, the benefit of the new mode consists. It is impossible, as we have shewn, for man not to have faith in the existence of a Supreme Being, who is infinite in wisdom, infinite in power, and infinite in goodness. True religion, therefore, does not consist in dogmatic beliefs or superstitious theories. It consists in reverence and gratitude to the Divine Being, and the proper discharge, by each one of us, of his duty to himself, his fellow-man, and every creature with which he may have relations, and whose condition may be improved by his good offices and kindness.

This leads us to the consideration of what is called moral evil. Of physical evil there is in reality none.

That which is so called—under the names of Labor, Pain, and Death—we have already disposed of. God, in the creation of man, did not expect him to fulfill all his duties, without running counter to many of the irrevocable and unchangeable laws to which he is amenable. This is conclusively proved by the peculiar constitution of man, which must have been his condition at the time of his creation. He is gifted with such capacities as would have been of no practical use to him unless to educate and guard him against violating laws, the effect of which he can better understand, and the importance of conforming to which he can better realize, when once he has broken them. This relates to the moral and spiritual, as well as to the physical nature of man. Man's body suffers pain, when he has violated the laws of bodily health; his spirit is degraded, when he has violated those which pertain to the spirit; and, if the violation be persisted in, the punishment will be repeated accordingly. These pains are sent in mercy to man, for the purpose of bringing him back to the path of law and duty, guiding him therein, and admonishing him to be more careful in future. These means of educating man, and of making God's care, justice, and goodness available to him to the extent of his needs—short-sighted as he is—were provided for at his creation. This view, we are aware, is in all respects at variance with the idea, that God created man sufficiently perfect to keep all His laws unbroken, or that God expected him to do so.

The existence of moral evil leads mankind the better to understand and to practice moral good. Men, in the aggregate, do vastly more good than evil; and they whose bad actions preponderate largely, or even moderately, over their good ones, are comparatively very few.

Good deeds make but little noise in the world; bad ones a great deal. The life of a considerable majority of mankind is largely made up of the practice of small virtues. Even so little a thing as a kind word, or a kind look, has soothed the aching heart, and caused the eye of the sorrowing and disconsolate to glisten with hope and happiness. These may seem trifles, when viewed separately; but when taken in the mass, they form a monument of praise, just as mountains raise their heads to Heaven, though composed of individual atoms of earth. Conspicuous virtues are no more acceptable to God than humble ones, and the smallest act of obedience to law, is as meritorious as the greatest. The widow's mite is as acceptable as the rich man's offering, and has its equal reward. Thankfulness and duty are the only roads to happiness. All God's blessings and good gifts were prepared and the conditions prescribed on which they were attainable, from the first. Man should be thankful for the abundance and excellence of these gifts; and especially thankful that they are not capriciously distributed, but are attainable upon the principle that like cause produces like effect.

And although those, which man in his short-sightedness may deem the most precious blessings, do not fall profusely on every individual, yet, if we take men collectively they will be found to be as much in accordance with their welfare as is consistent with their future destiny. Every man, whether he be rich or poor—whatever his joys, whatever his sufferings—is as happy as is well for him under existing circumstances. What may seem to be a man's partial loss in one way, may be more than compensated for in another manner. This fact is constantly exemplified. The possessor of wealth and indulger in luxury sometimes injures his health, impairs his faculty for sound sleep, and disturbs the serenity of his mind, by over-indulgence; while a poor man, who leads an active life and avoids excess, is rewarded by the priceless blessing of health of body and mind, which all the gold in the world could not purchase. In this, God's goodness and justice are most conspicuously apparent.

We now approach the apparently difficult, but in reality the simple, subject of prayer, as offered by individuals and by the churches. We have already said that God's good gifts are only to be obtained on the terms prescribed at the creation—terms which are never modified or altered, to suit the pleasure or supposed necessity of any one individual or of all mankind combined. Even if the whole human family should, at the same instant, pray most devoutly for the slightest change in God's original ordinances or purposes toward mankind, none could take place. The rain cannot be made to fall, because man prays for it. The pestilence cannot be removed by supplication to God; but by conformity to those physical laws, the breach of which produced the pestilence. This view is admirably illustrated and argued out by Mr. Buckle in his *History of Civilization in England*, from which we make a long, but very interesting extract.

"In the year 1853, the cholera, after having committed serious ravages in many parts of Europe, visited Scotland. There, it was sure to find numerous victims among a badly fed, badly housed, and not over-cleanly people. For, if there is one thing better established than another respecting this disease, it is that it invariably attacks, with the greatest effect, those classes who, from poverty or from sloth, are imperfectly nourished, neglect their persons, and live in dirty, ill-drained, or ill-ventilated dwellings. In Scotland, such classes are very numerous. In Scotland, therefore, the cholera must needs be very fatal. * * * * Under these circumstances, it must have been evident, not merely to men of science, but to all men of plain, sound understanding, who would apply their minds to the matter without prejudice, that the Scotch had only one way of successfully grappling with their terrible enemy, It behooved them to feed their poor, to cleanse their cesspools, and to ventilate their houses. If they had done this, and done it quickly, thousands of lives would have been spared. But they neglected it, and the country was thrown into mourning. Nay, they not only neglected it, but, moved by the dire superstition which sits like an incubus upon them, they adopted a course which, if it had been carried into full operation, would have aggravated the calamity to a frightful extent. It is well known that, whenever an epidemic is raging, physical exhaustion and mental depression make the human frame more liable to it, and are therefore especially to be guarded against. But, though this is a matter of common notoriety, the Scotch clergy, backed, sad to say, by the general voice of the Scotch people, wished the public authorities to take a step which was certain to cause physical exhaustion, and to encourage mental depression. In the name of religion, whose offices they thus abused and perverted to the detriment of man, instead of employing them for his benefit, they insisted on the propriety of ordering a national fast, which in so superstitious a country was sure to be rigidly kept, and, being rigidly kept, was equally sure to enfeeble thousands of delicate persons, and before twenty-four hours were passed prepare them to receive that deadly poison which was already lurking around them, and which hitherto they had just strength enough to resist. The public fast was also to be accompanied by a public humiliation, in order that nothing might be wanting to appeal to the mind and fill it with terror. * * * *

"This was the scheme projected by the Scotch clergy; and they were determined to put it into execution. To give greater effect to it, they called upon England to help them, and, in the autumn of 1853, the Presbytery of Edinburgh caused their Moderator to address a letter, ostensibly to the English minister, but in reality to the English nation, enquiring whether the Queen contemplated appointing a national fast-day.

"The letter, which, through the medium of the press, was sure to become well known and to be widely read, was evidently intended to act on public opinion in England. It was, in fact, a covert reproach on the English government for having neglected its spiritual duties, and for not having perceived that fasting was the most effectual way of stopping an epidemic. In Scotland generally, it received great praise, and was regarded as a dignified rebuke addressed to the irreligious habits of the English people, who, seeing the cholera at their doors, merely occupied themselves with sanitary measures, and carnal devices to improve the public health, showing thereby that they trusted too much to the arms of the flesh. In England, on the other hand, this manifesto of the Scotch Church was met with almost universal ridicule, and indeed found no favorers, except among the most ignorant and credulous part of the nation. The minister, to whom it was addressed, was Lord Palmerston, a man of vast experience, and perhaps better acquainted with public opinion than any politician of his time. He, being well aware that notions which the Scotch deemed religious the English deemed fanatical, * * * * directed a letter to be sent to the Presbytery of Edinburgh, which, unless I am greatly mistaken, will in future ages be quoted as an interesting document for illustrating the history of the progress of public opinion. A century ago, any statesman who had written such a letter would have been driven from office by a storm of general indignation. Two centuries ago, the consequences to him would have been still more disastrous, and would indeed have ruined him socially, as well as politically. For, in it he sets at defiance those superstitious fancies respecting the origin of disease, which were once universally cherished as an essential part of every religious creed. Traditions, the memory of which is preserved in the theological literature of all Pagan countries, of all Catholic countries, and of all Protestant countries, are quietly put aside, as if they were matters of no moment, and as if it were not worth while to discuss them. The Scotch clergy, occupying the old ground on which the members of their profession had always been accustomed to stand, took for granted that the cholera was the result of divine anger, and was intended to chastise our sins. In the reply which they now received from the English Government, a doctrine was enunciated, which to Englishmen seems right enough, but which to Scotchmen sounded very profane. The Presbytery were informed, that the affairs of this world are regulated by natural laws, on the observance or neglect of which the weal or woe of mankind depends. One of those laws connects disease with the exhalations of bodies; and it is by virtue of this law that contagion spreads, either in crowded cities, or in places where vegetable decomposition is going on. Man, by exerting himself, can disperse or neutralize these noxious influences. The appearance of the cholera proves that he has not exerted himself. The towns have not been purified; hence the root of the evil. The Home Secretary, therefore, advised the Presbytery of Edinburgh, that it was better to cleanse than to fast. He thought that the plague being upon them, activity was preferable to humiliation. It was now autumn, and before the hot weather would return a considerable period must elapse. That period should be employed in destroying the causes of disease, by improving the abodes of the poor. If this were done, all would go well. Otherwise, pestilence would be sure to revisit them 'in spite'—I quote the words of the English minister—'in spite of all the prayers and fastings of a united, but inactive nation.'

"This correspondence between the Scotch clergy and the English statesman is not to be regarded as a mere passing episode, of light or temporary interest. On the contrary, it represents that terrible struggle between theology and science, which, having begun in the persecution of science and in the martyrdom of scientific men, has, in these later days, taken a happier turn, and is now manifestly destroying that old theological spirit which has brought so much misery and ruin upon the world."

If God is perfect in knowledge, any attempt of priestcraft to dictate to Him, by means of prayer, what He should do, is pitiable ignorance or gross blasphemy. Jesus himself, says, "Your Father knoweth what things ye have need of before ye ask Him." God's laws are all-sufficient; and man's only business is to understand and obey them. To pray publicly or privately, may soothe the spirit of man, and raise him to a state of mental excitement and exaltation; but it can have no effect on

God's will. It may be asked how God's goodness is to benefit man, if he is to be subjected, and amenable to inflexible laws, which no prayer can mitigate or turn aside. The answer is easy. God organized and incorporated in man's system or nature, from the first, such qualities, faculties, and functions, as were necessary to fit him for being the medium and dispenser of God's blessings to himself and to his fellows. God placed within him conscience—"the voice of God"—the innate sense of right and wrong. He gave him also his reason and reflective faculties, together with instincts and intuitions, all of which point and lead to a belief in the immortality of the soul. All these, and others of a similar character, enable him to thread his way among the unchangeable and eternal laws of God, with a success which answers God's purpose in relation to his existence here and hereafter, and ought to secure thankfulness from him for the glorious bestowal of such a boon. He has been endowed, too, with such faculties as enable him, if he will, to understand the rationale of God's laws, whenever he studies them, and to recognize the harmony with which they all co-operate to work out a divine purpose. All animate and inanimate beings and things, it would seem, are allowed a certain free-will, and vacillate between two restraining laws which keep them within their proper bounds. The planets are prevented from getting too near the sun by centrifugal force, and from getting too far from him by that other restraining force called centripetal. These laws balance each other, and maintain and support the equilibrium of the universe.

The intellect of man is able to appreciate the utility of this, and of all God's laws. Hence it is clear that God has so constituted man, that, to a certain extent, he has the means of interpreting aright God's ways here upon earth. Thus is he allowed to enter into fellowship with his divine Maker, and enabled to argue from the things of time to those of eternity. Let him do this, and he will find abundant reason for the consolatory belief that not one human creature will be permitted to stray so far from the path of duty, as to bring upon himself utter and endless misery. He cannot help but have faith that God has made laws to restrain, and which ever will restrain humanity, as the planets and other heavenly bodies are restrained within their prescribed bounds. Thus instructed, he cannot ignore the impressions which he has received from the unmistakable manifestations of God's goodness toward him, or give his faith to a pretended revelation of God's character that consigns him to everlasting torment if he do not accept a faith inconsistent with itself. Why should God enable man to see and feel His goodness in this world of time, if He had no such goodness in store for him in the world of eternity? In this mortal state man has been so constituted, and his agency or control over his own acts has been so limited, that notwithstanding his lack of sufficient knowledge to enable him to conform to all the laws to which he is amenable—he is not permitted to depart so far from the right path, as to make it impossible for him eventually to attain the high state of bliss designed for him. He may bring upon himself penalties that may injure or kill his body; but he cannot forfeit his soul to everlasting misery. God has loved man too well, to put it in his power to do this; and too well not to put it in his power to work out for himself a higher degree of happiness in eternity than he can in this world, or than his limited faculties can conceive. All this may be fairly deduced from God's manifestations of goodness throughout all Nature, and the faith He has implanted in man's reason, conscience, and instinct, that his existence shall be—not a curse, or even a blank—but a transcendent blessing.

God's knowledge in relation to man is perfect. Man's liability to err, and the bounds which are set thereto, and the penalties which are attached to each breach of the law, are alike of God's ordaining. Who then, remembering these things, shall doubt that God has so adjusted one to the other, as that the punishment on the other side of the grave shall be, as here, for man's further education, and for his best interests and happiness? By analogy this should be so; and it is fair to infer that it is so, since the same God that has tempered and adjusted all things, so as to make life happy here, shall be equally our God— the God of goodness and wisdom—throughout all eternity.

The human soul is so attuned to what the ancients called "the music of the spheres," that all Nature draws it to the contemplation of a higher existence. Every living and every inanimate thing, and all the wondrous phenomena of the visible universe, seem to whisper to man to aspire and to be thankful. The moan of the wind, the blustering of the storm, the falling of the rain, the flash of the lightning, the rolling of the thunder, the lowing of the herd, the hum of the bee, the song of the bird, the fragrant loveliness of the flowers, the roar of the sea upon the shore, the gloomy grandeur of the ocean, the gurgling of the stream, the sigh of the forest leaves and branches, the sublimity of the snow-covered mountain-tops, the serene beauty of the morning and the evening, the majesty of night, the harmony of truth, the transcendent bliss when two souls are fused into one—when one heart beats in two bosoms, when the same soul is eloquent in mutual eyes—love to children, love to parents, the kind emotions and sympathies of the human family one to another, and to other living things these multifarious joys all preach the immutable truth, that God's beneficence pervades the universe, and that all tends to develop man's innate belief in His goodness, and prompts to praise and worship Him. Praise is joy; and the best worship is the obedience which, in its turn, produces the happiness of the worshipper. This is man's experience in time; and, if it be not destined to be his experience throughout eternity, God's goodness would be finite, which it is impossible to believe.

It has been urged by the preachers of Christianity and of nearly all known systems of theology that, however good God may be, He permits the existence of evil; and that man may prevail upon God by sacrifice and prayer, to remove or lighten its load. Most modern sects have discarded the idea of sacrifices for this purpose; but all insist, not only upon the efficacy, but upon the absolute necessity of prayer. These phases of belief originate in erroneous ideas of God's goodness.

Physical evil is but another name for pain; and pain, as has already been shewn, is in its purpose entirely benevolent—a warning that we have transgressed some law imposed upon us for our good. Moral evil is, in like manner, but another name for disobedience. If it were impossible for man to disobey any physical or moral law of God, he would be deprived, not alone of free-will, but of the capacity for improvement and of mental growth. He would be unable even to aspire to a better state of existence, or to qualify himself to enter it. There would be no propriety in his being placed in this world in a state of probation. There can be no probation, where it is impossible to go wrong. It is sometimes asked, how the injustice so often committed by man on man is to be reconciled with the shield which God has thrown around him, and all the inferior animals, for self-protection? The reply is, that so far as the corporeal part of man is concerned, and so far as intellectual agencies operate in this life, the protection is not perfect, else man's free agency would have no office. The protection provided is efficient only up to the boundary that circumscribes man's free will. Within that boundary man can work out for himself a higher or lower degree of happiness, according as he understands and conforms to God's laws; and it may be that the trials and vexations of this life will serve, by contrast, to increase the joys and happiness of the next. In fact, we can scarcely conceive what enjoyment would be, if we had no idea of the reverse. As regards the liability of man to encroach upon the rights of others, it must not be forgotten that God has given him various qualities, propensities, and incentives to action, in order that he may be used as an instrument, within certain limits, for carrying out God's purposes. These are, in the first place, that men shall contribute to the happiness and welfare of each other by kind offices and social intercourse; and secondly, that every individual shall secure a greater or less degree of happiness in this life and the life to come, according as he deserves more or less by his obedience. Now, while each individual may, in the exercise of his free-will, perform his part more or less perfectly, yet so strong in the right direction are the propensities established within him as motives to his conduct, that man, by the exercise of his free-will within its prescribed limits, accomplishes God's purpose while in the pursuit of his own happiness. This accounts for some of man's propensities being vastly stronger than others. Among the things which man has an agency in performing, and which God will not permit to fail, are, the perpetuation of the race of men, and the preparation of the soul of each man for the enjoyment of, at least some degree of happiness in time, and a high degree of happiness in eternity. Hence God has given man unusually strong propensities in relation to these two great duties of life. These press with resistless force to the accomplishment of their objects; and it sometimes happens, in impetuous natures, that they overstep their proper boundaries in these respects and run riot. But it is better for a man to be over-selfish, than to fail in the indulgence of these propensities to the extent of neglect in taking due care of his life and happiness. Thus the minor evil is consequent upon the ample means taken to ensure the greater good.

Man, in his early ignorance, that pain was not of itself an evil, but a necessary part of the divine government of the universe, was induced to pray to the Supreme Being for its removal. The custom still prevails; and it therefore becomes proper to enquire how it is that men should continue to ask God to perform miracles or acts of special providence in their favor, and sometimes on very frivolous pretexts. Did any man ever have proof positive that any prayer was answered? Events sometimes happen seemingly at the instance of prayer; but it is impossible to be assured, beyond the possibility of mistake, that the event in question would not have taken place, entirely independent of any prayer.

In the infancy of the race, when mental and material progress was naturally slow, the first idea of God, the divine Father, was based upon that of the human father, who tenderly supplied the wants of the child—even before the wants were made known, and who always listened with attention to the supplications of his offspring—when those supplications were for such blessings, benefits, or necessities, as ought to be supplied. In the manhood of the individual, these supplications cease; and each person arriving at maturity learns, as his father did before him, to depend upon his own exertions, in conformity with the laws of Nature, and to provide himself, and those dependent upon him with food, raiment, and shelter. In the manhood of the race, the same results ensue—though they are not acknowledged—and man practically perceives, though he may not admit the fact theoretically, that prayer to God for the supply of our wants is wholly unnecessary, inasmuch as God has provided beforehand for all things which pertain to man's happiness and enjoyment, with a profusion and variety greater than most of us can conceive. Man having outgrown his moral childhood should, therefore, be manly and mature enough in his intellect, to understand and act upon the knowledge, that God's favors and gifts can only be had by conforming to the conditions prescribed for all that live.

It is not insisted that prayer to God, to raise us miraculously from a bed of sickness, or to give us clearer views of His will and pleasure that we may serve Him the better, may not have some beneficial effect upon the mind of him who prays, though the act be irrational. In the case of sickness, if the means of recovery by Nature's appointed mode are properly applied, an unfounded faith that God will specially interpose, may excite a livelier hope of recovery, and thus indirectly be of benefit to the sufferer, for the reason that hope is half the cure, and tranquillity and buoyancy of spirit are healthful to the flesh. On the other hand there is danger that faith in prayer—as if that were the only panacea and specific—may lead to the systematic neglect of the true means of recovery. The man who asks God to stimulate him to worship and obedience by supernatural means, or who asks Him for health, or wealth, or length of life, or any other especial grace or favor, acts in effect as if God had been unmindful of him, and had not provided for his needs; and thereby, virtually, accuses his Maker of ignorance or neglect. It may be said, however, in defence of this man's conduct, that his prayer, though unanswered, is not without spiritual uses. Were a man in a floating boat to pull at a rope attached to the shore, having all the time perfect faith that he is pulling the shore to the boat, instead of hauling the boat to the shore, it would make no difference with him which was the result, so that the boat and shore came together at last. So, while a man prays God to come to him, he may be unwittingly drawing himself to God, through God's originally appointed or natural means, independent of prayer—while he imagines that God is coming to him by supernatural means, that is, at the instance of prayer. In this way man may conceive himself benefitted by the usual mode of prayer, and thus fail to recognize the true source of the benefit. But it is important to the highest worship of God, that man should have full faith that God originally provided for whatever is needful for him, so that he may understand that if he fail to enjoy these provisions on the terms primarily prescribed by God, it is through his own mistake or neglect, and not God's—as man's irrational prayer would imply.

Prayer is not worship; and the only worship that can be acceptable to God consists in obedience to His divine and beneficial laws, and in thankfulness and gratitude for the gifts so lavishly showered upon us.

The religion, which the spiritual necessities of mankind require, finds its only foundation in the teachings of God to all men, and is aptly illustrated in the precepts and pure teachings of Jesus—when disencumbered of Judaism and all the Mosaic mythology—to wit, adoration of God, and love and duty to man. This is the one true religion established in the hearts, consciences, and souls of all men from the beginning, which ever has been, and ever will be sufficient to the end, that, through God's wisdom, goodness and justice, the existence of each member of the human family shall result in the glorification of the Creator, and the happiness of His creatures—be the path travelled ever so tortuous or rough.

By the persistency with which Christian teachers of all denominations and sects—from the Pope down to the elected minister of the poorest chapel or meeting-house—continue to dwell on the allegory of the fall of Man, and the consequent supposed necessity of Christ's sacrifice, all people of emancipated intellect are driven from the churches in despair and weariness of spirit. The multitude, like those who followed Jesus to the mountain, hunger for the bread of life, and are presented with a theological stone, in which there is no mental or spiritual nutriment. God, according to the teachings of Moses, is a God of anger and to be feared, who could not be propitiated but with sacrifices and burnt offerings. God, according to His own teachings, is a God of perfect goodness, who requires no sacrifice from His creatures; nothing but faith and cheerful obedience to the benevolent laws which He instituted for their spiritual and physical happiness. The God of Moses did not know,

THE GOD OF MOSES. 71

and could not foresee, anything that was to happen in His own creation. The God of all, is all-wise; and to His omniscience nothing is hidden, in the past, the present, or the future. To reconcile these two systems, or to engraft one upon the other, as all the Christian churches have attempted to do, for more than eighteen centuries, is impossible. They are antagonistic, discordant, and irreconcilable. If one be true, the other must be false. If a theory supposed to be true at one time, ceased to be true at another, it can never have been true at all; for God's truths are eternal as Himself. The doctrine taught by God from the beginning, and which is ever being echoed and re-echoed in the souls of all men—that He is infinite in goodness as in all things, and that man's highest duty is to cultivate the sublime germ of love to God and man within himself, so that its legitimate fruits may be produced by contributing, as far as it is consistent with his duty to himself, to the happiness, and well-being of all God's creatures—this doctrine, this religion, this teaching, needs no support from Moses or his theology. It is the only known religion that may be safely stripped of all externals, and left in its beautiful simplicity, to appeal to the heart and intellect of the humblest, as well as of the most exalted of mankind. The mischief is that this religion has been adulterated with falsehoods, which, under the disguise of vital truths, have, as Jesus said, not brought peace into the world, but continual strife, and the sword, and theological dissensions; and probably these dissensions will never cease until religion is thoroughly purged of all false theology.

All the Christian churches, following Moses and the Old Testament, in one breath declare God to be a God of Love—to which all His works bear witness—and in the next that He is wrathful, revengeful, and cruel ; that He is a God who has determined to inflict, everlastingly, the most horrible torture on every individual of the human race, who shall in the course of his life commit a single sin, or fail to observe the least of His laws. Further than this, they declare that the human race merits this punishment, even though personally, they commit no sin, because Adam, the first man, sinned ; and that God's love is shewn by His permitting Jesus—himself God—to atone for Adam's transgression, though the benefits of this atonement are not to be extended to any one who does not have entire faith in its efficacy. This doctrine is so utterly at variance with the never-ceasing logic of Nature, and with the constant manifestations of God's goodness and justice, that to escape the dilemma, they who teach it, are led to resort to various subterfuges to make the faith acceptable to those on whom they would impose it. Out of these falsehoods and contradictions have grown the never-ending disagreements, disputes, and contentions of religious sects and their spiritual instructors—"blind leaders of the blind." It was these very contradictions and dissensions that brought about, not only, the crucifixion of Jesus, but all the wars that have been waged in the world for opinion's sake in relation to theological matters, since the days of Moses and the Prophets. Jesus said that he came not to send peace, but a sword. And it has been calculated that the wars which have been waged on account of the differences of opinion in or on doctrinal points have cost the lives of above two millions of people. Those engaged in, to establish Christianity, and those persevered in, against the Turks concerning the Holy Land, have cost many millions more. The wars of Charlemagne to christianize the Saxons, and of the Spaniards to convert the Moors and Americans, have deluged the earth with innocent blood. And the Inquisition alone, since its foundation in the fourteenth century, has burnt above one hundred thousand persons of both sexes, besides destroying twice that number by torture and the dungeon. To this point we shall have occasion to refer hereafter.

It may be asked, whether what the Christian churches preach and claim to be indispensable to man's salvation is altogether wrong. This is not asserted. No teaching addressed to man's religious nature can be entirely in error, which obtains such an ascendency over the minds of men. It has much truth, but a great deal of error; and what it has of truth is mixed up with error, in such a way as to render it extremely difficult for the mass of mankind to separate the one from the other. Priestcraft is fully aware of the value of theological fable, as a means of strengthening and consolidating its power over human affairs; and, lest the simple truths of Nature which all may study, should have their legitimate effect in assigning to the every-day duties of life their legitimate importance in making up the sum of man's religious duty, the Christian churches all insist that, if man's thankfulness to the one God be ever so great, and all the duties of life be ever so well performed, yet if faith in the necessity and efficacy of Christ's atonement for sin be lacking, he must suffer everlasting torment in hell-fire. Each sect claims to be the exclusive exponent of the means appointed by God to enable man to escape from this torment. Out of, and by means of this vast fraud and shameless inroad upon men's credulity, priests and governments that support them have filched from the toiling people millions of treasure, to support them in the exercise of their trade or profession.

The idea of Hell, hell-fire, and eternal torment, when properly considered, is an idea that is alike blasphemous and illogical. Not so with the idea of eternal progress toward infinite knowledge and happiness, which is a natural deduction from our earthly experience.

It is manifest from the nature of man, that if he could, in advance, read the future with certainty, it would unfit him for the affairs of this life and, by inference, for the part assigned him in the next. It is illogical to insist that God, in giving man his various faculties, did not intend that he should use those faculties to the best advantage, in all things pertaining to his duty, his happiness, and his welfare, both in relation to this life and the life to come. It is insisted, however, by the priesthood, that man must ignore his common sense and reasoning faculties, when he comes to deal with the affairs of the future life. The maintenance of this requirement can only be accounted for upon the idea, that the churches well know that, if man were to use all his faculties for the acquisition of knowledge and the ascertainment of truth in relation to his duty to his Maker, the hold which they have on the purses of the people would be weakened, or perhaps entirely lost. The only religion which has exercised its influence over the minds and conduct of men, from first to last—whether recognized or not—is that here advocated; and it will continue to exercise that influence, notwithstanding all the false teachings and adverse influences that have been, or may be brought to bear against it.

A ship is swept along by the Gulf Stream, on the way to its destination, although those on board may not be aware of the causes that are impelling it onward. They might indeed, from a want of knowledge on the subject, ascribe their onward course towards the wished-for haven to a cause totally different from the true one—even to a cause that was in reality retarding them, as theology retards religion. And more especially might this be the case with a portion of the voyagers, if there were others on board who from selfish motives were using means to deceive their fellow travellers as to the true source of their progress. In the same way, are not mankind carried onward by the vast stream of influences set in motion by God, from the first, upon which all the human family have been or will be embarked? This tide, bearing man to the final home which God has prepared for him, no human power can stay. Man may, from shortsightedness, or false teaching, or both, be unmindful, or even unconscious of the true channel through which God's blessings are continually conferred upon him; yet they flow on incessantly. God makes ample allowance for man's want of knowledge, and is patient and forbearing, ever educating him to broader truths, and leading him to a higher state. He has made sure too, that under the influence of Nature's teachings he will at last come within the fold prepared for him, and be enabled to appreciate aright the justice and wisdom of his great Benefactor. And He has further made sure that the true light, deep down in man's soul, and the faith and hope based upon the idea of one God, the Great First Cause of all, shall never be extinguished. Not all the false teachings or injurious influences of human power that were ever put in motion shall disturb this firm foundation. It is a germ of truth in the soul of man, which will most surely bring forth its legitimate fruits in God's own good time. It is nurtured and watered by Him, and it will enable man more and more to understand and appreciate His goodness, and advance nearer and nearer toward His perfections. The germ, in the seed of the fig tree, the vine, and every other plant and herb, is especially cared for by God, to the end that its vitality shall be preserved. In process of time, under the influences with which God has surrounded it, it is quickened and springs up into life. It is fostered and cherished by God, through Nature, and it flourishes and seemingly rejoices in the sunlight and the balmy air, ever pushing forward with increasing energy to the fulfilment of its destined office in the world. No human power can thwart God's purpose in this. He has willed—and His will is law—that the earth shall bring forth trees, shrubs, herbs, plants, flowers, and fruit, in order that this Eden in which He has placed man, may be filled with beauty for his sight and with abundance for his taste. But in this, as in other things, His bounty comes not single-handed. Through the same process by which He administers to man's sense of the sublime and beautiful, He supplies the physical necessities of all His creatures. Now, if He has so protected the germ in the mustard seed, and trained it with certainty to fulfil His design, shall He do less for man? Yet, according to the teaching of the Churches, we are asked to believe that—of all the things created by God—man was left in the most precarious condition, placed in the greatest jeopardy, least likely to fulfil the intentions of his Maker, and condemned, for no fault of his own, to be eternally punished with torments too horrible to comprehend. How utterly inconsistent, and at variance with all the dispensations of God's providence, which man meets at every turn in his life and experience, is this idea! God's goodness and tender care of man are manifest in thousands of ways; and the mildness of the punishment for a breach of His laws, and the evidently benign intention of such punishment, declare most emphatically that God, represented in any other light than as infinite goodness, is not the God who reveals Himself to the heart, the conscience, and the intellect of all men, at all times.

So far as man's career is traced—which is no further than the grave—no discoverable advantage accrues to those who assent to the doctrine of the fall of man through Adam, and his restoration through Christ; and no discoverable disadvantage befalls those who have not arrived at such a belief. Those who belong to the latter class, and who make up the great majority or more than three-fourths of the human race, are as good citizens, as good husbands, as good wives, as good parents, as good children, as good neighbors, and are equally as cheerful, equally as happy, and equally as honest as the small remnant who believe, or who pretend to believe, in the fall of man through Adam. The Christian proclaims that all who do not embrace the dogmas, on which the Churches are built, are under the condemnation of God, and are not allowed to participate in the benefits of His goodness, in the world to come. Now, since there is no apparent difference in the distribution of such benefits in this world, it is fair to infer there is none in the other. But since we cannot trace man thither, except by logical induction, which is not subject to positive confirmation, the Churches make the most of man's ignorance in this respect—an ignorance no greater than their own—and promise him transcendent benefits in eternity as the reward of his faith, and for his support of the Churches.

Man, by nature and for wise purposes, has a predisposition to credulity. He loves the marvellous and the mysterious. From this phase of his character proceeds the wonderful influence which the false doctrine of supernatural revelation has so long maintained over the human mind, through the incomprehensible mysteries contained in the Bible, based upon prophecy and miracles. The less man's reasoning faculties are developed, the greater is the attraction which the marvellous and miraculous have for him; and the readier is the credence he gives to them. Hence it is the least enlightened of our race, both in this and every other age of the world, who are the most liable to be led astray by tales of sorcery, witchcraft, and ghosts. And have not witchcraft and supernatural appearances of departed spirits as great a claim on our credulity, as the miracles of the Bible? The existing generation of men has advanced toward mental manhood, so far as to discard many of the superstitious fictions of the incipient stage of the human race; and would emancipate itself still more rapidly and completely than it is doing, but for the struggle made against it by the Churches. And they are now the only obstacle to man's entire deliverance from such a thraldom. Seeing, however, how much their influence, and their gain are endangered by the spread of learning and intelligence, they are the more tenacious and persistent in their efforts to uphold, and to root more deeply still into the minds of the people, a superstitious belief in the mysteries of the Bible. But this once mighty influence is on the wane. The light of irrefutable truth has dawned upon the mental vision of all the civilized nations upon earth; and the darkness of theological error will soon be forever dispersed. Let the Churches, if they be wise, look to this matter in time. The true and lasting interest of the clergy lies in conforming without delay to the imperative intellectual demands of the age. Unadulterated truth must be taught from the pulpit—if anything at all. The people will not, much longer, continue to listen to doctrines and dogmas, for the belief of which there exists in man not one single innate faculty commending them either to the judgment or to the heart; but which, on the contrary, cause his whole nature to revolt.

The Churches tell us that man cannot answer the just demands of God, and that, therefore, by necessity, he merits God's everlasting condemnation, and his own utter destruction; but the heart of man rejects the blasphemy, and realizes that God knows exactly how much and what allowances to make in behalf of man's short-sightedness. Man is so far inferior to his Maker, that He will make every allowance in calling man to account for his misdeeds. Indeed, God's justice demands that man's free agency, to which He Himself has set limits, should not be so far extended as that man's existence could possibly become a curse to him, or anything else than a blessing, either in time or in eternity. His manifest goodness in this world, to us and to all the various forms of animated life, is so self-evident, that all who honestly investigate the blessings and beauties of Nature, and correctly reason upon them, must be convinced of it. As we mount from Nature up to Nature's God, we find not only that "whatever is, is right," and must be right, but that whatever is, is good, and must be good. Were it not for that which we ignorantly designate as evil, good would not be known to us, and would not be properly appreciated. So far as we are imperfect beings, we are sure to make mistakes and to suffer for them; but the very correction must be seen to be beneficial to us; because it teaches us not to offend against God's laws again; and in this way the seeming evil is made instrumental in the training of man to his best estate. The same kindness, therefore, which is so eminently bestowed upon man in this world, will, we infer, be continued to him in the next. This we are bound to believe, because we know that God's goodness, like himself is infinite, and cannot fail or be withdrawn from any of His creatures—unless we admit God to be of changeable purposes, which we cannot do without denying His wisdom and perfection.

The most obvious and natural idea of the happiness reserved for man in eternity is, that it shall be a continuation and an augmentation of the purest and most ennobling joys which he has experienced in time; that his soul, perpetually thirsting for truth and knowledge, shall be permitted to see and understand those great mysteries of God, which have been partially concealed from him on earth; and that he shall forever approach nearer and nearer to the divine perfections, to which however he can never wholly attain; and that every step of his infinite progression shall be attended with loftier delights than the constitution of his physical frame could ever have permitted him to enjoy while on earth. God hath endowed man with various qualities and capacities, adapted to his present life; and made each a ministering angel to his happiness. Is not this an evidence that He will endow him in the future life with higher qualities and more enlarged capacities to comprehend, appreciate, and enjoy God's wisdom, goodness and glory, in an ever-advancing degree? The spirit of all men seems so to whisper; and God has given them faith, that the high poetic reveries of the soul shall not be disappointed.

These are things which God, indeed, has not permitted us to know; but on the other hand He has not permitted us to be without a lively hope that we shall at some time enjoy them. There is no complete, positive, or mathematical proof, that what we call the soul is immortal. All that we can learn about it comes through our intuitions, our instincts, and an innate consciousness of it, corroborated by the belief of all men, in all ages and in all countries, that a glorious eternity of some sort lies before us. If this be not the fact, as we fondly deem, then God has given to every human being a delusive faith in His kindness; an abiding trust in His goodness, never to be realized. This is inconceivable; it is at total variance with God's benign dispensations on our behalf here; and with the indubitable fact that it is impossible to destroy the smallest atom of matter that was ever created. Matter may be changed and transformed, but it cannot be annihilated; and if this eternity is the appanage of the physical substances and elements of which the universe is composed, shall it not also be the appanage of the soul? We cannot believe otherwise. We accept the proofs with as much faith and as thorough a conviction as we have in accepting proofs of mathematical science, though they are not based so entirely upon mere reason, as upon something which we feel to be superior to reason, and a more direct utterance of the voice of God. This cannot be a vain imagining. The unwritten poetry—that whispers to us of a life beyond the grave, pervades all Nature, and even comes to us more audibly from the starry universe than from the earth—proclaims that Time, which is but the turning of the small globe upon which we live, is not the measure of that far-seeing soul and that ample intellect which, though imprisoned for a while within the flesh, has so far transcended its carnal limits as to discover stars and whole systems so deep in the infinitudes of space, that the light projected by them, according to scientific calculation, takes a time almost beyond man's comprehension to travel from their place in creation to ours. Such facts and such discoveries teach us that the soul, which aspires so high, is justified in aspiring; that it came from God, and must approach nearer to him for ever. The line of that eternal progression is influenced, in some degree, by the operation of causes within man's own control.

Let those learned men, who are the chief dignitaries of the churches, look to the intellectual development of our times. They should be the allies, and not the foes, of human intellect. To them all the truths of science should be welcome, because they are divine. That true religion, which exists in the heart as well as in the soul, needs no fables to recommend it to our acceptance. The so-called sacred Books, to which they still call upon us to yield a slavish faith, should be acknowledged by them to be without that sanctity which cannot attach to them, if they be contradicted by Geology and by Astronomy, and by every new discovery of natural and physical truths. The stars alone are a perpetual reproof to the ignorant mythologies, with which the clergy still endeavor to mislead the people. Newton, Laplace, Leverrier, and Rosse, were greater teachers of religion than any Pope or Bishop, or other ecclesiastic, who ever lived or preached. If, instead of theological and doctrinal discourses founded upon historical errors and false ideas of God, the preachers and teachers, accepting the great truths of science, would preach God in all His works and religion in its purity,

THE CLERGY SHALL ACCEPT TRUTH. 83

conformably to the intelligence of the age—let the immediate consequences be what they might—their efforts would prove beneficial in the highest degree. Jesus so taught religion in the two commandments; for which teaching he was crucified. God is ever teaching it in its fullness. The time is ripening for this development. Uneasiness and doubt sit within the assemblies of all mythological worshippers. It is not only the sheep, but the shepherds, who see the approaching change, and know it to be inevitable.

>Great thoughts are heaving in the world's wide breast;
>   The time is heaving with a mighty birth;
>   The old ideas fall:
> Men wander up and down in wild unrest;
> A sense of change preparing for the Earth
>   Broods over all!
>
>But not to me—oh, not to me appear
>   Perpetual glooms; I see the heavenly ray;
> I feel the healthful motion of the sphere;
> I see the splendor of a brighter day.
>   Ever since infant Time began,
>   More or less darkness has been over man,
>   It rolls and shrivels up. It melts away!

The intellectual culture of the many, who are yearning for good, is more than a match for the learned priest-craft that domineered over the too credulous of former ages. The printing-press now speaks to the masses, and rescues them from the thraldom of the oracles that spoke of old.

Theologians declare that, in order to make man conform to God's will, he must have that will proclaimed to him in special language either by speech or writing, and hence infer the necessity for a Bible. Let us probe a little into this assumed necessity.

The most casual observer of animal life, if brought for a moment to dwell seriously on the subject, could not fail to acknowledge that God has a mode of instructing His creatures, which amply suffices for their requirements and His own glory. And if this be evident to the careless looker-on, the closer student will find a thousand curious proofs, alike in its fullness and its minuteness, that the original instructor must have been divine. But the routine of animal life being so far known and noted as to acquire among us the distinctive appellation of "natural," neither ordinary observer nor critical student dreams of attributing supernatural causes to any part of it. We speak of it as the course of Nature, the ordinance of the Almighty; and there let it rest. No one imagines that a special revelation tells the migratory race of birds when and where the seasons are propitious for them, or that an inspired messenger goes down to the depths to warn certain fish at certain periods that it were well for them to change their waters. We call it all, in a general way, "instinct;" while a few thinkers, perhaps, recognize in this self-same instinct the marvellous power and resources of God.

Now, we hold that instinct is implanted in man, no less than in the brute creation. But the instincts which apply to man's spiritual nature are of an essentially different order. Animal instinct concerns itself only with life and the means of living; and this being its sole end, it is restricted thereto; and the routine is limited, each after its kind.

Instinct in man is, we say, of far higher quality. That it is not confined to a mere making provision for the flesh—as is the case with animals—is manifest from the infinite variety of human pursuits and the constant changes in human condition. That it reaches up to something above and beyond this, to something intellectual and spiritual, to some mysterious but existing link between creature and Creator, is palpable, inasmuch as the recognition of an over-ruling Providence has been common among all races and in all ages whereof we have knowledge. To put it in plainer terms: instinct in animals, becomes in man natural religion. And as instinct is universal in the lower rank, so is natural religion universal in the higher. Is there not, then, a pitiful underrating of God's reach and ability, in the supposition that He limited to a chosen few the task of teaching scattered portions only of mankind their duty, and added supernatural contrivances to his broad and efficacious means of bringing men's souls into more and more sympathy with himself? God has revealed himself, indeed; but his revelation is innate in man, and from the beginning. It is instinct, that teaches bird and beast how to provide for their physical wants. Instinct in man, pertaining to his spiritual nature, points to his duty to God, to himself, and to his fellow-creatures. Instinct or intuition, and education under the wholesome restraints and training incident to God's unalterable laws—together with the natural attraction that causes man's spirit to gravitate in the direction of His Maker's—cannot fail eventually to realize to man all, and more than all his fond imaginings and hopes as to the happiness that God has in store for him.

Nor has God allowed any human soul to be without this dream of happiness beyond the grave, transcendently greater than any that this life permits. We cannot conceive it possible that He can disappoint, in the slightest degree, any such broad foreshadowing of his goodness That God has prompted man to lean upon him for solace, every human soul can testify. Who shall doubt the realization of this hope, since the author of it is the pilot to conduct to its consummation? This spontaneous inborn faith in future happiness is broad-spread as the human race, and is based upon the One God, the God who knows no change, neither shadow of turning, and whose far-reaching intelligence and omnipotent power created and fashioned the universe.

We say, this faith, so founded, over-rides or takes precedence—whether it be noted for the moment, or not—of all the so-called faiths supposed to rest upon the imagined God of change and miracles. This faith may not always be equally luminous, but it shall never fail in its office of lighting and cheering our onward and still onward way toward the perfection of Him who caused its existence. All faith not springing from within, and not maintained in man in the absence or in despite of artificial teaching, lacks the stamp of genuineness that God ever imprints upon what he has ordained. He has ordained that every man shall, sooner or later, recognize and appreciate His blessing. Nothing less is consistent with God's determinate will and manifested perfection.

The religion here advocated is God's regularly appointed means of governing mankind. It is at once the oldest and the newest in the world. It dates from the first created man, and is recorded anew in each succeeding child that is born into the world. It is stamped indelibly on every fibre of his nature, without alteration or amendment—is ever fresh and new, and adapted to his every want. All men are guided and governed by it. It is God's great light shining into, and reflected from every soul of man. Whenever there is a soul to receive, there is light to pervade it. Such is God's goodness and bounty. None can doubt the authorship of this religion; nor can any question the sufficiency of the supply of that which contributes to its exercise; or which makes it available to all men, at all times. Those who say that this light lures to evil and not to good—to the paths that run counter to God's design—that man is at enmity with God—should remember that God is the author of man's nature and propensities, and that therefore they undertake to censure, not merely man's opinions, but the works and ways of God.

Amid the contentions and clamor caused by the various antagonistic creeds, theologies, and dogmas, there are propounded for the mere faith of man—each sect claiming the monopoly of the road to bliss—man is being so quietly conducted along the true path to his welfare and happiness, by a religion which admits of no antagonism—by laws that cannot clash, but which co-operate harmoniously, and move on majestically and silently to the accomplishment of God's purposes—that the means by which the result is reached are unobserved. Such is the case in relation to the motion of the earth, of which we all partake; and yet we perceive it not, except through its results. It produces the various seasons, day and night, seed-time and harvest, summer and winter; and by it the panorama of the heavens passes in succession before the delighted gaze of the whole human family. All alike enjoy these sights and blessings, whether they are aware that the immediate cause of them is due to the motions of the earth, or not.

Some may not recognize the law that guides them; and, to this extent, their knowledge being more limited, their enjoyment may not be as full as that of others. But when applied to spiritual things, this is but a matter of time; every human soul will, sooner or later, arrive at such a knowledge and experience of God's goodness, wisdom, and glory, as to induce all to thank and praise and worship Him with all their hearts and powers. Our capacity for happiness will increase, with our training and education; and as all must pass under God, through the same process of training, all must at last arrive at the same appreciation of His goodness and glory—some, it may be, by a more tortuous course, and by the experience of greater trials and afflictions; but none the less effectually to the accomplishment of God's design. What we mean is, that God's mode of training can never fail to accomplish the end He has in view. It must prove effectual. All will experience the same résults, by having been made obedient to the same laws. The same causes, which operate upon all alike, will produce the same effects *in* all; else God would not be that impartial Being that we conceive Him to be, which is impossible. When a human soul is brought into existence, it is brought into existence for eternity, and however little progress it may make in the right direction during its sojourn on earth— whether it be taken hence in infancy or old age, or whether it has advanced tardily or rapidly in this state of probation—it matters not, this being, as we said, but a matter of time. God has ensured that it cannot fail in being brought to know and worship Him according to His good-will and pleasure, and to the attainment of supreme bliss. And as to the mode whereby man is called upon, while here, to exhibit his gratitude for the blessings and bounties bestowed upon him by his maker, let us see what sort of gratitude is the most acceptable to God.

Jesus, whom we admit to have been a very good teacher of natural religion, and who will be taken by

GOOD WORKS. 89

most readers as excellent authority in this respect, has given us some advice through his teaching to the scribes and Pharisees. When he was asked, "Why walk not thy disciples according to the tradition of the elders, but eat bread with unwashen hands?" his reply was: "Well hath Esaias prophesied of you hypocrites, as it is written. This people honoreth me with their lips, but their heart is far from me. Howbeit, in vain do they worship me, teaching for doctrines the commandments of men. For laying aside the commandments of God, ye hold the tradition of men, as the washing of pots and cups—and many other such like things ye do. Ye reject the commandment of God that ye may keep your own tradition, making the word of God of none effect through your tradition which ye have delivered; and many such like things do ye."

From this we should infer, that this mere lip-service—this religion of mere ceremonies—is not only not the worship which God requires, but that it is a hindrance thereto. Forms and ceremonies may be well as mere preliminaries or stepping stones to worship. They may tend to quicken and train to good acts the germ in man's soul whence all his goodness springs. But if they do not exercise a beneficial influence on him in relation to the right performance of the every-day duties of life—if they do not incite him to the actual achievement of good deeds—they are of no avail in the sight of God. Under their influence the religious sentiments may expand; but if they be not productive of something more, they are not in accordance with God's high purposes in relation to man. Can man expect to be the recipient of God's bounties without his doing the work which God has required of him? Action is the order of nature, and an active life of good works—the doing to others as we would be done by, with a profound sense of dependence upon God—is the whole duty of man. The line between that which is mere church-form, and that which is the substance of a religious life, should be distinctly marked. Instead of this the non-essentials are put in the foreground; hence, man's religious instincts and common sense should turn him from mere barren ceremonies to the legitimate field of action. The worship dictated by nature alone meets the spiritual wants of man. This is really the only common ground on which all can stand harmoniously. It has an inherent vitality and force, which will, under the enlarging civilization and mental progress of the day, drive superstition and priest-craft from the field, and disperse the dark clouds which have so long and so gloomily overshadowed the true light.

There exists in man an innate or spontaneous faith in the eternal goodness and justice of the divine ruler—a conviction that man's best interest is forwarded by his serving God according to His universal teachings. No power on earth can obliterate these teachings, or materially retard their influence, however they may seem to be smothered in some, by the mass of theological dogmas. It still governs all men's actions, whether they acknowledge it or not, or whether they are aware or not that it is the sole controlling influence which is actuating them for good, and restraining them from evil. The work of the age upon which we have entered is not to found a religion—God did that effectually at the first—it is to expose the errors which it has been attempted to be substituted for true religion. Every year furnishes additional proof, and carries conviction to increased numbers of the rising generation, that the Bible is full of untruths. This, irre-

TRUE BASIS OF RELIGION. 91

sistibly, leads to free and increased enquiry in relation to all that is recorded therein. A new spirit is abroad. Men no longer ignore their common sense, in judging of the claims of the Bible to reliability. Under this mode of scrutiny, conclusions and convictions adverse to Bible record are accumulating year after year. Learning, scientific research, and free thought are fast opening the eyes of all classes to the imposition to which they have been subjected by the teachings of a mere dogmatical faith. Those who say that the Bible must be taken in all its parts, as the only revealed word of God, say also, that man's natural faculties are utterly corrupt, depraved, and at enmity with God. If this be so—if man's mind is so wholly corrupt, and all his conclusions in relation to religion are so wholly unreliable—how can he comprehend aright the doctrines of the Bible and the Churches, which are not only at variance with all his intellectual faculties, but are instinctively repulsive. How is this innate conviction of the fallacy of the Bible doctrines to be overcome? Any proofs offered to man's reason, or any appeals made to his conscience, are ineffectual, if the faculties to which they are addressed are as vicious and incapable of sound conclusions as they are represented to be by the Church.

The Church doctrines carry with them their own refutation, if logically examined. If addressed for the first time to a mature, well balanced, and cultivated mind, would they not, at once, be rejected as unworthy of the slightest credence? This is well understood; hence, the effort, which is constantly being made, to imbue with them, the minds of children, and of others equally unsuspecting and pliable.

If the natural consciousness of mankind is the true basis of religion, and the hope of a blessed immortality, then it has a foundation which defies criticism—and which is beyond all possible apprehension of ever being disturbed. No higher foundation than God, the father of all, is possible; and no faith can be so satisfying and thorough, as that which is the inevitable result of the promptings of that innate consciousness which is most assuredly of God. All faith, based on ideas or conceptions derived from traditions of the supernatural, is but as chaff in comparison with that derived from the immediate promptings of God to each individual. It is inconceivable how it is possible to doubt this; or that the instruction, which God has given to all alike, is not the true guide to faith and to the doing of His will by His creatures. In fact, there is no faith or belief contrary to this, which has sufficient substance in it to control any man materially or to modify his conceptions of his religious duties. Hence all the faiths, which men have founded on other than the intuitions of the soul, go for nothing, and are impotent in respect to the eventual happiness of the soul. They are the result of education, of the instilling of error into the minds of men from early childhood, and had their origin in the greed for power and money. All views in relation to religion derived from the Bible and other sources, and which cannot be deduced from man's natural faculties independent of the Bible, must of necessity be open to the critical investigation of history. The closest, most advanced, and the most learned, of this is the most fatal to such doctrines. As an example of this, let the works of the Bishop of Natal be consulted. He establishes most conclusively, that the first six books of the Bible—the corner-stone of the whole canon—were not written by their supposed author, and that they are not historically true, much less divinely inspired and infallible.

Bishop Colenso's work can hardly be over-estimated for importance, when we consider its inevitable influence on the opinions of the masses. Of course, the fact of his established ability, his personal character, and his position as a dignitary of the Church, has had considerable influence in adding to the immediate publicity of his work.

Religion founded on human consciousness brings into requisition, and into harmonious union for its right understanding and practice, all the faculties and functions of our nature; not so with the theology founded on the Bible. A blind faith is there demanded in relation to doctrines which neither the head, the heart, nor the conscience can take any part in confirming. A conception of God, formed through all the faculties and functions of man acting in conjunction, presents Him as a being whom to believe in is to adore, and whom to adore is to obey.

While all men have a love of the novel and the marvellous, few men naturally give credence to the miraculous and supernatural. The human mind, in virtue of a constitutional bias, is prepared from the first to count on the constancy of nature's sequences which experience ever confirms. Similar causes always produce similar effects. This is indispensable to the being led through experience to any system of truth by which to guide our actions; yet those who under the teaching of the church from childhood, have given a tacit assent to doctrine of especial enactments of God at the instance of prayer or other cause, to provide for certain emergencies, have not even in this our enlightened day, the moral courage to deny altogether what they could not bring themselves to believe—that is to say, what did not appear to them to be in harmony with the dictates of reason, and the laws of nature. In order to know what man is by nature and apart from erroneous teaching, we ought to know what he has been under the various theological teachings that have prevailed in different ages and in the several quarters of the earth. The history of these distant ages and distant men—apparently so foreign to our modern interests—assumes a new charm, so soon as we know that it tells us the story of our own race, of our own family—nay, of our own selves. History gives us the thread which connects the present with the past. Many scenes, it is true, are lost beyond the hope of recovery; and the most interesting of all, the opening scenes of the childhood of the human race, are known to us by such small fragments only, that they do but make every word the more welcome, that bears the impress of the early days of mankind. So far as we can trace back the footsteps of man, even on the lowest strata of history, we see that the divine gift of a sound and sober intellect, and all the kind and gentle emotions belonged to him from the very first.

The human mind has an inborn reverence for the past, that it may the better divine the future, to ferret out which is the ruling passion of man, since the vast wondrous ways of God lay before him, and God as a magnet is ever drawing him thither. As man the more and more obeys this divine incentive, he the more and more perceives God's goodness, and discards former false views, and discharges many myths because they are not in harmony with his purer conceptions of God, and therefore must be false.

The mythic form of expression which prevailed in earlier ages is giving way before comparative philology, which has placed in our hands a telescope of such power, that the mist which the theologians would hold before our eyes is too thin to prevent God's perfections appearing the more and more to us. He is no longer a God of vengeance, but a God of infinite goodness.

Paul says, "Prove all things; hold fast that which is good." Many are the advantages to be derived from a careful study of other theologies, creeds and faiths, than our own; but the greatest of all is, that it teaches us to appreciate more truly what it is that constitutes true religion. Let us see what other nations as well as our own have had and still have in the place of religion; let us examine the prayers, the worship, the theology even of the most highly civilized races,—the Greeks, the Romans, the Hindus, the Persians,—and we shall then understand more thoroughly what it is, that they all agree upon as true, and what it is that they differ in, and in this way be enabled to discriminate between the essential and the non-essential in the diversified things which have been deemed worship at various times and in various countries.

Those who would limit the riches of God's goodness, and would hand over the largest portion of the human race to inevitable perdition, without having made themselves acquainted with the religion of those they condemn, do at the same time impute to God injustice, upon no better evidence than theology originating in superstition and priest-craft—they use ignorance as evidence, as though it were knowledge. It is true that until very lately the sacred books of three of the most important systems of faith, those of the Brahmans, the Buddhists, and the Parsees, were totally unknown in Europe, but this furnishes no valid excuse for those who consign all who do not embrace their own theology to eternal torment. The sincere and earnest seeker after truth (though he may have a deference for the Christian theology) as he becomes acquainted with the history and habits of the various great nations into which mankind is divided, cannot but ask himself the question whether if the heathen, (as they are disparagingly termed) should judge of us as the Christians judge of them by the worst phases of human character, (and that exaggerated,) if we would stand any better in their estimation than they do in the estimation of the Christians.

If the Indians had formed their notions of the influence of Christianity on man from the soldiers of Cortez and Pizarro, or if the Hindus had studied the principles of Christian morality in the lives of Clive and Warren Hastings, or, to take a less extreme case, if a Mohammedan, or Buddhist living in Christian countries, were to test the practical working of Christian charity by the spirit displayed in the journals of our various religious parties, their notions of Christianity would be about as correct as the ideas which thousands of educated Christians entertain of the character of the heathen religion. Even Christianity has been depraved into Jesuitism and Mormonism, and if we claim the right to appeal to the gospel as the only test by which our faith is to be judged, we must grant a similar privilege to Mohammedans and Buddhists, and to all who possess a written, and, as they believe, supernaturally revealed authority for the articles of their faith.

We cannot comprehend how any one who worships God in spirit and in truth, who holds that he is perfect in all things, that his goodness knows no bounds, can subscribe to the dogma that God determined from the first to elect a chosen few, as the recipients of everlasting bliss, and

INNATE PROMPTINGS OF THE HEART. 97

consigned much the largest portion of mankind to perpetual torment, for no fault of their own, but at the instance of an arbitrary will, the justice of which no man can comprehend. If the holding of such faith, if ascribing such character to God, is not sinning against Him, and debasing ourselves, we cannot conceive what is. God is a God of infinite goodness, not of vengeance; to be loved, not to be feared; to be worshipped for love's sake; not through fear of everlasting punishment.

How beautiful does this incentive to the worship of God appear, in comparison with that which wrings assent from us by the threat of torment! And more particularly when we take into consideration, that this threat of torment involves only a faith coming to us from uncertain authority, and repugnant alike to our innate perceptions of love and duty.

To present so dark and hideous a picture of God and of His mode of drawing men to Him, presupposes that there is not enough in the picture that God presents of Himself, to win man to love and worship Him.

The law implanted within the nature of man to regulate his physical system is expressed by the sensations, propensities, promptings, appetites, tastes, and checks, that God originally gave him, and that are indispensable to the perpetuity of the human race. In like manner, the soul of each individual must be guided, in its pursuit after happiness and well-being, by similar laws, which God has implanted within his moral nature; namely, by the innate, instinctive, irresistible promptings of the heart and spirit, after what is good, and true, and just, and kind, and lovely. Indeed, we all know by the necessity of the case that man has a consciousness and conviction within him that he possesses these perceptions and incentives, and that they are the infallible guides which God has placed there for his instruction and warning. The more faithful he is therefore to these instructions and warnings, the more happy he will be—just as the more faithful he is to the rules regulating the health of his body, the more sound will be his constitution, and the freer he will be from disease. To love God is to love His attributes; and the germs of that love being within us, all we have to do is to cultivate them, and to make them active. To strive to imitate Him, or, rather, to inculcate in our hearts a love of truth, justice, and goodness—the prime traits of character in the Almighty—is the worship and homage that are most acceptable to Him. But God is represented in the Bible, and by those who adhere to its teachings, as being endowed with attributes, purposes, and modes of action wholly inconsistent with the existence of such laws and incentives, to the acquisition and cultivation of virtue in the heart of man. The Bible is, moreover, utterly irreconcilable with itself. The Old and New Testaments, particularly, are at variance with each other, and on some of the most vital points. God Himself is represented as a Being endowed with the most opposite traits of character. In some places He is said to be a God of infinite goodness, love, and justice; in others, a God of hatred, revenge, cruelty, and injustice. He is represented as so unjust as to consign to everlasting punishment all those who are not His favorites; or, who will not, or cannot, believe in the very impracticable doctrine that Jesus must save them,—and that in a way which they cannot understand. And yet such incongruities are the very opposite to the doctrines of Jesus, whom Christian theologians profess to rely upon, as the best and most infallible guide to man. For, with the exception of some ideas which he entertained toward the latter part of his career, to the effect that he was the Messiah, and that he would come again at some future time to take possession of his kingdom, and reward his followers, and punish his enemies by bidding them to depart forever from his presence and province, which he denominated everlasting punishment—apart from this, we say, his religion was as much in unison with that written on man's heart and nature, as it could be. It was in perfect accordance with that which has just been advocated, and which is innate in man, and only needs to be developed by stimulation and cultivation. It was a reflection of God's laws, operating in the hearts of men. Whatever of good there is in man comes from this source and teaching, and from no other.

Again, the idea of the existence of a devil, and of the baneful influence ascribed to him over the minds, conduct and happiness of man, is in direct contradiction to God's infinite power, justice, and goodness.

If God created man with a free-will; and in His goodness allowed him the exercise of his free-will by setting before him things, all good in themselves, but by the use or abuse of which he would experience good or evil results; and if in the exercise of his free agency man sometimes chooses the evil—this is but the result of his short-sightedness, and the abuse of his free agency. It furnishes no grounds for the idea of the existence of such an evil spirit, as that which is said to run counter to the nature of God, and to tempt man to sin against Him. The idea of a Supreme Devil, or God of Evil, originated with the Persians, centuries before the Christian Theology was ever thought of. Yet it is curious to notice, in passing, how differently the Church has treated the Persian

Div, and the Cro God, who is common to all faiths. Out of the one true God, it has made a triform and triune Deity, scarcely less fantastic than certain divinities worshipped by Pagans; while the *Div*, or Satan, is allowed to maintain his potential unity, and figures in the Church's cheerful programme for this world, as going about like a roaring lion seeking whom he may devour; and in the next, as executioner-in-chief to an extremely wrathful judge.

Now it is against all reason to suppose, for a moment, that there is such an evil principle so embodied, and therefore *Div* cannot be admitted as a medium of temptation to man. When man errs, it is not the result of an innate viciousness; nor because he has anything placed before him which contains properties that are evil in themselves. It is because he is either ignorant of the nature of those properties, or because being careless or reckless in the exercise of his free agency, he indulges too freely in their use. Education only in addition to his innate perceptions, can regulate him in this matter. And to this end God has ordained that, whenever man oversteps the bounds of propriety, he shall suffer for it at once; or within such time that the punishment for delinquencies that are incident to man, while in the flesh, may serve the purpose of correction and warning. In this way, God's punishments, termed by the Church, "the vengeance of the Almighty," are all applied in mercy. There would be confusion and inconsistency and injustice in the idea, that man is to be chastised in a future state of existence for crimes committed in this, there can be no temptation beyond the grave to commit crimes that specially appertain to this life; and, therefore, such punishment would be retrospective and totally useless for

God's sole end of training and improvement. His is not punishment deferred. Neither is punishment by His laws appropriate after the offender has corrected himself. God's punishment, we repeat, is for the correction of the fault committed, with reference to future amendment. It is not—it would be absurd to say that it is—eternal punishment for faults which God notes down, and that He inflicts it in a revengeful spirit at some future time when it may be presumed that even the memory of their committal has passed away. No, this is unworthy of infinite goodness; and we hold it to be entirely irrational. The bare idea that God could for any offence, or for any cause whatsoever, determine that any of His creatures should be irrecoverably tormented, upsets at once the idea of the whole nature and perfections of God, and makes Him— not what the Bible describes Him to be, in some places, a God of love—but what it describes Him to be in other places, "a consuming fire," a revengeful, hateful, and malignant monster. How Christian people, who have any appreciation of the goodness and beauty of His character, can so debase Him, we are at a loss to understand. We can entertain no possible idea, in relation to God, other than that of His perfection. Hence, as perfection embraces all goodness, justice, and order, and as man's conception of these qualities—is of God's creating, it follows that man's ideas of good and evil—which are indissolubly associated with these qualities, are in the main, in accordance with God's own teaching.

All the creeds and theologies of the Bible and the Churches, which man's conscience rejects, and in which all the faculties of his mind combined fail to recognize, God's goodness, must, of necessity, be untrue. Shall traditional authority alone reverse all this? God has decreed otherwise. Men deceive themselves, when they give a formal or pretended adherence to such teachings. They will not be of the slightest service to men, either here or hereafter. Whenever such errors cease to be instilled into the pliant minds of children, and others, who are not accustomed to think for themselves, then will they be consigned to oblivion—their proper place. Then will the religion, which is an integral part of man, and which nature stimulates with never-failing effect, be left unadulterated with such unseemly dross as the theologians would heap upon it.

That happiness is the true and normal condition of life, and misery the exception, is evidenced in a thousand ways. All animated beings, whether rational or irrational, seek it, intuitively. As a rule of almost universal application, those who live the most joyful, buoyant, and happy lives, live the longest. Pleasurable sensations also, both mental and physical, not only attend all the duties and functions of life, but the legitimate exercise of every faculty affords its own peculiar pleasure; pain may sometimes result; but this is the extraordinary, and not the ordinary, rule. In the aggregate, the preponderance is largely in favor of pleasure. Pleasure, resulting from the performance of the duties of life, evidently springs from a double source. First, it is a spontaneous emanation from divine goodness, as a free-will gift to his creatures; and secondly, it is an incentive and guide to the requirements of peace and self-preservation, and to the practice of benevolence, love, friendship, and all other kindly impulses.

The happiness that man realizes from conscious existence, may rationally be taken as a guarantee that it is his normal condition; and whatever God addresses to his reason is never in vain or without a beneficent object. Man has implanted within him, by God, a religious instinct or tendency to glorify him. To live an innocent and joyous life is one mode of thanking God for existence. The insects that sport in the sunshine, the lambs that gambol in the fields, the birds that warble their merry or plaintive songs in the trees, and the children in their bright and gladsome spirits while at play, all thank God for their existence, in His own appointed way. With regard to these last, God has provided, through the laws of nature, for their guidance and care in a more marked manner; and man, who has come to riper years and is more under the control of reason, may well learn a lesson from them. To inculcate the idea that a melancholy spirit and a gloomy walk through life are more acceptable to God than the cheerful heart—which God is ever, in ten thousand ways, exhilarating, is an impediment to true religion. God intended that all His creatures should live serene and happy lives. This is pre-eminently apparent from the allurements so lavishly strewed in the path of all, to win them back from gloom and sorrow to sunshine and gladness. Cheerfulness begets cheerfulness; pain is exhaustive, tends to its own cessation. The action of the organs, in the production of pleasure, is promotive of their development and increased capacity. The same cannot be said of pain; therein the reverse is the rule. Pleasure tends to its own augmentation and perpetuity. Pain benumbs the nerves, and works its own diminution or extinction. Pain gives warning of impending dangers to life and happiness. Pleasure trains to religion and a blissful eternity. Such is the voice of God within us, and such is the voice of nature without us. But let it be borne in mind that the happiness, here spoken of, is that which is consistent with virtue, when indulged in to a rational or legitimate extent. Man may run into excess in the pursuit of happiness, or he may indulge in vice and dissipation, thinking happiness lies therein. In either case, the result will be the reverse of what he expects, for the choicest blessings of life are only precious when used in moderation. The vital and unextinguishable sense of right and wrong, the love of good, and the abhorrence of evil, which God has implanted in man's nature, together with the system of perpetual training through rewards and punishments which He has established must, and will ultimately prevail, and insure the ascendancy and triumph of the good, the right, and the true, against all adverse influences. Any other idea than this is an imputation against the righteousness of God's purpose, and the perfection of His work in creating man. When man brings to bear all the faculties of his mind— reason as well as instinct—with a view of ascertaining God's will and purposes in relation to him, and his proper duty to God, the result must be a more satisfying, a sounder, and a more abiding faith in the correctness of the conclusions arrived at, than can possibly be the case when his several faculties are at variance on the subject. A faith predicated on the infallibility of the Bible, which in many instances runs counter to itself, is not a safe guide to the future destiny of an immortal spirit, thirsting for enlarged supplies of knowledge and holiness.

What is termed evil in connection with the spiritual or mental part of man, results from his not being perfect, as God is perfect. This is a necessity. The creature must be lower than the Creator. But the enquiry, not unnaturally presents itself—why has God placed man so low? Why has He allowed so much seeming evil to exist that man's happiness and well being are apparently put in jeopardy? Why was man not endowed, at his creation, with a free agency so limited as materially to diminish the evil that now attends him? These are questions which are altogether beyond our present understanding. The proper answer is known only to God; but that it is best to be as it is, there can be no doubt. It is inconceivable that what God has done involves other than the greatest possible good. Man is to comprehend so much of God's purposes or ways, as is necessary for his good and happiness while in this life in order to prepare him for the next. God's infinite perfections guarantee this; and His benevolent purposes, in creating man, are beyond the possibility of question. To feel such trust in God as this acknowledgment implies, is man's highest privilege, and his indispensable solace. God has given him this abiding confidence, with its attendant charm of reliance, through such means as admit of no failure. A majority of mankind may never proclaim it in words; but nevertheless each and every human being, that ever came to consciousness, proclaims it in thousands of ways that are pleasing to God. The multitudes of cheerful spirits, and bright and happy upturned faces, that we meet daily, exhibit a never flagging hope of better things to come. This blessed hope is an emanation from God, to cheer us onward; and it betokens more and more precious treasures in store for us hereafter. For God can neither deceive, nor engender delusive hopes, to cheat or mislead his creatures.

Time, with its never ceasing tread, hurries man to his unseen destiny, and yet he trembles not, nor fears. Let all bless God in their hearts, that such is the glorious reward of this implicit trust—founded in the depths of each human soul, echoed from heart to heart, and chimed throughout all nature by its every aspect and mood. It must all be well for those who have the great, the just, the perfect God for their pilot and sponsor; and, vast as is the difference between the perfection of God and the frailty of short-sighted man, yet man is still encouraged to make efforts—though feeble they may be—to approach God's goodness and knowledge, and to start on the high career of assimilating himself to God's perfection. He finds that at each step he gains new accessions of strength, brighter light, and stronger aspirations and impulses to press onward. This encouragement and this help come from Him who knows the vastness of the object aimed at, the means to be used, and the degree of success that awaits the seemingly futile effort. These conceptions open to our view a prospect of stupendous magnificence and glory. They show that it is in reserve for man to progress through countless ages, adding knowledge to knowledge, and excellence to excellence, and to be ever approaching nearer and nearer to God's perfect holiness. They intimate that man is permitted to be an active and free agent, under God's supervision, in contributing to his own advancement and the carrying out of God's benign purposes. May not this view, to some extent, illustrate the wisdom of God in placing man so low, and with such a glorious career before him? May not the sum total of man's happiness be greater, as he is ever emerging from a dimmer to a brighter light—from one stage of happiness to another, still higher—ever advancing in his aims and longings for an existence far above, and superior to this, where he will be blessed with an increased knowledge of the mysteries of creation and God's wondrous ways? Does not this accord with what we know of our own natures and experience here? Is not our appreciation of the things around us assisted by contrast? Are not our very pleasures heightened by expectation? Each aim we have accomplished, begets higher aims, nobler purposes and increased energies, if we are but true to ourselves and our innate promptings and inspirations. Each and every gloomy, dark foreboding that lies in the path of life will ultimately, under God's inscrutable providence, be made subservient to our welfare and happiness. This is constantly being illustrated, during our brief sojourn on earth; and to an extent, and in ways so mysterious and unlooked-for, that the evidence of our senses leads us to the same conclusions as does faith, based upon God's wisdom, goodness, and justice, and manifested throughout all His works. God seems to take delight in making darkness available and subservient to the appreciation of the splendor of His works, and to a reverence and worship of Himself. The high sense of beauty, and the pious emotions that spring up within us on viewing the countless stars spangling the firmament, would be lost to us—but from being contrasted with the darkness of the night.— Viewed from the shaded side of earth and of life, the true glory of heaven is better seen, and the value of God's goodness and wisdom is more appreciated.

That species of evil which is denominated pain, and which relates to the physical, or material part of man, is unmistakably ordained of God for man's ultimate good. Matter, unlike the mind or spirit of man, is destined to dissolution and to a return to dust. Man, by his intuitions and by the other faculties of his mind, desires, and is led to the preservation of the body, to the fullest extent practicable. Without the instrumentality of pain, man would not be able to do his body the good offices and services which he does now, and which are indispensable to the continuation of his species, even for but a very brief space of time. Each and every sensation of bodily pain is a warning that the welfare of the body is endangered, and requires the good offices of its co-partner—the intellect—in its behalf. This monitor, pain, therefore, of all others, is the one most likely to be recognized and obeyed; and, in general, as the danger is more imminent, so is the monitor more persistent in his demands for an immediate attention to his warnings. As a general rule, whatever pertains to the health, vigor, and preservation of the body is attended with more or less pleasure; while whatever tends to its destruction is painful. We not only, therefore, have a sleepless sentinel on duty, to proclaim approaching danger; we have premiums offered for attending to the legitimate wants of our own bodies, and for striving to promote our own happiness. How beautifully and forcibly does this illustrate God's benevolence and more than fatherly care over us! The contemplation of it adds confirmation to confirmation, and faith to faith—if such a thing be possible—that man's greatest ultimate good is perfectly consistent with his seemingly lowly and apparently unfortunate condition here, moral and physical. It is an unmistakable evidence that God's consummate wisdom can bring beauty out of seeming uncomeliness, and clear up and disperse all the apparent gloom and imperfection, in His infinite perfection and brightness.

In the present world, man—so far as his body is concerned—is subject to casualty and the destructive powers of nature, equally with the lower animals. But as this life is only the beginning of an existence that will never end, and is under the Divine guidance, one can but have faith that it matters little at what period of time the transit, to the higher life, takes place. If it were important, life would not have been subject to the numerous contingencies that now beset it. And yet the teaching of God through our instincts, is to cling to life while we may, leaving the time of our departure to casualties beyond our control. In reflecting upon this, how comforting is it to know that we are the objects of God's goodness and care. We see but the threshold of our destined existence. We have but to strive unceasingly, and never to weary in well-doing, confidently leaving the issue to God.

But this subject of our existence here and hereafter, and of the connection between the two periods, may well bear to be further contemplated. This life, then, and this earth are but the time and place, the when and where, each human soul embarks for eternity. The longest life is but as a moment of time, in comparison with the soul's duration. The earth is but the stage whereon each human soul, among the myriads that are launched into eternity, is moulded, and—like the person—individually endowed with an identity peculiar to itself and resembling none other precisely. The belief that our individuality and identity in this world shall be preserved to us in the world to come—that we shall connect the consciousness of ourselves beyond the grave with that of ourselves here, and be so recognizable by others—is corroborated by a fact in our human experience, that cannot be gainsayed. Millions upon millions of inhabitants come and go upon the face of the earth; and yet no two among them bear such close resemblance as to prevent intimate acquaintances singling them out from all others. And as with the body, so with the soul. We, none of us have, an exact spiritual counterpart—a fact that is obvious to all students of the inner man, though not palpable at a moment's glance, as is the corporeal divergence. Now this being the case—the extreme difference between the most dissimilar persons being so small that they may be classed as a whole, and yet so distinctly marked that each stands out as it were alone—is it possible not to see herein a purposed design of God? And to what purpose can this point, more rational and more in accordance with His perfect plans, than that the probation, intended to lead man Heavenward, and barely dawning here on the longest-lived, shall continue when we go hence, through what is our morning, up to the splendor of an everlasting day? The more we contemplate God's wisdom and the harmonious workings of his systems, the more are we confirmed in this view? It is at least more probable that God will give the being, whom He himself created, an opportunity of learning to comprehend His mysteries, and of rendering Him homage, than that, after a mere comparative spasm of existence, man is at once promoted to a region of eternal bliss, or plunged into everlasting torment. That this cannot be so, and be consistent with God's justice, is the more manifest, when we remember that a large portion of the human race have their sojourn upon earth curtailed—by causes beyond their own control—to the hundredth part of that of others, and that surrounding circumstances must often alone determine man's progress towards the Heaven or the hell, which the theologians flaunt before him. We know that these same churchmen have great difficulty in reconciling this, their peculiar phase of God's character, with the other attributes wherein they clothe Him. The true solution of this whole difficulty is to clear away church theology and substitute in its place a wholesome belief that God has assigned eternity for the endless education and the mode and manner of it is of God's ordaining, who shall doubt its bringing all men to supreme bliss in God's good time?

Since no man can be wise, as God is wise, and since neither human reason, nor experience, can supply the deficiency, in working out his destiny under his free agency, instinct makes up for what he lacks in other respects. But since man, as now constituted and endowed, is always liable to deviate from right, and so bring more or less mental or bodily pain upon himself and others, some might say, why not have prevented the possibility of evil—if evil it be—by giving man such instincts as would have made it entirely unnecessary that he should be constituted a free and consequently an accountable agent? But will any one say that he would have preferred this? Would he not rather say: "The present system of limited agency is far more satisfactory to me? To have no control over my destiny annihilates my individuality. Rather let me have the responsibility which attaches to free agency, than the degradation which is involved in not having any share in shaping out my present life and future destiny. Rather let me, under the influence of volition and by actions that are my own, enter into the joys, sympathies, and griefs of life as it is. This best satisfies my nature, and the cravings of my spirit. Let me be loved, because of the peculiarity and personality which is the result of my own volition and acts; and let me love those whom I may love, because they have had a share in the making up of their own peculiar personality. In this is the crowning joy of life."

May not the crowning joys of Eternity be considered in a somewhat similar light? May not influences in a measure akin to this, ultimately prevail in perfecting man's love of his Maker? Intuition—as we have frequent occasion to remark—renders it imperative that man should acknowledge a God above him. So far, there is no exercise of free-will. It is only an acquaintance with God's works and an insight into His dealings with man, that can convert this knowledge into reverence. Herein, the free-will is partially exercised. But it is only a thorough appreciation of God's infinite loveliness, that can impart full impulse to volition, and transform this reverence into love that is worthy of its object. Nature endues a mother with affection for the child born of her—unattractive, ugly, peevish, troublesome though it be. This is instinct. How much more intense is her attachment, if the little being be supremely fair and gifted with every infantile grace? This is love. So it may be with man hereafter, when, in another stage of his existence, the marvellous beauty of God's character and attributes are gradually revealed to him. We believe, indeed, that God has predetermined to make His self-constituted and self-sustained perfection apparent to all men.

We believe that every man will eventually love Him, and strive more and more to serve Him—not alone from those spontaneous movements within, that impose no restraint on his own free agency, but also from these emotions that emanate from his own free-will.

The instincts of man, which have reference to his spiritual or divine nature, are the primary foundation of man's religion. The office of the reasoning faculties is distinct from that of the instincts. The instincts are more necessary, because they are ever shedding upon our onward path a light indispensable to us, in groping our way through this chequered scene. They are the inexhaustible fountain, whence is drawn every noble purpose,

GOD'S LAWS UNCHANGEABLE. 113

every incentive to good, kind, and generous deeds. Man, as a free agent, acting under and by force of his reason and all his faculties, other than instinct, would stumble, fall, and utterly fail in his progress through life; but as it is, he has ever with him a safe pilot—a guardian angel, as it were, guided by a higher mind than his own. There are certain duties that God has assigned to man during his stewardship here, the proper performance of which is too important and too difficult of understanding to be entrusted to man's reasoning faculties alone, even when of the highest order and fully matured, much less when the reverse is the case. Instinct is indispensable to the welfare both of the body and soul. It is given by God to ensure that, while man is to a certain extent entrusted with working out his own destiny, God's benevolent purpose towards him shall ultimately prevail. And while there is, judging from observation here, a vast difference in the endowment of individuals, in relation to all those faculties of the mind which are subject to cultivation and improvement, there is little or no difference in relation to instinct—the office of which is so important, that all God's living creatures have it, in ample strength and in ample time. This is not the case with those other faculties called mental. These are developed, in process of time, according to our advantages, by observation, by experience, by comparison, and by study. This being so, the improvement of them exhibits itself at different periods and in different degrees, in different individuals. This is manifest to all men. We all recognize it in this life, however it may be in the next.

Does God govern mankind entirely by laws established at the first—co-eval with the creation of man; or has he subsequently, and from time to time, enacted and made operative new laws to meet unforeseen contingencies? Is God moved from day to day and from hour to hour by prayer, or otherwise, to reverse or modify his general laws for the government of men, by means of what are termed special providences? If men are to be held accountable for the breach of God's law, justice demands that the law should be stable and sure, not vacillating or shifting, the same deed being right to-day, and wrong to-morrow, and *vice versâ;* otherwise, man is without a reliable rule of conduct, and his never varying instinct and innate perception of right and wrong have no parallel in the laws of God, no immovable standard of moral right by which he can constantly direct his course.

Now, plain and undeniable as seem the conclusions here suggested, they are directly in the face of those of Christian theology; they cannot both be true; and if the Christian theology be true, then God—contrary to Bible phraseology—is a being of change; and this makes the inference irresistible, that He was not equal to adjusting all things aright from the first, but only after trial, observation, and second thought. If this view of God is to be taken as glorifying and worshipping Him, we not only fail to perceive that such is the fact, but deem such view most irreverent.

With a view to bringing the light to be derived from history to bear on the question, as to whether God's government was perfect from the first, or required subsequent radical amendments and a never ending round of adjustments called special providences, by way of testing the rationale of what is termed supernatural revelation, we will state a supposed example. Let us say that five persons have appeared upon the earth at various periods, but all after many generations of men had lived and died thereon. Each of these persons claimed to be entrusted by God with a message of vital importance to every member of the human family; the character and import of which had never before been made known to man. The pretended new communication from God was to the effect, that every individual must have an unwavering belief that a certain person, who was then, or had been, or was to come, upon the earth, was the only medium through which men could be saved; that all who had this faith would receive eternal happiness, and all who had it not, eternal damnation. Up to this point, each of these five persons delivered similar messages; but here they diverged. Each now personally, or by followers, was declared to be the one designated by God as he to whom the faith in question must be given in order to obtain salvation. Suppose that these five messengers were named respectively, Christ, Zoroaster, Buddha, Godama, and Mohammed, each claiming to be the only Saviour of mankind.

Now this supposed case furnishes substantially the facts that have actually taken place among men; and the result is that faith, more or less strong, has been divided between the several persons named as Saviours. The number professing faith in Jesus—or living in so-called Christian countries—comprises about one-third of the inhabitants of the globe. This being the case, is there any tenable reason why the Christian theology should be held right, and all the others wrong? We deem them all alike fallacious. God sends his laws for the government of mankind into the world, by each and every inhabitant thereof—each being his own messenger; and as the law enjoined by this message is of the same import at all times and in all places, this message demands our faith in preference to any other.

Again: if a man claims that he was the first person to whom God made known a new law, to be added to His former laws for the government of mankind—which had answered their purpose for generation after generation of men, but which now required amendment and addition—we cannot credit him. We have unbounded and unextinguishable faith, that God is perfect and unchangeable, and that His laws to govern man must have been perfect and all-sufficient from the first. We cannot put faith in any one who pretends that God added to His original code, a vital and imperative law for man's government, long after many men had lived and died. None, we say, who hold that God is perfect and unchangeable, can possibly credit such a story; neither can they reconcile it to their views, that God, who makes sure that all his ways are perfect, should confide to a single individual an all-important message intended for the benefit of each one of the human race.

To those whose conception of God is no higher than one involving additional enactments, alterations, and especial providences, as unforeseen occasions may require for the government of the world, another difficulty presents itself. If, according to their theory, it becomes necessary for God to bring forward through the especial messenger, for the regulation of man's relations with his Maker; and if two persons appear simultaneously, each claiming to be from God; both giving contradictory versions of the claimed will of God—how, under these circumstances, are the advocates for the supernatural to determine which is the true and which the lying messenger? The Bible itself, will not certainly give them much aid in distinguishing the false from the true, if we may judge by its many warnings. Ahab consulted four hundred prophets; they were all impostors, with the exception of Micaiah. "The prophets," saith the Lord to Jeremiah, "prophesy lies in my name; I sent them not, neither have I commanded them; neither spake I unto them: they prophesy unto you a false vision and divination, and a thing of nought, and the deceit of their heart;" and elsewhere, "Thus saith the Lord of hosts, hearken not unto the words of the prophets that prophesy unto you; they make you vain; they speak a vision of their own heart, and not out of the mouth of the Lord." Jesus, himself, did not implicitly rely upon his own universal recognition. "Then," said he, "if any man shall say unto you, Lo, here is Christ, or there, believe it not. For there shall arise false Christs and false prophets, and shall shew great signs and wonders; insomuch that, if it were possible they shall deceive the very elect."

Christian theology then, has no other foundation than the conflicting claims of numerous prophets and miracle-workers; a majority of whom, according to Bible narrative, are false. We fail to perceive that any one of them has more claims to be credited than another; and must consequently conclude that they are all alike incredible.

Saying we believe in Jesus, is unintelligible, unless we specify the nature of our belief, inasmuch as various descriptions of belief have been connected with the name of Jesus. During the few years of his public career, he assumed three distinct positions before the world, while, during the first half century after his death, yet another and totally distinct position was assigned to him.

Belief in Jesus, has therefore, been construed to signify—in the first place, that he was a teacher of the way to the inheritance of eternal life; secondly, that he was the Messiah, the person designated by the prophets, to rule over the Jews forever on earth; thirdly, that he was destined to reign forever over a new world—after the destruction of the old one—to be inhabited by the righteous only; fourthly and lastly, that he is co-equal with God, and the Saviour of all men who entertain this belief.

Now these several offices—three of which were assumed by Jesus, while the fourth was thrust upon him after his death—differed so essentially from each other, as to render it absolutely impossible that they could all have been fulfilled. Passing by Jesus' first and unobjectionable position—that of a teacher of divine truths, or in other words, of natural religion—we ask, how could he reign everlastingly as King of the Jews on the earth that then was, and yet reign everlastingly also on a new earth which he was to build up from the ashes of the old one? It is just as plain that Jesus has never ruled here in any Kingship as that the earth never has been destroyed according to his prediction. What he predicted therefore, with so much eloquent earnestness, is both impossible according to reason, and flatly contradicted by facts. Adding to this the fourth office thrust upon Jesus, the puzzle is complete. Where shall we turn for a reliable guide to true belief? we say that men should turn to the One God, Jehovah. He points unmistakably to the first and only religion, which Jesus taught with signal effect, and which embraced his true mission, and the only rational portion of his course.

JESUS' SECOND COMING. 119

All the early followers of Jesus clung to the first and third of the beliefs enumerated above, and confidently looked for the destruction of the earth that was to be replaced by a new one, and for Jesus' second coming to rule over them forever thereupon. They clung to this belief and this expectation, up to, and long after the time predicted by Jesus for its fulfilment. In fact, the expectation of a coming millenium, so-called, upon earth, over which Jesus is to rule forever, has not yet entirely died out. The belief and expectation, no doubt originated in the declarations of Jesus himself, which assumed a very definite form, as he drew toward the close of his career. "For," said he, "as the lightning cometh out of the east, and shineth even unto the west ; so shall also the coming of the Son of man be. For wheresoever the carcass is, there will the eagles be gathered together. Immediately after the tribulation of those days shall the sun be darkened, and the moon shall not give her light, and the stars shall fall from Heaven, and the powers of the heavens shall be shaken. And then shall appear the sign of the Son of man in Heaven ; and then shall all the tribes of the earth mourn, and they shall see the Son of man coming in the clouds of Heaven with power and great glory. And he shall send his angels with a great sound of a trumpet; and they shall gather together his elect from the four winds, from one end of Heaven to the other. Now learn a parable of the fig-tree : When his branch is yet tender, and putteth forth leaves, ye know that summer is nigh. So, likewise, ye, when ye shall see all these things, know that it is near, even at the doors. Verily, I say unto you, This generation shall not pass till all these things be fulfilled. Heaven and earth shall pass away, but my words shall not pass away."

These citations embody Jesus' reply to the question of his disciples: "Tell us, when shall these things be? and what shall be the sign of thy coming, and of the end of the world." Jesus, moreover, elsewhere likened his coming Kingdom of Heaven, to a net which is made instrumental in dividing the godly from the ungodly. Some further light is also thrown upon the literal signification of Jesus' announcement, by Peter's words, in his second Epistle, " But the day of the Lord will come as a thief in the night; in the which the heavens shall pass away with a great noise, and the elements shall melt with fervent heat; the earth also, and the works that are therein shall be burned up. * * * Nevertheless, we, according to his promise, look for new heavens and a new earth wherein dwelleth righteousness."

With reference to the expected destruction and renovation of the earth, Mr. Lecky, in his "*History of European Morals*," has a comprehensive foot note: "The belief," says he, "that the world was just about to end, was, as is well known, very general among the early Christians, and greatly affected their lives. It appears in the New Testament, and, very clearly, in the epistle ascribed to Barnabas in the first century. The persecutions of the second and third centuries revived it, and both Tertullian and Cyprian strongly assert it. With the triumph of Christianity, the apprehension for a time subsided; but it reappeared with great force when the dissolution of the empire was manifestly impending, when it was accomplished, and in the prolonged anarchy and suffering that ensued. Gregory of Tours, writing in the latter part of the sixth century, speaks of it as very prevalent; and St. Gregory the Great, about the same time, constantly expresses it. The panic that filled

Europe at the end of the tenth century has been often described. The fulfillment of these predictions of Jesus and his disciples in relation to the destruction of the world by fire, like those in respect to his second coming, has been so long delayed beyond the expected time, that the theologians have been obliged either to abandon them as fallacious, or to assign to them a meaning totally different from the obvious and originally received one, deduced from the plain meaning of words. The new world is still to be created, just as Jesus' promised throne of David remains still unoccupied.

The great craving of man's spirit is for the discovery of truth. To gain an insight into the mysteries of the universe, gives other and higher delight, than merely to admire its beauties. The first faint symptoms of this passion—for such it is—are exhibited in early childhood. The inquisitive boy either cuts the bellows, to see where the wind comes from, or takes a watch to pieces, to find what makes it tick. During adolescence and maturity, the zest for knowledge increases in intensity with the discovery of each new truth; and as truths are ascertained, and multiply, and their wonderful harmony with each other, is observed, the dawning of light within the soul gains strength and becomes more luminous.

The poetical part of man's nature has its foundation in truth and harmony—the great characteristics of God. The poetic instinct is the legitimate offspring of the intuitions that apply to man's higher nature and destiny; and these in conjunction with his other faculties, form the ladder, as it were, upon which he ascends heavenward. When the spirit soars into the higher regions of imagination, under the excitement of a sense of the beautiful, harmonious, and truthful, it is but God's mode of giving man a ray of that sublime light, which shines brighter and brighter as he presses forward in the right direction—an indication that the soul is capable of a more exalted state of existence and happiness than it has yet realized, or than the things of this earth can reveal. It is the whispering of God, to allure man to the sure path that leads to his more congenial abode—to his true destiny. This perception and natural leaning, by and through our instincts, to the well-being and happiness of ourselves and our species, is analogous to that which incites the bird of passage to mount upon its wings, and speed its way from colder regions to the warmer climes of the South, there to pass the winter season, and then again to return to the North, the better to rear its young. The still, small voice, that charms the bird hither and thither, communicates not an idle tale; it is truth, big with utility, involving life and death. The bird that pours forth its tuneful strains, perched upon the tree-top, sings not in vain; in Nature's good time, his mate, the harbinger of love and gladness, and fruitfulness, will come, and God's all-wise and benevolent purposes will be answered. And so of that chant of love which Nature causes to vibrate in the virgin and unwedded heart. It is but the budding of the highest bliss, that earth has in store for humanity. It is God's mode of making his children subservient to the accomplishment of his great ends. All Nature is full of melody, to those who know how to listen. Music, sometimes the more enchanting for being dimly audible, is ever attuning the emotional soul to the lovely and the sublime, and training it to a higher and higher estate. Unwritten poetry, we say, pervades all nature. Man is attuned to its harmony and its inspiration. The infinite fancies and fond imaginings of man are not without an actually existing object, either here or elsewhere; neither are they without utility. They contribute, immeasurably to the charms of life. They foster hope, that blessed boon to man. They stimulate to nobler deeds, and lead to loftier aspirations. Fiction and poetry, which transport and thrill the soul in books do but portray some truth or truths recognized already as existing in nature. If not, the spirit heedeth not; the charm is wanting, and the springs of life go still unquickened. Poetry may, not inaptly, be likened to the flowers that contain the embryo of luscious fruit, and that are all the sweeter and more attractive because they promise something more valuable than the present sense enjoys. Not that the flowers themselves are without real utility. By their fragrance and beauty, they furnish a feast to some of the organs of man, no less than does the fruit to others. There is no quality or organ of man's nature. either of body or mind, that is devoid of utility. No such anomaly can emanate from the Deity. Man's body, it is true, cannot subsist on music, but it furnishes a rich feast to his higher being. It can, and does, feed that part of his nature, wherewith he is enabled to appreciate and enjoy the harmony of God's works. As truth after truth is added to the store of man's knowledge in relation to God and his works, the more and deeper is he impressed with the glory of the author of the universe and the wonderful harmony and accord of all created things.

This advance in knowledge, and appreciation of God's greatness and goodness, we deem, will be without end. The lower animals, and the physical part of man's being, find the means of satisfying their wants and cravings in things pertaining to earth. Not so with the human soul; it has longings not satisfied in this life, qualities and powers for the enjoyment of a nobler and higher existence, which find not the means of their realization here. There is nothing waste and nothing meaningless in the feelings and faculties, wherewith living creatures are endowed. For each desire there is a corresponding object; for each faculty there is room and opportunity for exercise, either in the present life or in futurity. But for the immortality of the soul, man's endowments would not be in harmony with his destiny. He would be an exception to God's universal order and fullness of all things—an anomaly in nature irreconcilable with the known and only conceivable attributes and ways of God.

It is evident from the wide-spread and extensive practice of using idols in devotional service, that it proceeds from some strong, legitimate trait in human nature. All the prominent errors of man so proceed. Among the powerful propensities which God has given to man is a restless desire to search after, and penetrate into, the wonderful mysteries of the spiritual and physical universe. But for this thirst for, and advancement in, and acquaintance with the knowledge and ways of God, man would fail to prepare himself for his future destiny as God intended he should. Man, in his eagerness to see God, climbs the tree, as did Zaccheus, or builds a tower as did Nimrod. In primitive times the lowly in intellect and culture endeavored to portray God, the incomprehensible, by the help of tangible things; and having singled out a figure or symbol, availed themselves of it as giving some idea of God. They, then, through such a symbol, poured out their spontaneous adoration to that mysterious Being, whose wisdom, through His works, they saw pervading all things, yet not otherwise visible to the physical eye. God, however, designed man for development and advancement, as he did the child in his progress from infancy to manhood. The appliances and helps suited to these ends, for one age and stage of growth, are unsuited to a more advanced one. The present state of knowledge, cultivation, and intellectual development in all civilized nations is such, that man should now allow nothing to stand in the way between his own spiritual eye and the great Spirit which fills the universe.

There is no room or occasion for a second or third person in the Godhead. The Spirit of God pervades the universe. It is an Infinite Mind, and must, of necessity, be a unit. What God wills to do, and what God executes, is without effort. No other idea is consistent with Infinity. The utility or possibility of there being two or three co-equal infinite Gods is as incomprehensible to man, as that there can be two or three infinite divisions of space; or that there can be two or three independent existences of time. Yet, two, and even three, co-equal Gods are claimed as the Rock on which the Christian Church is founded. This is idolatry.

The Christian Church claims, too, the infallibility of the Bible, notwithstanding irrefutable evidence to the contrary, and thereby again sets up an idol. The worship of Jesus and the Virgin Mary is as much idolatry as is the worship of the sun, the moon, the stars, and other objects, worshipped by what are called idolatrous nations. They who worship God through these material objects, which are symbolical of the true light emanating from Him who is infinite, and ineffable light itself, are much more excusable, in view of the greater intelligence claimed by Christians in these later times.

The various trains of thought and reasoning which lead men from a consideration of the natural world to a conviction of the existence, the power, the providence of God, do not require, for the most part, any long or labored deduction, to give them their effect on the mind. The notion of such supremacy is universal and innate. In many nations, in many periods, this persuasion has been mixed up with much that was erroneous and perverse. But the opinions of the intellect or the fictions of the fancy, do not weaken the force of such conviction. The belief of a supreme and presiding power runs through all these errors; and while the perversions are manifestly the work of caprice and allusion, and vanish at the first ray of sober enquiry, the belief itself is substantial and consistent, and grows in strength upon every new examination. It is an assurance that the mere existence of a law, connecting and governing any class of phenomena, implies a presiding intelligence, which has preconceived and established the law. We cannot, then, represent to ourselves the universe governed by general laws, otherwise than by conceiving an intelligent and conscious Deity, by whom any such laws were originally contemplated, established, and applied.

The impression which thus arises, of design and intention exercised in the formation of the world, or of the reality of a Prime Cause, operates on men's minds so generally, and increases so constantly on every additional examination of the phenomena of the universe, that we cannot but suppose such a belief to have a deep and stable foundation. Indeed, science shows us, far more clearly than the conceptions of every-day reason, at what an immeasurable distance we are from any faculty of conceiving *how* the universe, material and moral, is the work of the Deity. But with regard to the material world, we can at least go so far as this;—we can perceive that events are brought about, not by insulated interpositions of divine power, exerted in each particular case, but by the establishment of general laws. This, which is the view of the universe, proper to science, whose office it is to search out these laws, is also the view which, throughout this work, we have endeavored to keep present to the mind of the reader. We have attempted to show that it combines itself most readily and harmoniously with the doctrines of Natural Religion, that the arguments for those doctrines are strengthened, the difficulties which affect them removed, by keeping it steadily before us. We conceive, therefore, that the religious philosopher will do well to bear this conception in his mind. God is the author and governor of the universe, through the laws which He has given to its parts, the properties which He has impressed upon its constituent elements: these laws and properties are, as we have already said, the instruments with which He works: the institution of such laws, the selection of the quantities which they involve, their combination and application, are the modes in which He exerts and manifests His power, His wisdom, and His goodness: through these attributes, thus exercised, the Creator of all, shapes, moves, sustains and guides the visible creation.

How strongly then, does science represent God to us as incomprehensible! His attributes as unfathomable! His power, His wisdom, His goodness, appear in each of the provinces of nature which are thus brought before us; and in each, the more we study them, the more impressive, the more admirable do they appear. When, then, we find these qualities manifested in each of so many successive ways, and each manifestation rising above the preceding by unknown degrees, and through a progression of unknown extent, what other language can we use concerning such attributes, than that they are *infinite?* What mode of expression can the most cautious philosophy suggest, other than that He, whom we thus endeavor to approach, is infinitely wise, powerful, and good?

But with sense and consciousness, the history of living things only begins. They have instincts, affections, passions, will. How entirely lost and bewildered do we find ourselves, when we endeavor to conceive these faculties communicated by means of general laws! Yet they are so communicated from God, and of such laws He is the law-giver. At what an immeasurable interval is He thus placed above everything which the creation of the inanimate world alone would imply; and how far must He transcend all ideas founded on such laws as we find there! But we have still to go further, and far higher. The world of reason and of morality is a part of the same creation, as the world of matter and of sense. The will of man is swayed by rational motives; its workings are inevitably compared with a rule of action; he has a conscience which speaks of right and wrong. These are laws of man's nature no less than the laws of his material existence, or his animal impulses.

All the laws which govern the moral world are expressions of the thought and intentions of our Supreme Ruler in relation to man. All the contrivances for moral no less than for physical good; for the peace of mind and other rewards of virtue, for the elevation and purification of individual character; for the civilization and refinement of States, their advancement in intellect and virtue; for the diffusion of good and the repression of evil; all the blessings that wait on perseverance and energy in a good cause; on unquenchable love of mankind, and unconquerable devotedness to truth; on purity and self-denial; on faith, hope, and charity; all these things are indications of the will, and future intentions of that God of whom we have endeavored to track the footsteps upon earth, and to show his handiwork in the heavens. "This God is our God, for ever and ever." And if, in endeavoring to trace the plan of the vast labyrinth of laws by which the universe is governed, we are sometimes lost and bewildered, and can scarcely, or not at all, discern the lines by which sorrow, and vice, and injustice from man to man, fall in with a scheme directed to the strictest right and greatest good, we yet find no room to faint or falter; knowing that these are the darkest and most tangled recesses of our knowledge; that into them science has as yet cast no ray of light; that in them reason has as yet caught sight of no general law by which we may securely hold: while, in those regions where we can see clearly; where science has thrown her strongest illumination upon the scheme of creation; where we have had displayed to us the general laws which give rise to all the multifarious variety of particular facts; we find all full of wisdom, and harmony, and beauty; and all this wise selection of means, this harmonious combination of laws, this beautiful symmetry of relations, directed, with no exception which human investigation has yet discovered, to the preservation, the diffusion, the well-being of those living things, which, though of their nature we know so little, we cannot doubt to be the worthiest objects of the Creator's care. We find if we never experienced pain, we should be every moment injuring ourselves without perceiving it. Without the excitement of uneasiness, without some sensation of pain, we should perform no function of life, should never communicate it, and should have none of its pleasures. Hunger, which compels us to take our required nourishment, is the commencement of pain. *Ennui*, which stimulates us to exercise and occupation, is a pain. Love itself is a longing which becomes painful until it is met with corresponding attachment. In a word, every desire is a want, a longing, a beginning of pain. Pain is therefore the main-spring of all the actions of animated beings. Inasmuch as want involves pain, and since all our pleasures proceed from the gratification of our legitimate wants, it is apparent that God can, and does cause, even pain and want to pave the way to man's happiness and well-being.

That all foreseeing Power, who is the guardian of our infirmities, has supplied to human weakness what human wants required. There is a principle in our mind, which, to us, is like a constant protector. It may slumber, indeed, but it slumbers only at seasons when its vigilance would be useless. It awakes, at the first intimation of danger ; and it becomes more watchful and vigorous, in proportion to the violence of the attack which it has to dread.

It is well that man is constituted independently of his own will, and that he has so little power in shaping the circumstances amid which he moves. He would have needed a far more comprehensive view than he is equal to, both of what is best for men in a community, and for man as an individual, had he—a creature of such brief and narrow survey—been left with the fixing either of his own principles of action, or of his relation with the external world. That constitutional shame—that quick and trembling delicacy—a prompt and ever-present guardian, appearing as it does in very early childhood, is most assuredly not the result of our anticipating either present or distant consequences. Thus, with reference to our animal instincts, to which we have already alluded. Other forces than those of human prudence and human principle seem to have been necessary for restraining within legitimate bounds a most powerful and fascinating incentive, which, when improperly indulged, is deteriorating to the moral character; and which, when once permitted to lord it over the habits, so often terminates in the cruel disruption of families and the irretrievable ruin and disgrace of the offender. It is not by any prospective calculation of ours that natural modesty acts herein as a strong precautionary check. It is directly implanted by One, who sees the end from the beginning, and has made it available to all men at all times by a monitor set up within us. Conscience, as the supreme arbiter of all our actions, superintends all our senses, passions, and appetites, and judges how far each of them is either to be indulged or restrained. When conscience prevails over the other principles of our nature, then every man is led, by the very make and mechanism of his internal economy, to feel that this is as it ought to be; or if these others prevail over conscience, that this is not as it ought to be. The object of conscience is the subordination of the whole inner man to its dictates, and its proper, its legitimate business, is to prescribe what man shall be and what he shall do.

Righteousness, it is felt, would not have been so enthroned in the moral system of man, had it not been previously enthroned in the system of the universe. This is not a local or geographical notion. It is not, therefore, the peculiarity of one creed, or of one country. It circulates at large throughout the family of man. We can trace it in the religion of savage life where theology has not found its way; it mantains its authority over the artificial theology of a more complex and idolatrous paganism. Neither crime nor civilization can extinguish it; and whether we find it in the fierce and frenzied Cataline, or in the tranquil contemplative musings of Socrates and Cicero, we find the impression of at once a righteous and a reigning sovereign.

The law of conscience may be regarded as comprising all those virtues which the hand of the Deity has inscribed on the tablet of the human heart; and it is an argument, for these being the very virtues which characterize and adorn Himself, that they must have been transcribed from the prior tablet of His own nature.

Conscience speaks the same language, and owns one and the same moral directory all the world over. True to her office she gives forth the same lessons, in all the countries of the earth. Let the mists of passion and artificial education be only cleared away; and the moral attributes of goodness and righteousness and truth will be seen undistorted, and in their own proper guise—and there is not a heart or a conscience throughout earth's teeming population, which could refuse to do them homage. In spite of the occasional diversity of moral judgments which are vastly less wide and numerous than is generally supposed, there is a fixed standard of morals, to the greater principles of which, a full and unanimous homage is rendered from every quarter of the globe. On the whole, then, it is evident that conscience is founded on human nature, and forming a constituent part of it, and may be regarded as a faithful witness for God, the author of that nature, and as rendering to His character a consistent testimony. This ascendant faculty of man, which may be termed the divinity within us, notwithstanding the occasional sophistry of the passions, is on the whole, representative of the Divinity above us. Whenever an act of iniquity or an outrage is done to the law of conscience, there is felt a reaction within, which tells that the outrage is resented. Then it is that conscience makes most emphatic assertion of its high prerogative, and, instead of coming forth as the benign and generous dispenser of its rewards to the obedient, it comes forth like an offended monarch in the character of a severe avenger. In that instant pleasure and instant pain, wherewith conscience follows up the doings of man, we behold not only a present judgment, but a present execution of the sentence, to the end that immediate repentance and amended ways may follow.

God is the rewarder of virtue. He hath so constituted our nature that, in the very flow and exercise of the good affections, there shall be the oil of gladness. There is instant delight in the first conception of benevolence. There is sustained delight in its continued exercise. There is consummated delight in its happy smiling, and prosperous result. Kindness and honesty and truth are of themselves and irrespective of their rightness, sweet unto the taste of the inner man. Malice, envy, falsehood, injustice, irrespective of their wrongness, have of themselves, the bitterness of gall and wormwood.

It is thus manifest that a state of well-doing stands associated with a state of well-being. The special virtue of temperance is not more closely associated with the health of the body, than the general habit of virtue is with a wholesome and well conditioned state of the soul. There is then no derangement, as it were, in the system of our nature—all the powers, whether superior or subordinate, being in their right places, and all moving without discord and without dislocation. In short, God has so framed the creatures of His will, as that their perfect goodness and perfect happiness are one.

To educate and win man to his greatest happiness, and true destiny, God has spread diversified loveliness over the panorama of visible things, thrown innumerable walks of enchantment around us; turned the sights and sounds of rural scenery into the ministers of exquisite enjoyment; and caused the outer world of matter to image forth in profusion those various qualities which please or powerfully affect us in the inner world of consciousness and thought. God, we say, has thus multiplied our enjoyments, and invested them with such qualities as suit the constitution of the human mind. He has pencilled them with the very colors or moulded them into the very shapes which suggest either the graceful or the noble of the human character.

He has so formed our mental constitution, and so-adapted the whole economy of external things to the stable and everlasting principles of virtue, that in effect the greatest virtue and the greatest happiness go hand in hand. But the union of these two does not constitute their unity. Virtue is not right because it is useful; but God has made it useful, because it is right. He both wills virtue, and wills the happiness of his creatures—this benevolence of will, being itself, not the whole, but one of the brightest moralities in the character of the Godhead. He wills the happiness of man, but wills his virtue more; and accordingly, has so constructed both the system of humanity and the system of eternal nature, that only through the medium of virtue can any substantial or lasting happiness be realized. Finally, it is worthy of special note that while conscience exercises the same authority and gives the same lessons, approves and disapproves of the same things all the world over, it never condemns in matters concerning the thousands of disputed creeds and theologies abroad in the world; may not this be taken as proof positive that dogmas and doctrines form no part of genuine religion?

The Christian theology being entirely based upon supernatural or special providences in contradistinction to the absolutely stable and unalterable laws of God, we cite a passage hereupon, from the writings of Dr. Chalmers. It will be seen that the views here expressed are completely adverse to the idea of vacillating and shifting laws, such as theologians pretend to recognize in God's government of the affairs of this world.

"This disposition to count on the uniformity of Nature, or even to anticipate the same consequents from the same antecedents, is not the fruit of experience, but anterior to it; or at least anterior to the very earliest of those of her lessons which can be traced backward in the history of an infant mind. Indeed, it has been well observed by Dr. Thomas Brown, that the future constancy of Nature is a lesson, which no observation of its past constancy, or no experience could have taught us."

At whatever stage of the experience the inference may be made, whether longer or shorter, whether oftener or seldomer repeated—the conversion of the past into the future seems to require a distinct and independent principle of belief; and it is a principle which, to all appearance, is as vigorous in childhood as in the full maturity of the human understanding. The child who strikes the table with a spoon for the first time, and is regaled by the noise, will strike again, with as confident an expectation of the same result as if the succession had been familiar to it for years. There is the expectation before the experience of Nature's constancy; and still the topic of our wonder and gratitude is, that this instinctive and universal faith in the heart should be responded to by objective nature, in one wide and universal fulfillment.

The proper office of experience, in this matter, is very generally misapprehended, and this has mystified the real principle and philosophy of the subject. Her office is not to tell, or to reassure us of the constancy of Nature; but to tell what the terms of her unalterable progressions actually are.

The human mind from its first outset, and in virtue of a constitutional bias co-eval with the earliest dawn of the understanding, is prepared and that before experience has begun her lessons, to count on the constancy of Nature's sequences. But at that time, it is profoundly ignorant of the sequences in themselves. It is the proper business of experience to give this information; but it may require many lessons before that her disciples be made to understand what be the distinct terms even of but one sequence. Nature presents us with her phenomena in complex assemblages; and it is often difficult, in the work of disentangling her trains from each other, to single out the proper and casual antecedent with its resulting consequent, from among the crowd of accessory or accidental circumstances by which they are surrounded. There is never any uncertainty as to the invariableness of Nature's successions. The only uncertainty is as to the steps of each succession and the distinct achievement of experience is to ascertain these steps. And many mistakes are committed in this course of education, from our disposition to confound the similarities with the samenesses of Nature. We never misgive in our general confidence that the same antecedent will be followed by the same consequent; but we often mistake the semblance for the reality, and are as often disappointed in the expectations that we form. This is the real account of that growing confidence, wherewith we anticipate the same results in the same apparent circumstances, the oftener that that result has in these circumstances, been observed by us—as of a high-water about twice every day, or of a sunrise every morning. It is not that we need to be more assured than we are already of the constancy of Nature, in the sense that every result must always be the sure effect of its strict and casual antecedent. But we need to be assured of the real presence of this antecedent, in that mass of contemporaneous things under which the result has taken place hitherto; and of this we are more and more satisfied with every new occurrence of the same event in the same apparent circumstances. This too is our real object in the repetition of experiments. Not that we suspect that Nature will ever vacillate from her constancy—for if by one decisive experiment we should fix the real terms of any succession, this experiment were to us as good as a thousand. But each succession in Nature is so liable to be obscured and complicated by other influences, that we must be quite sure, ere we can proclaim our discovery of some new sequence, that we have properly disentangled her separate trains from each other. For this purpose we have often to question Nature in many different ways; we have to combine and apply her elements variously; we have sometimes to detach one ingredient, or to add another, or to alter the proportions of a third—and all in order, not to ascertain the invariableness of Nature, for of this we have had instinctive certainty from the beginning; but in order to ascertain what the actual footsteps of her progressions are, so as to connect each effect in the history of Nature's changes with its strict and proper cause. Meanwhile, amid all the suspense and the frequent disappointments which attend this search into the processes of nature, our confidence in the rigid and inviolable uniformity of these processes remains unshaken—a confidence not learned from experience, but amply confirmed and accorded to by experience. For this instinctive expectation is never once refuted, in the whole course of our subsequent researches. Nature, though stretched on a rack, or put to the torture, by the inquisitions of science, never falters from her immutability; but persists, unseduced and unwearied, in the same response to the same question; or gives forth, by a spark, or an explosion, or an effervescence, or some other definite phenomenon, the same result to the same circumstances or combination of data. The anticipations of infancy meet with their glorious verification in all the findings of manhood; and a truth which would seem to require Omniscience for its grasp, as co-extensive with all Nature and all history, is deposited by the hand of God, in the little cell of a nursling's cogitations. In the instinctive, the universal faith of Nature's constancy we behold a promise. In the actual constancy of Nature, we behold its fulfillment. When the two are viewed in connection, then, to be told that Nature never recedes from her constancy, is to be told that the God of Nature never recedes from his faithfulness. If not by a whisper from His voice, at least by the impress of His hand, He hath deposited a silent expectation in every heart; and He makes all Nature and all history conspire to realize it. He hath not only enabled man to retain in his memory a faithful transcript of the past, but, by means of this constitutional tendency, this instinct of the understanding, as it has been termed, to look with prophetic eye upon the future. It is the link by which we connect experience with anticipation—a power or exercise of the mind co-eval with the first dawnings of consciousness or observation, because obviously that to which we owe the confidence so early acquired and so firmly established, in the information of our senses. Nature never disappoints, or which is equivalent to this, the Author of Nature never deceives us. The generality of Nature's laws is indispensable, both to the formation of any system of truth for the understanding and to the guidance of our actions. But ere we can make use of it, the sense and the confident expectation of this generality must be previously in our minds; and the concurrence, the contingent harmony of these two elements; the requisite adaptation of the objective to the subjective, with the manifest utilities to which it is subservient; the palpable and perfect meetness which subsists between this intellectual propensity in man, and all the processes of the outward universe—while they afford incontestable evidence to the existence and unity of that design, which must have adjusted the mental and the material formations to each other, speak most decisively, in our estimation, both for the truth and the wisdom of God.

We have long felt this close and unexcepted, while at the same time, contingent harmony, between the actual constancy of Nature and man's faith in that constancy, to be an effectual preservative against that scepticism, which would represent the whole system of our thoughts and perceptions to be founded on an illusion. Certain it is, that besides an indefinite number of truths received by the understanding as the conclusions of proof more or less lengthened, there are truths recognized without proof by an instant act of intuition—not the results of a reasoning process, but themselves the first principles of all reasoning.

There is a comfort in being enabled to vindicate the confidence which Nature has inspired—as in those cases, where some original principle of hers admits of being clearly and decidedly tested. And it is so of our faith in the constancy of Nature, met and responded to, throughout all her dominions, by nature's actual constancy, the one being the expectation, the other its rigid and invariable fulfillment. This perhaps is the most palpable instance which can be quoted, of a belief anterior to experience, yet of which experience affords a wide and unexcepted verification. It proves at least of one of our implanted instincts, that it is unerring; and that, over against a subjective tendency in the mind, there is a great objective reality in circumambient nature to which it corresponds. This may well convince us, that we live, not in a world of imaginations—but in a world of realities. It is a noble example of the harmony which obtains, between the original make and constitution of the human spirit upon the one hand, and the constitution of external things upon the other; and nobly accredits the faithfulness of Him, who, as the Creator of both, ordained this happy and wondrous adaptation. That we are never misled in our instinctive belief of nature's uniformity, demonstrates the perfect safety wherewith we may commit ourselves to the guidance of our original principles, whether intellectual or moral—assured, that, instead of occupying a land of shadows, a region of universal doubt and derision, they are the stabilities, both of an everlasting truth and an everlasting righteousness with which we have to do." This is directly opposed to special providences, without which Christian theology is baseless.

Our ideas of the moral attributes of God must be derived from our own moral perceptions. It is only by attending to these, that we can form a conception of what His attributes are; and it is in this way we are furnished with the strongest proofs that they really belong to Him. The peculiar sentiment of approbation with which we regard the virtue of beneficence in others, the peculiar satisfaction with which we reflect on each of our own actions as have contributed to the happiness of mankind, and we may add, the exquisite pleasure accompanying the exercise of all the kind affections, naturally lead us to consider benevolence or goodness as the supreme attribute of the Deity. It is difficult, indeed, to conceive what other motive could have induced a Being, completely and independently happy, to have called his creatures into existence. The evils which we suffer are parts of a great system conducted by Almighty power, under the direction of infinite wisdom and goodness.

The creation of beings endowed with Free-will, and consequently liable to moral delinquency, and the government of the world by general laws—from which occasional evils must result—furnish no solid objection to the perfection of the universe. When man, ignorantly or knowingly, violates any of God's laws, he receives the punishment consequent upon his action and best for his ultimate welfare. Such punishment is therefore in accordance with God's goodness and justice—utility being the sole principle of action, as well in regard to punishments as rewards.

The various duties of life agree with each other in one common quality, that of being obligatory on rational and voluntary agents; and they are all enjoined by the same authority—the authority of conscience. These duties, therefore, are but different articles of one law, which is properly expressed by the word Virtue; or still more unequivocally, by the phrase, The Moral Law.

The practice of morality is facilitated by repeated acts; and, therefore, the word Virtue may with propriety be employed to express that habit of mind which it is the great object of a good man to confirm. "He that ruleth his spirit feels himself greater than he that taketh a city." "It is pleasant," says Dr. Tillotson, "to be virtuous and good, because that is to excel many others. It is pleasant to grow better, because that is to excel ourselves." We are under an obligation to right, which is antecedent, and, in order and nature, superior to all other.

Dr. Clarke has expressed himself nearly to the same purpose. "The judgment and conscience of a man's own mind concerning the reasonableness and fitness of a thing, is the truest and most formal obligation, for, whoever acts contrary to this sense and conscience of his own mind, is necessarily self-condemned, and the greatest and strongest of all obligations is that which a man cannot break through without condemning himself. So far, therefore, as men are conscious of what is right and wrong, so far they are under an obligation to act accordingly." This view of human nature is the most simple, so it is the most ancient which occurs in the history of moral science. It was the doctrine of the Pythagorean school, as appears from a fragment of Theages, a Pythagorean writer, published in Gale's *Opuscula Mythologica*. It is also explained by Plato, in some of his dialogues. Adam Smith says, "Upon whatever we suppose our moral faculties to be founded; whether upon a certain modification of reasons, upon an original instinct called a moral sense, or upon some other principle of our nature, it cannot be doubted that they are given us for the direction of our conduct in this life. They carry along with them the most evident badges of their authority, which denote that they were set up within us to be the supreme arbiters of all our actions; to superintend all our senses, passions, and appetites; and to judge how far each of them was to be either indulged or restrained. Since these, therefore, were plainly intended to be the governing principles of human nature, the rules which they prescribe are to be regarded as the commands and laws of the Deity, promulgated by those vicegerents which he has thus set up within us. * * * * By acting according to their dictates, we may be said, in some sense, to co-operate with the Deity, and to advance, as far as in our power, the plan of Providence."

Again: "Therefore, all things whatsoever ye would that men should do to you, do ye even so to them; for this is the Law and the Prophets." (Matthew vii. 12.) This golden rule was embodied in the words of Confucius, the Chinese sage, five hundred years before Christ; and again by Hillel, a Hebrew president, thirty years before Christ. But all men have been under its influence, and have been actuated by it, to a greater or less extent, since the existence of man, independent of its having been spoken or written. The principle upon which the saying is founded is innate—imperative, in a degree, and none can disregard it.

The generality or constancy of Nature's laws is indispensable, both to the formation of any system of truth for the understanding, and to the guidance of our actions. The stability of God's law, we say, is indispensable to our being educated to its observance, and yet the churches inculcate, that it is vacillating or being changed from day to day, at the instance of prayer or other causes moving God to reverse his general laws, the better to provide for some special and unforeseen contingency. On this one question, as to whether God's purposes and ways are unchangeable or whether they are vacillating, hangs the truth or fallacy of the pretended fall of man, and the Christian scheme, for his restoration. Mr. Buckle has well observed that the ancient superstition is now slowly though surely dying away, which represented the Deity as being constantly moved to anger, delighting in seeing His creatures abase and mortify themselves, taking pleasure in their sacrifices and their austerities, and, notwithstanding all they could do, constantly inflicting on them the most grievous punishments, among which the different forms of pestilence were conspicuous. It is by science, and by science alone, that these horrible delusions are being dissipated. Events, which formerly were deemed supernatural visitations, are now shown to depend upon natural causes, and to be amenable to natural remedies. Man can predict them, and man can deal with them. Being the inevitable result of their own antecedents, no room is left for the notion of their being special inflictions. This great change in our opinions is fatal to theology, but serviceable to religion. For, by it, science, instead of being the enemy of religion, becomes its ally.

That this remarkable improvement, the relieving of religion from dogma, is due to the progress of physical science, is apparent, not only from general arguments which would lead us to anticipate that such must be the case, but also from the historical fact, that the gradual destruction of the old theology is everywhere preceded by the growth and diffusion of physical truths. The more we know of the laws of Nature the more clearly do we understand that every thing which happens in the material world, pestilence, earthquake, famine, or whatever it may be, is the necessary result of something which had previously happened. Cause produces effect, and the effect becomes, in its turn, a cause of other effects. In that operation, there is no gap, and no pause. The chain is unbroken; the constancy of Nature is unviolated. Our minds become habituated to contemplate all physical phenomena as presenting an orderly, uniform, and spontaneous march, and running on in one regular and uninterrupted sequence. This is the scientific view. It is also the religious view. Against it, we have the theological view; but that which has already lost its hold over the intellect of men is now losing its hold over their affections, and is so manifestly perishing, that at present no educated person ventures to defend it, without so limiting and guarding his meaning, as to concede to its opponents nearly every point which is really at issue.

"While, however, in regard to the material world, the narrow notions formerly entertained are, in the most enlightened countries, almost extinct, it must be confessed that, in regard to the moral world, the progress of opinion is less rapid. The same men, who believe that Nature is undisturbed by miraculous interposition, refuse to believe that man is equally undisturbed. In the one case, they assert the scientific doctrine of regularity; in the other, they assert the theological doctrine of irregularity."

"The doctrine that God governs the world by supernatural and irregular means instead of never varying laws, is not only unscientific, but it is eminently irreligious. It is, in fact, an impeachment of one of the noblest attributes of the Deity. It is a slur on the omniscience of God. It assumes that the fate of nations, instead of being the result of preceding and surrounding events, is specially subject to the control and interference of Providence. It assumes that there are great public emergencies, in which such interference is needed. It assumes that, without this interference, the course of affairs could not run smoothly; that they would be jangled and out of tune; that the play and harmony of the whole would be incomplete. And thus it is that the very men, who at one moment proclaim the divine omniscience, do at the next moment advocate a theory which reduces that omniscience to nothing, since it imputes to an All-wise Being, that the scheme of human affairs, of which He must from the beginning have foreseen every issue and every consequence, is so weakly contrived as to be liable to be frustrated; that it has not turned out as He could have wished; that it has been baffled by His own creatures; and that, to preserve its integrity, its operations must be tampered with and its disorders redressed. The great Architect of the Universe, the Creator and Designer of all existing things, is likened to some clumsy mechanic, who knows his trade so ill, that he has to be called in to alter the working of his own machine, to supply its deficiencies, to fill up its flaws, and to rectify its errors."

"Those who cling to these errors, do so from the influence of tradition, rather than from complete and unswerving belief. From the beginning, there has been no discrepancy, no incongruity, no disorder, no interruption, no interference; but all the events which surround us, even to the furthest limits of the material creation, are but different parts of a single scheme, which is permeated by one glorious principle of universal and undeviating regularity."

ERRONEOUS IDEAS OF HEAVEN. 147

Faith in an existence beyond the grave involves by necessity the belief that man's spiritual individuality, his consciousness of personal identity, is preserved to each individual; else the faith, with which God has inspired him in relation to happiness in another world, would be a delusion. Man can have no conception of future happiness, or attach any value to the idea of it, apart from associations with his present existence, or unless he blends with it some recollection of his past existence, peculiarities, and identity. Let a man contemplate his mind and spirit waking up in eternity as from a sleep, with all their faculties in full vigor, co-operating and performing their normal functions as when united to the body here, and possessing all the peculiarities that distinguished them individually, yet without the slightest remembrance or consciousness of his former being—would such a future be deemed of the smallest worth by any one? If we are not to know ourselves in the next world and to associate our existence here with that of the world to come, then it matters little whether it be another or ourself that secures a more or less happy state in eternity, or any existence whatever beyond the grave.

In the infancy of the human race, when men were slowly elaborating forms of speech to give utterance to their thoughts, and communicate with their fellows, words were invented, that, however originally useful in themselves, have helped, in the progress of time, to circumscribe the intellect they were intended to enlarge. Such words, to this day, exercise a prejudicial effect, and convey false meanings and impressions. Thus the Bible accounts of Heaven and Hell give an altogether erroneous idea of the imaginary states which they profess to prefigure. Heaven is represented as a place above the earth—a place heaved-up, like a vault or arch over the earth, in which God is supposed to dwell. The discovery that the earth is a globe, and not an extended plane, ought to suggest an idea of Heaven more correctly applicable to the fact; for it makes the words "up" and "down" mathematically incorrect, and pertinent only to that apparent plane commanded by the human eye. Still, however, not only the ignorant, but the educated, continue to speak of "Heaven" as a place above the earth—as the abode of God—a place inhabited in eternity only by those who believe in certain doctrines which are inculcated here, and where the enjoyments prepared for them are, according to most creeds, far more carnal than spiritual, and pertain to the things upon which the sensual are most addicted to set a value. For the faithful Christian, there are crowns of gold, to be worn in a city which is paved with gold, whose foundations are garnished with all manner of precious stones, and whose twelve gates are of pearl. There are beautiful bowers and fountains, and lovely "houries" for the eternal delight of the good Mussulman. There are happy hunting grounds for the immortalized Red Indian.

In like manner, the word "Hell," which originally meant a "hole," or the "grave,"—has been used to create an idea opposite to Heaven—the heaved-up abode of bliss, and to signify a place below the earth—a place of eternal punishment—the abode of the Devil, the representative of the principle of evil, where unbelievers will be tormented forever in fire and brimstone. Astronomy ought to make an end of both of these erroneous ideas, for it proves that the universe is the abode of God— the universe that embraces the earth, the stars, and every other system that pervades the infinity of space. There

ATTRIBUTES OF GOD. 149

is therefore no room for Hell. The glorious universe swallows up every atom of space that exists. If the terms are admissible in any sense, Heaven is in reality a comparatively advanced state of happiness here and hereafter, brought about by obedience to God's laws. Hell, in like manner, is the state of mind, here and hereafter, produced by disobedience to those laws. It is, within certain limits, for man himself to decide or control, by his own conduct, the amount of either that shall be his portion.

At every step in a train of argumentation, we are in the habit of affirming one thing to be true, because of its logical connection with another thing known to be true. But, as this process of derivation must have a limit, it is obvious that at the starting point to which some, at least, of these trains of reasoning are traced back, there must be truths which—instead of borrowing their credibility from others—announce themselves immediately to the mind, by the original and independent and inherent evidence pertaining to them.

Now, among those primary convictions of the understanding—these truths which come by necessity, firsthanded from God to man—we shall, for our present purpose, cite only the one from which all others radiate, to wit, the existence of a God who is the Creator and Ruler of the universe—including man. Upon this undisputable truth—we claim—may be founded with implicit confidence, the following propositions: That He who made the universe has no peer, no equal, is One and indivisible: That He is absolute in power; and that there is no devil or other being disputing His sway, or at enmity with Him. That He is infinite in justice and goodness, and hence could not have so ordained man and his surroundings, as to permit of other than eventual supreme good to each human being.

We hold that these views in relation to God, naturally flow from the bare contemplation of Him, whose knowledge and power were and are equal to creating and sustaining the universe. We hold also, that experience, which shall never end, commences betimes in the life of each man, to confirm him the more and more in his early conceptions of God's excellence and glory.

This prime conviction of the existence of a God, and the natural deductions from it, practically over-ride all false teaching, come it from whatsoever source it may, and is ever confirming the true. We have said that a self-evident truth, which must by necessity come to the mind of every man first-hand, is the only reliable basis, no less than the continuous cement of all sound reasoning. Where do the Christian Churches find this basis and this cement? Is it in their traditions, in their theologies borrowed from the ancients, in their fabulous records contradicted by history, in the unfulfilled predictions of their oracles, in their miracles, which will not bear the test of science, in their self-bestowed certificates of their own infallibility, in the bloody doings of their hierarchy during the dark ages, in their repulsive creed that dooms the vast majority of mankind to everlasting anguish?

Furthermore, the need of a base, or foundation—corresponding in solidity, and of universal acceptation with that of the existence of a one Omnipotent and indivisible God—whereupon to rest the doctrines peculiar to the Christian theology, as distinguished from natural religion, is visible in the multiplicity of Christian sects, in their wars and persecutions among themselves in other times and in their divisions and heart-burnings of to-day. This

GOD IN NATURE. 151

again brings up the question which distinguishes theology from religion.

God hath so constituted us, that we thirst for knowledge, adapted to our taste for the beautiful; and He has formed the world without, to awaken echoes in the soul within, so as to promote at one and the same time the enlargement of the experience, the quickening of the understanding, and the refinement of the feelings.

Each class of objects furnishes its quota of evidence. The physical works of God give indications of power and skill. The providence of God exhibits a governing and controlling energy. Our spiritual natures lift us to the conception of a living and spiritual God.

The phenomena, which prove the existence of God, also demonstrate that he delights in the happiness of his creatures. How delightful to find that every adaptation indicating design also indicates benevolence, and that we have as clear evidence of the goodness as of the very existence of God. Let it be observed, too, that the mind, as its general conceptions expand, will also have its idea of God expanded. When Nature is viewed in a narrow spirit, it may leave the impression that there is an unseemly warfare, and that there are numberless contradictions in the universe. The light of knowledge, as it rises, dispels these phantoms, and discloses among apparent incongruities and contentions, a unity of being in the Creator and Governor of all things.

The workings of conscience in the soul, besides furnishing a curious subject of inquiry, carry us down into the very depths of our nature, and thence upwards to some of the highest of the Divine perfections. It is by this light, which God has furnished to all men, and the training resulting from his unalterable laws, that God's goodness will become more and more apparent.

We have seen that in Judaism, Mahommedanism, Hindooism, Buddhism, Christianity, and every description of creed under the sun, the will of a living Being is asserted as the ground of all things; they all speak of Him as declaring Himself, and as exercising a continual, not an occasional, government over men. The universal recognition of a Divine, personal, unseen, Sovereignty; of One who is not sought out by men, but who calls them to do His work, is the foundation, and strength of actual religion. He calls upon them to obey a Will; each act of obedience brings them into closer acquaintance with Him who gives the command.

Man is taught that the evil which he is conscious of in himself, and which he sees in others, comes from unlikeness to the perfect Being in whose image he is created. He has but a glimpse of the Divine purposes and character, but it is such a glimpse, as is suitable to his necessities. He is taught that righteousness is a reality; that the government of the world is based upon it; that wrong and oppression are not meant to triumph.

But such a Revelation as this, could never merely be delivered to men as a book of sentences or maxims; it must come forth in a history of Divine law and human acts. It must show how the Divine Will directed events by means of a never-varying law and disciplined men for that perfect good, that knowledge of himself which He had designed for them. It must show how He cultivates the faculties which He has given to His creatures, how He enables them to overcome the darkness and difficulties in the midst of which they are struggling. Thus securing the predominance of right over wrong, and virtue over vice, and the clearer and clearer view of God's goodness and perfection.

In primitive times men in striving to comprehend the characteristics of God, resorted by way of illustration, to those traits in human character, which are quite at variance with His nature. In many cases this course misleads rather than edifies. Such passions and emotions, while especially adapted to the necessities of finite beings of limited power and knowledge and liable to err, have no counterpart in God's higher nature. His infinite power, knowledge, foresight, justice, goodness, in short, His supreme perfections preclude any such emotions, passions, or qualities, as repentance, anger, pity, hope, fear, love, mercy, hatred, forgiveness, surprise, gladness, levity, revenge, disappointment, rejoicing, or jealousy. Nothing can take place which God did not foresee would take place at the time of establishing His perfect design, to be worked out under the unalterable laws that He ordained for the purpose. Since, therefore, it is man's high privilege to advance in the knowledge and appreciation of God's goodness and perfections, in contemplation of Him we should avail ourselves of the highest intellectual culture at our command. In this way, we confirm, and add to the original conception of God, taught us by natural religion. This will lead us to a vastly more elevated idea of God, than those teachings which inculcate that He is finite and vacillating, and which reduce Him to a level with His dependent, short-sighted creatures. Love, mercy, and forgiveness can not apply to God in the sense in which these emotions are understood and expressed by man. Justice, and goodness supersede them. God's ordinances regulated by His infinite wisdom are such, that the exercise of mercy and forgiveness would be less just and beneficial to man than otherwise, both in this life and the life to come. It is far better for God to exact to the utmost that penalty which He has attached to man's misdoings, not as punishment, but as remedy—inasmuch as it is imposed upon him with the sole object of training and fitting him to the destiny that God originally designed for him. A jury sometimes recommends a criminal whom they have condemned to the mercy of the court, because they are not altogether satisfied that the culprit is guilty by the strict interpretation of the law, or because they find mitigating circumstances in his case. Not so with God—He is enabled by His perfect fore-knowledge and wisdom to make sure that the crime and the punishment are in exact fitness to each other; and since they are so adjusted for man's best interests, it would be unmerciful to destroy this fitness, by the relaxation of any portion of the penalty originally attached to man's misdoings. The same considerations apply to love. If God's original laws are strictly just, and all-sufficient for carrying out His perfect purpose—and who shall doubt it—any exercise of love that would alter man's original relation to those laws, would be unjust to him. God's justice is exact to the most minute point, and admits of no amendment. Any exercise of love or mercy, on God's part that would reverse His original decrees, presupposes God to be fallible or unable to ordain all things aright from the first.

The parable of the Prodigal Son is intended to inculcate the idea that God rejoices more over the repentance of a sinner, than over the well-doing of a just man. What a striking example of the unwarrantable application of human passions to the Deity is this! It is natural that a father should experience an agreeable surprise and elation at the return of a wayward son to duty. But God has ordained that he who sins shall assuredly repent; and what God has imperatively ordained to take place can afford Him no surprise or rejoicing at its consummation. Every event or issue is the even flow of the purpose He foresaw and intended from the beginning; therefore, the parable in question is not a true illustration of the attributes or emotions of God. Sincere repentance tends, most forcibly, to turn men from their evil ways; and, therefore, Jesus did well when he charged his Apostles to preach repentance, but inconsistently when he inculcated the idea that repentance brings remission of the penalty due to sin. This is impossible, inasmuch as the punishment which sin entails is the sole cause of the repentance. The effect of punishment and repentance for sin were never meant to be retrospective; but are intended to warn us against the commission of sin in future. For instance, the burnt child dreads the fire. This wholesome dread in no wise assuages the pain of the burn; but it is an important lesson to the child to enable it to steer clear of similar dangers, and the more effectual, as the pain is more severe. God's goodness and justice are here shewn in exacting the penalty, and thereby producing the repentance; since repentance leads to man's best interests.

Even the appellation of Father, accorded to God by Jesus—much as it has done and is calculated to do in giving some appreciation of God's goodness and care over His creatures—falls as far short of giving the true idea of the extent and beneficial exercise of God's goodness, as weak man falls short of God's perfection. God, in dispensing happiness to His creatures, goes to the extreme bounds that is well for them, but never beyond. God, knowing all things, does all things with a perfection beyond man's conception. Neither Father, nor any other human idea or figure of speech, can fully represent God's goodness to His creatures. Jesus says truly, "there is none good but God."

This view of divine government involves a much more elevated idea and worship of God, than any other. The perfect foreknowledge and power of God enabled Him so to constitute man, and to ordain such laws for his government, as to meet the exact requirements under every possible contingency, without addition, amendment, alteration, or abatement. In this perfect work is the strongest possible manifestation of God's equal justice and goodness to all men. The high and the humble are alike amenable to His unalterable laws; and those laws are in exact accordance with man's best interests.

INTRODUCTION TO BIBLE CRITICISM.

God's instructions to man through Nature, in relation to his duties here, are so plain and unmistakable that they cannot but be understood alike by all men, in all ages of the world. Hence the inference is irresistible that whatever is claimed to be a revelation from God in relation to man's duty, whether in and through the Bible, by miracles, or through any other means whatsover, if it be not so plain and devoid of obscurity as to be understood, in this way, by all men, cannot have emanated from God.

No man is bound to accept, as true, any averment in the name of religion, which is repugnant to the dictates of his own conscience, or inconsistent with the justice and goodness of God. It was never intended that anything should be received as infallibly true, except that which we perceive intuitively, or which is palpable from observation, or subject to unmistakable demonstration.

The character of the proof of the three following assumptions is such that universal assent is given to them; first, the truth of the existence of the One God, Jehovah; second, the immortality of the soul; third, that it is man's duty and interest to conform to the moral, and other laws pertaining to his being.

Strong conclusions ought not to be drawn from improbable statements or imperfect premises. God requires that we should believe only so much as can be fairly deduced from the premises, or only so much as the credibility of the statement warrants.

God has given us our mental faculties to enable us to discriminate between truth and error, and he who makes not this use of them arrives at truth, if at all, by mere chance.

We cannot come to a full conviction of the truth of a proposition, except on evidence which we deem full and infallible. Every substantial structure must have a foundation proportionally substantial.

Maintaining these axioms, we now proceed to remark upon the Bible, assuming that if in its entire scope, it be a true revelation from God, as Christian theology claims it to be—whether its contents be derived from natural or supernatural sources, or in part from each—there should be perfect harmony throughout. No one can, consistently, object to subjecting the claimed truth of the Bible to the most rigid test, either by comparing its various parts, one with the other, or with the established facts of Nature, or with the moral consciousness of man; or by any other available mode of investigation. The Bible should be able to withstand the most rigid scrutiny, when viewed in connection with whatever truths may serve to throw light upon it; and it should be proof against such logical deductions as may be brought to bear against it.

We believe the Bible to be true, only so far as its teachings are in accordance with the teachings of God to all mankind, through their natural faculties, holding that there is no such thing as supernatural revelation. We believe also that all pretended deviations from the order which God established at the beginning are unproved, and have their origin and advocacy, in human ignorance or fraud. Evidence of this is furnished most abundantly in Bible record, as we shall attempt to show. Bible authority will also be claimed as legitimate, for the purpose of controverting dogmas and doctrines that are professedly founded on its contents.

VAGUENESS OF PROPHECIES.

All the prophecies, and most of the parables of Jesus, are so extremely vague and uncertain in their meaning (if any meaning they have) as to be susceptible of innumerable interpretations, all equally plausible, if compared one with another; and yet not one of the constructions put upon the Bible text, is sufficiently plain to be for a moment relied on as a guide to that duty, and faith upon which, the churches aver, hangs man's eternal welfare. And even those portions of the Bible, which are less obscure than some to which we have alluded, are made to have a far-fetched spiritual significance, totally at variance with the wording. This answers a double purpose. First, it rescues the dogmas, creeds, and theologies of the churches and clergy, partially from discredit and overthrow; and secondly, whenever a figurative mode of expression is substituted for the plain meaning of words, it operates so that there can be no end to equivocation and misrepresentation. Hence, each of the many sects finds material for a specious building up its respective tenets, and each can make it appear that its church is the only gate through which to pass on to eternal bliss. None are wanting in zeal in pushing their peculiar views, (all of which depart more or less from the early teachings of

Jesus,) solely for the love of the dear people; and yet they are ever mindful of the toll which the wayfarer must pay at their gate. Let us look at a few examples of this mode of interpretation.

The plan of salvation taught by the Churches, is through faith in the divinity of Jesus. This involves the question whether the Prophets were or were not supernaturally endowed, and enabled to designate, centuries beforehand, the identical person who afterwards was claimed to be both God and man, co-equal with Jehovah; and whether Jesus was he whom they designated as that person.

In order to prove that he was, resort is had to complicated prophecies, visions, dark sayings, and dreams, all of them most vague and uncertain in their interpretation—if indeed they have any definite meaning. This very much confuses church teaching; but it holds church-goers in wonderment and awe, at the profundity of the Teacher who claims to penetrate and expound this deep, and to them unfathomable, system—a system from which it is claimed that most vital truths are extracted, and without a knowledge of which truths, and the aid of their Teachers, they—the less knowing—are led to believe that they would be irrevocably lost.

As to the visions, dreams, and prophetic utterances of mere men, as mediums for promulgating laws that are to be accepted and binding on other men, some few remarks may be pertinent. A man declares that God has supernaturally revealed to him a new law, to be obeyed by all other men; and that God has attached to the neglect of said law the penalty of everlasting torment. Now how can we know this to be true, without supernatural revelation, to assure us that the prophet himself bears a true

SUPERNATURAL INSPIRATION INCREDIBLE. 161

message from God? It is the essence of a law, that he who is commanded to obey, should have a knowledge of the authority of him who promulgates that law. But there is no intuition or natural sense within us tending to the recognition of these prophecies, utterances, dreams, and visions, as being from God. Hence we are not bound to obey what is called supernatural revelations, having no reliable evidence of their truth, further than the mere assertion of him who claims to have a message from God.

Now, if God ever speaks to man supernaturally, (which we feel assured he never does,) the fact can only be known by those to whom God has so spoken. No man can possibly bring home to another's understanding, how he can have been spoken to directly and supernaturally, unless the one to whom he addresses himself has also been spoken to supernaturally. If a man perceive the course which he supposes to be proper for himself and others to pursue, through his intuition, conscience or natural sense, it is easy to explain to another how God communicated this, His will, because God has in like manner so communicated with all men. In this way we can give more or less credit to communications, coming through others, when they say that those communications were received in a natural way: yet only when they bear evidence of having been so received, and in proportion to the credibility of the person; and so far as the character of what is communicated may be consistent with reason. But if a man says he has been supernaturally inspired to communicate God's will to men, and he communicates that which is a new thing, unheard of before by any one, strange, and not in itself in conformity with man's natural reason, intuitions, instincts, and conscience—is it obligatory on any second person to shape his conduct, in accordance with such pretended supernatural communication? What possible claim can such a man have on the credulity of others as having truly received from God a correct exposition of His will?

God has shown—and beyond the ability of man to throw a shadow of doubt on the subject—that He makes His will and laws, for the government of all lower animals, perfectly efficient. His ends and purposes, through the instincts and intuitions implanted in each respective race, at the first, operating uniformly and universally, are, we have a right to conclude, exactly suited to the bringing about of the results which He intended at the creation. That this analogy holds good in relation to man, may be doubted by some, but cannot be disproved. No good reason can be advanced why God should govern all the lower animals by a mode entirely in accordance with His perfect foreknowledge and infinite power, and yet govern mankind in a way most palpably inferior, so much so as to require (according to popular theology) that each one of the human family, should report to God by words of mouth, such special amendments to his general laws as they may think necessary to their individual welfare. Now this is equivalent to attributing to God an absence of that foresight, power and infinite perfection which He has made so manifest throughout all His work. We are, therefore, under the thorough conviction, that God governs man by His immutable laws, first established, operating alike upon every individual, for his best interest, and requiring no alteration or amendment. This alone is consistent with God's foreknowledge, justice, power, goodness and majesty.

FAILURE OF PRECISE PREDICTIONS. 163

All the prophecies which admit of a definite construction, both as to the things predicted and the time of their coming to pass, have entirely failed to come to pass. The following furnishes an example: And as he sat. upon the Mount of Olives, the disciples came unto him privately, saying: "Tell us when shall these things be, and what shall be the sign of thy coming, and of the end of the world?" (Matthew xxiv. 3.) The answer to these questions, we may fairly infer is contained in the following language made use of by Jesus: "Immediately after the tribulation of those days shall the sun be darkened, and the moon shall not give her light, and the stars shall fall from heaven, and the powers of the heavens shall be shaken. And then shall appear the Son of man in heaven, and then shall all the tribes of the earth mourn, and they shall see the Son of man coming in the clouds of heaven with power and great glory. And he shall send his angels with a great sound of a trumpet; and they shall gather together his elect from the four winds, from one end of heaven to the other. Now learn a parable of the fig tree. When his branch is yet tender and putteth forth leaves, ye know that summer is nigh. So likewise ye, when ye shall see all these things, know that it is near, even at the doors. Verily I say unto you, This generation shall not pass till all these things be fulfilled." (Matthew xxiv. 29, 34.) And again: "Verily I say unto you, There be some standing here which shall not taste of death until they see the Son of man coming in his kingdom." (Matthew xvi. 28.) Now these prophecies admit of no prevarication or shuffling, as is the case with most of them; and there can be no doubt that when Jesus made the prediction, that His second coming in person in the clouds of heaven, with power and great glory, should take place before the generation of men to whom He was then speaking should all pass away, he fully believed it would be fulfilled within the prescribed time, which is distinctly marked in the most unmistakable terms. The failure is complete. No person can argue to the contrary, with any show of candor. This, of itself, in all fairness, is fatal to the pretensions of Jesus' divinity, and is highly damaging to all His claims based upon the prophecies of the Old Testament. Strauss remarks on this subject; "Here we stand face to face, with a decisive point. The ancient Church clung to this part of the doctrine of Jesus, in literal signification, nay, it was, properly speaking, built upon this foundation, since without the expectation of His near return, no Christian whatever, would have come into existence. For us, Jesus exists only as a human being. To a human being no such thing as he here prophesied of himself, could happen. If he did prophesy it of himself, and expect it himself, it proves that he conceived himself to be that which he was not."

"All these things spake Jesus unto the multitude in parables; and without a parable spake he not unto them: That it might be fulfilled which was spoken by the prophet, saying, I will open my mouth in parables; I will utter things which have been kept secret from the foundation of the world."—Matthew xiii. 34, 35. Here he, who is claimed as God, is represented as making it a studied point to shape his conduct in accordance with prophecy. But while Jesus shaped his sayings and conduct specially with a view of making them thus conform, his followers put a construction on them not warranted by the text, and thus gained for him that credence without which he would not now stand before Christendom as he does.

PARABLE OF THE LOST SHEEP. 165

Now, as to the parable of the Lost Sheep: "Then drew near unto him all the publicans and sinners, for to hear him. And the Pharisees and Scribes murmured, saying, This man receiveth sinners and eateth with them. And he spake this parable unto them, saying, What man of you, having an hundred sheep, if he lost one, doth not leave the ninety and nine in the wilderness, and go after that which is lost until he find it? And when he hath found it, he layeth it on his shoulders, rejoicing. And when he cometh home, he calleth together his friends and neighbors, saying unto them, Rejoice with me, for I have found my sheep which was lost. I say unto you, that likewise joy shall be in Heaven over one sinner that repenteth, more than over ninety and nine just persons which need no repentance."—Luke xv. 1, 11. This teaching is of doubtful utility, if nothing more. It indicates that a person's character is elevated by wrong-doing. God's mode of reclaiming the erring is by shewing them their folly through the upbraidings of conscience or by other punishments, thereby producing a sense of degradation or pain and unhappiness. This produces repentance and amended ways by necessity, sooner or later, and always in God's good time, which we deem better than rejoicing over the sinner, since it is God's mode of training to virtue. It is obvious that God's mode is directly opposed to the deductions of Jesus from the parable on this subject.

Again: the Parable of the Prodigal Son: "Father, I have sinned against heaven and in thy sight, and am no more worthy to be called thy son. * * * But the father said to his servants, bring forth the best robe, and put it on him, and put a ring on his hand, and shoes on his feet. And bring hither the fatted calf and kill it; and let us eat and be merry. Now his elder son was in the field: and as he came and drew nigh to the house, he heard music and dancing: And he called one of the servants, and asked what these things meant. And he said unto him, thy brother is come, and thy father hath killed the fatted calf, because he hath received him safe and sound. And he was angry, and would not go in: therefore came his father out and entreated him. And he answering, said to his father, Lo, these many years do I serve thee, neither transgressed I at any time thy commandment; and yet thou never gavest me a kid, that I might make merry with my friends. But as soon as this thy son was come, which hath devoured thy living with harlots, thou hast killed for him the fatted calf."—Luke xv. 21, 23, 25, 30.—This represents wrong-doing; and repentance therefor, as being more commendable than a uniform course of correct conduct. This is not in accordance with the self-respect which God has implanted within the nature of man, neither is it in accordance with the aggregate sense of right. The human father of the parable may be supposed to be in doubt as to whether his erring son would ever return to duty and to his home, and may be considered as acting but the natural part of a Father, in rejoicing at the unexpected return of his wayward child. But God, knowing and controlling all things, can never (like the human father) be in doubt, can never be surprised, can never rejoice over an unexpected occurrence. Hence, the Parable here in view, is inappropriate when applied in this way.

Furthermore: "There was in a city a judge, which feared not God neither regarded man. And there was a widow in that city; and she came unto him saying, Avenge me of mine adversary. And he would not for awhile but afterward he said within himself; though I fear not God, nor regard man, Yet, because this widow troubleth me, I will avenge her, lest by her continual coming she weary me. And the Lord said, hear what the unjust judge saith."

"And shall not God avenge his own elect which cry day and night unto him, though he bear long with them? I tell you he will avenge them speedily."—Luke xviii. 2, 3, 4, 5, 6, 7, 8.

Now the prominent teaching of this parable is that God will avenge only his own elect, and that, for the sole purpose of getting rid of the annoyance of their long-continued importunities. But how much does this view conflict with that unbounded goodness and long forbearance which all Christians of the present day ascribe to God! If it be said that it was designed to applaud and encourage long-continued pleading and importuning for the redress of grievances, or the avenging of our adversaries, then we answer that it is not in accordance with the following teaching of Jesus : " Your Father knoweth what things ye have need of before ye ask Him." "Use no vain repetitions." "Not every one that saith unto me, Lord, Lord, shall enter into the Kingdom of Heaven, but he that doeth the will of my Father which is in Heaven." All which passages go to prove, that it is his works, and not much speaking that are acceptable to God.

And still another: When a certain rich ruler asked Jesus what he must do to inherit " eternal life," his reply was to this effect : "If thou wilt be perfect, go and sell all that thou hast and give it to the poor, and thou shalt have treasure in Heaven ; and come and follow me. For, verily, I say unto you, A rich man shall hardly enter into into the Kingdom of Heaven."—Matthew xix., 21, 23.

Again, "It is easier for a camel to go through the eye of a needle, than for a rich man to enter into the Kingdom of God. When his disciples heard this they were exceedingly amazed, saying, Who then can be saved?"—Matthew xix. 24, 25. And again: In the parable of the rich man and Lazarus, the following occurs: "Son, remember that thou in thy life-time receivedst thy good things, and likewise Lazarus evil things; but now he is comforted, and thou art tormented."—Luke xvi. 25. "Blessed be ye poor, for yours is the Kingdom of God." "But woe unto you that are rich, for ye have received your consolation."—Luke vi. 20, 24. The teaching of these parables and sayings can have but one object, that is, to represent poverty and suffering as virtues, and the true road to Heaven, and to make riches an insurmountable obstacle to future happiness. Self-preservation is the strongest law which God has implanted within man; and out of this grows the incentive to acquire, and store up the necessaries and luxuries of life; the legitimate doing of which increases a man's usefulness to himself and fellow-men. This is so universally recognized, that the instructions of Jesus on the subject are entirely disregarded by the disciples of Christianity, not excepting the clergy, which practically falsifies the Bible, whereof it is said every word must be received as truth.

Again: "These twelve Jesus sent forth, and commanded them, saying, Go not into the way of the Gentiles, and into any city of the Samaritans enter ye not; But go rather to the lost sheep of the House of Israel."—Matthew x. 5, 6. "I thank thee, O, Father," said Jesus, "because thou hast hid these things from the wise and prudent, and hast revealed them unto babes."—Matthew xi. 25. This is inconsistent with the idea that

Jesus' mission was to raise all who fell through Adam, and of his being the Saviour of all mankind.

Again : "But I say unto you, Love your enemies, bless them that curse you, do good to them that hate you, and pray for them which despitefully use you and persecute you."—Matthew v. 44. "Ye have heard that it hath been said, an eye for an eye, and a tooth for a tooth. But I say unto you, That ye resist not evil; but whosoever shall smite thee on thy right cheek turn to him the other also, And, if any man will sue thee at the law, and take away thy coat, let him have thy cloak also. And, whosoever shall compel thee to go a mile, go with him twain. Give to him that asketh thee, and from him that would borrow of thee turn not thou away."—Matthew v. 38, 42. These injunctions are at variance with the well-defined characteristics of human nature, and consequently unsuited to the practices of every-day life, inconsistent with self-preservation, and a becoming dignity and self-respect.

Lastly : "Now, when Jesus was risen early the first day of the week, he appeared first to Mary Magdalene. * * * Afterward he appeared unto the eleven. * * * And he said unto them, Go ye into all the world, and preach the Gospel to every creature. He that believeth and is baptized, shall be saved, but he that believeth not shall be damned. And these signs shall follow them that believe. In my name shall they cast out devils; they shall speak with new tongues. They shall take up serpents; and if they drink any deadly thing it shall not hurt them; they shall lay hands on the sick, and they shall recover."—Mark xvi. 9, 14, 16, 17, 18. Now, since nothing is said to the contrary, it is fair to presume that these things were spoken by Jesus as pertaining to all future time. But will any one pretend that in these days there is a verification of the truth of these declarations? Rather, is it not apparent that the reverse is the case?

A man born in a Mohammedan country believes in Mohammed. A Chinese believes in Confucius; and so with the followers of every other system of theology on the face of the globe. All, or most of the founders of the different systems, claim supernatural origin and endowments for themselves, or are believed to have possessed them, by their followers. People who are educated to believe in a particular faith, think that on such belief depends their salvation. Now, could we have any better proof than this, that one has as little foundation as the other, to rest upon—not even excepting the Christian theology? There is no merit or demerit, no salvation or condemnation, either for belief or non-belief, in any of these theologies. God is too just and good to ordain that the doom of an immortal soul shall be determined by the merest accidental circumstance, in no way involving the voluntary action or accountability of the individual soul.

The early teachings of Jesus are comprised in his enjoining the duty of love to God and man, which he repeatedly says is all that is necessary for salvation. These teachings, however good in themselves, had nothing new or peculiar in them, but were taught, substantially, and with equal, if not with greater force and fullness, by Zoroaster, Confucius, Buddha, Mohammed, and all the other founders of theology and great Teachers of religion and morals. Did not the Greek and Roman philosophers, Aristotle, Socrates, Plato, Democritus, Pythagoras, Epicurus, Pindar, and Solon, recognize as a rule of conduct, the great principles of moral deportment contained in the

CHRISTIANITY NOT ORIGINAL. 171

early teachings of Christ, to wit, love of God and good works? Indeed, all nations on the face of the globe, as far back as history will carry us, have in substance, advocated and been governed by this religion, which is common to all.

Every doctrine, creed, theology, dogma or faith, that has ever been claimed to be, or which has gone by the name of religion, other than natural religion, has been embraced by a portion, only, of the different nations and peoples of the earth; springing up during one age of the world, gone in the next. On the contrary, all agree, and at all times and in all places, that love to God and love to man, and the conforming to the moral law, is the bounden duty of every accountable member of the human family. But here the boundary of harmony on religious subjects is reached. This universal religion has been, and is, preached and urged upon the observance of mankind, in connection with thousands of different doctrines, creeds, theologies, ceremonies, and forms, which are claimed as essential parts of worship: each sect contending for its own peculiar views, in relation to doctrines, creeds, and theologies, with such pertinacity and bitterness, as to cause wars, that have resulted in the massacre of millions upon millions of human beings, and that continue to be the source of most lamentable contentions and criminations, and of irreligious conduct generally. It is submitted therefore, whether this state of facts, which is verified by history, does not indicate, unmistakably, what it is that constitutes the religion which God intended and insured for universal adoption by nations and individuals, or, in other words, whether it does not furnish a sure criterion, by means of which the wheat and the chaff may be distinguished each from the other.

The principal written codes connected with the worship of God in various countries, and which have been more or less the cause of disastrous wars and disgraceful feuds among men, are the following: the Zend Avesta of the Parsees; the Vini Pidimot of the Burmese Empire; the Rig Veda of the Hindoos; the Koran of the Mahommedans; and the Bible of the Christians. But we would ask, is it at all a part of the duty which God exacts of man, to pay homage to, or to worship, any of the persons, whom these books or records glorify? Godama, Mahomet, Zoroaster, Buddha, and Jesus, all claim to be either gods or supernaturally endowed by God. Which of them shall we acknowledge? We would submit also, that, whereas the Sun, the Moon, the Stars, and many other symbols, have been adopted by various sects, either as substantial parts or as adjuncts of worship, so also does the Christian theology require divine honor to be paid to the Virgin Mary, and that three Gods be worshipped instead of the One living and true God. Wherein, we ask, lies the difference? May there not be a good side and an evil side, in all these cases alike—good, inasmuch as the symbol leads up to the God above it—evil, whenever and wherever devotion stops short at the symbol?

It is very important that the truth on this subject should be determined, and be set forth by those among us who make a profession of teaching. But, bound by the rules of their Church and constrained by habit, the clergy advocate a certain set of special tenets, even whilst the most learned and sensible men among them acknowledge, in their own hearts, that what may be called the technicalities of their faith are not based on reliable evidence. Intelligent observation of God's dealings with the human race around them, and a careful study of the record of

SIMPLICITY OF TRUE RELIGION. 173

past ages, lead them to the just conclusion that the religion which God teaches is love for Himself and His laws, and the golden rule, " Do unto others as you would they should do unto you." Yet they lack the moral courage to preach this sublime and simple doctrine, preferring, in deference to custom and in fear of giving offence, to reiterate Biblical stories that are disproved by investigation, or that have much in common with other creeds which they affect to despise.

And yet how pathetically do these same Christian clergymen appeal for pecuniary aid, to the end that they may convert the Heathen! Their object, meanwhile, is not to promulgate the practical religion which Jesus taught with such wonderful effect both by precept and example, and which consists entirely of love to God and good will to man; neither is it to inculcate morals based on good works taught in the law of God. It is their own Christian theology, which they are bent upon instilling into the Heathen mind, its main point being a theoretical belief in man's fall through Adam, and resurrection through Jesus. It is evident, or it should be, indeed, to all reasonable minds, that God sent His only true and all-sufficient religion to the Heathen in common with all men. Else what becomes of all those who either never heard of Jesus; or, if they did, have no more desire to believe in him than a Christian has to believe in Mohammed, or to become an Israelite?

The theology—for means of sending which to the Heathen each creed, sect, and denomination of Christians so pathetically pleads—consists of dogmas and theologies tacked on to the pure religion of Jesus and of Nature. Each has a different dogma, each has variations in its faith. How are the Heathen to choose between one and another?

In all countries, whether Heathen or Christian, there are those who mingle the spurious with the good; consequently Heathen teachers have false gods and false theologies of their own, which they trade in, with equal results as the Christians. They see that the same is done in Christian countries, and they laugh at the idea of a comparatively small number of Christians dictating creeds and theologies to the balance of mankind, quadrupling them in number, and as likely to be right as themselves. Hence it is just as reasonable to suppose, that the Heathen should attempt to benefit Christian communities, by sending them their Bibles, which contain moral codes and precepts equally as good, and, in fact, dogmas and theologies as ingeniously contrived, as well authenticated, and as plausible in their claim to divine origin as the Christian Bible. Their oracles, too, whose names are taken to designate the various theologies which prevail among them, have as valid a claim, by miracles and prophecies, to supernatural endowments (or to Divinity itself) as have the Christian Churches on behalf of Jesus. But it is not Jesus himself, who is reponsible for the system which has been engrafted on his name. It is his professed followers who have perverted his teaching. His answer was, when he was asked, "Master, which is the great commandment in the law?" "Thou shalt love the Lord thy God with all thy heart, and with all thy soul, and with all thy mind. This is the first and great commandment. And the second is like unto it. Thou shalt love thy neighbor as thyself. On these two commandments hang all the law and the prophets."—Matthew xxii, 37, 38, 39, 40. And when, again, he was asked,

"Good Master, what good thing shall I do, that I may have eternal life?" His answer was, "Why callest thou me good? there is none good but one, that is God: but if thou wilt enter into life, keep the commandments. He saith unto him, which? Jesus said; Thou shalt do no murder, Thou shalt not commit adultery, Thou shalt not steal, Thou shalt not bear false witness. Honor thy father and thy mother; and, Thou shalt love thy neighbor as thyself."—(Matthew xix, 17, 18, 19.) In all this, he does not require, but actually declines, having any honor done to himself as a condition of entering into eternal life. All that he requires is, that a man should love God, the Father, and do those good works which He prescribes for him to do. If there had been anything else, would not Jesus have told him what it was? It was a most momentous question which had been asked of him. It was necessary, therefore, that he should be most precise and accurate in answering it; and yet he did not say, "believe in me; through me alone, and the shedding of my blood, canst thou be saved," but simply, "keep the commandments." "Not every one that saith unto me, Lord, Lord, shall enter into the kingdom of heaven," said he, on another occasion, "but he that doeth the will of my Father which is in Heaven."—(Matthew vii, 21.) And this will of the Father he exemplified in his own life. He "went about all the cities and villages, teaching in their synagogues, and preaching the gospel of the kingdom, and healing every sickness and every disease among the people."—(Matthew ix, 35.) .

The worship of the Father alone, by good works, and not by praying to and worshipping him, Jesus, was the requisite, as he conceived, for entering into the kingdom of heaven. Jesus, in this, practiced what he preached.

He went about diligently and zealously preaching natural religion, healing the sick, and rebuking those who thought that they could get to Heaven by crying to him "Lord, Lord!" instead of exhibiting in their daily conduct a life of good works: so that we have the express authority of Jesus for saying, that love to God and kind offices one toward another is the whole duty of man, which again is in accordance with THE FIRST AND ONLY TRUE RELIGION.

Bible descriptions of God and His attributes purport to be derived from God Himself, through His supernatural revelation, to particular individuals. But this revelation, if such it be, represents God as intensely human, both in form and character. It ascribes to Him many of the weaknesses and faults, and much of the short-sightedness, of the frailest of men; and it is totally unlike the revelation which He has made of Himself to all men, through the works of Nature. He has written Himself upon the broad face of the Universe, and in the depth of men's soul's, in such legible characters, and established such laws in relation to man, as to ensure that His will shall be done and man's happiness secured in God's good time. In addition to this, He has portrayed Himself, in every phase of creation, with a beauty and grandeur, that man becomes more and more capable of appreciating.

Now, we ask, shall this sublime record, which God has made of Himself, be for a single moment tarnished by a forced conjunction with views of Him that are impious? If so, let those suffer the damaging consequences, who teach such doctrine. Yet we are told that these descriptions of the Almighty must be believed in as infallibly true, by all men, as a condition of happiness beyond the grave. And what are they? Read what the writers of the Christian Bible say, and then judge for yourselves. Very few quotations will suffice to show in what abominable form the Creator has been represented, by those who declared themselves to be his messengers.

In the first place, he is represented as being addicted to furious anger, and this to such a degree that, were any of his creatures to manifest the same disposition, they would be looked upon as monsters. Take the following examples: "The fierce anger of the Lord"—Numbers, xxv. 4; "The anger of the Lord shall smoke"—Deuteronomy, xxix. 20; "Through the anger of the Lord it came to pass"—2 Kings, xxiv. 20; "Let the Lord be angry"—Genesis, viii. 30; "And provoked the Lord to anger"—Judges, ii. 12; "The children of Israel have only provoked me to anger"—Jeremiah, xxxii. 30; "And I will tread down the people in mine anger, and make them drunk in my fury"—Isaiah, lxiii. 6.

Hatred and a fierce thirst for vengeance are attributed to him in a similar manner: "I hate robbery for burnt offerings"—Isaiah, lxi. 8; "Because the Lord hated us"—Deuteronomy, i. 27; "Therefore have I hated it"—Jeremiah, xii. 8: "There I hated them, * * * I will love them no more"—Hosea, ix. 15; "Jacob have I loved, but Esau have I hated"—Malachi, i. 23. To illustrate the Almighty's revengeful tendencies, turn to Exodus, xx. 5, where we are told that he will visit the iniquities of fathers upon the children, nay even upon four generations of unborn children; to Deuteronomy, vii. 10; "He repayeth them that hate him to their face, to destroy them;" to Isaiah, xlvii. 3; "I will take vengeance," lxiii. 4, and; "The day of vengeance is in mine heart;" to Romans, xii. 9; "Vengeance is mine;" and especially to—1 Samuel, xv. 2, 3,—"Thus saith the

Lord of Hosts, I remember that which Amalek did to Israel. * * * Now go and smite Amalek, and utterly destroy all that they have, and spare them not; but slay both man and woman, infant and suckling, ox and sheep, camel and ass."

Jealousy also, such as we find attributed to certain gods and goddesses in Pagan mythology, is set down as one of God's characteristics: "I, the Lord, thy God, am a jealous God"—Exodus, xx. 5; "They provoked him to jealousy with strange gods"—Deuteronomy, xxxii. 16; "He is a jealous God"—Joshua, xxiv. 19; "Then will the Lord be jealous for his land"—Joel, ii. 18; "God is jealous and the Lord revengeful"—Nahum, i. 2; "I am jealous for Jerusalem"—Zechariah, i, 14; "I will give thee blood in fury and jealousy."—Ezekiel, xvi. 38.

Even ignorance is attributed to the Almighty, the words that follow being put into His mouth—Genesis, xviii. 21: "I will go down now, and see whether they have done altogether according to the cry of it which is come unto me, and if not I will know." Job also represents the Omnipotent as condescending to ask Satan about His doings, as if He were not also omniscient.

They presume even, these writers under so-called inspiration, to speak of His indulgence in scornful laughter; as in Psalm, ii. 4, "He that sitteth in the heavens shall laugh, the Lord shall have them in derision," and again, lix. 8, "Thou, O, Lord, shall laugh at them, thou shalt have all the heathen in derision."

Fickleness and alternation of purpose, common human infirmities, are represented as among His peculiarities. In Genesis we are told that "it repented the Lord that He had made man on the earth, and it grieved Him at His heart." Yet it must be owned, the sacred writers

GOD'S EVIL PASSIONS. 179

are not unanimous in attributing to God this tendency to change of mind. Thus, in Exodus, xxxii. 14, we read, "The Lord repented the evil which He thought to do unto His people;" and in 1 Samuel, xv. 29, "The strength of Israel will not repent, for He is not a man that He should repent." It is written in Psalms, cxvi. 45,—"He repented, according to the multitude of His mercies;" in Jonah, iii. 10, "God repented of the evil that He had said;" and in Jeremiah, xviii. 8, "If a nation turn, I will repent of the evil." Yet we find in James, i. 17, "The Father of lights, with whom is no variableness, neither shadow of turning."

It would perhaps be almost sufficient to have cited the Lord's alleged repentance over the superior being of his own creation, which the same authority tells us, He had pronounced "very good;" but we cannot omit to remind the reader of the very curious story of Moses pleading with the Lord, as it stands in Exodus, xxxiii. 7–14. The Lord told Moses that the Israelites were a stiff-necked people, given up to idols, and announced their consequent fate in these strange words: "Now, therefore, let me alone, that my wrath may wax hot against them, and that I may consume them." But Moses was emphatic and plain-spoken in his remonstrance, for such it may be justly termed. "Turn from thy fierce wrath," says he, without flinching, "and repent of thy evil against thy people." We know what ensued; "And the Lord repented of the evil which he thought to do unto his people."

But let us pass on, from the attempt to assimilate the Creator and the creature, so far as passions and sensations are concerned, and observe how this degrading process has been applied to corporeal resemblance. Head, feet, arms, hands, eyes, mouth, nostrils, back and bosom, figure more or less frequently—but always with a familiarity that ought to be revolting—in the Biblical descriptions and allusions.

"Ephraim is the strength of my head," says the Psalmist, lx. 7; Isaiah, lix. 17, puts "a helmet of salvation upon his head;" and St. John the divine—Revelations, xix. 12—saw in a vision that "on his head were many crowns." The footsteps and the feet of the Almighty are often referred to; as in Isaiah, vi. 2,—"With twain He covered his face, and with twain He covered his feet;" Psalm, lxxvii. 19, "Thy footsteps are not known," and lxxiv. 3, "Lift up thy feet;" Revelations, i. 15, "His feet like unto fine brass." Further than this, we find, Psalm, cviii. 9,—the homely expression: "Over Edom will I cast out my shoe," coupled with that other most undignified phrase: "Moab is my wash-pot."—The arms of the Almighty are often mentioned, sometimes as bared for the execution of His vengeful purposes, sometimes as opened for sheltering the righteous.—The hand of the Lord, as though it were a human hand, appears still more frequently in the sacred Scriptures.—Psalm, lxxv. 8—"In the hand of the Lord there is a cup, and the wine is red." 1 Samuel, v. 6—"But the hand of the Lord was heavy upon them of Ashdod;" Numbers, xi. 23—"Is the Lord's hand waxed short?" Exodus, ix. 3—"The hand is upon thy cattle;"—Psalm, lxxiv. 2; "Why withdrawest thou thy hand, even thy right hand? Pluck it out of thy bosom." This last citation serves to illustrate how the Lord God is supposed to have a bosom, being more direct than that one in John, i. 18, "The Son which is in the bosom of the Father."—So constant are allusions to the Almighty's mouth, and to what proceedeth out of it, that we limit ourselves to one note-worthy instance. In the Book of Numbers, xii. 8, God is made to say with reference to Moses: "With him will I speak mouth to mouth, even apparently, and not in dark speeches, and the similitude of the Lord shall he behold."—As to the eyes of God, reference to them, in as it were a physical sense, is continual. Thus, in Proverbs, xv. 3, we read: "The eyes of the Lord are in every place, beholding the evil and the good;" in Deuteronomy, xxxii. 10—"He kept him as the apple of His eye;" and in Psalm, xxxiv. 15,—"The eyes of the Lord are upon the righteous." The verse last quoted concludes thus, "and his ears are open unto their cry," which reminds us that we omitted the "ears," when naming the bodily points wherein God and man are familiarly assimilated in the Scriptures. Mention is also made of the Almighty's nostrils. "By the blast of God they perish," says Job, iv. 9—"and by the breath of His nostrils are they consumed." David, 2 Samuel, xxii. 9, asserts that, because God was wroth, "There went up a smoke out of His nostrils, and fire went out of His mouth, which kindleth coals." Is it not somewhat strange, that expressions, precisely similar, are applied by Job, xli. 20, 21—to his description of the leviathan:- "Out of his nostrils goeth smoke. * * * His breath kindleth coals." Furthermore, Isaiah, lxv. 5—makes the Lord, with reference to "a rebellious people," use this expression: "These are a smoke in my nose, a fire that burneth all the day;" and in Leviticus, xxvi. 31—Jehovah declares: "I will not smell the savor of your sweet odors." On the other hand, in Genesis, viii. 21—we are told how the Lord God, inhaling the scent of Noah's sacrifice on emerging from the ark, "smelled a sweet savor."—Lastly, as though to lower still more these associations and similitudes, so derogatory to all reverential feeling, Holy Writ informs us that the Divine Being has a back. Jeremiah, xviii. 17, puts this phrase in his mouth: "I will scatter them as with an east wind before the enemy; I will shew them the back, and not the face, in the day of their calamity;" and Isaiah says, xxxviii. 17—"Thou hast cast all my sins behind thy back." Moses also—Exodus, xxxiii. 23, makes the Lord say, in anticipation of the promised interview: "And I will take away mine hand, and thou shalt see my back parts, but my face shall not be seen."

We have thus glanced in detail at some of the instances, in which the mysterious Founder and Ruler of the Universe is vulgarized and falsified in the Bible, by human beings presuming to attribute to Him a share in their own mental and corporeal faculties. To them might be added the profane and inadmissible idea of Jehovah speaking to Moses "face to face, as a man speaketh unto his friend,"—Exodus, xxxiii. 2;—of God riding upon a cherub and flying,—Psalm, xviii. 10;—of the Lord being "a man of war," and of his wearing a "vesture" or a "breast-plate;" of the Lord coming down to see the Tower of Babel,—Genesis, xi. 5. As well might it be thought in accordance with God's justice, that He should, through Moses, enjoin the Israelites to borrow jewels of gold and silver from their Egyptian neighbors, when on the point of departure through the Red Sea. They must have known, as God must have known, that the pretended borrowing would be nothing better than fraud and robbery.—Exodus, xii. 35, 36.

It has been well asked whether a mandate ever issued from the lips of a blood-thirsty Oriental despot more terrible than that concerning Amalek, which is quoted above; and whether we, at the peril of our salvation, are to believe that such an injunction came from the Creator, rather than from the mouth of the cruel-minded Samuel, who "hewed Agog in pieces before the Lord in Gilgal." To this may be added the query, with reference to several of the foregoing citations, whether any Christian would tolerate, in the way of illustration, a statue or picture, wherein the Almighty Father was depicted as a human being inflamed with human passions; though, when the ear alone is appealed to, we not only tolerate the idea, but cling to it with such passionate earnestness as to persecute with the extreme of resentment any one who will not adopt it as an article of his creed. How, also, can the God who affirms, "I am the Lord, I change not," (Malachi, iii. 6,) be described by different individuals, as constantly varying, unless they themselves were giving utterance to their own human conceptions of what a God should be; and even, in this, differed amongst themselves? Is it not more rational, to believe that God has been clothed with human attributes by man, rather than than that the Lord of all creation puts on the contemptible dress worn by mortals who live in one of the smallest of the worlds which He has made? Surely such considerations should serve to wean us from that blind reverence to the identical words of Scripture, in which most of us have been educated. Nor can this reverence be justified by affirming that the language, to which we have taken exception, is only conventional or metaphorical. Who shall dare to say that God cannot give such a description of Himself as is consistent with His attributes, except through a certain phraseology? The idea is impious, as every thoughtful mind must recognize. At the same time it must be owned, that this habit of incorporating humanity with the God-head has taken hold of all nations in all time, and has, so to say, been rubbed into all theologies. How far this arises from man's inability to comprehend what lies outside of and beyond himself, is touched upon elsewhere; but there can be no doubt that it has been fostered, in large degree, by what a writer already cited, has termed the exigencies of the priesthood.

Without the fiction, says he, that the Almighty heard and spoke in reply to a special class only, the hierarchy could not exist. They feign, therefore, to have divine powers—a pretension readily conceded, by those who are unable or unwilling to think for themselves. By this division of labor, the ecclesiastic becomes as implicitly trusted as the lawyer or the physician. But, as there is in all educated men a propensity to search out the foundation of the claim to superiority which is advanced by professional men generally, so also is there, in some, a strong determination to examine the claims of those who assume the power to dictate to the Almighty, what He is to do with mortals when they become immortal.

If investigation and the light of modern science, acting upon our finer sense, overthrow our faith in the Bible, as an inspired record, they lead us to a more profound acknowledgement of the Almighty's power, justice, and wisdom. "God is a spirit, and they who worship Him must worship Him in spirit and in truth." This is altogether a different thing, from a blind reliance upon the utterances of prophets and the interpretations of priests.

The most pernicious error of church teaching is, that sin can be compounded for, that the just punishment due to sin can be evaded through what theologians call "The scheme of salvation." Now the natural effect of this popular dogma is, that those who believe, or think they believe, such teaching concern themselves more about the escape they are to make from punishment, than they do about the shunning of sin. While men act upon the idea that the penalty for sin can be avoided or bargained for, they are comparatively indifferent to any work of self-discipline, or the correction of their faults. All this is at direct variance with the teachings of God, through His natural laws. He therein recompenses every man according to his works. In this there is no prejudice, no favor, no spite, no partiality, no escape from just penalty, no possibility of losing a just reward, no bargaining, no compromise, no evasion, no substitution. Any one of these would be less just and good, than for God to exact the whole penalty attached to the breach of His inexorable law. He punishes to correct, to bring to repentance, to save to the blissful end in store for us.

The third chapter in Genesis professes to give an account of man's first sin, and has been made the basis of that fundamental article of the Christian faith, "The fall of man." The conclusions drawn from this chapter are not warranted by the words of the narrative, which we shall now proceed to show.

Not once in the Old Testament, either in the law or in the Prophets, is the story at all alluded to. All their notions of God and man were totally at variance with the idea of man having been made originally perfect. Jesus never alluded to this in any of his discourses; on the contrary, he declares that there is none perfect but God; and this, taken in connection with the fact that he nowhere intimates that man fell through Adam, ought to be conclusive with all who believe in Jesus' divinity, that man was no more perfect at the Creation, than he was in Jesus' day, or in our own. The first time that Moses' story is appealed to as historical, is in the writings of the Apostle Paul. It is upon his probable acceptance of the narrative, in an unwarranted literal sense, and upon false inferences drawn by him from it, that the prevailing idea of the utter corruption and curse of mankind, through the fall, and of their recovery or redemption by the substitution of a victim in their place, is founded.

But see what serious results this leads to. All who believe the doctrine of Christian theology which is based upon man's supposed original perfection and subsequent fall, it is said, will be saved: but all who do not believe in it will be damned. To admit this is to represent God as cursing the whole human family, for the sin of one of their number; and only removing that curse from those who believe in the shedding of the innocent blood of a victim, of whom but a small minority have ever heard.

The error which lies at the root of this delusion is the idea, that man was originally made perfect; and that he fell from that state of purity and perfection, dragging with him his whole posterity. Now we boldly assert that Adam and Eve were not created spiritually perfect as God is perfect, but perfect as God intended that man should be. The story itself not only does not say that they were; it gives not the remotest intimation of such a thing. They are represented as believing a serpent, or perhaps the evidence of their own senses, rather than the words of God, and as soon as they are tempted they yield at once.

The fact is, they could not have been made perfect. There is no such thing as perfection in any created being. If there were, there would be more Gods than one: for whatever is perfect is God.

But this inference is evaded by a qualification. Theologians tell us that they mean relative perfection—not that man could be made perfect as God is perfect, but that he was made good and happy. This we admit; God could not make anything but what is good and happy. But He could, and did make beings, who, when they were produced by His wisdom and goodness, were not only without a knowledge of physical cause and effect, but without a knowledge also of moral cause and effect. All that took place with regard to man's experience of good and evil was, that being created with a free-will he at once put that free-will into full exercise, and of course learned what he did not know until the experiment was tried.

Again, there is not a word in the story about everlasting death, or the torment of the soul. "Ye shall surely die," was understood by Adam and Eve as referring to the death of the body; because the narrator goes on to describe their being driven out of Paradise, lest they should eat of the tree of life, and live forever. Nothing can be plainer than that natural death is here meant. This view of the subject is further enforced by the following declaration, "Unto dust shalt thou return." The Apostle Paul quotes it in that sense, when he says, "By one man sin entered into the world, and death by sin, and so death passed upon all men, for that all have sinned," though the first part of this assertion is shown elsewhere to be inaccurate, inasmuch as science proves that death had entered the world long before the date assigned by theologists. Again, there is no allusion whatever to a substitute or sacrifice as the mode of removing the curse, and appeasing the wrath of God. There is not a single word spoken by God to Adam and Eve about redemption or atonement. If such a theory had been true—if the narrative in Genesis were supernaturally suggested—it would surely have contained some intimation of it, when God pronounced the curse. This being a matter of the very highest importance, not only to Adam and Eve, but also to their posterity, we cannot conceive, the goodness of God precludes the bare idea, that he could have withheld it from man.

The answer to this is, that God did, at once, inform Adam of his intention; that He gave him a distinct and unmistakable intimation of it when He said, "I will put enmity between thee and the woman, and between thy seed and her seed: it shall bruise thy head and thou shalt bruise his heel."—Genesis, iii. 15. But how can this be called a plain and unmistakable intimation of the scheme of salvation? It is as dark a parable as any that could be constructed; and we think it so obscure, except as to the natural enmity that exists between the two, that it would be useless to argue on it.

Turn, in the next place, to the statement, "And the Lord God took the man and put him into the garden of Eden, to dress it and to keep it."—Gen. ii. 15.

Church theology inculcates the idea that labor was imposed upon Adam in consequence of his first transgression; but it is evident, from the above text, that previous to Adam's sinning, as it is called, the dressing and keeping of the garden was enjoined on him. This, no one can deny, was bodily labor, by any fair interpretation. Adam was also required to give names to every living creature. Could he have done this, except at the expense of mental labor, even though every beast of the field and every fowl of the air was brought to him for this purpose?

As a consequence of Adam's eating the fruit, God cursed the serpent who tempted him, through Eve, as well as the

THE STORY OF THE FALL OF MAN. 189

ground upon which he trod; neither of which is supposed to be morally accountable. The curse on the serpent, such as it was, in any sense is applicable only to his physical nature.

And the curses, referred to, which pertain to man, do not necessarily grow out of man's moral offence. The fair inference is the reverse of this. The sin, according to the narration, was prompted by the craving of man's animal nature, not at the expense of any moral delinquency, such, for instance, as appropriating the fruits of a fellow-being's labor, in a dishonest way. For, according to the story, Adam and Eve were the only persons then upon the earth, and being in harmony, it is said, in partaking of the fruit; their action consequently involved no sin—one against the other.

A sense of shame, occasioned by the sudden discovery of the nakedness of one's person does not involve the idea of moral degradation; it rather indicates a lively perception of the propriety of things; and when this state of things is accompanied with strenuous efforts to hide the nakedness which caused the shame, as in Adam's and Eve's case, it is highly deserving of praise. If the story be credited, such must have been the view which God took of the matter, when he sympathized with them to the extent of helping the naked pair out of their dilemma by clothing them with skins, thus rewarding instead of punishing them and showing that their course met God's approbation, instead of condemnation. Hence, the eaters of the forbidden fruit could not have been deemed guilty by God, at least, in a moral point of view, else he would have left them to the punishment, which under his unalterable laws ever attaches to moral delinquencies. This view is fully sustained by the narrative of the matter in question ; the only punishment which is indicated therein, being death of the body, and labor, which we assert is a blessing, and not a curse.

There is another view of this subject, which is adverse to theologians. The reading of Genesis leaves the impression, that a very short time only could have elapsed between the eating of the fruit, which it is alleged brought death into the world, and the time of God's clothing the naked pair with the skins of animals. Now, if it be true that, up to the eating of the fruit by Adam, none of God's creatures had died, it begets the query, how it came to pass that that there were skins of animals immediately at hand in a fit condition for comfortable clothing.

If, to account for these inconsistencies, it be said that God can do all things that he wills to do, we answer that when men say God has done things totally inconsistent with his uniform mode of action, and give no reliable proof of the truth of their assertion, we have a right to infer even more ; and to be quite sure that the story has its origin in man's imagination and not in the doings of God. This story in Genesis rests upon the sole authority of Moses; it is irrational, improbable, and contradictory to itself; but worse than this, the Church has founded a theology upon it, totally unwarranted by the wording or spirit of the narrative.

The gist of the theological system consists in their claiming that Adam's alleged sin tainted his moral nature; and this enables them to transfer the final test of the truth or fallacy of their dogma beyond the grave. Thus, they elude detection of their error, since no man returns thence to confront them.

One of the evils inflicted upon Adam according to the narrative was additional labor, not labor primarily.

ITS INCONSISTENCIES.

The ground, by virtue of the curse, became harder to till, outside, than within the garden in which he was first placed. It was, therefore, the body, and not the moral nature of Adam, that had to pay the penalty, if penalty it be to labor, which we deny.

And again, Eve was visited with increased pain in child-bearing, and not with any new source of sorrow. This also pertains to the body. It is not a consequence of moral guilt, not entailing inward reproaches, as when one offends against the laws of chastity, for example. And if these evils in our physical nature do terminate in the death of the body, the death of the body is an advantage, because it leaves the soul untrammelled, and enables it to draw nearer to God, who is the source of happiness.

"And the Lord God said, behold the man is become as one of us to know good and evil."—Genesis, iii. 22. If this be true, God looked upon man, after his transgression, as more like Himself than before. He certainly became a wiser being; and we cannot understand how wisdom can be a curse to man. It brought with it a knowledge, that if we offend against the laws of God we must suffer for it. But God was too good to allow us to go on suffering in this world forever, for our short-sightedness and folly: He therefore made it impossible for us to do so, by allowing death to terminate our career. That man might not go further, and take and eat of the fruits of life, and live forever, God allowed death to be made the gate, through which we are to pass to a state of everlasting progression in wisdom and felicity.

But to go further into this incredible narrative—"And they were both naked, the man and his wife, and were not ashamed."—Genesis, ii. 25. This happy state of nudity and innocence, then, was that which they gloried in, before the fall. But what next? When they discovered, by eating of the fruits of the tree of knowledge of good and evil, that the condition in which they were was unseemly, they experienced a sense of shame, as indicated by their use of fig leaves, and they were afraid, and went and hid themselves; and so, when God found them thus, in order to hide their nakedness, we are told, "Unto Adam also and to his wife did the Lord God make coats of skins and clothed them."—Genesis, iii. 21.

These, then, are the consequences of Adam and Eve's eating of the fruits of the tree of knowledge of good and evil. Being redeemed or saved from them, of course the converse becomes the proper order of things. So that, when a man is redeemed or saved to eternal life by the plan of salvation through Jesus, he might go naked and feel no shame!

Again, "Therefore the Lord God sent him forth from the garden of Eden to till the ground from whence he was taken." (Genesis, iii. 23.) It appears from the scope of this verse, that God turned Adam out of Paradise to till the ground outside of its limits, not because he ate of the fruit by means of which he had assimilated himself to God by gaining a knowledge of good and evil, but rather lest Adam should partake of the tree of life, and live forever, and thus reverse one of the results of his partaking of the fruits of the tree of knowledge, to wit, the mortality of the body. So God compromised the matter, being content to let all the consequences of eating the forbidden fruit remain, except that the body should return to the dust whence it was taken. And to make quite sure that Adam did not render this inoperative, He placed a guard over the tree of life. This, we conceive to be the natural rendering of the story of "The Fall," and this, if any credence is to be given to it at all, must be much nearer the truth than the different and far-fetched construction which the Christian Churches put on it when they deduce from it the doctrine that man fell from the original state of innocence, that he must be redeemed therefrom by the sacrifice of Christ, and that our salvation depends on our belief in this complicated dogma.

We submit then, is not the course which is attributed to God, in the fable we have just criticised, an imputation against His omnipotence, His wisdom, and His stability of purpose? His laws are immutable; they never vary; and from the first they were framed for man's best interests and happiness. The death of the material portion of animals is one of those laws, which was in the order of things from the first. Had it been otherwise, the increase of the human race, at the rate at which men have multiplied since the creation, would have been sufficient to fill the earth so full, that they could not find standing room, not to say food enough to subsist upon. No, God has a more beneficent purpose in view, than to make earth man's continual abiding place. He places us here, that he may train us for a much higher and wider state of existence beyond the grave. Death, then, was no accident; neither was it visited upon man as a punishment for his delinquencies, but as an important step in his advance toward God.

What theologians term "The Fall of Man," is based by them upon the fable in the first book of Moses, called "Genesis," the substance of which is as follows: The first human pair was placed in the garden of Eden, where everything around them was in perfect harmony with their nature, their tastes, and their appetites: "And the Lord God planted a garden eastward in Eden: and there he put the man whom he had formed. And out of the ground made the Lord God to grow every tree that is pleasant to the sight, and good for food."

In the first place, it is said, or may be inferred from subsequent words, that in some respects Nature itself was very different from what we find it now. Originally, there were no such things as thorns, or briars, or noxious weeds and plants infesting the ground and annoying and perplexing the man, who was placed upon the earth to enjoy perpetual happiness thereon. These things sprang up at, and in consequence of the sin of Adam.

"And unto Adam he said, Because thou hast hearkened unto the voice of thy wife, and hast eaten of the tree of which I commanded thee saying, Thou shalt not eat of it: cursed is the ground for thy sake: in sorrow shalt thou eat of it all the days of thy life. Thorns also and thistles shall it bring forth to thee; and thou shalt eat the herb of the field."

The elements also were so propitious, and the climate so congenial and healthy; that they suffered no inconvenience from the former, nor could the seeds of disease be implanted within them by the latter, although their physical construction was precisely what it is now. "They were both naked," implying that, having neither the rigor of coldness in winter nor the fierceness of heat in summer to contend with, their bodies did not therefore require any protection in the way of clothes. This is further implied by the theological view, that man—if he had not fallen—was to live without labor, and hence could not have provided himself with clothing. Since animals also were to live forever, man could not be clothed with their skins;

and yet, contrary as it may seem to this idea, God made them garments, or coats of skins, as soon as their sense of shame made it necessary. Again, "For in the day that thou eatest thereof thou shalt surely die," implies that but for an act of disobedience—which he might or might not commit—neither death, nor its antecedents, pain and disease, could have ever visited them. Neither was the nature of the animals what it subsequently became. They were all peaceful and happy and harmonious, none carnivorous; but all gregarious and living upon herbs: "And to every beast of the earth, and to every fowl of the air, and to everything that creepeth upon the earth, wherein there is life, I have given every green herb for meat." Man himself was an entirely different creature to what he became, immediately after eating the fruit of which God his Maker had commanded him not to eat. He was good and holy and just and true; and consequently he was perfectly happy.

This is, substantially, a picture of what is presented to us from the pulpit, concerning man and his estate before he ate of the forbidden fruit. It is what is claimed by theologians as a fair deduction from the account given in the Book of Moses, to which we have referred.

But is it in accordance with the facts or phenomena of Nature, and with the wisdom of God? If this dogma of the Church be true, it results in lowering the attributes of the Almighty, and in representing Him as a Being whose laws and plans, pertaining to all created things, were liable to be thwarted by a single act of His creature man; and to the extent of necessitating an entire revision of those laws and those plans. It results in an imputation upon His omnipotence, His wisdom, His goodness, and His unchangeableness. It results in the theory that man—both constitutionally and morally—is not the same being that he was at his creation, or at the time when he was first called to take upon him the original organism of his type. In a word, it results in the imputation that God, who, according to His very nature, never varies nor modifies nor adapts His laws to any contingency, was—instead of being supreme—so far subject to the caprice of man as to be compelled to abandon His original plan, and reconstruct or re-organize His laws pertaining to the vegetable, animal, and spiritual affairs of our globe. Now God is a Being of absolute powers and perfections, of infinite wisdom and goodness; and by necessity, in carrying out His designs at creation, He must have made everything perfect both as a whole and in its several parts, so that entire harmony ensues and no revision or amendment is admissible. God made man with such faculties, physically and mentally and morally, as in His wisdom He deemed best. He is omniscient and unchangeable. He cannot therefore be turned aside in His purposes. That infinite goodness and wisdom, which originally governed Him in His designs toward man, must ever remain intact. Man was made perfect, as man, and no higher, else he would have been something more, or other, than man. Nothing is conceivable of God, than that everything which He has created, and the laws by which His creation is governed, have been and must be from first to last in perfect harmony each with the other, and with His will and pleasure. It is indispensable that they should be. But how does this accord with Christian theology, according to which, a single breach of Adam's duty wrought a total change in most, if not all, of God's original ordinances in relation to man, the lower animals, and even the plants?

Let us look at this matter more closely. If God's original design in regard to man and His ordinances for the accomplishment of His designs were in exact conformity with each and every part of His general plan, nothing wanting, nothing useless; and if His original plan and purpose was what theologians assert it to have been—then certain properties and affections, which now pertain to our nature, had no use or part in that organization. Up to the time of Adam's first transgression, there could have been no repugnance to evil, since evil was not then contemplated by God. There could have been no preference for the good, since there was nothing contrary thereto, there being no evil with which to contrast the good. Conscience could have had no existence in man. Sin being a surprise to God, conscience to rebuke it could have had no part in God's original design. Modesty, that exquisite trait in the nature of man, could have had no part in his original constitution, since God did not foresee that the first pair would do that which made their nakedness appear in a new light to them. And yet, according to the narrative, the instant it was called into requisition, modesty very naturally performed the duties of its office—even before God had called the offenders to account for doing that which required its first blush. This shows that man was at first as now; and is of itself fatal to the theological deduction from the narrative as it stands. And now, before proceeding to show at some length, how absurd is the theological view of the consequences entailed upon certain parts of animal creation by Adam's fall, we interpolate one remark that properly belongs to a more general consideration of the subject. Theologians hold and repeat unceasingly that death is but the passage or gate to heaven which opens to those who believe. If this be so, it follows—according to the doctrine that Adam and all his posterity were originally intended to dwell forever in this lower world—that if Adam had not sinned we should all have been deprived of that blissful abode, which we are led to believe is a transcendantly more happy place than was even Paradise itself! So that, notwithstanding man is said to have done very wrong in disobeying God, yet he did the very best that he could for his own advantage. The Church, perhaps, may be able to reconcile this difficulty, when it explains why man is permitted to eat meat, though God said to him: "Thou shalt eat the herb of the field." God's perfection is a guarantee of the exact fitness and harmony of His creation as a whole, and as seen in the various laws, means, and appliances for carrying out His purposes. There is nothing wanting, nothing useless—each and every part being indispensable to the accomplishment of His perfect end. Now this involves that, if God's original purpose in creating what pertains to this earth was in accordance with the theory of the Christian theology on the subject, to wit,—that all God's creatures were to live forever happy, and in harmony with each other, committing no breach of His laws, having no pain, misery, or discomfort, either of body or mind—then, the instant Adam first disobeyed these laws, the harmony and fitness of all must have been changed, to produce another harmony under the condition of things as they now exist. Adam, himself, must necessarily have been reorganized. He must instantly have been so transformed, as to adapt him to his present wants and his present nature. In fact this change relates alike to all men, to the intuitions, instincts, and physical structure of all, and to every property of the body and mind of all.

INSTANT CHANGE IN ANIMAL LIFE. 199

And thus also with the lower creation. All the birds, fishes, animals, and insects, that are now carnivorous, must have had their instinctive propensities altered. New means of capturing, eating and digesting such food as they now eat must have been instantly furnished them, to accommodate them to the new order of things—an immense work to be performed, as it seems to us, on account of so unimportant a transaction as that to which it is attributed. The beasts and birds of prey must have been provided with sharp fangs and hooked claws, to enable them to secure their victims; and the appliances which they have for masticating flesh, must have been given them at the same time. All the animals and birds that feed upon carrion must have had their cravings of appetite adapted to such food, and their sense of smell made surprisingly keen, to apprise them of its locality at long distances. The hen must have been gifted with the instinct, that causes her to call her chickens under her wings, when the hawk is in sight. The dog must have had the instinct given him, that warns him of danger when he smells a snake whose bite he, intuitively, knows to be fatal. The instinct that makes living things flee, or otherwise strive to protect themselves, when their natural antagonist presents itself, must also have been called into requisition. In fact, all the instincts and propensities that pertain to the preservation of life, and to defence at the approach of a natural enemy, must have been given to all living things, the moment death became inaugurated because of Adam's sin.

Again, all living creatures, that, in their living state, are designed as food, for other living creatures, must have had their means and propensity for propagating their kind materially increased, to answer to the state of things that then came about.

If God's purposes were, that animated things should not prey upon each other, why did He make such numerous kinds and species of animals, birds, insects and fish, with organs, functions, instincts and propensities, especially adapted and only calculated for the purpose? Why did He not endow them with those other faculties absolutely necessary for maintaining life according to what theologians call God's original plan? That God from their creation, intended that one creature should prey upon another, is strongly indicated by the fact, that those animals, birds and fishes of the larger series, which are not liable to be used as food by others, propagate their kind in much less abundance than do those which are made to be devoured: What vast, but what appropriate disproportion is there between sharks and herrings, between hawks and sparrows, between tigers and buffaloes, between swallows and insects on the wing!

Again: it is certain that, to maintain the order and fitness of things which God designed, animals of all kinds require a certain area or space for their occupancy, in proportion to their numbers. It is also apparent that the aggregate of animal life is materially increased by the different kinds and varieties of species that exist; and that the well-being of each is promoted by the existence of not over a certain number of another kind. That is to say, there might have been too many of one or more kinds to produce the best result. If this be true, it is probable that the devouring of one by another is among the means that Nature uses for preventing this inconvenience. There is another provision of Nature apparently tending to the same end—it has been ordained that an insect shall, under

DEATH INDISPENSABLE. 201

certain contingencies, deposit its eggs in or on the body of another living insect or animal of a different species. The effect of this is to increase the number of one, and to diminish that of the other kind. This provision of Nature, whereby insects and other animate things feed one upon another and upon the eggs of each other, is, we say, among the arrangements of God to maintain an equilibrium, or proper proportion between the kinds, and to prevent the earth from being overstocked, as it soon would be under the theological version of God's original decrees.

The same arrangement prevails with regard to the birds of the air, and the beasts of the field and forest. Life and death are linked together, and depend on each other by and through God's ordinances in such a way that it is not possible that it can have been anything else than His original purpose that they should both prevail. The preying of one species of animated nature upon another is totally at variance with the dogmas of the theologians on this very subject. They say that it was God's original design that all living things that came into being on the earth or in the waters should live forever. The fallacy of this is at once shown by the use of figures. At the rate at which living things now multiply, the number would very soon be so great, if all continued to live, that further increase in numbers would be totally impracticable. This result would render all the provisions that now exist for the production and consequent perpetuation of animal life perfectly useless. And yet these embrace so wide a range and are so intimately interwoven with the organs, functions, and instincts of animal nature that it is impossible to conceive that God's plan for perpetuating the inhabitants of the world was not at first as now. It is impossible to conceive, for example, that the beautiful and pure relationship which exists between parents and children should not remain an ever-living and active principle—a never-ceasing symbol, in some degree parallel to the relationship that exists between God, who is a Father and more than a Father, and all His happy children, here and hereafter—a monument of His benign goodness to all the children of men. To return to our point: even the living things of the sea must have had their nature greatly changed. Before death came into the world through Adam's sin, they must have fed on the fruits and herbs of their own expansive and aquatic fields. It is true that the primary source whence food is derived for the growth and support of animals is in the air, in the water, and in the earth. It is also true that animals cannot draw their support directly from the inorganic matter contained in these elements. It can only be converted into pabulum adapted to their support by and through the instrumentality of plants. Vegetation, therefore, links together animal life and inorganic matter. Vegetation is the prime medium in bringing the means of life and animation out of inert matter. On the land, where plants are in greater abundance and enjoy more of the elements of thrift than is the case in the sea, their office is performed more extensively; and the pabulum suitable for the sustenance of both large and small animals is furnished in much greater abundance than is the case in relation to those which inhabit the waters, and derive their support through the medium of animalcules. Out of this results the important office of the animalcules that exist in such vast numbers in water. They save up and accumulate, as it were, the comparative lesser supply of food by aquatic plants. When inorganic matter has once passed through the medium of plants into suitable food for animals, it is retained in that state

THE FOOD OF ANIMALS. 203

through the instrumentality of animalcules, which serve as a guard over every avenue of its return into its original state. In this way abundant means of food is furnished to all the grades of aquatic animal life; and thus the otherwise too scanty vegetation of the waters is made sufficient to the end in view. The plant product—the organic matter, be it vegetable or animal—is seized upon in all its stages of decomposition by the animalcules which exist in myriads, and is thus converted into their own tissue, and turned back into animal life in its various grades, they themselves being preyed upon by larger classes of animals. Now, all this is a part of a vast, complicated, and yet harmonious system ordained by God, and made to operate in perfect accordance with all his other systems. This perfect whole is entirely at variance with the idea of the theologians, that God's original purpose was that each individual creature in the sea, as well as on land, should live forever on vegetable matter alone—that is to say, if the inhabitants of the waters were to exist in anything like the numbers in which we find them now. If vegetable matter only was to be food for them, such food must have been vastly increased in quantity. Otherwise, not one aquatic animal could exist, in proportion to the thousands that now teem in the waters. And the same would have been the case, in a less degree, with land animals, if all were dependent on vegetable food alone and one did not prey upon the other. We conclude, therefore, that, if the theological view of the original ordinances of God in relation to animal creation is right, then the animalcules found both in fresh and salt water, in which decaying vegetable or animal matter exists, had no office, or at least not their present use in the economy of Nature.

Let us look now at another branch of this interesting subject. To ensure that the face of the earth shall be perpetually clothed with verdure, most beautiful to the eye and most pleasing to the taste, God has caused the seeds of innumerable varieties of plants to be produced in superabundance, to be wafted by the winds or carried by the waters over and through hill and dale and valley, and sowed by the birds of the air and the beasts of the field and forest. Numerous and manifold are the seeds thus scattered abroad; and these take root and spring up, in proportion to the space and fertility of the soil requisite for the rearing of healthy specimens. The multiplicity of seeds, and the varied and ample mode of distribution that prevails, not only ensures that there shall be no lack in numbers and dissemination; it furnishes an abundance from which to select the best samples. This God has provided for by His unalterable laws, as well in the vegetable as in the animal world. And those laws operate in favor of the specimens of each variety, whose incipient stage gives the best promise for future excellence. The young tree or bush, that makes haste—if we may so speak—to shoot above and over-top its neighbors, receives upon its branches and leaves more light, more air, and more of the rays of the sun, so essential to its growth, than is the case with the less thrifty of its kind standing near by. This is true, in various degrees, with every variety of plant and herb. To that which hath, more is given. The unthrifty fall a prey to the strong of their own, or other kinds; and this applies with equal, if not with greater force, to animal as to vegetable life. The weak and unthrifty have impediments thrown in their way that the strong know not of. To the same end, is the greater belligerent propensity of male than of female animals. It is in order that the progeny may be sired by the more healthy and vigorous of the respective kinds; and hence a higher grade of excellence is maintained among the animal tribes than would otherwise be the case. From this rivalry for precedence in the animal department of nature, as well as the vegetable, death frequently ensues. Even death, we say, so far as we can see, is ordained to the end that life may be more abundant, beautiful, and excellent; that freshness, buoyancy, and the green leaf may predominate. Was this forced unexpectedly upon Omnipotence, by the sin of Adam, or was it originally ordained as the result of God's wisdom and goodness? Although we may not comprehend the length and breadth of God's logic in all this, nevertheless our faith is complete that it is and was right, first and last—Christian theology to the contrary, notwithstanding. The present order has, most unquestionably, much to do with the keeping of all the things of the earth, fresh, beautiful, and more comely than would otherwise be the case.

Upon the whole, it is evident, therefore, that the laws pertaining to the animal and vegetable portion of the world were, at the first, adjusted to the order of things as they now exist. Death and decomposition were intended constantly to contribute to a new organization of life and beauty. If not, Adam's one mistake operated to convict God of millions of mistakes, involving a radical change in man, and the lower animals to suit them to present circumstances. Now, which of these two propositions is the more credible, and more in accordance with true religion and reverence for our Maker—that God made the blunder in question, or that the story has its origin and advocacy in the priesthood? Grant that there was a time when the first man had not performed any act either good or bad, pertaining to the duties for which he was held responsible. So circumstanced, he was, of course, without committed sin, and therefore personally innocent. Is not this true, at some time, with regard to every man that ever arrived at a moral accountability? In this respect, at least, it is evident that all men—including Adam—start, on a perfect equality, to traverse their course through time and in eternity. Now, that Adam was, from the first, gifted with some agency over his volitions and actions, and that his original nature and knowledge was not such as to ensure that he would not err in the exercise of his limited agency, is shown by the Bible story of his fall. That he did err, precisely after the manner of all men, as soon as he was put to the test, is also shown by the same account.

It is, therefore, difficult to see how it can be said that Adam in any way differed, from first to last, from the present type of humanity. Standing as a figure of the first man, Adam was, at one period of his existence, guiltless of any committed or personal sin, and to that extent, in God's sight he was innocent, true and good. Every man, arriving at a state of accountability, is precisely in the same condition. But, say the Churches, man's nature is corrupt; he is at enmity with God; and this was brought about by Adam's sin,—where is the evidence? If all men, at one period of their lives, advance from the same stand-point, all men like Adam, being fallible, are not only liable—but they are sure to err. Adam so erred, without having been subject to the taint of corruption—as the theologians have it—by the sin of any preceding man. The Bible narrative on this subject leads to the inference, that, very early after he was put to the test of choosing the good and avoiding the evil—which is literally the business of life with all men— he did precisely the same thing that all other men do. At times he did what is right ; and at times he did what is wrong. It is in that way we gain experience, and are trained to the practice of virtue. God alone is always right, always good ; and the idea that He originally created man short-sighted and liable to err, as we now see him, militates nothing against His goodness, since He has ordained that which shall be effectual to the diminution of man's ignorance and the supplying of his short-comings, by His own infinite knowledge and perfection. God has never been thwarted, disconcerted, nor interfered with, in the slightest degree, by either man or devil. He is supreme in all things. His plans and doings were all perfect from the first, and need no altering. They cannot be altered. The very idea of God, when contemplated in the fullness in which it is man's highest privilege to view Him, amounts to demonstration that He is unchangeable. This alone is consistent with the perfections of God, and in direct opposition to the teachings of Christian theology. We insist, therefore, that man and all the lower animals that now inhabit the earth bear the same stamp and impress that God originally gave them ; and that human nature is ever the same in its incipient stage—subject to be assimilated more and more toward God's perfections, under the influence and teaching of His unchanging laws, ordained for the purpose at man's creation. This may, figuratively, be termed the partaking of the tree of knowledge of good and evil. None are shut out from it. All eat of it, even in this first stage of our existence ; but with various degrees of success; and in God's good time, none will fail to profit by it. We shall eat, and live forever.

If on the other hand, it shall be alleged that God foresaw what Adam would do in the matter in question, and provided all things before-hand so as to meet the exact case, so say we ; and Adam as the representative of mankind, is now as at first, and as God intended he should be from the first.

In relation to the origin of man, we cite the following extracts from Humbolt and other German writers, which in substance repudiate the Hebrew tradition:

"We do not know," says Wilhelm von Humbolt in an unpublished work, "either from history or from authentic tradition, any period of time in which the human race has not been divided into groups. Whether the gregarious condition was original, or of subsequent occurrence, we have no historic evidence to show. The separate mythical relations, found to exist independently of one another in different parts of the earth, appear to refute the first hypothesis : and concur in ascribing the generation of the human race to one pair. The general prevalence of this myth has caused it to be regarded as a traditionary record, transmitted from the primitive man to his descendants. But this very circumstance seems rather to prove that it has no historical foundation, but has simply arisen from an identity in the mode of intellectual conception, which has everywhere led men to adopt the same conclusions regarding identical phenomena ; in the same manner as many myths have doubtless arisen, not from any historical connection existing between them, but from an identity of human thought and imagination. It is in vain that we direct our thoughts to the solution of the great problem of the first origin; since man is too intimately associated with his own race, and with the relations of time, to conceive of the existence of an individual, independently of a preceding generation and age."

"Nothing remains but to embrace the opinion, that the distinct characteristics of the human race were imprinted at all times; or that in general mankind does not descend from one man and woman,—from Adam and Eve—but from several human pairs."

"Inasmuch, as it has never yet occurred to anybody to sustain that all figs have sprung from a solitary primitive fig, even as little can any one admit the whole of mankind to be derived lineally from a single human pair. Wherever the conditions of life were found, life has sprung forth."

According to these views, the whole story in the Book of Genesis relating to Adam and Eve—which is the sole authority as to the first human pair being placed in the Garden of Eden—is altogether fallacious, a view in which we entirely concur.

Now, as the Christian theology is wholly based on the story taken in its literal significance, upon the authority of a single person who is claimed to have recorded it two thousand years after its supposed occurrence, there is certainly left but a very slender foundation, whereon to build one's hopes or fears of eternal salvation or destruction.

We find that, according to Bible narrative, Adam was created in such a condition of life that had he not broken the commandment of God, he would have enjoyed it in the paradise of Eden, everlastingly. But he ate of the tree of knowledge of good and evil, of which God had told him: "Thou shalt not eat of it; for in the day that thou eatest thereof, thou shalt surely die." And now, lest he should put forth his hand, and eat of the tree of life and

14

live forever, God thrust him out of Paradise. By which it appears, that if Adam had not sinned, he would have had an eternal life on earth, both bodily and spiritually. But, as he did, physical mortality became the lot, both of him and his posterity. Not that actual death then entered; for Adam then could never have had children; whereas, he lived long after, and saw a numerous progeny spring up around him. Where therefore it is said, "In the day that thou eatest thereof, thou shalt surely die,"—Genesis, ii. 17; and, "unto dust shalt thou return,"—Genesis, iii. 19; it must needs be meant that his body would become mortal, and be sure to suffer death.

But, added to this idea, the theology of the Christian churches teaches also, that Adam's sin degraded the spiritual nature of mankind. This doctrine is not warranted by the language of the Bible. "For God doth know, that in the day ye eat thereof, then your eyes shall be opened; and ye shall be as gods, knowing good and evil."—Genesis, iii. 5. "And the Lord God said, Behold, the man is become as one of us, to know good and evil; and now, lest he put forth his hand, and take also of the tree of life, and eat, and live forever: Therefore the Lord God sent him forth from the garden of Eden, to till the ground from whence he was taken."—Genesis, iii. 22, 23.

Now, it is difficult so perceive how man's arriving at a knowledge of good and evil, and thereby assimilating himself to God, is to be construed into man's degradation or fall. Is it not rather an advance in the right direction? Does not knowledge tend to elevate, rather than to degrade? Some knowledge must be had of evil, in order to lead us to the highest appreciation of the good, the true, and the right. God therefore trains man in the direction of his own perfections, by rewarding virtue and punishing vice, which tends to constantly increasing knowledge of good and evil; and thus man is conducted to the happy destiny which God designed for him.

But to proceed with the argument on the theory that man did fall, and that it became necessary that some one should restore him.

If, as it is said, Jesus has made satisfaction for the sins of all that believe in him, and therefore recovers to all believers that "Eternal life" which was lost by the sin of Adam, it must, in this sense, be recovered for them on earth. Herein, alone, is it that the comparison of St. Paul holds good, when he says, "As by the offence of one, judgment came upon all men to condemnation, even so by the righteousness of one, the free gift came upon all men to justification of life."—Romans, v. 18, 19; or as he more perspicuously expresses it, in those other words of his: "For as in Adam all die, even so in Christ shall all be made alive."—1 Corinthians, xv. 22.

The place then, wherein men are to enjoy eternal life, which Jesus hath obtained for them, can be none other than here, where, having first obtained it, they lost it; and where, last of all, they recover it again, through him. For if, as in Adam all die, that is, if in Adam all have forfeited paradise and eternal life on earth, and returned to dust again; even so in Christ shall all be made alive, that is, all shall be made alive on earth, in the flesh. If this, we say, be not the meaning of the words, then words fail to convey any adequate idea of the text. The Psalmist not only corroborates, but he strengthens this view of the subject. "For there," says he, that is on Mount Zion, (the place which is made to represent Jerusalem upon earth,) "the Lord commanded the blessing, even life forever more."—Psalm, cxxxiii. 3. John also, in the Revelations, does the same thing: "To him that overcometh, I will give to eat of the tree of life, which is in the midst of the paradise of God."—Revelations, ii. 7. This was the tree of Adam's eternal life, which, from the wording of the fable, was evidently intended to be on earth. But, for our further confirmation, the same Apostle says again, "I, John, saw the holy city, the new Jerusalem, coming down from God out of heaven, prepared as a bride adorned for her husband."—Revelations, xxi. 2. And again, to the same effect, he remarks, "And he carried me away in the Spirit, to a great and high mountain, and shewed me that great city, the holy Jerusalem, descending out of heaven from God,"—Rev. xxi. 10; implying that the new Jerusalem, the paradise of God, at the coming again of Jesus, should come down to God's people from heaven; and not that they should go up to it from earth. This differs nothing from that, which the two men in white clothing,—that is, the two angels, said to the Apostles who were looking upon Jesus ascending: "This same Jesus, who is taken up from you into heaven, shall so come, as you have seen him go into heaven."— Acts, i. 11. This is equivalent to saying that Jesus will come down to govern them under his Father, here, eternally; and not take them up, to govern them in Heaven above. It answers also to the restoration of the kingdom of God instituted under Moses, which was a political government of the Jews on earth.

Now—referring again to the first part of the argument— if Adam and Eve had not sinned, and had lived on the earth, together with their posterity, forever, it is manifest that the earth could not have contained the aggregate. If immortals could have generated as mankind do now, the earth, in a short space of time, would not have sufficed for them to live in.

Again, the joys of that "life eternal," in Scripture language, are all comprehended under the name of Salvation. Now, to be saved, is to be secured, either respectively against special evils, or absolutely against all evils—comprehending want, sickness, and even death itself. If, therefore, man was created an immortal being, not subject to corruption, and having nothing in him that tends to dissolution, and if he fell from that state of happiness by the sin of Adam, it follows that to be saved from sin, in his case, is to be saved from all the evils and calamities that sin brought upon him. , So that the meaning of the Scriptural term, "remission of sins," is one and the same with salvation from death and misery. This is manifest from the words of Jesus, when he cured a man sick of the palsy, He began by saying, "Son, be of good cheer, thy sins be forgiven thee" (Matthew, ix. 2;) and, being murmured at by the Scribes for this act, asked them, " Whether is it easier to say, Thy sins be forgiven thee, or to say, Arise and walk?" (Matthew, ix. 5.) Of course, he meant that the two things were synonymous—that " Thy sins be forgiven thee," and " Arise and walk," would produce the same effect. Reason, too, teaches us that since death and misery are, according to Bible teaching, the punishments of sin, redemption from sin must also be redemption from death and misery ; that is to say, absolute salvation.

But salvation may also be a special remedy against particular evils—and what are they? Examples are the best means of teaching us. " And he said, the Lord is my rock, and my fortress, and my deliverer; the God of my rock; in Him will I trust; He is my shield and the horn of my salvation, my high tower and my refuge, my Saviour—thou savest me from violence. I will call on the Lord, who is worthy to be praised: so shall I be saved from mine enemies." (2 Samuel, xxii. 2, 3, 4.) "And the Lord gave Israel a Saviour, so that they went out from under the hand of the Syrians; and the children of Israel dwelt in their tents, as beforetime." (2 Kings, xiii. 5.) Now, these quotations, and many others of a similar character, which could be selected, most unquestionably have reference to the realization of an earthly salvation, which is described and marked out precisely at length in the following passages from the book of Isaiah: "Look upon Zion, the city of our solemnities; thine eyes shall see Jerusalem, a quiet habitation, a tabernacle that shall not be taken down; not one of the stakes thereof shall ever be removed, neither shall any of the cords thereof be broken. But there the glorious Lord will be unto us a place of broad rivers and streams; wherein shall go no galley with oars, neither shall gallant ship pass thereby. For the Lord is our judge, the Lord is our law-giver, the Lord is our King; he will save us. Thy tacklings are loosed; they could not well strengthen their mast; they could not spread the sail; then is the prey of a great spoil divided; the lame take the prey. And the inhabitants shall not say, I am sick; the people that dwell therein shall be forgiven their iniquity." (Isaiah, xxxiii. 20, 24.) In these words we have the place from whence salvation is to proceed, namely, "Jerusalem," "a quiet habitation;" and the eternity of it, "a tabernacle that shall not be taken down," &c. Is it not, therefore, evident that the Scriptures foretell that salvation shall be on this earth? If this is not sufficiently emphatic, examine the following texts from the same prophet. "And they (that is, the

Gentiles who had any Jew in bondage) shall bring all your brethren, for an offering unto the Lord out of all nations, upon horses and in chariots, and in litters, and upon mules, and upon swift beasts, to my holy mountain Jerusalem, saith the Lord, as the children of Israel bring an offering in a clean vessel into the house of the Lord." "And I will also take of them for priests and for Levites, saith the Lord." (Isaiah, lxvi. 20, 21.) Whereby it is manifest that the chief seat of God's kingdom, which is the place from whence the salvation of the Gentiles was to proceed, was Jerusalem.

But, to pursue this subject still further: The prophet Joel, in describing the day of judgment, says that God will "shew wonders in Heaven, and in earth, blood, and fire, and pillars of smoke; the sun shall be turned into darkness, and the moon into blood, before the great and terrible day of the Lord come. And it shall come to pass that whosoever shall call upon the name of the Lord shall be delivered: for in Mount Zion and in Jerusalem shall be deliverance." (Joel, ii. 30, 31, 32.) Obediah, in his single chapter, says the same thing: "Upon Mount Zion shall be deliverance, and there shall be holiness; and the house of Jacob shall posess their possessions" (verse 17)—that is, the possessions of the heathen. These possessions he designates more particularly in the following verses, by the title of "the Mount of Esau," "the Land of the Philistines," "the fields of Ephraim," "of Samaria," "Gilead," and "the cities of the South;" and then he concludes with these words, "the kingdom shall be the Lord's." All these places are said to be for salvation, and for the kingdom of God, after the day of judgment upon earth.

By examining the term "world," as made use of in the Bible, this will become still more apparent. There we have it referred to in three different senses, as the old world, the present world, and the world to come. Of the first, St. Peter speaks in the following language, "And spared not the old world, but saved Noah the eighth person, a preacher of righteousness, bringing the flood upon the world of the ungodly."—2 Peter, ii. 5—which evidently means the world that existed from Adam, to what is called the Deluge. Of the present world, Jesus himself thus speaks, "My kingdom is not of this world; if my kingdom were of this world, then would my servants fight that I should not be delivered to the Jews."—John, xviii. 36.—Jesus means the world then actually around him, which was then, and which is now, inhabited by the human race, as contradistinguished from the world over which he expected to rule at his second coming. And of this world to come to which Christ alluded, the Apostle Peter again enlightens us: "Nevertheless we, according to his promise, look for new heavens, and a new earth wherein dwelleth righteousness."—2 Peter, iii. 13. This is also that world, whereunto Christ coming down from heaven in the clouds, with great power and glory, shall send his angels, and shall gather together his elect from the four winds, and from the uttermost parts of the earth, and thenceforth reign over them under his Father, everlastingly.

The only article of faith, which the Scriptures make simply necessary to salvation, is this, that Jesus is "The Christ." By the name of Christ, at that time, was understood "The king;" the anointed one; the one whom God had before promised, by the prophets of the Old Testament, to send into the world, to reign over the Jews, and over such nations as should believe in him, under himself, eternally; and to give them that eternal life, which was lost by the sin of Adam, namely, life everlasting in the flesh upon earth. The aim of all the Evangelists, who give us such a graphic description of the life of Jesus, was to establish that One article of Faith, that Jesus is "The Christ." The sum and substance of Matthew's Gospel is this, that Jesus was of the stock of David, and that he was born of a Virgin. These are considered perhaps, the strongest marks by which the true Christ was to be identified; but they are not all. They are confirmed, we are taught, by the following corroborative evidence. The Magi came to worship him as such, that is as "The King of the Jews." Herod, for the same cause, sought to kill him. John the Baptist proclaimed him. He declared himself; and his Apostles also preached, that he taught the law, not as a scribe, but as a man of authority—that is, as a man in a supreme position. He cured diseases by his word only, and did many other miracles, which were foretold the Christ should do. He was saluted king, when he entered into Jerusalem. He forewarned his disciples, and others, to beware of any except himself, who should pretend to be Christ. He was taken, accused, and put to death, for saying he was that king. The cause of his condemnation, written on the cross, was, "Jesus of Nazareth, The King of the Jews." All these, and many other examples of a like character, teach, (and teach nothing more nor less than this,) that men should believe that "Jesus is the Christ." We gather these quotations from the History of Jesus, written by Matthew. The other three Evangelists who wrote of him, with some few discrepancies, additions, and subtractions, say pretty much the same things. The whole and sole design therefore of the Evangelists, was to impress and establish this one idea.

Indeed John makes it the sum total of his history. "These things were written," says he, "that ye might believe, that Jesus is the Christ, the Son of God; and that believing ye might have life through his name,"— John, xx. 31—that is to say, life everlasting upon earth in the flesh. The Apostles, even in the lifetime of Jesus, were sent to preach the kingdom of God: "And he sent them to preach the kingdom of God."—Luke, ix. 2.— And again, "As ye go, preach, saying, The kingdom of heaven is at hand."—Matthew, x. 7. Now what can we gather from this, but that he sent them to preach that he was "The Messiah," "The Christ," "The King," which was to come? Their preaching, likewise, after his death, was the same. This is manifest from an account which Luke gives in the Book of Acts, of a riot which such preaching occasioned at Thessalonica. "The Jews," says he, "which believed not, moved with envy, took unto them certain lewd fellows of the baser sort, and gathered a company, and set all the city on an uproar, and assaulted the house of Jason, and sought to bring them out to the people. And when they found them not, they drew Jason and certain brethren unto the rulers of the city, crying, these that have turned the world upside down, are come hither also, whom Jason hath received; and these all do contrary to the decrees of Caesar; saying that there is another King, one Jesus."—Acts, xvii. 5, 6, 7.

Jesus himself, no doubt, at one period of his life, favored this idea. The following suggestion which he made to the Jews with reference to himself evidences that he did, "Search the Scriptures; for in them ye think ye have eternal life; and they are they that testify of me." John, v. 39. Of course he could have reference, in these words, to no other writings than those of the Old Testament, the New Testament not then being in existence. Admitting then that the Old Testament Scriptures do bear all the marks whereby men might have known Jesus when he came among them—such as those to which we have before referred, to wit: that he should descend from David; be born at Bethlehem, and of a Virgin; and that he should do great miracles by which it should be known that he was come to be a temporal King; and, The King of the Jews;—which he never was—still, does this warrant theologians in putting a totally different construction on it, by going further and saying that he was not only a temporal king, but that he was the King of Kings, and Lord of Lords? What authority have they for doing this? We shall presently shew.

The principal evidence, which Christians have to produce in support of the Divinity of Jesus is the working of miracles. In order to claim credence for his miracles, they are necessarily compelled to admit the validity of the miracles of Moses and of the Old Testament generally, some of which are said to have been wrought by persons who were considered types of Jesus. We will examine into the nature of these first, therefore. Now it must be admitted that there are some references made in the Scriptures themselves, to the power of working wonders, even by men who were represented to be at variance with God and His people. In fact, the ability to perform such acts is conceded to them. But they are also said to have been produced by magic and incantation.

For example, when we read that after the rod of Moses had been cast on the ground, and had become a serpent, (Exodus, vii. 2,) the magicians of Egypt did the same by their enchantments. Again, after Moses had turned the waters of the Egyptian streams, rivers, ponds, and pools of water into blood—Exodus, vii. 22—the magicians did so likewise by their enchantments. And again, when Aaron had, by the power of God, brought frogs upon the land—Exodus, viii. 6—the magicians also did so by their enchantments, and they " brought up frogs upon the land of Egypt."

Now, enchantment is not, as many think it, a working of strange effects by spells and words, but imposture and delusion wrought by legerdemain; and so far is it from being supernatural, that the impostors, who practice it, resort neither to the study of science nor of nature. All they do is to impose upon the ignorance, stupidity, and superstition of the most credulous. So that all that miracle-working consists in is this, that the enchanter has made himself master in the art of deception. It is, therefore, not a good or laudable thing to do; it is bad, wicked, and detestable; and abhorrent to every sensible mind.

What a reputation for miraculous powers (before the science of the course of the stars was discovered) might not a man have gained, had he truly foretold, that on a certain day or at a certain hour, the Sun would be darkened! A juggler, also, by handling the appliances of his profession, (if such tricks were not now ordinarily practised,) might gain for himself such renown for ability to work miracles, as would suggest that he was aided by the devil, at least, if by no higher power.

But when we take a more sensible view of the matter, and look upon the impostures which are wrought by confederacy, there are few things, (however impossible they may appear,) that cannot be done or seem to be done. And, however, glaring the fraud may be, it still finds dupes enough ready to believe in it. Two men conspiring, one to seem lame, the other to cure him with a charm, might deceive many; but many conspiring—one to seem lame, another to cure him, and all the rest to bear witness to the cheat—might deceive many men.

The seeming miracle of raising Lazarus from the dead, (if it were ever enacted;) was, no doubt, the result of collusion; so also was the raising to life of the ruler's daughter, and of the son of the widow of Nain. We hesitate not to say the same in regard to all other instances, where the gaining of credence in miracle-working has been attempted.

None of the miracles, with which the old histories are filled, took place at a period of scientific culture. Scrutinizing observation, which has never once been deceived, teaches us that miracles never happen, save in times and countries wherein they are believed without examination, and before persons whose minds are already prepared to believe them. No miracle ever occurred, in the presence of men capable of testing its mysterious character. Neither common people, nor men of the world, are able to apply the test. It requires much precaution and long habits of scientific research. In our days, have we not seen almost all respectable people made dupes of by the grossest frauds and the most puerile illusions? Transactions said to be marvellous and attested by the whole population of small towns, have—thanks to a severer scrutiny—been satisfactorily explained. And, if it can be proved that no contemporary so-called miracle will bear to be inquired into, is it not probable also, nay, is it not more than probable, that the miracles of the past, which have all been performed among an ignorant populace, would equally present their share of illusion, were it possible to criticise them in detail?

It is not, then, in the name of this or that philosophy; but in the name of universal experience, that we banish miracles from history. Up to this time the performance of a miracle has never been proved.

In the aptitude of mankind to give too hasty belief to pretended miracles, therefore, how very wisely put, is the caution in the beginning of the thirteenth chapter, and again, at the end of the eighteenth chapter of Deuteronomy—that we take not any for prophets, who teach any other religion, than that which God, through his messenger, Moses, hath established; nor any, though he teach the same religion, whose prediction we do not see come to pass!

Jesus taught another religion than that of Moses; and his prediction, that his second coming would be during the lifetime of some who heard him so predict, did not come to pass. By this it is proved, that the Bible test of a reliable worker of miracles is adverse to the pretensions set up in behalf of Jesus. He also failed to establish his claim, in relation to having been sent of God to be temporal ruler of the Jews, either by miracles or otherwise. Unfulfilled also is the idea of Jesus in relation to the destruction of the earth by fire, and the formation of a new one in its place, wherein he claimed that the righteous alone were to dwell, and were to be ruled over by him. All of this was to take place, according to Jesus' own prediction, before the then generation should pass away; yet now, after eighteen hundred years, it remains unaccomplished.

We add a few remarks in regard to the pretended miracles, described by the writers of the New Testament as having been worked by Jesus.

There is undoubtedly a class of diseases which may not be cured by a charm, or by the force of imagination, or immediately by soothing influences.

Of this sort was that of the woman with the issue of blood of long standing. Yet there is another class of complaints, or conceits, which may be so cured, or at least appear for a time to be so. Hence, the account given in the Gospels, in many cases, corresponds to appearances exhibited at the time. When Jesus dismissed the woman having the issue of blood, with the words, "Thy faith hath made thee whole," he could not have expressed himself more modestly, and, it may be, that he spoke not altogether inappropriately. She may in some degree have been benefitted by her faith; but she could not have been instaneously and entirely cured of a disorder, like the one in question. Faith, hopefulness, and buoyancy of spirits have a marked tendency to produce beneficial effects, and generally do so in almost all descriptions of diseases. But this in a way altogether natural, never supernatural or miraculous. The firm belief which many persons had in Jesus as a wonder-worker, no doubt had more or less influence, for a time at least, as is evident from the fact that in his home at Nazareth, by reason of the unbelief of the people, it was only in a few cases that he had succeeded.—Matthew, xiii. 58. It was supposed, at the period in question, that there were processes, more or less efficacious, for driving diseases away. On this account, the occupation of exorcist or conjurer was a regular profession, like that of physician, and it may be fairly assumed that Jesus had, in his lifetime, the reputation of possessing the profoundest secrets of this art. Many singular incidents were related, in connection with his cures, in which the credulity of the people gave full scope for his encouragement, as at this day. In Syria, they regard as mad, or possessed by a demon, people who are only somewhat eccentric. A gentle word in such cases often suffices to drive away the demon. And such were, doubtless, the means employed by Jesus. At that time, also, the fashionable form of complaint among the Jews was, possession of devils, which accounts for his popularity as a caster of them out. We have seen this morbid condition re-appearing in our own days, in connection with the newly arisen belief in spirits and devils. Nervous and mental diseases, which otherwise would have appeared simply in the form of convulsions, periodical craziness, and the like, appeared in connection with that superstition as madness, produced by demoniacal possession, that could only be removed by operating on the delusion. There is every probability that, as to the cause of this disease, Jesus shared the ideas of his age. Hence, on account of its frequently yielding to his denunciation, in the name of God, he considered this fact a sign of the Messianic times, though he laid the less stress upon the fact as regarded himself and his disciples, because he saw the same effect produced by others whom, in this respect, he placed without hesitation on a par with himself.

In cases of cure of this kind by the imagination, it could not but happen sometimes that, with the excitement, the imagined relief produced by it also passed away, so that the old complaints returned. Jesus himself speaks of such relapses, not merely with reference to sick persons who had been cured by himself, but generally, so that we may be sure that they had happened in his own experience, as well as in that of others. As regards the re-possession, he explains it as the return of the devil that

DIFFERENT MIRACLES. 225

had been driven out, with a fresh accession of strength. We infer from this, that he looked upon the cause of these complaints as a supernatural one, and his power of removing them as by no means absolute.

Now we have to speak of quite another description of miracles, said to have been enacted by Jesus, which involves the question, whether God's laws in relation to physical nature are invariably the same. The affirmative is at this day so well established by science and every other available test, that to argue the subject is frivolous. We therefore deem it impossible, that Jesus should ever, by a mere blessing, have enormously increased existing means of nourishment. It is impossible, that he could have changed water into wine. Nor can he, in defiance of the law of gravity, have walked upon the water without sinking. He cannot have recalled really dead men to life. Narratives of this kind have their existence in fable only; never in fact. The gross ignorance and the dark superstition of the people, in Jesus' time, make it perfectly intelligible that even cures, effected by means obviously natural, were considered as miracles.

If Jesus could cure some diseases supernaturally by the mere word of command, why not all? Why resort to manipulation, and the applying of spittle and clay to the eyes of the blind, and the cleansing with water, according to Bible narrative? Here is evidently a judicious discrimination between complaints which may be affected purely by the imagination, and those in which it was deemed necessary to resort to material appliances. Natural means were evident, while credit was given (for whatever good may have resulted) to supernatural means.

Again, the most wonderful and startling of all the miracles said to have been performed by Jesus, was that called the raising of Lazarus. If this ever had the appearance of being performed, it is certain that Lazarus was not dead; and the presumption is, that Jesus knew it. This is to be inferred from the fact that he, himself, intimated to his disciples that Lazarus was only asleep. Let any candid reader examine the following narrative with a critical eye, and see if something of this kind of collusion cannot be detected in it: "Therefore his sisters sent unto him, saying, Lord, behold he whom thou lovest is sick. When Jesus heard that he said, This sickness is not unto death, but for the glory of God, that the Son of God might be glorified thereby. These things said he; and after that he saith unto them, Our friend Lazarus sleepeth; but I go that I may awake him out of sleep. Then said his disciples, Lord, if he sleep he shall do well. Howbeit Jesus spake of his death; but they thought that he had spoken of taking of rest in sleep. Then said Jesus unto them plainly, Lazarus is dead. And I am glad for your sakes that I was not there, to the intent ye may believe; nevertheless let us go unto him. Jesus saith unto her, Said I not unto thee, that if thou wouldst believe thou shouldst see the glory of God? Then they took away the stone from the place where the dead was laid. And Jesus lifted up his eyes and said, Father I thank thee that thou hast heard me. And I knew that thou hearest me always; but because of the people which stand by, I said it, that they may believe that thou hast sent me. And when he thus had spoken, he cried with a loud voice, Lazarus, come forth. And he that was dead came forth, bound hand and foot, with grave clothes; and his face was bound about with a napkin. Jesus saith unto them, Loose him and let him go. Then many of the Jews which came to Mary, and had seen the things which Jesus did, believed on him."

According to the testimony of the Apostle Paul, it was a national peculiarity of the Jews to desire signs from a man in whose doctrine they were asked to believe. Moses was supposed to have spoken to the people, before the suppression of the rebellious adherents of Korah.—Numbers, xvi. 28,—"Hereby ye shall know that the Lord hath sent me to do all these works; for I have not done them of mine own mind." "The Jews," St. Paul remarks, "require a sign, and the Greeks seek after wisdom."—1 Corinthians, 22.

As the national legend of the Hebrews had attributed to Moses, one of the most eminent prophets, a series of such miracles as might then be read in the books held sacred by them, it was natural that miracles should, in like manner, be expected of every one who claimed to be a prophet or the Messiah, and that a Teacher should not be held in full estimation by the people if he were without this proof of having received credentials from above. Accordingly, it is quite certain, as we read in the Gospels, that on more than one occasion, when Jesus put forward pretensions which none but a Prophet could put forward, he was met by the demand for an accrediting sign. "Master," said they, as we read in the Gospel of Matthew, " we would see a sign from thee." On two other occasions, likewise, they accosted him with the expressions of a wish of this kind, and for what they define more accurately as a sign from heaven,—Matthew, xvi. 1 ; Mark, viii. 2. But Jesus refused to comply with their demands. Up to this time, his pretension went no further than that he was a teacher sent from God. He relied upon the excellence of the doctrine that he taught, as an evidence that he was sent; and this he declared. He, therefore, returned a summary answer to the demand for a sign. No sign whatever, said he, shall be given to this evil and adulterous generation. By the term "generation," we understand him to mean his contemporaries generally, whose want of susceptibility and whose perversity in the case of the Pharisees and Scribes, came under his observation in a particularly glaring manner. It was not until later, and probably after he had conceived the idea that he was the promised Messiah, that he saw the policy of yielding—as he did—to the importunities for a sign. The answer that Jesus gave to the messengers of the Baptist, who were sent to him in consequence of a series of miracles which he was then performing, and to which he appealed as a proof of his Messianic commission, appears to stand in direct contradiction to his refusal to perform signs and wonders. When John the Baptist sent to ask Jesus whether he was the promised Messiah, or whether they were to look for another, John must have been in doubt, whether those miracles—similar ones to which had been performed by the Prophets in the Old Testament—did also, on this occasion, announce only a Prophet, or, lastly, and once for all, the Messiah. The sequel has shown that Jesus was not the expected Messiah, inasmuch as he never occupied the throne of David. But, however Jesus might disclaim the performance of material miracles, it was supposed, according to the mode of thought of the period, and of his contemporaries, that miracles he must perform whether he would or not. As soon as he was considered a Prophet—Luke, vii. 16—and we cannot doubt that he might attain this character as well as the Baptist, even without the performance of

JEWISH TESTS OF THE MESSIAHSHIP. 229

miracles—miraculous powers were attributed to him, they came of course into operation. From that time, wherever he showed himself, sufferers regularly crowded upon him in order only to touch his garments, because they expected to be cured by doing so.—Matthew, xiv. 36; Mark, iii. 10, vi. 56; Luke, vi. 19. And it would have been strange indeed, if there had been no cases among all these, in which the force of excited imagination, or impressions half spiritual and half sensuous, produced either actual removal or temporary mitigation of disease. Such effect was ascribed to the miraculous powers of Jesus.

But, besides, and beyond these signs as a test of the truth of the mission of a prophet, there were other means by which the Jews examined his claims, and particularly the claims of one aspiring to the Messiahship. Their conceptions of the Messiah, though different in different persons, agreed nevertheless in this—that the Messiah, after the opening of his kingdom, would continue to reign over his followers for a period far exceeding the natural duration of human life. According to Luke, his dominion was, absolutely, to have no end: "He shall be great, and shall be called the Son of the Highest: and the Lord God shall give unto him the throne of his father David: And he shall reign over the house of Jacob forever; and of his kingdom there shall be no end."—Luke, i. 32, 33.

This idea we find borrowed from the prophets David, Isaiah, Daniel, and others, where the duration of his reign is said to be a thousand years, as in Revelations, xx. 4. If he died at last, this death was to happen to all life on earth, for the purpose of bringing about a change into the super-terrestrial state. But in no case could he die, until he had finished his work and executed all that was expected of him. In no case could he be cut off, as a condemned criminal, submitting to superior power.

Now both these contingencies had occurred to Jesus. His ministry, as the pretended Messiah, was broken off; and it was broken off by the violence practised against him by the Jews, even before it had fully begun. The case, then, immediately after the decease of Jesus, between the Jews of the ancient faith, and his adherents, stood as follows. The former said, "Your Jesus cannot have been the Messiah, because the Messiah is to continue forever. He was not to die until after a long period of dominion as the Messiah, at the same time enjoying earthly life as all others. But your Jesus has died before the time by a disgraceful death, without having done anything expected of the Messiah." On the other hand, the latter said, "As Jesus, our Messiah, died so early, the prophecies, which promise to the Messiah that he shall endure forever, can only have meant that his death should not subject his soul to a continuance in hell, nor his body to corruption."—Psalm, xvi. 10; Acts, ii. 21; but that he should migrate into a higher life with God, from whence he will return to earth at his own time, in order to bring to a conclusion his work that was interrupted through your guilt." Now which interpretation is the most credible and probable? Let us look further.

All the prophecies, that can, with any consistency, be construed to have any relation to the office of Jesus' Messiahship, point to his sitting on the throne of David in the capacity of an earthly king, and thence redeeming the Jews from personal, and, perhaps, incidentally from some degree of spiritual and mental bondage.—Isaiah, ix. 6, 7.

THE THRONE OF DAVID. 231

That the Jews, at the time of Jesus' ministry among them, so understood it, will be seen by the following citation: "There came wise men from the east to Jerusalem, saying, Where is he that is born King of the Jews? for we have seen his star in the east, and are come to worship him. * * * And when he—Herod—had gathered all the chief priests and scribes of the people together, he demanded of them where Christ should be born. And they said unto him, In Bethlehem of Judea, for thus it is written by the prophet: And thou Bethlehem, in the land of Juda, art not the least among the princes of Juda; for out of thee shall come a Governor that shall rule my people Israel."—Matthew, ii. 1, 2, 3, 5, 6. This is further evinced by the inscription which Pilate caused to be put on the cross upon which Jesus was crucified, to wit: "Jesus of Nazareth, The King of the Jews," and to which the Jews objected, saying, "Write not The King of the Jews, but that he said, I am King of the Jews."—John, xix. 21. He was accused then by the Jews, of claiming to be their king; and it is evident that the accusation was a just one.

Indeed, even after his death, it was still the belief of the Apostles that he was a Prince and a Saviour, and that he was raised up to sit on the throne of David. In the first sermon that Peter preached (which was on the day of Pentecost,) he addressed himself thus to the assembled multitudes that surrounded him: "Men and brethren let me freely speak unto you of the patriarch David, that he is both dead and buried, and his sepulchre is with us unto this day. Therefore, being a prophet, and knowing that God had sworn with an oath to him, that of the fruit of his loins, according to the flesh, he would raise up Christ to sit on his throne," &c.—Acts, ii. 20. And when this same Apostle, and some others of his brethren had been arrested for preaching, in his name, after the alleged resurrection and ascension of Jesus, Peter in his defence remarked, "Him hath God exalted with his right hand to be a Prince and a Saviour, for to give repentance to Israel, and forgiveness of sins."—Acts, v. 31.

This proves that they still adhered to the idea that his mission was to save the Israelites from bondage,.through the medium of his being their Prince ; and from their sins, by preaching repentance to them. But, was the son of Mary, the wife of Joseph, who was called Christ, sent to sit upon the throne of David?

This was the question that was fairly presented to the Jews, both by Jesus and his disciples before his death, and by his Apostles after his death ; and it is quite certain that it took a political phase, and was canvassed, on the side of the Apostles, with equal skill and ardor, as are such questions now. The point at issue was, belief or non-belief, as to whether Jesus as the appointed of God, was to occupy the throne of David. Human nature and political intriguing having the same sway over men's minds then as at present, it is not improbable that all things, which were promised to those that believed, were so promised in order to swell up a majority, so that Jesus might be declared a King by acclamation, and the leaders in that doctrine be thus enabled to divide the spoils. By the flatteries of his immediate followers, and of those who espoused his cause, he was made to believe without doubt that he was the person selected by God to serve in the capacity here indicated ; and hence, in view of his princely honors and the high source of his appointment, he allowed others to call him, and called himself, "Christ," "Lord,"

JESUS' PROGRESSIVE IDEAS. 233

and "the Son of God," as was the manner of the Jews, in relation to persons who were held in high estimation.

This was his attitude, and these were his claims, when the question was being agitated, by the people, as to his title to the Jewish throne. They were instilled and fostered within him by the fanaticism of his followers, who repeatedly proclaimed with shouts and acclamations, that he was the promised Messiah—The King whom the Jews expected to reign over them.—Mark, xi. 9. We read in St. Matthew's Gospel that the multitudes that went before and that followed, cried, saying, " Hosanna to the Son of David, Blessed is he that cometh in the name of the Lord, Hosanna in the Highest." And again, in St. John, " that when he perceived that they would come, and take him by force, and make him a King, he departed again into a mountain himself alone." This he did, probably, because, by his far-sightedness, he saw that the time had not yet come for him to assert his right to the position. There being, at that moment, no general movement of the populace to support him in his claim.

When Jesus had completely given up his association with Judaism he was filled with revolutionary ardor. The innocent aphorisms of the first part of his prophetic career, in part borrowed from the Jewish rabbis anterior to him, and the beautiful moral precepts of his second period, are exchanged for a decided policy. The Messiah had come ; and he was the Messiah. The Kingdom of God was about to be revealed ; and it was he who would reveal it. It was by crises and commotions that it was to be established. " From the days of John the Baptist," saith he, "until now, the Kingdom of Heaven suffereth violence, and the violent take it by force ;" (Matthew, xi. 12 ;) and again, " The law and the prophets were until John; since that time the Kingdom of God is preached, and every man presseth into it."—John, xvi. 16.

He had previously contented himself with quietly teaching the doctrines of purity and truth. Now he presented a different attitude before the world. He was above, and beyond, a mere simple teacher of morality. He was a prophet, and more than a prophet, and to be obeyed. A kingdom was to be established by him.

In his paroxysm of heroic will, he believed himself all powerful. If the earth would not submit to this supreme transformation, it must be broken up, purified by fire, and by the breath of God. A new heaven and a new earth would be created, and instead of men it would be peopled with the angels of God.

A radical revolution, embracing even nature itself, was now the fundamental idea of Jesus. But much darkness mixed itself with even his most correct views. Sometimes strange temptations crossed his mind. In the desert of Judea, Satan had offered him the kingdoms of the earth. Not knowing the power of the Roman Empire, he might, with the enthusiasm there was in the heart of Judea, which ended soon after in so terrible an outbreak, hope to establish a kingdom by the number and the daring of his partisans. Many times, perhaps, the supreme question, presented itself—will the kingdom of God be realized by force or gentleness, by revolt or by patience? Much vagueness no doubt tinged his ideas. Our principles of positive science are offended by certain of the dreams contained in the programme of Jesus.

There was a contradiction between belief in the approaching end of the world, and the general moral system which he advocated in prospect of a permanent state of humanity. He prepared his disciples for treating the civil powers with contempt by not deigning to make any defence when brought before them. He wished to annihilate riches and power; and it was his dream to effect a great social revolution, in which rank would be overturned, and where all authority in this world would be humiliated except his own, he fancying himself destined to have supreme rule.

He gradually became more and more imperious. At about thirty years of age, he made the proclamation of his Messiahship, and the affirmation of the coming catastrophe in which he was to figure as judge, clothed with the full powers which had been delegated to him by the Ancient of days. "The Father," said he, "judgeth no man, but hath committed all judgment unto the Son,"— John, v. 22; evidently imagining that he, to whom the title of the Son was given, would be appointed to judge his fellow-creatures. His family were strongly opposed to him, and plainly refused to believe in his mission or pretensions. The Nazarenes, much more violent, wished, it is said, to kill him by throwing him from a steep rock: "And all they in the synagogue, when they heard these things were filled with wrath, and rose up, and thrust him out of the city and lead him unto the brow of the hill whereon their city was built, that they might cast him down headlong."—Luke, iv. 28, 29.

If Jesus conceived that he was the Messiah, and referred the prophecy in Daniel to the Messiah, and expected in accordance with it, to come with the clouds of heaven in his own person, as proclaimed by him, he not only appears to us in the light of a fanatic, but we see also an unallowable self-exaltation in a man's (and it is only of a human being that we are everywhere speaking) so putting himself above every one else, as to contrast himself with them as their future judge. And, in doing so, Jesus must have completely forgotten how he had on one occasion disclaimed the epithet of good, as one belonging to God alone.

The title of "Son of David" was the first which he accepted, probably without being concerned in the innocent frauds by which it was sought to secure it to him. The universal belief was, that the Messiah would be son of David, and like him would be born at Bethlehem. The first idea of Jesus was perhaps not precisely this. But public opinion on this point made him do violence to himself. The immediate consequence of the proposition, "Jesus is the Messiah," was this other proposition, "Jesus is the son of David." He allowed a title to be given him, without which he could not hope for success. In this, as in many other circumstances of his life, Jesus yielded to the ideas which were current in his time, although they were not precisely his own. He associated with his doctrine of the "kingdom of God" all that could warm the heart and the imagination. It was thus that we have seen him adopt the baptism of John, although it could not have been of much importance to him. "The woman saith unto him, I know that Messias cometh, which is called Christ, when he is come, he will tell us all things. Jesus saith unto her, I that speak unto thee am he."—John, iv. 25, 26. It is evident that Jesus made no such announcement in relation to himself during the early part of his ministry. The remark of the woman, and his reply, is proof that no such idea was then current. And this is corroborated by John while imprisoned, sending to inquire of Jesus whether he laid claim to being the expected Messiah. Now if the character and

OBJECT OF CHRIST AND APOSTLES. 237

mission of Jesus was what the theologians claim, it is incomprehensible why his course and conduct in each and every part, and as a whole, should not have been more in conformity with our conception of a fair representation of normal man and a perfect God than was the case. Jesus was probably led to imagine that he was the expected Messiah by the homage done to him by his admirers, and those who deceived themselves about him. This idea, however, he abandoned as far as he himself was concerned; and he must have felt, (and felt most bitterly at the last,) that he had been deceiving himself as to his true position, otherwise he would not have exclaimed as he did, "My God, my God, why hast thou forsaken me?" Mark, xv. 34.

This one acknowledgment, of his subordination to God, made so exactly after the manner of an ordinary man disappointed in his aim and unexpectedly brought to the last struggle of life, should set at rest, as we conceive, the assumption that he was either the predicted Messiah or co-equal with God. When he answered the woman as he did, it is probable that he thought himself to be what he said he was. He thought, likewise, no doubt, that by gaining the confidence and credence of the people in him as the Christ, it would favor his ascension to the throne, as the King of the Jews. The great desideratum with him and with his Apostles was, to induce the people to believe that the person, then among them, was the Christ, was the identical person to whom the Prophets pointed as destined to rule as King over the Jews perpetually, upon earth. A majority of such believers being obtained, the road was plain and the way sure, to the aggrandizement of both him and themselves. And so confident were they in their expectations of success, that politician-like, they began to squabble and to importune him, in advance, for the honors and spoils that would fall to the lot of each, when he should have attained to the throne. That this squabbling for place had relation to temporal affairs—matters pertaining to this life—and not to those beyond the grave, is shown by the Gospel itself. St. Luke says, (ix. 46,) "Then there arose a reasoning among them, which of them should be greatest;" and again, xxii. 24 to 29,—And there was also a strife among them which of them should be accounted the greatest. And he said unto them, The kings of the Gentiles exercise lordship over them; and they that exercise authority upon them are called benefactors. But ye shall not be so; but he that is greatest among you, let him be as the younger; and he that is chief, as he that doth serve. For whether is greater, he that sitteth at meat, or he that serveth? is not he that sitteth at meat? but I am among you as he that serveth? Ye are they which have continued with me in my temptations. And I appoint unto you a kingdom, as my Father hath appointed unto me. That ye may eat and drink at my table, in my kingdom, and sit on thrones, judging the twelve tribes of Israel." Now, no one will deny, we presume, that this has reference to temporal affairs, and that it was so understood by those to whom it was spoken. If so, it evidently accounts for the Apostles being stimulated to use every available device for the purpose of making and retaining believers; and it is corroborated by the kind of teaching or belief which Jesus was so solicitous to inculcate in relation to himself, as shown by reference also to Gospel authority. St. Matthew, xxii. 41, 42, says: "While the Pharisees were gathered together, Jesus asked them, saying, What think ye of Christ? whose son is he? They say unto him, The son of David." Again, "And Jesus answered and said, while he taught in the temple, How say the scribes that Christ is the son of David."—Mark, xii. 35. His motive in asking these questions is unmistakable, and shews how anxious he was to have his lineal descent traced from the house of David, and consequently his title to the throne of the Jews established, and believed in, and publicly proclaimed. Hence his declaration : " Whosoever therefore shall confess me before men, him will I confess also before my Father which is in heaven. But whosoever shall deny me before men, him will I also deny before my Father which is in heaven."—Matthew, x. 32, 33.

The importance of confession before men is manifest; and especially in such a case as this, where Jesus was to be proclaimed as King. It is not at all an uncommon thing for men of influence to declare, and commit themselves in favor of a certain political tenet, or on the side of an individual who is an aspirant for a high position in the government of a country ; and it is often the case, that the public announcement of such a course gives éclat and impetus to the cause or party interest which is being pushed forward. A large portion in all communities, who do not take the trouble to think for themselves, is continually, heedlessly, and thoughtlessly following the lead of prominent men.

Viewed in this light, the public avowal of Jesus had a two-fold advantage, first, of binding the new disciples more firmly to the new faith, and secondly, of increasing the popularity of the pretender. But when viewed in relation to religious matters, one cannot avoid calling to mind that precept which condemns such a course, and which teaches us to be more modest and retiring. " He that exalteth himself shall be abased; but he that humbleth himself shall be exalted." This will occur to us more strongly, when Jesus' avowal is viewed in relation to the ostentation of the Pharisees, who sounded a trumpet before them in the synagogues and in the streets, that they might be seen and heard of men, as Jesus himself had noted and condemned.

All conceivable good was promised for simply believing in Jesus' divine right to the throne of his ancestors, and the public committal to such espousal of Jesus' pretensions, by baptism. The Apostles, like the politicians of our day, had learned from experience, that one party is constantly winning back some portion of the converts which the other had made; hence, the policy of sealing the new faith with a public pledge and formal act.

This temporal or worldly interest, it is evident, was the great and only object that led and stimulated Jesus, and his disciples, to encourage such zeal in the belief and pledge in question. In all such efforts to propagate the interests of their Master, the conduct of the Apostles, was true to the instincts of the most adroit politicians—fully up to the best party manœuvring of our day—and lacks nothing in the adaptation of the means to the ends, provided double-dealing and false pretenses are conceded to be admissible in such matters. But, when men teach that all, who do not believe that Jesus was the person to whom the prophets had reference in their predictions, when they assigned a king to the Jews, will be condemned by God to everlasting torment, they teach what is opposed to every rational and just view that can be taken on the subject; and, as it has never been propounded to nor heard of by one in a thousand of the men born into the world, it is impossible that anything, which places God so directly at variance with even man's sense of justice, can be true.

When Jesus undertook to teach natural religion, which is love to God and good will towards men manifested by good works, he struck at the root and influence of the whole system of the Jewish religion and priesthood. In speaking of God as the Father of all mankind, he incurred their displeasure, and raised their ire beyond measure; because they claimed that they alone were the children of God. When he denounced their ceremonials, their sacrifices, their pride, and their self-righteousness, he brought upon himself a storm of persecution and abuse which, at last, instigated them to murder him. That he disapproved of, and highly condemned their whole ceremonial law and teaching, as works of supererogation and hypocrisy, the following denunciations against them, proves: "If ye had known what this meaneth, I will have mercy and not sacrifice, ye would not have condemned the guiltless "—Matthew, xii. 7; "For, laying aside the commandment of God, ye hold the tradition of men as the washing of pots and of cups; and many other such like things ye do "—Mark, vii. 8; "Ye reject the commandment of God that ye may keep your own tradition "—Matthew, vii. 9; "And when thou prayest, thou shalt not be as the hypocrites are; for they love to pray standing in the synagogues, and in the corners of the streets, that they may be seen of men "—Matthew, vi. 5; "They think that they shall be heard for their much speaking "—Matthew, iii. 7; "Your Father knoweth what things ye have need of before ye ask Him "—Matthew, vi. 8.

Now, what could have been better calculated to raise against Jesus the fierce indignation of the priests, than such an unmitigated condemnation of the very things they most trusted in, and from which they derived their great power and influence. The religion which he taught, and which harmonizes so beautifully with the true instincts of natural religion, could not but become popular with the common people, and to such an extent, that the priesthood were alarmed lest they should lose their long enjoyed ascendency. The result was, that they could not rest satisfied until they had succeeded in having Jesus arraigned before the Roman authorities, on the double charge of laying claim to be King of the Jews, and blasphemy; "But the Jews cried out, saying, If thou let this man go thou art not Cæsar's friend: whosoever maketh himself a king speaketh against Cæsar."—John, xix. 12; "Then the high priest rent his clothes and saith, What need we any further witnesses? Ye have heard the blasphemy."—Mark, xiv. 63, 64. The plan adopted by his enemies was to convict him by the testimony of witnesses; and, by his own avowal of blasphemy and outrage against the Mosaic religion, to condemn him to death according to their law; and then to get their verdict sanctioned by Pilate, the Roman Governor. The fatal sentence which Jesus had really uttered: "I am able to destroy the temple of God, and to build it in three days," was cited by two witnesses. To blaspheme the temple of God was, according to the Jewish law, to blaspheme God Himself. "And whoso shall swear by the altar sweareth by it, and by all things thereon. And he that sweareth by the temple, sweareth by it, and by him that dwelleth therein."—Matthew, xxiii. 21, 22. Now, these crimes were punished by the law with death; "And thou shalt speak unto the children of Israel, saying, Whosoever curseth his God shall bear his sin. And he that blasphemeth the name of the Lord, he shall surely be put to death."—Leviticus, xxiv. 15, 16. Accordingly, with one voice, the assembly declared him guilty of a capital crime, which decision being confirmed by Pilate, his execution took place. His conviction and death, under the foregoing circumstances, it is well known, were brought about at the instigation and by the hatred of the priesthood, in consequence of his espousal and persistent teaching of the religion of the heart and conscience. He, it was, we all know, who was the great champion and defender of the simple doctrines of love to God and love to man, apart from the sacrifices and ceremonies of the Jewish ritual. This, as we have said, greatly incensed the priests, because it brought into disrepute their whole system. It diminished the influence which they had gained through their ceremonies and sacrifices, and made them (themselves) unpopular. And, having crucified him under these false pretenses, by this act, they caused him to become a thousand fold more potent to do the very thing they sought to get rid of by procuring his death. This admirable trait in human character—the enthusiastic espousal of the cause, and the yielding of our sympathies on the side of the oppressed and ill-used—so increased his popularity, that the views which he took of religion, and his power of discrimination between the good, the false, and the true, only served the more to increase the popularity of natural religion. At the same time it is to be observed that all this occurred in the midst of the Jews, whose natural leanings and old habits induced them, in course of time, to graft upon the purer doctrines, that Jesus taught, a portion of their own rites and ceremonies. Among these, sacrifice was pre-eminent. But what was worse still, they took, as the basis of their creed and worship, the sacrifice of the death of him, to whom such a creed and worship were so obnoxious as to merit and receive his most unsparing and untiring opposition. And in this connection it is important to bear in mind, that Jesus himself said not a word to justify this interpretation of his death. On the contrary, he said everything that he could against the principle of Judaism, on which it all rests. His course in this respect is most significant; and if candidly considered, from a common sense point of view, will, as we conceive, leave this fundamental doctrine of the Christian Church without a rational foundation to rely on. There is not the faintest allusion in any of Jesus' discourses or parables, to his being a sacrifice for sin, or to God's requiring any blood to be shed before he would forgive sinners. With this indisputable fact before us, it is incomprehensible, how they, who now teach this doctrine, can justify themselves in allowing this Jewish excrescence to be grafted upon the religion originally taught by Jesus. We can, to some extent, excuse the Jews for carrying with them the doctrines to which they had been accustomed for ages, but for others, who look with aversion upon the Jewish sacrifices, even of animal life, there can be no excuse. The result is, that a leading doctrine of Christian theology has come down to us from that very class of men, who hated and stoned Jesus and put him to death. This is not only a different mode of worship from that which he taught, but it is at direct variance with it.

The Churches teach that Jesus came to abolish the old Jewish law and its ceremonies, and especially that part of the law which relates to sacrifices; and that, as a substitute, therefore, he offered the shedding of his own blood upon the cross as an atonement for the sins of the people.

Now, this teaching Jesus himself contradicts. He says he came to bear witness to the truth of the moral law, and to call sinners to repentance. When he is asked what is necessary to be done that we may inherit eternal life, he gives full and explicit directions, comprised in what we term the commandments. In them we do not find that sacrifice of himself, or of anything else, is mentioned.

When he is asked the question referred to, he does not seem to have entertained the idea that he was the predicted Messiah. Neither did he imagine that he was to be made a substitute for the sacrifices of the Jewish religion. Hence, he had nothing whatever to say about salvation through his atonement.

The young man, who enquires of Jesus as to the conditions of entering into eternal life, is told to keep the commandments. He says he has done so, from his youth up. He is then told that, on account of this, he is not far from the Kingdom of Heaven. But the reason, assigned for his not absolutely attaining thereunto is that he does not exercise charity. He is allowed, therefore, to go away with the impression, that if he can only do this he is safe ; and yet we are told by the theology of the times, that there was something else necessary to which Jesus did not make the remotest allusion.

Now, all this is irreconcilable and at variance with God's indisputable justice and goodness. It is impossible to conceive that God should punish any one of His creatures everlastingly, for not believing that, which they never had the slightest intimation that it was any part of their duty to God or man to believe. We defy any one to find one single passage in the whole New Testament, wherein Jesus declares it necessary, or wherein he even solicits belief in himself as a sacrifice. He calls upon men, we admit, to believe in him, as being the predicted Messiah and as a true teacher ; but never as a true Saviour of the souls of men beyond the grave, by any other means than the saving efficacy of the doctrine which he taught.

In order to shew still more convincingly that Jesus did not teach that anything else was necessary for salvation than good works, and that no such thing as sacrifices, either of slain beasts or of himself, was in any way required, we now refer to the occasion when we were taught upon what principle we shall all be judged. Jesus there imagines himself to be the arbiter, who is to decide between men and their God ; and, in so doing, assimilates men under two conditions to a promiscuous flock of sheep and goats. As a shepherd, says he, divideth his sheep from the goats so will he divide the good from the bad ; and he will set the sheep—those who represent the good— on the right-hand, but the goats—the bad—on his left. "Then," he continues, "shall the King say to those on his right-hand, Come ye blessed of my Father, inherit the kingdom prepared for you from the foundation of the world. For I was a hungered, and ye gave me meat : I was a stranger and ye took me in : Naked and ye clothed me : I was sick and ye visited me : I was in prison and ye came unto me. Then shall the righteous answer him, saying, Lord, when saw we thee a hungered and fed thee ? or thirsty and gave thee drink ? When saw we thee a stranger and took thee in ? Or when saw we thee sick, or in prison and came unto thee ? And the King shall answer and say unto them, Verily I say unto you, Inasmuch as ye have done it unto one of the least of these my brethren, ye have done it unto me." He then goes on to address, in their own proper character, those on His left in a correspondingly diverse manner.

THE OLD TESTAMENT ON SACRIFICE. 247

What then are the conditions here laid down, as those upon which men are to be acquitted or condemned, by the most solemn tribunal sitting upon men's actions that could be pictured to the imagination? Are they, whether a man believed in this dogma, or that dogma? Whether the Jew attended to the strict observance of the sacrifices and ceremonies of his religion, or not? Whether the Christian believed in the sacrifice of Christ or not? Whether the Mahommedan believed in Mahommed or not? The Hindoo in Juggernaut? or the Chinese in Confucius? Nothing of the kind. Belief in no man is required. Faith in no system is expected. The offering of no sacrifice is looked for. What is requisite is simply this, doing unto others as we would they should do unto us. Love to God, and love to man, manifested by our works of charity and goodness, an amplifying, so to say, of Jesus' final exhortation to the rich man already mentioned.

But the Bible furnishes other evidence tending to the same conclusions. The Old Testament is so full of the condemnation of sacrifices and other superstitions from the pens of prophets and others that only a limited number of examples can be selected for these pages. What said Samuel to King Saul, after the latter had returned from the slaughter of the Amalekites, and brought with him the best of the sheep and the oxen for sacrificial purposes, contrary to the instructions which he had received to slay all and spare none, neither man nor woman, infant nor suckling, 'ox nor sheep, camel nor ass? "Hath the Lord as great delight in burnt offerings and sacrifices, as in obeying the voice of the Lord? Behold, to obey is better than sacrifice, and to hearken than the fat of rams."—1 Samuel, xv. 22. What saith the Psalmist?

"Sacrifice and offering thou didst not desire; mine ears hast thou opened; burnt offering and sin-offering hast thou not required."—Psalm, xl. 6. And again, "For thou desirest not sacrifice; else would I give it thee: thou delightest not in burnt offering."—Psalm, li. 16. What saith the wise man, Solomon? "Keep thy foot when thou goest to the house of God, and be more ready to hear than to offer the sacrifice of fools."—Ecclesiastes, v. 1. What say the prophets Isaiah, Jeremiah, Hosea, and Malachi? "To what purpose is the multitude of your sacrifices unto me? saith the Lord: I am full of the burnt offerings of rams, and the fat of fed beasts: and I delight not in the blood of bullocks, or of lambs, or of he-goats."—Isaiah, i. 11. "Bring no more vain oblations: incense is an abomination unto me: the new moons and Sabbaths, the calling of assemblies, I cannot away with: it is iniquity, even the solemn meeting."—Isaiah, i. 13. "To what purpose cometh there to me incense from Sheba, and the sweet cane from a far country? your burnt offerings are not acceptable, nor your sacrifices sweet unto me."—Jeremiah, vi. 20. "They sacrifice flesh for the sacrifices of mine offerings, and eat it: but the Lord accepteth them not; now will he remember their iniquity, and visit their sins."—Hosea, viii. 13. "The Lord will cut off the man that doeth this, the master and the scholar, out of the tabernacles of Jacob, and him that offereth an offering unto the Lord of hosts."—Malachi, ii. 12.

Lastly, we cite this remarkable passage from Hosea, vi. 6. "For I desired mercy, and not sacrifice; and the knowledge of God more than burnt offerings." Twice did Jesus himself make distinct reference to this injunction, and emphasize its plain language by application to actual circumstances. When the Pharisees reproached him for eating with publicans and sinners, he said, "Go ye and learn what that meaneth, I will have mercy and not sacrifice." When they reproached his disciples for plucking ears of corn on the Sabbath day, he told them, "If ye had known what this meaneth, I will have mercy and not sacrifice, ye would not have condemned the guiltless."

And Jesus' adoption of Hosea's very language leads us on, from the Old Testament to the New. Nor herein is there need of further proof, than this adoption affords, that Jesus himself attached no importance to sacrifices. As to ceremonies this is the estimate that he set upon them: "Woe unto you, Scribes and Pharisees, hypocrites! for ye pay tithe of mint and anise and cummin, and have omitted the weightier matters of the law, judgment, mercy and faith." Nevertheless, one scribe may be excepted, he of whom St. Matthew relates that he approved Jesus' outspoken doctrine, to the effect that true religion consisted in loving God with all the soul, and loving man as one's self. This, saith the scribe, is more than whole burnt-offerings and sacrifices. And when Jesus saw that he answered discreetly, he said unto him, "Thou art not far from the kingdom of God."— Mark, xii. 34. Surely one sentence of denunciation, from him who is considered the head and front of Christianity, ought to suffice for uprooting a system based essentially upon the very principle denounced by him. Jesus throws contempt upon sacrifice. The Christian churches exalt and magnify it as the *sine quâ non* in man's salvation. Pay no heed to sacrifices, says Jesus. His churches say, practically, let us make Christ himself part and parcel of the system that he repudiates!

Not having been influenced by personal contact with Jesus, St. Paul—apart from his frequent reference to the comparative merits of faith and good works—appears never to have freed his mind from a certain ideal connection between sacrifice and salvation. It is true, he warns the Corinthians, that "circumcision is nothing and uncircumcision is nothing, but the keeping of the commandments of God;" and that he tells the Hebrews, that "it is not possible that the blood of bulls and of goats should take away sins." But he tells these latter also, that "without blood is no remission;" nay, he goes further still, and would have the Hebrews believe, that the sacrifice of Christ was needed on Christ's own behalf! So astounding is this dogma, that it seems to have staggered the Church itself, if one may judge by the eloquent silence of the preachers in regard to it. The precise expression runs thus,—Hebrews, ix. 12:—"Neither by the blood of goats and calves, but by his own blood, he entered in once into the holy place." Furthermore, the very phraseology used by Paul, on two occasions, shows how this sacrificial notion was rooted in him. He exhorts the Romans "to present their bodies a living sacrifice, holy, and acceptable unto God;" and the Jews to "offer the sacrifice of praise to God continually."

It has been established that Jesus nowhere either taught, or gave countenance, in any way to the worship of sacrifices, or to any other kind of worship, except that enjoined by natural religion. The same cannot be said, however, with regard to his Apostles, after his death. It was then, that they began to foist their own habitual traditions upon his unincumbered doctrine and thus to make worship widely different from that which he had advocated. Nor had they any consistency about them.

They blew hot and cold, almost in the same breath. Sometimes they preached one thing and sometimes another. Take for example, that most inconsistent man of all, Peter, termed by one branch of Christians, the infallible founder of their Church, and in whose power they put the keys to unlock and lock, both heaven and hell. What absurdities is he not responsible for. Examine the first sermon which he preached, as recorded in the second chapter of the book of Acts.

This was an important occasion. It was an occasion when, we are told, men from almost every country on the face of the earth were gathered together at Jerusalem; and for the first, and perhaps the last time, heard an exposition of the doctrine of salvation from the mouth of one who might be looked upon as qualified to teach it.

But what does Peter say, in this discourse, about either the old sacrifices of the Levitical priesthood, or the sacrifice of Jesus upon the cross? Not one word. He speaks of Jesus as a man—a man, mark you—a man approved of God; as having, by the determinate counsel of God, been taken and crucified and slain; as having been raised from the dead; as having ascended to heaven; and as having been made both Lord and Christ. But he does not utter a single syllable about Jesus having been made a sacrifice; still less does he insist, as the Church does, that unless we believe in him as such, we cannot be saved. No. Is it to be inferred then, that those persons present from every nation under heaven, were to comprehend this new and complicated dogma by intuition, and were then to go and preach or tell it to their friends? Or are we not rather in a more sensible and natural manner, to say, that Peter neither intended, nor did they understand anything of the kind? The latter deduction is assuredly the first one, and is corroborated by Peter's continued silence on this point—when he, together with the other Apostles, was asked by those who were so much concerned: "Men and brethren, what shall we do?" His reply was: "Repent and be baptized every one of you, in the name of Jesus Christ, for the remission of sins"—the baptism signifying a pledge to adhere to the teaching of Jesus as the way to righteousness. Again, not one word was said about Jesus being crucified as a sacrifice for sin. The omission is the more striking from the fact that Peter was fresh from communication with him. That he subsequently fell back into his old ways is on record. His Master was not with him, to keep him on the right path. He had been slippery in his dealings with Jesus, himself, and is accused, by his associate Paul, of having played fast and loose in the matter of circumcision, and in that of eating with the Gentiles. Be this as it may, in course of time, they all conspired to make Jesus a substitute for those sacrifices with which they were so fully imbued, that they could not cease to cling to them; although they found that those of the Jewish order were too gross and too much opposed to his own teachings to be intermingled with his more refined teaching. When we say all, we should probably except St. James. It is to be noted that, in the five chapters of his general Epistle, he does not once allude to the sacrifice of Jesus, and very sparingly to Jesus himself, save when he declares that "the coming of the Lord draweth nigh." In one memorable verse also, he gives his views of "pure religion and undefiled before God and the Father," which consists in comforting the afflicted, and leading a pure life—not in believing that man is saved only by the death of Christ. In another verse, he says concisely, "Thou believest that there is one God; thou doest well,"—not two Gods, or three.

The Church argues an analogy between the sacrifice of Christ on the cross, under what it calls the new dispensation, and animal sacrifice, as practised under the old. Now it is shown elsewhere, from the Old Testament, that the whole system of sacrifice was rather tolerated than approved by God. At the same time, there is not the slightest evidence that Jesus and his disciples ever participated in the sacrificial services of the Jewish synagogue, though they frequented it, to read, or to teach, or to pray therein. This we say is remarkable, and adds another proof that Jesus and his Apostles, at all events during his lifetime, never countenanced, by any means whatever, sacrifices of any kind. Indeed we are told that he took a scourge of small cords and drove out the buyers and sellers of the things that were used in the Temple, and in this way shewed his displeasure at their being brought there at all, for any such purpose.

We submit from the evidence here presented, whether any sober-minded man can conscientiously, and without misgivings, stand by a system, that God so unsparingly denounced, and that Jesus himself never approved.

With a view of discussing this question, in its every phase, we proceed further to confirm what has hitherto been said, in a more general way. Epiphanius says of the Ebiontes—Heares, xxx. 16—that in their pretended Gospel of Matthew there occurs this expression of Christ: "I am come to do away with sacrifices, and if you do not cease to sacrifice, the anger of God will not cease from you."

This horror of bloody sacrifices the Ebionites had in common with the Essenes. Jesus had a conviction that reconciliation with God was only attainable by purely inward means. And hence his displeasure at the gross materialism of the sacrificial service.

Thus did Jesus, not only by words, "have mercy and not sacrifice"—Matthew, xii. 7—but by his example, condemn the whole system. And yet how remarkable it is that this very system was at length engrafted upon the pure natural religion which he advocated!

Renan says, one idea, at least, which Jesus brought from Jerusalem, and which henceforth appears rooted in his mind, was that there was no union possible between him and the ancient Jewish religion. The abolition of the sacrifices which had caused him so much disgust, the suppression of an impious and haughty priesthood, and, in a general sense, the abrogation of the law, appeared to him absolutely necessary. From this time he appears no more as a Jewish reformer, but as a destroyer of Judaism. Certain advocates of Messianic ideas had already admitted that the Messiah would bring a new law, which should be common to all the earth. The Essenes, who were scarcely Jews, also appear to have been indifferent to the temple and to the Mosaic observances. But these were only isolated or unavowed instances of boldness. Jesus was the first who dared to say that from the time of John, the Law was abolished: "The law and the prophets were until John: since that time the Kingdom of God is preached, and every man presseth into it."—Luke, xvi. 16. That is to say, independent of any sacrifice. Now, the Churches claim that the law of God required for the remission of sins, up to the time of the shedding of the blood of Christ, the sacrifices enjoined by the ceremonial law; and that this shedding of his blood was accepted by God as a crowning and final sacrifice for the remission of the sins of all who believe in its efficiency. This is not in accordance with Jesus' declaration that the law prevailed not after John, whose death took place before that of Jesus. Consequently, before the shedding of Jesus' blood there was no sacrificial law in existence, and therefore it could not have been substituted for, or abrogated by the shedding of Jesus' blood as they claimed.

When Jesus was driven to extremities, he lifted the veil entirely, and declared that the Law had no longer any force. On this subject he used striking comparisons. "No man putteth a piece of new cloth into an old garment, neither do men put new wine into old bottles."— Matthew, ix. 16, 17; Luke, v. 36. This was really his chief characteristic as a teacher. Jesus was no longer a Jew. He was in the highest degree revolutionary; he called all men to a worship founded solely on the fact of their being children of God. He advocated the religion of humanity, established, not upon blood, but upon the heart. He proclaimed the rights of man, not the rights of the Jew; the religion of man, not the religion of the Jew; the deliverance of man, not the deliverance of the Jew.

Following out these principles, Jesus despised all religion which was not of the heart and conscience. The vain practices of the devotees, the exterior strictness which trusted to formality for salvation, had in him a mortal enemy. The love of God, charity, and mutual forgiveness, were his whole law. Nothing could be less priestly. The priest, by his office, ever advocates public sacrifice, of which he is the appointed minister. We should seek in vain in the Gospel for one religious rite recommended by Jesus. Those who imagined they could win the Kingdom of Heaven by saying to him, "Rabbi,

Rabbi," he rebuked; and proclaimed that his religion consisted in doing good.

Among the various books, or so-called, divine records, which are claimed to be supernaturally inspired, there are none so obscure as the Bible. The teachings or sayings, of Jesus, which are recorded in the Bible, are mostly in parables or riddles, whose meaning is so vague and uncertain that no two persons would be likely to put the same construction upon any one of them. Jesus adopted and continued this course of teaching to the perplexity and astonishment of his disciples, notwithstanding he was constantly importuned for his reasons for so doing. In which cases, when he answered at all, he said he did so, that the prophecies might be fulfilled, or to prevent the wise and prudent and the multitudes generally, from receiving and understanding the truth—his teachings being intended only for his disciples and babes. This is inconsistent with the idea of Jesus being either God, or the Saviour of men. We cannot conceive of God's shaping His course, professedly and especially, to suit the vague prophecies of men, that He might the better gain credence to His being God. Besides, such a course is adverse, by its obscurity, to the Church's version of the mission of Jesus, which teaches that he came to give light, and thereby everlasting life to all men. He who came to be the Saviour of all men, could not, surely, studiously, hide the means of salvation from any. The preceding remarks have been suggested by the following Bible quotations, which seem to us to be entirely at variance with the idea, that Jesus came to be the Saviour of all men.

"And the disciples came, and said unto him, Why speakest thou unto them in parables." "He answered

OBSCURITY OF THE BIBLE. 257

and said unto them, Because it is given unto you to know the mysteries of the kingdom of heaven, but to them it is not given." "For whosoever hath, to him shall be given, and he shall have more abundance: but whosoever hath not, from him shall be taken away even that he hath. Therefore speak I to them in parables: because they seeing, see not; and hearing, they hear not; neither do they understand." "And in them is fulfilled the prophecy of Esaias, which saith, By hearing ye shall hear, and shall not understand; and seeing ye shall see, and shall not perceive:" "All these things spake Jesus unto the multitude in parables; and without a parable spake he not unto them:" "That it might be fulfilled which was spoken by the prophet, saying, I will utter things which have been kept secret from the foundation of the world."—Matthew, xiii. 10, 11, 12, 13, 14, 34, 35. "I thank thee, O Father, Lord of Heaven and Earth, because thou hast hid these things from the wise and prudent, and hast revealed them unto babes."—Matthew, xi. 25. "And when he was alone, they that were about him with the twelve asked of him the parable." "And he said unto them, Unto you it is given to know the mystery of the kingdom of God: but unto them that are without, all these things are done in parables." "That seeing they may see, and not perceive; and hearing they may hear and not understand, lest at any time they should be converted, and their sins should be forgiven them."—Mark, iv. 10, 11, 12. Such is the Bible version of the sayings of Jesus. Their import is totally inconsistent with his pretended divine mission. It is not in harmony with Peter's remark, that God is no respecter of persons. Neither does it accord with the idea that God's creatures are all alike the objects of His care and goodness. If

17

Jesus came, as a messenger from God, out of love and kindness to mankind, to enable all to obtain eternal life through his teaching, then it would seem, according to the best human understanding, that all his teachings should be such as all men could unmistakably comprehend and avail themselves of. God's teaching is heard and heeded throughout the universe. To this premeditated obscurity in the teachings of Jesus, and of the Bible record generally, is due in a great measure the number and variety of sects, and the difficulty in coming at anything definite on the subject of religion or even theology.

It is well to notice some of the results of the many constructions that have been put upon the Bible, In illustrating its various readings and their results, we quote from sundry authorities mentioned here below. The innumerable sects and parties into which Christianity is divided—each laying claim to exclusive sanction and authority from the Bible—each declaring its own views right, and all who differ from it wrong, are each supported by Scripture texts of the most plausible aspect. "The Trinitarian denounces the Unitarian, and the Unitarian the Trinitarian; and both unite in condemning the Roman Catholic in some of his peculiar doctrines. The Armenian denounces the Calvinist's views, as a system consisting of human creatures without liberty,—doctrine without sense,—faith without reason,—and God without mercy."—*Archd. Jortin.* The Calvinist on the other hand represents Armenianism as "delusive, dangerous, and ruinous to immortal souls."—*Close's Sermons.* And the Unitarians declare them both to be "mischievous compounds of impiety and idolatry."—*Disc. on Priestly.* Archbishop Magee, on the other hand, denounces the Unitarian system as "embracing the most daring impieties that ever disgraced the name of Christianity; and declares that if Unitarianism be well founded, Christianity must be an imposition." All sects join in denouncing the Methodists "as misled fanatics, alienated from all knowledge of the true God."—*Divine Truth.* The Church of England denounces the whole body of dissenters "as accursed, devoted to the devil, and separated from Christ,"—*Canon,* v. vii; and the Bishop of London—*Letters on Dissent.*—declares them "to be actuated by the devil, with the curse of God resting heavily on them all." "The dissenters are not slow in retaliating on the Church of England. They say that it is an obstacle to the progress of truth and holiness in the land, that it destroys more souls than it saves, and that its end is most devoutly to be wished for by every lover of God and man."—*Christian Observer.* "The Roman Catholics declare their Church to be 'the only true one,' while all others join in denouncing them as the 'scarlet whore of Babylon,' and a combination of idolatry, blasphemy, and devilism.'"—*Cuns. Apostasy.* "The Romanist retorts again, by consigning every sect and description of religionists to eternal damnation as heretics and schismatics, and their clergy as desecrating thieves and ministers of the devil."—*Rheims' Test.*

It would be an endless task to enumerate the names and tenets of the various sects which constitute that "chaos of confusion" denominated "the Christian Church," all derived from this one book, the Bible, which is declared to be an emanation from the Almighty, and a revelation of His will to all men.

From the rapid advancement of civilization, the increase of the wealth and the luxuries of life, the clergy of modern times have found it necessary to make further changes and modifications in the religion of Jesus, so as to accommodate it to their own views and the peculiarities of the times. His name is still assumed as the foundation of their religion; but little attention is paid either to His precepts or example. In reality, only the shadow of the religion taught by Jesus now remains.

In view of all this, can the reader hesitate to acknowledge, that a religion so divided against itself has no claim, either to be the true religion, or of divine origin? Can any one imagine for a moment how, amidst such an infinite mass of obscure texts, contradictory opinions, and glaring discrepancies, all seriously derived from the pages of this book, that it is a correct and useful system of religion?

Truth belongs to all times and to all men. That the truth is not evident in Scripture is proved by the innumerable sects into which Christianity has split; for when truth is clear and evident it is impossible to divide people into parties or factions. What would be the true religion, if there were no sects? That in which all minds must necessarily agree. Sectarianism and error are but synonyms; for "the word of God" can convey but one meaning. We would only ask how many meanings have the Scriptures, the assumed word of God, conveyed—count the different sects!

People in all ages, from the inborn delight which man derives from the wonderful and mysterious, have, at all times and in all places, been readily persuaded to lend their belief to the supernatural and the invisible. Hence, one great cause of the enormous superstructure in the Christian religion, of prophecies and miracles, of dreams and visions, of angels and devils, and other supernatural and invisible agents, which have been worked up into the few simple and truthful precepts, which Jesus, during the early part of his public career, enforced with so much zeal and eloquence.

No great events in history have happened without having given rise to a cycle of fables. At a certain period in his career Jesus began to imagine that he saw in himself traits of character corresponding to the Messiah. Perhaps a sagacious observer might have recognized from this point the germ of the narratives which were to attribute to him a supernatural birth, and which arose, it may be, from the idea, very prevalent in antiquity, that the incomparable man could not be born of the ordinary relations of the two sexes, or in order to respond to an imperfectly understood chapter of Isaiah, which was thought to foretell that the Messiah should be born of a virgin. At times they connected him, from his birth, with celebrated men, such as John the Baptist, Herod the Great, Chaldean Astrologers, who, it was said, visited Jerusalem about this time, and two aged persons, Simeon and Anna, who had left memories of great sanctity. It was, especially, after the death of Jesus that such narratives became greatly developed. That he never dreamed of making himself pass for an incarnation of God, is a matter about which there can be no doubt. Such an idea was entirely foreign to the Jewish mind; and there is no trace of it in the Gospels. Certain passages, expressly exclude this idea, and we only find it indicated in portions of the Gospel of John, which cannot be accepted as expressing the thoughts of Jesus. Sometimes he even seems to take precautions to put down such a doctrine. The accusation that he made himself God, or the equal of God, is presented, even in the Gospel of John, as a calumny of the Jews. In this last Gospel he declares himself to be less than his Father.—John, xiv. 28. Elsewhere he avows that the Father has not revealed everything to him. He is Son of God, but so are all men. He calls God his Father. Every one should feel that God is more than a father. "All who are raised again will be sons of God."—Luke, xx. 36. The divine son-ship was attributed in the Old Testament to beings whom it was by no means pretended were equal with God—Genesis, vi. 2; Job, i. 6; ii. 1; xxviii, 7; Psalm, ii. 7; lxxxii. 6; 2 Samuel, vii. 14. The word "son" has the widest meaning in the Semitic language, and in that of the New Testament. The transcendent idealism of Jesus never permitted him to have a very clear notion of his own personality. He is his Father, his Father is he. He lives in his disciples: he is everywhere with them.—Matthew, xviii. 20; xxviii. 20. His disciples are one, as he and his Father are one.—John, x. 30; xvii. 21. In general, the later discourses of John, especially chapter xvii., express one side of the psychological state of Jesus, though we cannot regard them as true historical documents.

No idea of the laws of nature marked the limit of the impossible, either in his own mind, or in the minds of his hearers. The witnesses of his miracles thanked God "for having given such power unto men."—Matthew, ix. 8. He pardoned sins.—Matthew, ix. 2. He was superior to David, to Abraham, to Solomon, and to the prophets.—Matthew, xii. 41, 42; xxii. 43. We do not know in what form, nor to what extent these affirmations of himself, were made. Jesus ought not to be judged by the law of our petty conventionalities. The admiration of his disciples overwhelmed him, and carried him away. It is evident that the title of Rabbi, with which he was at first contented, no longer sufficed him. There was no supernatural for him, because there was no nature. Intoxicated with infinite love, he forgot the heavy chain which holds the spirit captive; he cleared at one bound the abyss, which the weakness of the human faculties has created between God and man. The belief.that certain men are incarnations of divine faculties or "powers," was wide-spread. For nearly two centuries, the speculative minds of Judaism had yielded to the tendency to personify the divine attributes, and certain expressions which were connected with the Divinity. Thus, "the breath of God," which is often referred to in the Old Testament, is considered as a separate being, the "Holy Spirit." In the same manner the "Wisdom of God," and the "Word of God" became distinct personages. This was the germ of the process which has engendered the hypothesis of Christianity, and all that dry mythology, consisting of personified abstractions, to which resort is had when desiring to pluralise the Deity.

Jesus appears to have remained a stranger to these refinements of theology, which were soon to fill the world with barren disputes. It was John the Evangelist, or his school, who afterwards endeavored to prove that Jesus was the Word, and who created, in this sense, quite a new theology, very different from that of the "kingdom of God."—See John, Gospel, i. 1-14; 1 Epistle, v. 7. The essential character of the Word was that of Creator and of Providence. Now, Jesus never pretended to have created the world, nor to govern it. His office was to judge it, to renovate it. The position of president at the final judgment of humanity, was the essential attribute which Jesus attached to himself and the character which all the first Christians attributed to him.—Acts, x. 42.

At all events, the strictness of a studied theology by no means existed in such a state of society. All the ideas we have just stated, formed in the mind of the disciples a theological system so little settled, that the Son of God, this species of divine duplicate, is made to act purely as man. He is tempted—he is ignorant of many things. He corrects himself. Comp. Matthew, x. 5, with xxviii. 19. He is cast down, discouraged. He asks his Father to spare him trials—He is submissive to God as a son.—Matthew, xxvi. 39. "He who is to judge the world does not know the day of judgment."—Mark, xiii. 32. He takes precautions for his safety.—Matthew, xii. 14-16; xiv. 13. Soon after his birth he is concealed to avoid powerful men who wish to kill him.—Matthew, ii. 20. In exorcisms, the devil cheats him, and does not come out at the first command.—Matthew, xvii. 20; Mark, ix. 25. In his miracles we are sensible of painful effort, through exhaustion, as if something went out of him.—Luke, viii. 45, 46; John, xi. 33, 38. The need Jesus had of obtaining credence, and the enthusiasm of his disciples, heaped up contradictory notions. To the Messianic believers of the millenarian school, and to the enthusiastic readers of the books of Daniel and Enoch, he was the Son of man: to the Jews holding the ordinary faith, and to the readers of Isaiah and Micah, he was the Son of David: to the disciples he was the Son of God, or simply the Son. Others, without being blamed by the disciples, took him for John the Baptist risen from the dead; for Elias; for Jeremiah, conformable to the popular belief that the ancient prophets were about to re-appear, in order to prepare the time of the Messiah.—Matthew, xiv. 2; xvi. 14; xvii. 3. Honesty and imposture are words which, in our rigid consciences, are opposed, as two irreconcilable terms. In the East, they are connected by numberless subtle links and windings. The authors of the Apocryphal books of "Daniel" and of "Enoch," for instance, men highly exalted, in order to aid their cause, committed, without a shadow of scruple, an act which we should term a fraud. Two means of proof, miracles and the accomplishment of prophecies, could alone, in the opinion of the contemporaries of Jesus, establish a supernatural mission. Jesus, and especially his disciples, employed these two processes of demonstration, where Jesus had conceived that the prophets had written only in reference to him. He recognized himself in their sacred oracles; he regarded himself as the mirror in which all the prophetic spirit of Israel had read the future. In many cases, these comparisons were quite superficial, and are scarcely appreciable by us. They were most frequently fortuitous, or insignificant circumstances, in the life of Jesus, which recalled to the disciples certain passages of the Psalms and Prophets, in which, in consequence of their constant pre-occupation, they saw images in him.—Matthew, i. 23, iv. 6, 14; xxvi. 31, 54, 56; xxvii. 9, 35. The exegesis of the time consisted thus almost entirely in a play upon words, and in quotations made in an artificial and arbitrary manner.

As to miracles, they were regarded at this period as the indispensable mark of the divine, and as the sign of the prophetic vocation. The legends of Elijah and Elisha were full of them. It was commonly believed that the Messiah would perform many.—John, vii. 34; Esdras, xiii. 50. In Samaria, a few leagues from where Jesus was, a magician, named Simon, acquired an almost divine character by his illusions.—Acts, viii. 9. Jesus was therefore obliged to choose between these two alternatives—either to renounce his mission, or to become a miracle-worker. It must be remembered that all antiquity, with the exception of the great scientific schools, and their Roman disciples, accepted miracles; and that Jesus not only believed therein, but had not the least idea of an order of nature regulated by fixed laws. His knowledge on this point was in no way superior to that of his contemporaries.

The lapse of time has changed that which constituted the power upon which the Christian theology is founded, into something offensive to our ideas. Criticism experiences no embarrassment in the presence of this kind of historical phenomena.

With reference to our argument that there is One God, and one only, we next invite the reader's attention to forty-three selected texts, affirming that fact.

1. "Thou shalt have no other gods before me."—Exodus, xx. 3.

2. "Unto thee it was shewed, that thou mightest know that the Lord is God; there is none else besides him."—Deuteronomy, iv. 35.

3. "Know therefore this day, and consider it in thine heart, that the Lord he is God in heaven above, and upon the earth beneath: there is none else."—Deuteronomy, iv. 39.

4. "Hear, O Israel: the Lord our God is one Lord."—Deuteronomy, vi. 4.

5. "See now that I, even I, am he, and there is no god with me: I kill, and I make alive; I wound, and I heal; neither is there any that can deliver out of my hand."—Deuteronomy, xxxii. 39.

6. "There is none holy as the Lord; for there is none besides thee: neither is there any rock like our God."—1 Samuel, ii. 2.

TEXTS IN FAVOR OF ONE GOD ONLY.

7. "Wherefore thou art great, O Lord God: for there is none like thee, neither is there any God besides thee, according to all that we have heard with our ears."—2 Samuel, vii. 22.

8. "For who is God, save the Lord? and who is a rock, save our God"?—2 Samuel, xxii. 32.

9. "And he said, Lord God of Israel, there is no god like thee in heaven above; or on earth beneath, who keepest covenant and mercy with thy servants that walk before thee with all their heart."—1 Kings, viii. 23.

10. "And Hezekiah prayed before the Lord, and said, O Lord God of Israel, which dwellest between the cherubims, thou art the God, even thou alone, of all the kingdoms of the earth; thou hast made heaven and earth."—2 Kings, xix. 15.

11. "Now therefore, O Lord our God, I beseech thee, save thou us out of his hand, that all the kingdoms of the earth may know that thou art the Lord God, even thou only."—2 Kings, xix. 19.

12. "Thou, even thou, art Lord alone: thou hast made heaven, the heaven of heavens, with all their host, the earth and all things that are therein, the seas and all that is therein; and thou preservest them all; and the host of heaven worshippeth thee."—Nehemiah, ix. 6.

13. "That men may know that thou, whose name alone is Jehovah, art the Most High over all the earth."—Psalm, lxxxiii. 18.

14. "For thou art great, and doest wondrous things: thou art God alone."—Psalm, lxxxvi. 10.

15. "Behold, God is my salvation; I will trust, and will not be afraid: for the Lord Jehovah is my strength and my song; he also is become my salvation."—Isaiah, xii. 2.

16. "O Lord of hosts, God of Israel, that dwellest between the cherubims, thou art the God, even thou alone, of all the kingdoms of the earth, thou hast made heaven and earth."—Isaiah, xxxvii. 16.

17. "Now, therefore, O Lord our God, save us from his hand, that all the kingdoms of the earth may know that thou art the Lord, even thou only."—Isaiah, xxxvii. 20.

18. "I am the Lord; that is my name: and my glory will I not give to another, neither my praise to graven images."—Isaiah, xlii. 8.

19. "For I am the Lord thy God, the Holy One of Israel, thy Saviour; I gave Egypt for thy ransom, Ethiopia and Seba for thee."—Isaiah, xliii. 3.

20. "I, even I, am the Lord; and besides me there is no Saviour."—Isaiah, xliii. 2.

21. "I am the Lord, and there is none else, there is no God besides me: I girded thee, though thou hast not known me."—Isaiah, xlv. 5.

22. "That they may know from the rising of the sun, and from the west, that there is none besides me: I am the Lord, and there is none else."—Isaiah, xlv. 6.

23. "Verily, thou art a God that hidest thyself, O God of Israel, the Saviour."—Isaiah, xlv. 15.

24. "For thus saith the Lord that created the heavens, God himself that formed the earth and made it, he hath established it, he created it not in vain, he formed it to be inhabited: I am the Lord, and there is none else."—Isaiah, xlv. 18.

25. "Tell ye, and bring them near; yea, let them take counsel together: who hath declared this from ancient time? who hath told it from that time? have not I the Lord? and there is no God else besides me; a just God

and a Saviour: there is none besides me."—Isaiah, xlv. 21.

26. "Look unto me, and be ye saved, all the ends of the earth; for I am God and there is none else."—Isaiah, xlv. 22.

27. "Remember the former things of old: for I am God, and there is none else; I am God, and there is none like me."—Isaiah, xlvi. 9.

28. "Thou shalt also suck the milk of the Gentiles, and shalt suck the breast of kings: and thou shalt know that I the Lord am thy Saviour and thy Redeemer, the Mighty One of Jacob."—Isaiah, lx. 16.

29. "I will not execute the fierceness of mine anger, I will not return to destroy Ephraim: for I am God and not man; the Holy One in the midst of thee; and I will not enter into the city."—Hosea, xi. 9.

30. "Yet I am the Lord thy God from the land of Egypt, and thou shalt know no god but me: for there is no Saviour besides me."—Hosea, xiii. 4.

31. "And the Lord shall be king over all the earth; in that day shall there be one Lord, and his name one."—Zechariah, xiv. 9.

32. "And he said unto him, Why callest thou me good? there is none good but one, that is God: but if thou wilt enter into life, keep the commandments."—Matthew, xix. 17.

33. "And Jesus said unto him, Why callest thou me good? there is none good but one, that is, God."—Mark, x. 18.

34. "And Jesus answered him, The first of all the commandments is, Hear, O Israel; the Lord our God is one Lord."—Mark, xii. 29.

35. "And the scribe said unto him, Well, Master, thou hast said the truth: for there is one God; and there is none other but he."—Mark, xii. 32.

36. "And Jesus said unto him, Why callest thou me good? none is good, save one, that is, God."—Luke, xviii. 19.

37. "And this is life eternal, that they might know thee, the only true God, and Jesus Christ whom thou hast sent."—John, xvii. 3.

38. "As concerning therefore, the eating of those things that are offered in sacrifice unto idols, we know that an idol is nothing in the world, and that there is none other God but one."—1 Corinthians, viii. 4.

39. "Now a mediator is not a mediator of one; but God is one."—Galatians, iii. 20.

40. "One Lord, one faith, one baptism."—Ephesians, iv. 5.

41. "Now unto the King eternal, immortal, invisible, the only wise God, be honor and glory forever and ever. Amen."—1 Timothy, ii. 5.

42. "For there is one God, and one mediator between God and men, the man Christ Jesus."—1 Timothy, ii. 5.

43. "Thou believest that there is but one God; thou doest well: the devils also believe, and tremble."—James, ii. 19.

Here we have forty-three selected texts, affirming that there is but one God. Five of these are the sayings of Christ himself. Nine declare that God Jehovah is our Saviour or salvation, and one is the endorsement of a Scribe to the affirmation of Christ, that the Lord our God is one Lord. Now this is remarkable. If Christ is God, why is he not so accredited both in the Old and New Tes-

FURTHER PROOFS. 271

taments? This is not the case in either one or the other. It is easy to make an assertion we admit, and if that assertion is unsupported by good and reliable evidence, it is of no account. But if a man makes an assertion on the authority of competent testimony, that assertion is entitled to our respect and belief. Now, it is asserted by a large majority of the Christian Churches that Christ is God: but whence do they derive their evidence to support them in such an assertion? We know of none that carries any weight with it, and there is certainly none in the Book which they rely upon as infallibly true. We assert that Christ was not God; and this, on the testimony of God Himself, and the man Jesus, whom the Churches deify. Can God lie? He says, He is not a man that He can lie: nor the Son of Man that He can repent. No one can fail to see then, from the numerous foregoing texts, that we have abundant Bible authority in support of the unity of the Godhead; and that man's final deliverance from infirmity and affliction will be wrought out for him by the One God, who is both his Creator, Preserver, and Redeemer.

By way of further proof, however, we will devote some space to viewing the subject through a variety of phases. If Jesus had been God, why did he, at the time of his death, commend his soul to God? This we are told that he most certainly did. "And about the ninth hour Jesus cried with a loud voice, saying, Eli, Eli, lama sabacthani? that is to say, My God, My God, why hast thou forsaken me?" "And when Jesus had cried with a loud voice, he said, Father into thy hands I commend my spirit: and having said this, he gave up the ghost."

Jesus, it is said, was to be a propitiation for the sins of mankind, on the assumption that he was God, and man, and without sin. But is this assumption consistent with the assertion, that each and every part of the Bible is true? To be without sin, the Bible says, is to be good. Sin, therefore, presupposes the absence of goodness. Was Jesus good in this way? As we have before shown, he says himself, that there is none good but one, that is God. He therefore, could not be without sin, neither could he be that propitiation for sin that he is said to be, being not without sin.

Again, it is said that after his resurrection, Mary met him, and, we presume, was about to take hold of him, when he said unto her, "Touch me not; for I am not yet ascended to my Father; but go to my brethren and say unto them, I ascend unto my Father, and your Father; and to my God and your God." Now, Jesus here represents himself as standing in the same relation to God, as did the woman to whom he was addressing himself. He calls God his Father, in the same sense that he calls Him her Father. If he, as he is said to have declared, was one with the Father, how could he be Father to himself? This is absurd. It makes the theory of the Divinity of Jesus simply ridiculous.

Again, "Believest thou not that I am in the Father; and the Father in me? the words I speak unto you I speak not of myself; but the Father that dwelleth in me, he doeth the works." The Father dwelleth in every man in the same sense.

"For both he that sanctifieth and they who are sanctified are all of one: for which cause he is not ashamed to call them all brethren." "Then, answered Jesus, and said unto them, Verily, Verily, I say unto you, The Son can do nothing of himself, but what he seeth the Father do: for what things soever he doeth, these also doeth the

Son likewise. For the Father loveth the Son, and showeth him all things that himself doeth; and he will show him greater works than these, that ye may marvel."

"And he saith unto them, Ye shall drink indeed of my cup, and be baptized with the baptism that I am baptized with: but to sit on my right hand, and on my left, is not mine to give, but it shall be given to them, for whom it is prepared of my Father." This is precisely the reply that any man, seeking to establish a kingdom, might make to such a question.

"Jesus saith unto them, my meat is to do the will of him that sent me, and to finish his work," which was, to exhort to repentance, and love to God and man. "For I have not spoken of myself; but the Father which sent me, he gave me a commandment, what I should say, and what I should speak." "And I know that his commandment is life everlasting; whatsoever I speak, therefore, even as the Father said unto me, so I speak."

So say the Quakers, and others, who conceive that they have a call to preach.

"Jesus saith unto them, If God were your Father, ye would love me: for I proceeded forth and came from God; neither came I of myself, but he sent me."

"If ye keep my commandments ye shall abide in my love: even as I have kept my Father's commandments, and abide in his love."

Any preacher of the Gospel might without any breach of propriety, so remark to his flock.

"At that day ye shall know that I am in my Father, and ye in me, and I in you." That is, the preacher and congregation alike, serving God, each in his appropriate way, may have the same mind as the Father within each of them.

"He that hath my commandments, and keepeth them, he it is that loveth me, and he that loveth me shall be loved of my Father, and I will love him, and will manifest myself to him."

"That they all may be one; as thou, Father, art in me, and I in thee, that they also may be one in us; that the world may believe that thou hast sent me." Now, Jesus might, with the greatest propriety, make use of such language as this; and yet be nothing more than a teacher, in whom was a large supply of God's illuminating mind and goodness. He did, no doubt, earnestly and eloquently, set forth, in the most graceful and glowing colors, much that was pure in the eyes of men, and make it attractive to them; and, having the faculty to do this, he found a ready witness and response in the hearts of his hearers. All this, however, is by no means an evidence that he was more than a teacher of extraordinary ability.

During a considerable portion of his three years ministry, Jesus fully persuaded himself that, by divine right, he was entitled to the throne of David. He did not believe himself to be God, or to be equal with God; but without doubt he felt assured that he was the person designated by the prophets, who was to be the earthly ruler and deliverer of the Jews; and this led him to act in conformity with the idea. He fell naturally into the custom of the times, by identifying himself with wonder-workers. He performed what are called miracles, as many others did, to impress the people with a deeper sense of the validity of his claim to so exalted a position.

Like other men, he was created "in the image of God;" St. Paul says of him, (Colossians, i. 15,) "who is the image of the invisible God." But this did not make him God, any more than it did other men, who are created in that image. An image is not the thing itself. Conspicuous traits in him were, a vivid perception of the truth as written upon the hearts of men, an apt mode of presenting it in its purity and beauty, and intense zeal in portraying it. "To this end," say he, " was I born, and for this cause came I into the world, that I should bear witness unto the truth. Every one that is of the truth, heareth my voice."—John, xviii. 37. And this "truth" comprised the two absorbing ideas of his life—the one that he was appointed to mount the throne of David, and the other that he was sent of God to preach and teach the way to heaven by the practice of religion in its purity. Throughout nearly the whole of his ministry, he manifested extraordinary zeal and made the most strenuous efforts in inculcating this double belief. Nor, considering his enthusiasm and the personal gifts with which he was graced, need we wonder that many of those about him, gradually caught his spirit and espoused his cause. With this his course of conduct was consistent; but totally inconsistent with his being God or co-equal with him.

The terms Christ, Messiah, and The Anointed One, are synonomous. This will serve to explain how Jesus conceived himself to be entitled, by virtue of the prophecies, to each or any of these appellations, and saw therein his right to the throne of David determined. It was in fact, only with respect to these two pretensions that the claims of Jesus were upheld before the Jewish people. It was not until very late in his lifetime that he conceived the idea of the destruction of the world, and the creation of a new one wherein the righteous only should dwell, being ruled over by himself everlastingly in the flesh.

The meaning which church doctrine gives to belief in Jesus, at this day, is totally at variance with each and all of the views entertained of himself, and finds no warrant either in the letter or spirit of his teachings, or in the example which his life furnished when rationally interpreted. This makes church theology a thing totally different from the religion of Jesus. The terms of salvation and the only ones that he prescribed were love of God, the Father, good works, and kind offices one towards another.

Neither does he anywhere intimate, in any of his sayings or teachings, that these terms of salvation were to be at all changed, added to, or diminished after his death. It was left for the Apostle Paul, many years later, to put forth a doctrine totally dissenting from that which Jesus had taught with such marked effect during his ministry. This doctrine of Paul, it is well known, is the basis of the Christian theology of our day. In this, the main features are, that Jesus voluntarily gave up his life to redeem from the consequences of original sin all who should have faith that he did actually suffer death for this express purpose, that such atonement was both indispensable and efficacious to the end in view, and that the real worth of the sacrifice consists in the fact that the victim was co-equal with God.

If the death of Jesus imposes a belief in this dogma as an absolutely essential requisite to eternal life, it may be answered, that belief therein is utterly beyond man's will, seeing that it is inexplicable in itself and runs counter to all we learn by study of God's dealings with the world. It is, moreover, wholly out of the reach of those who never heard of it, comprising by far the majority of those beings whom God created in his own image. Furthermore, we ask, is the death of Jesus to give the lie to his life? He preached, while alive, a doctrine that he who runs may read. Is he, when dead, to be made the centre-piece of a new and incomprehensible theory, under which the burden of man's sins is to be shifted off his own shoulders? If this be so, while at the same time all the laws and obligations imposed by God upon man are left in force, then most assuredly the way to eternal life has not been facilitated, but impeded by this vicarious offering on the cross. We hold that the death of Jesus works no change in the requisites for our mode of salvation. He himself never claimed that it involved any change whatever. We contend, therefore, that Paul was at fault, in promulgating the idea that it did. Paul, too, is evidently at variance on these doctrinal points with James, and with Peter also during Jesus' lifetime at least, and until after Peter's own first sermon was delivered, and yet it is from their conflicting views that the present system of Christianity is derived, and by them that it is sustained.

According to the authority of the Apostle Paul and the Churches that identify themselves with his views, the particular kind of faith or belief in Jesus, which they make indispensable for salvation, could have had no existence before the death of Jesus. And the belief which they imperatively demand is not that he *will* die at some specified or indefinite time; but that he *did* die. The faith therefore upon which Paul and the Christian churches rely for salvation, finds no analogy, precedent, or support in the faith inculcated by Jesus, and avowed by his Apostles during his lifetime. The new creed, for so it may well be called, materially changes the order of worship, or of Divine Service. Jesus himself made God the Father the crowning object of his worship. The Churches, on the contrary, put Jesus prominently in the foreground. God the Father whom Jesus acknowledged as the source and fountain of all that is good, being comparatively kept out of sight.

The extreme views of Paul and the fickleness of Peter hereon do not need any further elucidation; but the subjoined passage from the Epistle of James (chapter ii.) serves to show that this Apostle maintained that men have been, and may be justified solely through good works and the grace of Jehovah. And this view conforms with the largely preponderating weight of evidence in the Scriptures: to wit, that Jehovah is the one and only true God, Redeemer, and Saviour of mankind, in proof of which we have elsewhere cited voluminous texts. The Apostle James says, "What doth it profit, my brethren, though a man say he hath faith, and have not works? can faith save him? If a brother or sister be naked, and destitute of daily food, And one of you say unto them, Depart in peace, be ye warmed and filled; notwithstanding ye give them not those things which are needful to the body; what doth it profit? Even so faith, if it hath not works, is dead, being alone. Yea, a man may say, Thou hast faith, and I have works; shew me thy faith without thy works, and I will shew thee my faith by my works. Thou believest that there is one God, thou doest well: the devils also believe and tremble. But wilt thou know, O vain man, that faith without works is dead? Was not Abraham our father justified by works when he had offered Isaac his son upon the altar? Seest thou how faith wrought with his works, and by works was faith made perfect? And the Scripture was fulfilled which saith, Abraham believed God, and it was imputed unto him for righteousness and he was called the Friend of God. Ye see then how that by works a man is justified, and not by faith only."

Abraham, it is true, is described as offering sacrifice; but it was in accordance with custom, his whole-souled faith being based on God-Jehovah, not Jesus. Therefore, the only belief necessary in connection with good works, to insure salvation, is belief in the Almighty Jehovah; and this is in flat contradiction to the doctrine of the Churches. Thus we have Paul and the Churches, on one side of this vexed and dogmatical question; and Jesus, James, Natural Religion, and the balance of Biblical authority, on the other.

There is nothing in the Bible from Jesus shewing that he ever entertained the idea that man was created perfect and fell from that state through Adam, or that his (Jesus') crucifixion would prepare the way for man's restoration in accordance with the scheme of Christian Theology, neither does the Bible furnish a single unequivocal declaration from Jesus to the effect that he claimed himself to be co-equal with God; nor does it contain a solitary word from him, that could bear such construction, which he did not subsequently explain away, or which has not since been proved to be erroneous.

In denying having claimed to be God, when the Jews were about to stone him for what they deemed equivalent to such a claim, he asserts that he made no such declaration, or anything that could be construed into such, and cites the Jewish laws, customs, and practices in support of his assertion.—John, x. 33, 34, 35, 36.

Furthermore, it is plain from the following texts, that the term God, as applied to Jesus, does not necessarily mean God the Creator of the universe: "Your eyes shall be opened, and ye shall be as gods knowing good and evil."—Genesis, iii. 5; "And the Lord said unto Moses, See I have made thee a god to Pharaoh."—

Exodus, vii. 1; "Who is like unto thee, Oh, Lord, among the Gods?"—Exodus, xv. 2; "For the Lord your God, is God of Gods."—Deuteronomy, x. 17; "Among the gods there is none like unto thee, O, Lord."—Psalm, lxxxvi. 8; "Thou, Lord, art high above all the earth; thou art exalted far above all Gods."—Psalm, xcvii. 9.

Again, what could be more emphatic than the following language of the Apostle Paul? "For, though there be that are called gods, whether in heaven or in earth—as there be gods many and lords many. But to us there is but one God, the Father of whom are all things, and we in Him; and one Lord Jesus Christ by whom are all things, and we by Him."—1 Corinthians, viii. 5, 6; "For, therefore, we both labor and suffer reproach, because we trust in the living God, who is the Saviour of all men, especially of those that believe."—1 Timothy, iv. 10.

Now, within these three texts, three points are laid down with decisive clearness. One is that the living God is the Saviour of all men, as distinguished from Jesus, who is nowhere, in the Bible, absolutely called the living God. Another is, that there is but one God, the Father of all men, and consequently the Father of Jesus. The third is, that all men are in God the Father and He in them. The expression of Jesus, "the Father is in me, and I in Him," implied nothing more than that relationship which exists between God and every one of mankind. The same is true as to his saying, "I and my Father are one"—that is, I and my Heavenly Father are one in purpose. Every man is an instrument in God's hands for the accomplishment of his ends; and inasmuch as God has made sure that man shall co-operate with Him to serve these ends, in the way and to the full extent of His original intention—every man in a certain sense is one in purpose with God. It is evident that this is all, that Jesus could have meant by the expression. The closing sentence in the last of the texts above quoted may perhaps be taken as illustrative of the changing or mixed nature of Paul's religious views. A Pharisee himself, and the son of a Pharisee, and brought up at the feet of Gamaliel, he had nevertheless emancipated himself from Jewish tradition, and was content to preach that true and only religion which makes—to use his own words—" the living God the Saviour of all men." Not yet an advocate of that awful doctrine of the church, which dooms the great bulk of mankind to everlasting torment, he had, as it were, a foretaste of its exclusiveness; and this found vent in his mild phrasing, especially of those that believe. But whatever Paul's trimming, or meaning, all men believe that there is a God to whom they are accountable, know right from wrong, and believe that virtue is more estimable than vice. But some men shape their daily conduct under the influence of this belief, and actuated by their agency more in accordance with their duty to God, their neighbor, and their own welfare, than others. Every man, owing in some measure to the various circumstances which surround him, is at different times more or less governed by varying influences. Hence, exhorting men to repent of their evil deeds, and to practice good works, is among the services which one man may render to another; and in this Jesus made himself conspicuous. He exhorted men to be mindful of and to practice the religion of the heart and conscience; and no doubt with marked success and excellent effect. And since such practice is the important thing, the all-in-all, for this and the future life, and, as the most stimulating influence thereto came to the many by and through Jesus' instrumentality, under the natural promptings originally implanted in man, it might with truth be said that the things that were all-important came from God, by and through Jesus, in a natural way. Thus simply is explained the expression in the text, "Christ by whom are all things, and we by him."

The exhorting men to repentance and the practice of good works, we say, was one among the services by which Jesus made himself conspicuous. Repentance was the great, the predominant theme of his life. It was more on his lips than any other. His name was more intimately associated with it, than with any other. It is evident, therefore, that he conceived that the great want of the Jewish people, and particularly of the Jewish priesthood and others in authority, was repentance. And it was for his persistent cry to this end, and his pretensions to the Messiahship, that he suffered persecution and death. On these two ideas he staked his all. And being instrumental in causing the Jewish people to repent and return to a more consistent course, his disciples continued the work in his name and under its prestige.

It is important here, however, to observe, that, according to the record, Jesus in his last and most important interview with his disciples, spoke not a single word that can, by the remotest inference, be construed as enjoining upon them to preach or inculcate belief or faith in certain claims, since set up on his behalf. These were, that he was co-equal with God, and that belief or faith in such asserted dogma was indispensable to salvation. This omission assists greatly in determining the much disputed question of his relationship with God. As we before remarked, there is no Bible record to show in a plain and unmistakable manner, that Jesus, out of his own mouth,

JESUS NEVER CLAIMED DIVINITY. 283

ever pretended to be co-equal with God, the Lord Jehovah. On the other hand, there are numerous sayings of his which disclaim, or are inconsistent with, any such pretensions. Take, for example, the following citations. He had spoken of God as his Father: on account of which, "The Jews took up stones and stoned him. Jesus answered them, many good works have I showed you from my Father; for which of these works do ye stone me? The Jews answered him, saying, For a good work we stone thee not: but for blasphemy, and because that thou being a man makest thyself God. Jesus answered them, Is it not written in your law, I said ye are Gods? If he called them Gods unto whom the word of God came, and the scripture cannot be broken; Say ye of him whom the Father hath sanctified, and sent into the world, Thou blasphemest, because I said, I am the Son of God? If I do not the works of my Father believe me not. But if I do, though you believe not me, believe the works: that ye may know, and believe, that the Father is in me, and I in him."—John, x. 31–38. This is equivalent to saying that it did not follow, nor did he intend it to be so understood, that because he said, "the Father is in me and I in him," he therefore claimed equality with God the Father, and Creator of all mankind. In justification of himself, he cites the license, which the Scriptures give, to call those men gods unto whom the word of God came. It is evident, therefore, from this explanation of his having said, "I and my Father are one," that he meant that he was God, only in the ordinary sense of the word; that by diligently doing the works of the one God, as others had done unto whom the word of God came, he had the same claim to such an honorable estimation and title. In the event, however, of their not yet being prepared to acknowledge even this subdued claim, he took the precaution to refer them to the result of his works, as proving that he was engaged in promulgating God's will, less entangled with error than was the case with their then accepted teachers.

It may be well to bear in mind, too, that the Apostle Paul nowhere gives Jesus the title of the Living God; neither did he believe him to be the Saviour of men. He speaks clearly to this point in two texts, one of which has been already quoted: "For therefore we both labor and suffer reproach, because we trust in the Living God, who is the Saviour of all men."—1 Timothy, iv. 10; "As concerning therefore, the eating of those things that are offered in sacrifice to idols, we know an idol is nothing in the world, and that there is none other God but one."—1 Corinthians, viii. 4.

Christian theology maintains that Jesus came into the world and took on him the form of a man, for the express purpose of suffering crucifixion as a propitiation for the sins of the world. This is in direct contradiction to Jesus' own declared views on the subject. He says: "To this end was I born, and for this cause came I into the world, that I should bear witness unto the truth."—John, xviii. 37. In other words, he meant that his mission was to preach natural religion, love to God, love to man, and good works, uncontaminated by the dogmas of the Jewish priests. This view is confirmed out of his own lips, in another place: "I will have mercy, and not sacrifice: for I am not come to call the righteous but sinners to repentance."—Matthew, ix. 3. In fact what he here conceived to be his relation to God and man corresponds exactly with what any conscientious minister of the Gospel might say of himself, and forces the conviction that he esteemed

INGENUITY OF THE PRIESTS. 285

himself nothing more than man, in any sense of the word. This estimate is consistent with the every-day practice of his life. "And Jesus went about all the cities and villages, teaching in their synagogues, and preaching the gospel of the kingdom, and healing every sickness and every disease among the people."—Matthew, ix. 34.

No other view than this, of his own conception of his vocation and office can, in our judgment, be derived from the Bible. None other, we think, can be reached by any fair and rational construction, unbiased by preconceived opinions imbibed from the false and forced constructions of those who make it their business to mystify and entangle the dogmas, theologies, and creeds of their own invention with true religion—with the religion of nature—with the religion of which Jehovah is, at once, the founder, the great high-priest, and the preserver, and of which Jesus was, in much of his teachings—though not the author—a remarkably true and zealous expounder. At the same time, while there is no reliable proof that Jesus is God, there is much to the contrary, which ought, as we conceive, to be conclusive to all. The negative evidence is so strong, that no one can pretend that Jesus ever occupied the throne of David in the capacity predicted, or in any other. This alone, in all fairness should suffice for the total discredit of all the prophecies upon which his Messiahship has been based; and would do so, were it not for the ingenuity, adroitness, learning, mental ability and persistence, of the leading priests in ancient and modern times. The former, in an age when superstition and ignorance favored their designs, stimulated by pecuniary interest, and a greed for domination, ensnared their unsuspecting victims into a web of the marvellous and mysterious, which for the unenlightened has a charm so intricate, so subtle, and so strong, that generations of intellectual culture were required to extricate men from its toils. As to the modern priesthood, while the craving for wealth and power equally subsists in them, the moment the fallacy of their teaching is detected, they shape and twist their theology, interpreting this passage of scripture symbolically, and that one literally, as serves the occasion, so that it becomes well nigh impossible to bring them to an acknowledgment of the untenableness of their position. Thus, if they cannot elude detection as to the hollowness of many among their ingeniously contrived devices, they at least find some loop-hole for escape; and the more they are pressed to the wall by the intelligence of the age, the more vehemently they cry out: "He that believeth and is baptized shall be saved; but he that believeth not, shall be damned." Nor could there be a more striking instance of clerical perversion, than occurs in reference to this denunciation. It is applied from a thousand pulpits, to the whole complicated theory of original sin and redemption by the blood of Christ. Under what circumstances did Jesus utter it? With respect to the scheme, as it is well called, of salvation? Not at all. Immediately preceding the record of these words, is this verse, (Mark, xvi. 14:) "Afterward he appeared unto the eleven as they sat at meat, and upbraided them with their unbelief and hardness of heart, because they believed not them which had seen him after he was risen." Not a word here touching sin or sacrifice. It is only unbelief in his personal identity—the unbelief of his own disciples then before him—that is so unceremoniously denounced by Jesus. But the time is fast approaching, when all this cloud of error will be dispersed, and the craft of a profession rendered futile. Human

CHARACTER OF JESUS' PRECEPTS.   287

physical slavery has been compelled to succumb, at the mandate of educated honesty. The enslavers of human intellect must, ere long, lose their prestige over the intellects of others, and cease to prey upon the pecuniary substance of their fellow-men. Conscience, common sense; and culture, are fast gaining the mastery over church theology and a dogmatic priesthood.

The doctrine of Jesus is nowhere more plainly laid down, than in his own description of the view that will be taken of the conduct of men by the final judge of the world. "I was," says he, "a hungered, and ye gave me meat: I was thirsty, and ye gave me drink: I was a stranger, and ye took me in: Naked and ye clothed me; I was sick, and ye visited me: I was in prison, and ye came unto me." In reply to the enquiry, when these things were done in his behalf, the King says, that, "Inasmuch as they were done to the least of his little ones, they were done unto him."—Matthew, xxv. 35, 36. Such is what Jesus considers to be requisite for entering into the Kingdom of Heaven, that is to say, good works, which are, practically, love to God and love to man. He conceives that there is nothing further required. The grand aim of his own life, at least of the earlier parts of it, seem to have been to manifest such a disposition. I am come, said he, on another occasion, "not to destroy, but to fulfill the law;" and the context shows that he had reference to the moral law of God, which was over him in common with all mankind. He therefore exhorted all about him to strive for this one thing, to become obedient to the laws of God, that they might be like Him—God. "Be ye, therefore, perfect," said he, "as your Father also is perfect."—Matthew, v. 48. His precepts and teachings in detail, too, were all of this same character. "Blessed are the merciful," said he, "for they shall obtain mercy. Blessed are the pure in heart, for they shall see God. Blessed are the peace-makers, for they shall be called the children of God."—Matthew, v. 7, 8, 9; "Do not commit adultery; Do not steal; Do not bear false witness; Defraud not; Honor thy father and mother."—Mark, x. 19; "Forgive men their trespasses."—Matthew, vi. 14; "Whatsoever ye would that men should do to you, do ye even so to them, for this is the law and the prophets."—Matthew, vii. 12. Now, what a catalogue of good works does he here collect which, while they have no reference to any peculiar sentiments of his own, are accepted and inculcated by him, as the teaching of God to all men, through their intuitions; and proper sense of right; and which he considered himself as much bound to obey as ourselves. And that he and others who lived by this rule, might be acknowledged as so doing, he gave a test whereby men might judge in this matter: "Ye shall know them by their fruits," said he; and again, "A good man out of the good treasure of his heart bringeth forth good things." He was a good man, but he claimed to be nothing more. He nowhere speaks of himself as God—on the contrary he almost invariably calls himself, "The Son of Man;" and defends himself from the charge of calling himself God, when using expressions that were so construed, on the plea that such expressions were allowable under the Jewish usages, without implying that he made himself God. That this is his estimate of himself may be seen still more clearly. He quotes from the Old Testament—and, "The first of all the commandments" is 'Hear, O, Israel; the Lord our God is ONE LORD.'" He thus emphatically acknowledges that there is but one God, which is equivalent to denying that he himself was God. But if this is not deemed sufficient, hear what he says further: "Worship the Father in spirit and in truth."—John, iv. 23 ; "Jesus said unto them, My meat is to do the will of him that sent me."—John, iv. 34 ; " I speak not of myself; the Father which sent me gave me the commandments."—John, v. 37 ; "My Father is greater than I."—John, xiv. 28. Now, are not these expressions equally applicable to, and proper to be made by all men, who are teachers of true religion? So far as our knowledge extends, through our natural instincts and intuitions, there neither is, nor can be, any intermediate grade of being or beings between God and man.

But is it claimed that he was sent by the Father, and that he was endowed with supernatural powers, because he said, "And this is life eternal that they might know thee, the only true God, and Jesus Christ whom thou hast sent."—John, xviii. 31. In the same sense God sends every man into the world. It is the light of God in the soul of man which is his true Teacher; "That was the true light which lighteth every man that cometh into the world."—John, i. 9; "Behold the Kingdom of God is within you."—Luke, xvii. 21; " Fear not, for it is the Father's good pleasure to give you the kingdom."—Luke, xii. 32. " Blessed are they who hear the word of God and keep it,"—Luke, xi. 28,—that is, blessed are they who hear and obey the voice of conscience and the teaching of the external universe ; "He that doeth truth cometh to the light that his deeds may be made manifest that they are wrought in God."—John, iii. 21; "Jesus answered them, my doctrine is not mine, but his that sent me,"—John, vii. 16,—it would be well if all teachers could conscientiously say this; "Jesus cried and said, he that believeth on me, believeth not on me, but on him that sent me."—John, xii. 44; which is of extreme significance in determining this question, as it is equivalent to saying that belief in him is a mere figure of speech, to indicate belief in the God Jehovah. From this it is evident that, wherever Jesus speaks of man's welfare as being advanced by love to, and belief in him, he simply means that man is to believe in and love and practice the doctrines which he is urging on the attention of his hearers, and these are always of one and the same import:—love to God and man. Take collectively those exhortations of Jesus which are recorded in the Bible; and, although they are not always in harmony or consistent with each other, the only rational deduction and conclusion to be drawn from them is, that he conceived himself to stand in the same relation to God as other men, except that he was inculcating a purer doctrine than that taught by those about him. And it is this separation of true religion from error, at a day when it was so pre-eminently needed, that made him dear to the people of that period and his remembrance precious to succeeding generations. His saying, "believe in me," meant nothing further than believe in the doctrines which I teach, and which go by my name, thus implying that he is but as other men, who advocate religion in its purity.

By thus associating himself with other men in the duties of his office and ministry, it is evident that, according to his view, they all stand in the same relation to God; that he and they are all alike the recipients of God's love—all alike subject to his laws, will, and guidance. The only difference between him and those about him was, that he set himself up as their Teacher, and that they acknowledged themselves to be his disciples.

This view of Jesus and his vocation is far better supported by his own sayings and doings, than the position, attributes, and functions assigned to him by the Christian Church. It may be that, at times, he went a little beyond the natural teaching of God to all men—no doubt he did in some of the kindly feelings and offices, which he conceived should be entertained and practised by men one towards another. Perhaps in some particulars they are too refined for general observance and application. Indeed, it will be at once recognized that they are more than average human nature is capable of manifesting. Of such kind are these: "But I say unto you that ye resist not evil: but whosoever shall smite thee on thy right cheek, turn to him the other also. And if any man will sue thee at the law, and take away thy coat, let him have thy cloak also. And whosoever shall compel thee to go a mile, go with him twain. Give to him that asketh thee, and from him that would borrow of thee turn not thou away. Ye have heard that it hath been said, thou shalt love thy neighbor, and hate thine enemy. But I say unto you, Love your enemies, bless them that curse you, do good to them which hate you; and pray for them which despitefully use you and persecute you."— Matthew, v. 39, 40, 41, 42, 43, 44.

Still, making allowance for these exaggerations, we maintain that the only practicable mode of manifesting ardent love to God is the actual performance, with lively diligence, of those things which are just, and true and good. This is inculcated by Jesus in most impressive terms, some of which we have quoted, and his seal is put upon the worth of this practical faith, by his emphatic saying, with reference to charities; "Inasmuch as ye have done it unto one of the least of these my brethren ye have done it unto me." Whoever follows this course faithfully and sincerely, we insist is a religious man in the fullest sense of the word, notwithstanding the combined declarations of all Christendom to the contrary.

The denunciations of Jesus were as emphatic as they could be against those who incidentally perverted his teachings, which, though imparted by God to all men without Jesus' aid, were so enthusiastically enforced by him as to produce great uneasiness and consternation amongst the corrupt rulers and priesthood of his time— indeed, so much so, as to cause him to be falsely accused and murdered on the cross, under pretence of judicial authority. Among the rebukes administered by Jesus to the priesthood of his day are there not some as applicable now, to that same class of individuals, as they were then? "For laying aside the commandment of God, ye hold the tradition of men, as the washing of pots and cups; and many other such like things ye do. Ye reject the commandments of God that ye may keep your own tradition." "Making the word of God of none effect through your tradition, which ye have delivered: and many such like things do ye."—Mark, vii. 8, 9, 13.

To the simple teachings of Nature and Jesus, theologians add that of natural depravity of man. This idea is false in its conception. It is an imputation against the wisdom and goodness of God, and blasphemous in its character. It implies that God is neither Omnipotent nor Omniscient; that He is unable to create and control all things aright according to His will and pleasure.

Exciting terror in the minds of men, by teaching the doctrine of eternal torment, is another imputation against God's infinite goodness. These and many others of a similar nature, we hesitate not to say have had their origin in the attempts of dishonest and designing men to defraud their more honest and unsuspecting fellow-creatures. Examples of this we have, even amongst the earliest, and perhaps more sincere followers of Jesus; nay, even amongst those who are called his Apostles. Take the well-known story of Ananias and Sapphira as a sample: "Neither was there any among them that lacked: for as many as were possessors of lands or houses sold them and brought the prices of the things that were sold, And laid them down at the Apostles' feet: and distribution was made unto every man according as he had need.

" And Joses, who by the Apostles was surnamed Barnabas, (which is being interpreted, The son of consolation,) a Levite, and of the country of Cyprus. Having land, sold it, and brought the money, and laid it at the Apostles' feet."—Acts, iv. 34, 35, 36, 37. "But a certain man named Ananias, with Sapphira his wife, sold a possession. And kept back part of the price, his wife also being privy to it, and brought a certain part and laid it at the Apostles' feet. But, Peter said, Ananias, why hath Satan filled thine heart to lie to the Holy Ghost, and to keep back part of the price of the land? While it remained, was it not thine own, and after it was sold, was it not in thine own power? Why hast thou conceived this thing in thine heart? Thou hast not lied unto men, but unto God. And Ananias hearing these words, fell down and gave up the ghost: and great fear came on them that heard these things. And the young men arose, wound him up, and carried him out and buried him. And it was about the space of three hours after, when his wife, not knowing what was done, came in. And Peter answered unto her, Tell me whether ye sold the land for so much? And she said, Yea, for so much. Then, Peter said unto her, How is it that ye have agreed together to tempt the spirit of the Lord? Behold the feet of them which have buried thy husband are at the door, and shall carry thee out. Then fell she down straightway at his feet, and yielded up the ghost; and the young men came in, and found her dead, and carrying her forth, buried her by her husband. And great fear came upon all the church, and upon as many as heard these things."—Acts, v. 1—11. The idea attempted to be inculcated by these representations is, that God was so incensed and offended with the persons who withheld a part of their possessions for their own use, instead of giving it all to the Apostles, that He, instantly, by an especial act, struck them dead. Now, this we hold to be entirely at variance with God's dealings with his creatures at this or any other time and place, and the promulgation of such a story was, as we conceive, a trick, a cheat, for the purpose of extorting money from and gaining domination over those susceptible of being so wrought upon through their fears. If it shall be suggested as possible that the death of these persons took place in accordance with the natural workings of God's universal and never-varying laws, we reply: Had it been Ananias alone who was said to be stricken dead, we might attribute his death to the effect of sudden shame or fear acting upon a system deranged by high nervous excitement. Rare as such cases are, they are not entirely inconsistent with the physical laws of our being, nor altogether beyond our natural experiences. But, when a second person, after so brief an interval, is put through the same identical process of cross-questioning, condemnation, and collapse, even the most extreme credulity takes alarm and shies off. One fortuitous coincidence between Peter's denunciation and the breaking of human heart strings might be received as a possible circumstance. Two such fortuitous coincidences, coming one close upon another, pass all bounds of credibleness. If it be claimed that the persons of the day of the early Apostles had more tender consciences in regard to lying or false pretence than those of our day, and, therefore, might be more likely to die from a sense of shame on account of having been detected in making false representations, it so happens that we are not without means of testing the susceptibility of the Apostles themselves, which at least should not fall below that of the common people about them. It appears from Bible record that Peter, the veritable Apostle who accused Ananias of lying, spoke falsely when he denied knowledge of Jesus thrice in succession. But, when detected, he neither fell dead from shame, nor was he stricken down by the Almighty. Again, the character and the false spirit of Judas are indicated by his betrayal of Jesus into the hands of his enemies, and by his own thieving propensities. All this proves that human nature was no better in the time of Peter and Judas, than now; and this puts it beyond possible credibility that Ananias and his wife died (if death there was) of a broken heart.

This leaves no alternative but to refer their death to a supernatural cause. Now, we appeal to the rational and common-sense men of our day, whether, if at this time, and in any part of the world, an occurrence of the kind under consideration was said to have taken place as a supernatural and especial exhibition of God's vengeance, for the cause assigned by the Apostle Peter, it would receive the slightest credence? And yet, this is the version that Peter gives of the pretended phenomena. We further submit whether the claiming of Peter, that God in his vengeance smote two persons dead in quick succession, for the cause assigned, does not come with a particularly ill grace from a person notoriously untruthful, from one whom Jesus denounced as Satanic, and as savoring not duly of the things of God. It is further submitted, whether if the death of the persons in question did occur at the time and place, and under the circumstances narrated, is it not more likely that it resulted from foul play, instigated by the Apostles for base purposes, rather than that the immediate cause of death was the upbraidings of conscience, fear, or the supernatural visitation of God manifested for the express purpose of frightening people into putting all their property at the disposal of the Apostles. And this trick, as we deem it, had for a time the expected effect; and "great fear came upon all the Church and upon as many as heard these things." These people were evidently made to fear lest they should not conform to the wishes of the Apostles, and thereby subject themselves to the summary vengeance of God invoked by them. And, we are told that "by the hands of the Apostles were many signs and wonders wrought among the people. . . . . And of the rest durst no man join himself to them." Unclean spirits also, as we say, were pretended to be cast out, another false pretence for the gaining of power. "And believers were the more added to the Lord, both men and women."

We have no doubt but that the character of this belief was that, if they—that is, all upon whom great fear came—did not blindly follow the bidding of the Apostles in relation to the giving up all their property to them, they could not escape the vengeance of the Lord, which

THREAT OF ETERNAL PUNISHMENT. 297

the Apostles would invoke against them. This presents a dark picture of human nature; but the odium pertains but to a comparative few—the mass of mankind are of the better sort.

We are happy to believe that a large majority of the enlightened men of our day and country not only disbelieve, that the man and his wife were stricken down by God for the reason assigned by the Apostles; they also are shocked by the hypocrisy, and perchance the murderous spirit, involved in the affair. But the Apostles were not without their competitors and imitators in this respect. There were at that time many different churches, doctrines, and creeds, some of which preceded them. The leaders of the earlier sects, perceiving that the new comers were even more greedy than themselves—claiming not only a part of men's substance, but the whole—feared lest there would be nothing left. On this account, and on account of the growing influence of the Apostles, they often came in conflict with each other; and one of the results of these feuds, is thus set down. "The high priest rose up, and all they that were with him, which is the sect of the Sadducees, and were filled with indignation. And laid their hands on the Apostles, and put them in the common prison."—Acts, v. 17, 18.

We trace, also in this transaction, the germ of that dominating and grasping spirit which was carried to so revolting a pitch by the Christian Church, during the dark and middle ages, as is seen elsewhere in this work. And yet, there are many practices, in some of the Christian Churches, at the present time, which are only a little less glaring and despicable.

A striking analogy exists between Peter's intimidating process for raising revenue for the Church, and that which yet so extensively prevails. We allude especially to the menacing of the people by threats of everlasting punishment if they do not embrace a particular dogma or article of faith to the exclusion of many others. Might it not be said, therefore, that herein Peter is the symbolic foundation of the Church, which is so faithful to his propensities, and which, we augur, will not be able much longer, to withstand the flood of light, common sense, and reason, that menaces it, both in this and other countries?

We proceed to point to some of the other devices, that are resorted to at the present day, for swelling the coffers of the Church, and which we conceive to be altogether unjustifiable. Prominent among them is the preaching of mystical and wonder-exciting dogmas and theologies, and the exhibition of imposing ritualism, ceremonies, and paraphernalia, the invention and traditions of men, so appropriately condemned by Jesus in these pertinent words: "For laying aside the commandments of God, ye hold the tradition of men. * * * Making the word of God of none effect through your traditions." Again, the fable of Purgatory is instrumental in extracting large sums from those who are made to believe that their deceased friends are suffering terrific torments therein, and can only be released from it by the prayers of the Church, which prayers can only be procured by money forthcoming. The granting of indulgences by the Church, which in plainer language means the privilege to sin, and absolution from the consequences of sin—neither of which God ever grants—may also be named as prolific and disgraceful sources of revenue to the Church. Representing God as punishing the smallest sin everlastingly, with the most excruciating torment, in a wrathful and vindictive spirit—unless the sinner has full faith that Jesus is

JESUS NOT A SAVIOUR. 299

co-equal with Jehovah, and that he (Jesus) is the only Saviour of men from everlasting punishment, entailed on them by reason of the sin of Adam—is another of the whips with which they scourge the people. This threatening with God's vengeance all, who are not within the pale of the Church, is of the same character as the farce enacted by the apostles before mentioned, and is resorted to with a similar view. Its object is to frighten into their net all those who are susceptible of being so operated upon, and thus, incidentally, to swell the church's gain. Such an intimidating process cannot be persisted in by the clergy, with an eye single to the spiritual and temporal welfare of their hearers, while at the same time they have a full knowledge of the existence of such Bible testimony as is here cited; "Yet I am the Lord thy God from the land of Egypt, and thou shalt know no God but me: for there is no Saviour beside me."—Hosea, xiii. 4; "I am the Lord thy God, the Holy One of Israel, thy Saviour." Isaiah, xliii. 3; "I, even I, am the Lord; and beside me there is no Saviour."—Isaiah, xliii. 11; "And all flesh shall know that I the Lord am thy Saviour and thy Redeemer, the Mighty One of Jacob."—Isaiah, xlix. 25; "We trust in the living God, who is the Saviour of all men, especially of those that believe,"—1 Timothy, iv. 10; and we insist that all men believe, as we heretofore endeavored to show. The appellation of the Living God is nowhere in the Bible applied to Jesus. Peter called him the Son of the Living God, but we have before shown that this might be applied to other men as well as to Jesus. In addition to the foregoing, however, there are in the Bible a dozen or more texts, directly affirming that there is but one God, and not a word positively declaring that Jesus is God—co-equal with Jehovah.

But further proof of the erroneous dogmas and declarations of the Church can be furnished: "All flesh shall see the salvation of God."—Luke, iii. 4, 6; "And the glory of the Lord shall be revealed, and all flesh shall see it together: for the mouth of the Lord hath spoken it."—Isaiah, xl. 5. These texts give assurance that each human being will be saved by The Lord God-Jehovah, to the enjoyment of His glory—not by Jesus, as some assert. They are also irreconcilable with the church dogma, that the majority of mankind will be the subjects of God's everlasting vengeance. If it shall be objected that there is Bible authority for such a dogma, and sufficient for it, then we say that this does but show that the Bible is fallible, and the production of fallible men, since God cannot contradict himself.

If the human soul is placed upon earth as a preparatory measure to fit it for an existence in eternity, the natural inference is, that the soul retains the main characteristics throughout, and there is nothing in the so-called word of God, to contradict this idea. The soul naturally craves constant progression from one state to that of another. A continued state of rest, even unattended with pain or want, cannot afford happiness, nothing short of progress from incident to incident, from new interests to new interests, can satisfy the soul—to be happy it must be in harmony with the gravitating influence which is ever leading it on the great mission of assimilating itself to its Maker. Restlessness is one of the great features with which God has endowed the soul, to the end that it may never cease seeking Him and finding out more and more the wondrous ways and mysteries of God, and glorifying him—and yet the theologians tell us that beyond the grave the blessings of Christ's kingdom shall be peace and

THE SPIRIT RESTLESS. 301

quietness forever. "And my people shall dwell in peaceable habitations and in sure dwellings, and in quiet resting places."—Isaiah, xxxii. 18. This is adverse to the great purposes of God. The course of the human spirit is onward.

Man, so far as we know, is the only created being endowed with qualities capable of comprehending and appreciating the wisdom, goodness and glory of God. Shall his brief existence upon earth, while there is an eternity before him, be the limit of time allowed to complete his strivings to know God, the inexhaustible— no; the normal condition of the human soul is neither perpetual rest in peace or perpetual torment, but a never ceasing activity in cultivating and bringing itself more and more to the appreciation of its Maker. The following is quite as wide of the true nature of the soul as the foregoing theological view. The Bible narrative in relation to our first parents, is so construed by the Church, as to inculcate the idea that Adam and Eve and all their posterity, were originally intended by God to live a life of ease, and without labor, pain, care, death, or anything else to disturb them from a perfect state of peace, happiness and quietness, instead of experiencing the vicissitudes incident to an active life of good works. A further construction of the theologians put upon this fable, would, if true, present the matter thus—

If the first human pair had not eaten of the forbidden fruit, no one of the human family would have perceived that their nakedness was uncomely in the presence of others; in other words, there would have been no such trait in human character as modesty. The inauguration of modesty appears from the Bible narrative to have been the very first consequences of disobedience of command, and it is apparent, as the story goes, that God recognized the sensation of shame which Adam and Eve experienced in consequence of their nakedness as being praiseworthy, inasmuch as he, without delay, assisted them in administering to it by making both for Adam and Eve coats of skins and clothing them. Another inference from the narrative in question is, that but for the disobedience of our original parents, no one of the human family would ever have became so assimilated to God as to know good from evil. The further inference is that man, by his first breach of divine law, learned that the true enjoyment of life and existence consisted in acting in conformity to the law, which is equivalent to the partaking of the tree of life.

Now admitting, for the argument, that these Bible narratives are other than fables, it follows that but for original sin we should have been without modesty, without any knowledge of the difference between good and evil, without any assimilation to God, and without knowledge of the way which leads to life eternal—in short, on a level with the brute creation.

Now, if all these consequences of original sin are to be abolished according to the Church version of the subject, by resurrection through Christ, would we be the gainers by such restoration, to the original ignorance and absence of shame of nudeness imputed to our first parents before they had eaten the forbidden fruit.

It has been remarked that Jesus was persuaded, during the latter portion of his ministry, that he was sent to be "The King of the Jews," and to preach a purer doctrine to the people than that which was taught through means of the Jewish priesthood. He was also surrounded by those who favored these ideas, and who were constantly urging his claims to such a position and to such an office. When they had succeeded in convincing themselves on this point, they were naturally desirous to bring others to the same conclusion. And there can be no doubt, but that he also caught the spirit, and lent his voice to the cry, "believe and be baptized!" This cry, from habit, and from the consciousness that the doctrine which he preached, led to life and happiness here and hereafter, was constantly in his mouth. In this way he was gradually led to associate himself with it. "Ye believe in God," said he, "believe also in me."—John, xiv. 1. But that it was nothing more than the doctrine, which he proclaimed as the way to eternal life and in which he solicited belief, we infer from the record of John the Evangelist, who speaks of him in these words; "The same came for a witness, to bear witness of the Light, that all men through him might believe."—John, i. 7. When this plain language is considered in connection with the fact, that he denied that he was God or co-equal with God, it fully warrants the view of his office and religious sentiments which is taken in this work.

Now, the interpretation which the Churches put upon belief in Jesus, and the one here adopted, cannot be received together. So great is the difference between them, that they are totally inconsistent with each other. Jesus either meant that eternal life would result from belief in his doctrine of love to God, and good works, or he meant that belief in his being co-equal with God insured eternal life. If he meant that the latter must be added to a life of good works, it is inconceivable why he did not make such a declaration in plain and unmistakable terms, which he never did, at least there is no such record in the Bible. On the other hand, he did declare repeatedly and explicitly, in the plainest words and in the most impressive manner possible, that the sum total of the requirements for the inheritance of eternal life is, love to the One God, love to man, and good works. Such a belief as this, when taken in the sense here advocated, shows "the Religion of Jesus" to coincide and harmonize with the religion of the heart, the conscience, and the common sense of all mankind. In short, it is in unison with the religion of nature and of the God of nature, and shares this marked feature with the actuating principle that underlies the religion of every people on the face of the globe, however debased by the infusion of absurd dogmas and the practice of repulsive rites.

The church mode of interpreting the words of Jesus makes our eternal happiness depend on our ability to believe certain obscure passages of the Bible, containing accounts of what one person says in relation to another!

If belief comes at all, it must, of necessity, be involuntary. No man can have a real, honest faith, of the kind just mentioned, except through intuition, or upon evidence that is irresistibly convincing. Belief, therefore, not being a matter of free agency, there can be no merit in its adoption, whereas, on the contrary, good works, which a man may, or may not do, constitute the only acceptable mode of manifesting love to God.

Man's moral accountability to God, for his conduct here can have reference only to those actions over which man himself has any control, that is to say, those which, by virtue of his free agency, he may do or leave undone at his own will and pleasure. Belief in Jesus as a God and a Redeemer, which the system of Christianity demands as indispensable to salvation, is not among the actions that man can control at will; neither is it among the convictions that come to us spontaneously, or by the inevitable consequences of nature's universal teaching. It is not like the assurance that there is an overruling Intelligence, to whose laws we are each and all accountable. Hence, the belief in question, if binding on us at all, must of necessity be founded upon evidence, the sufficiency or insufficiency of which it is in the capacity of the reasoning faculties to scan, weigh, and determine.

Again: "He that believeth on the Son hath everlasting life; and he that believeth not the Son shall not see life: but the wrath of God abideth on him."—John, iii. 36. This suggests the inquiry, what does believing on the Son mean? Is it that his teaching, or that believing on him, personally as the Son, leads to everlasting life? If we may rely upon the explanation from Jesus' own mouth to believe in him, was to believe in his teaching, and his teaching is not his own, but God's. He said himself—John, vii. 16,—"My doctrine is not mine, but his that sent me." In his solitary prayer, also recorded by St. John in the 17th chapter of his Gospel, Jesus says, in the 6th verse: "I have manifested thy name unto the men which thou gavest me out of the world, and they have kept thy word;" in the 8th verse, "For I have given unto them the words which thou gavest me;" and again, in the 14th verse, "I have given them thy word." Thus it is clear, on his own testimony, that it was God's doctrine that Jesus taught. What, also, said Paul, narrating to Agrippa his own course, after his own conversion? "Whereupon, O King Agrippa, I was not disobedient unto the heavenly vision, but shewed first unto them of Damascus, and at Jerusalem, and throughout all the coasts of Judea, and then to the Gentiles, that they should repent and turn to God, and do works meet for repentance." This is Paul's view of the obligations of Christianity, in the way of teaching, even though the vision that set him to work was in the form of the Lord Jesus. Paul also, in the midst of Mars Hill, at Athens, proclaimed—Acts, xvii. 24, 27, 28,—the "unknown" God whom the Greeks ignorantly worshipped as "the God that made the world and all things therein." He added, furthermore, the remarkable declaration, that the Lord is not far from every one of us: "For in him we live, and move, and have our being; as certain also of your poets have said, For we are also his offspring." Herein we detect the recognition of that great first principle of all religion which is implanted in us by God himself, and a contradiction of the human dogma that consigns all men to perdition, outside of a chosen few of the elect.

Just in proportion as a man teaches and practices the laws pertaining to his existence, in more or less purity, the more or less conspicuously does God appear in him. Now, if any preacher of the present day were to commence teaching the truths relating to man's well being here, and to his happiness hereafter, unencumbered with church dogmas, as were the teachings of Jesus, his hearers would know at once that his doctrine came from God. Their minds and consciences would both bear witness to it; and it would seem to those, who first heard it, like a miracle, because of its novelty. That a religious teacher of our day should inculcate love to God manifested by acts of kindness, one towards another, as the total requisite for man's highest enjoyment, would seem almost incredible. And yet, such was the teaching of Jesus, both by precept and example. It was his everyday vocation, pursued with untiring zeal, before he conceived the idea that he was the Messiah. No wonder Nicodemus expressed himself as he did. He instantly recognized that the great celebrity which Jesus had obtained, grew out of the excellency and purity of the doctrines which he taught; that he was admirably adapted to his mission of promulgating and enforcing unadulterated truth; and of so pointing out the way that leads to eternal life, as to justify him in saying, "I am the way, the truth, and the life."

But the religion, which Jesus associated with belief in himself, is more fully illustrated by his last charge to his disciples, when to push forward the good work which he had commenced, he sent them to teach all nations, to take his mantle upon them, to avail themselves of his renown as a teacher, to assume his office, and to hand down to all posterity the doctrines with which his name and fame were identified. He charged them to preach repentance, which is the turning point to a better course—that which works an aversion to sin, and which leads to a higher life. All this shows that he believed in himself as a teacher of God's laws in relation to man. His course and teaching evince that his genius lay particularly in that line, as was the case also with Zoroaster, Mohammed, Buddha, Confucius, and other celebrated founders of religious systems and expounders of morals. In him, as in the above mentioned persons, that peculiar faculty was most extraordinarily developed. He had a happy facility for laying bare divine truths, and disentangling them of the bewildering mazes into which designing men had woven them, for base purposes.

Such we believe to have been the character of Jesus; and we believe, also, that his endowments, like those of the persons cited above, although extraordinary, were natural and not supernatural. In virtue of such qualities, he became obnoxious to the grasping priesthood of the day, whom he never spared, and by whom he was relentlessly pursued, dragged before the tribunal, speciously accused, and finally murdered.

But, if Jesus conceived that belief in him signified that which his followers claimed for him, and that he was God as they claim, we cannot comprehend how it was that he did not make the subject so plain and unmistakable that all mankind would have had their duty placed squarely before them. Neither can we understand why their eternal doom, for not exercising such a belief in him, was not so emphatically taught them by natural intuition, or other evidence, that they could not have misunderstood him. How far this is from the fact, is indicated by the number of sects into which Christianity is split.

And yet those who profess to be his disciples teach, that if men do not blindly believe, just what they propound for them to believe, they are, for their contumacy, to be condemned to everlasting punishment, and this too, as before shown, in the face of an imperative law of nature, which makes either intuition, or other evidence, indispensable to belief. We persist that the individual mind of the person to whom belief, in anything, is propounded, must be the final and sole arbiter. Therefore every real—not blind—belief, in relation to Jesus, is totally involuntary, and beyond man's control, and consequently, involves neither merit nor demerit.

This holds good, also, in relation to those who have never had any such dogma presented to their minds; and, is, therefore, not among the things for which God holds them accountable. No one can believe a proposition without convincing evidence of its truth, or withhold belief in the face of such evidence. Nor can any man comprehend how it is, that the simple fact of arriving at a state of

NO GOOD RESULTS FROM THIS BELIEF. 309

mind called belief in the divinity of Jesus, and his sacrifice for sin, should entitle the believer to everlasting bliss, while, at the same time such belief offers no suggestion of, or stimulant to good works.

Action is the order of nature. It is, therefore, not alone sufficient that man should have a proper conviction of his duty—he is required to act in accordance with it as well; but church doctrine says, " whosoever believeth on me—meaning Jesus—shall inherit eternal life." And this is repeated, again and again, without addition, subtraction, or qualification.

On the isolated acceptance of this question of belief hangs everlasting bliss; on the converse everlasting death, say the clergy. We hold that no state of the mind can receive countenance from God which is not productive of an active life of good works. Jesus taught this, and it was the only, and the entire requisite which he made for the inheritance of eternal life.

How can an impression or a conviction that there are two Gods, or three Gods, in place of one God, be of any effect in inciting men to the performance of what all recognize as duty—to the exercise, for instance, of charity, which St. Paul himself declares to be greater than faith or hope ? Is there any specific or magnified virtue in a subdivided Godhead ? Does it tend to clear up any of the mystery, in which the Supreme Being has, for the present, been pleased to enwrap himself from our knowledge, or to enhance our ideas of his wisdom and power; to be told that Divinity is triune ? Are the attributes of the Almighty more comprehensible or more striking, when they are parcelled out into three divisions; the Father's portion being mainly wrath, the Son's portion being mainly mercy, and the Holy Ghost's business being mainly that of a medium? We think they are not. We can understand why it was, in Pagan mythology, that Cerberus, the dog who kept the gates of hell, was represented with three heads. Thereby it might be supposed that his ability to bark and bite was tripled. But that entry through the gates of Heaven should also be guarded, as it were by a triplex ideal—that conveys through it a sense of weakness, rather than of strength—seems to us a human device more strange and more unwarrantable. Yet the theologians say that such belief is indispensable to salvation, and that salvation is at once secured by it. This involves the idea that a transcendant change takes place in every new convert from a belief in one God to a belief in three Gods, from the moment of imbibing the new notion; and this is the turning-point according to them, between everlasting bliss and perpetual torment. Carrying out this view, they assume a position, which we deem inconsistent with the teaching of Jesus himself, who is claimed as the basis of their creed. It is that—however barren of good works a man's life and conduct may have been, or however vicious he may have been up to the last hour of his existence—at this latest moment a belief in Jesus being God and Redeemer acts as an infallible passport to Heaven. Now, this is tantamount to a belief, that entertaining a bare idea for a few moments suffices to ensure eternal happiness, in despite of a life of sin, while a life of well-doing, without the entertainment of this idea, is counted but as dross, and cannot save. We say, on the contrary, such promptings of the human heart, as are implanted by God, though still under man's free control, tend exclusively to train him to good works as between man and man. Shall then the merit of a virtuous and useful life be made to hinge upon credence in a certain number of Gods? Shall what is meritorious to-day, be damnable to-morrow and *vice versâ?* It is indisputable, that individuals are constantly shifting, from one side of this question to the other, which involves, according to Christian theology, that the individual, so often as he may change, becomes instantly blessed or cursed, a saint or devil, a meet personage for Heaven or for Hell. And here it may be said in passing, that we agree with Jesus, who implies that Heaven and Hell are in men's consciences, and as applicable to this side of the grave as to the other. In Matthew, xii. 28, he says: "The Kingdom of God is come unto you;" and in Luke, xvii. 21—he speaks more strongly still: "Behold the Kingdom of God is within you." If this be so, and if the difference of the beliefs in question works the momentous difference that theologians maintain, it is past comprehension why it does not exhibit itself in a way not to be mistaken, between the conduct and condition of those espousing the two sides respectively. Why is the visible state of the individual the same when he enjoys Heaven by virtue of belief in the Trinity, and when he is transferred thence to Hell as a consequence of his belief in the one God Jehovah only? Again, if it be suggested that Jesus' mode of salvation, which is by good works, and the church's mode, which is by faith alone in Jesus, may be used in conjunction, we say that this betrays a suspicion that the church may be wrong, and consequently that both may be wrong. To make this appear more absurd, let us place them once more one against the other. Jesus claims that on his mode of salvation hangs all the law and the prophets, and that it is the only and all-sufficient one. The church claims that their mode of salvation is the only one given under

Heaven, whereby men may be saved, and that it is consequently all-sufficient. Now, two all-sufficient and only modes of salvation combined are superfluous and ridiculous.

It has been observed by a writer, often quoted, and from whom much is borrowed in this instance, that Jesus sought in every way to establish as a principle that his Apostles were as himself.—Matthew, x. 40, 42; xxv. 45; Mark, ix. 40; Luke, x.; John, xiii. 20. It was believed that he had communicated all the marvellous virtues to them, which he claimed to have been delegated to him.

They prophesied and cast out demons, although certain cases were beyond their power.—Matthew, xvii. 18, 19. They also wrought cures, either by the imposition of hands, or by the anointing with oil.—Mark, vi. 13; James, v. 14; one of the fundamental processes of Oriental medicine. Lastly, like the Psylli of old, or like certain Bengalese of our day, they could handle serpents; and they could drink deadly potions with impunity.— Mark, xvi. 18; Luke, x. 19. But, whilst with the lapse of time all this pretence of supernatural power becomes more and more repugnant to our perceptions of truth, there is no doubt that it was generally received by the primitive Church, that it held an important place in the estimation of the world around, and that without it the Christian theology would never have existed. Charlatans, as generally happens, took advantage of this movement of popular credulity. Even in the lifetime of Jesus, many, without being his disciples, cast out demons in his name. The true disciples were much displeased at this, and sought to prevent them. But Jesus, no doubt, saw that it was better policy not to interfere with them.— Mark, ix. 38, 39; Luke, ix. 49, 50. It must be observed, moreover, that the exercise of these claimed gifts had to some degree become a trade. Carrying the logic of absurdity to the extreme, certain men pretended to cast out in the name of Beelzebub, the prince of demons.

They assumed that this sovereign of the infernal regions must have entire authority over his subordinates, and that in acting through him they were more likely to make the intruding spirit depart.—Matthew, xii. 24, 28. Some even sought to buy from the disciples of Jesus the secret of the miraculous powers, which had been confided to them.—Acts, viii. 18, 19. This shows that there were those of that day, who esteemed these pretended miracles as but an ingenious trick, which might be performed by any one who was instructed in the mode and manner of effecting them.

It was only after the death of Jesus, that particular Christian churches were established; and they were constituted purely and simply on the model of the synagogue. Nor did they draw within their folds all those who had been more or less intimately associated with Jesus in person. Joseph of Arimathea, Lazarus, Mary Magdalen, and Nicodemus did not, it seems, become members of these churches, clinging in preference to the tender and respectful recollections which they had individually preserved of him.

It is to be observed, also, that there is no trace in the teaching of Jesus, of an apparent canonical law, ever so slightly defined by him. It may be assumed, on the contrary, that the idea of a newly written code and articles of religious faith, could never have been entertained by him, for he deemed the true record to be inscribed on men's hearts and already transcribed into the moral commandments extant in the Jewish law. Not only did he not write; but it would have been useless and adverse to the spirit of such an infant sect to get up any so-called sacred books, inasmuch as they believed themselves to be on the eve of the great final catastrophe. It cannot be too often repeated that, when Jesus speaks of his kingdom as not being of this world—John, xxviii. 36—he means the world which was then, and is now inhabited by the human race, and that his world to come is the one described in 2 Peter, iii. 13—in these words: "Nevertheless, we, according to his promise, look for a new heavens and a new earth, wherein dwelleth righteousness." The first Christian generation lived almost entirely upon delusive expectations and dreams. They conceived themselves on the eve of seeing the then world come to an end; they looked for a new one, and they regarded as useless everything which only served to prolong the then state of things upon that earth wherein they were living. Possession of property was interdicted.—Luke, xiv. 33; Acts, iv. 32, and v. 1, 11. Although several of these disciples were married, there was to be no more marriage, on becoming a member of the sect.—Matthew, xix. 10, and following. The celibate was greatly preferred; even in marriage, continence was recommended. Revelation, xiv. 4. At one time the Master seems to approve of those who should mutilate themselves, in prospect of the coming kingdom.—Matthew, xix. 12. Cessation from generating one's kind was sometimes considered as a sign and condition of fitness for the impending change.—Matthew, xxii. 30; Luke, xxii. 35. The rule that Jesus sought to institute, was severe in the extreme. He required from his associates a complete detachment from the ordinary participation and interest in worldly matter, in absolute devotion to his work of evangelizing the world. Jesus, during the latter part of his lifetime, apparently believed that the impossible could be attempted with impunity. He made no concession to necessity. He boldly preached war against nature, and total severance from ties of blood. "Verily I say unto you," said he, "there is no man that hath left house or parents, or brethren, or wife, or children, for the kingdom of God's sake, who shall not receive manifold more in this present time, and in the world to come life everlasting." The Kingdom of God here spoken of, is the kingdom to be established upon earth; and the world to come is like the present one, but in a regenerated state. His followers were not to carry with them either money or provisions for the way, not even a scrip or change of raiment. They must practice absolute poverty, living on alms and hospitality. The Father would send them his spirit from on high, which would become the principle of all their acts, the director of their thoughts, and their guide through the world. If driven from any town they were to shake the dust from their shoes, declaring always the proximity of the kingdom of God, that none might plead ignorance. "Ye shall not have gone over the cities of Israel," added he, "till the Son of man be come."

In his severe view of the exigencies of religion, Jesus went so far as to abolish all natural ties. His requirements had no longer any rational bounds. Despising the healthy limits of man's nature, he demanded that man should exist only for him, that man should love him alone. "If any man come to me," said he, "and hate not his father, and mother, and wife, and children, and brethren, and sisters, and his own life also, he cannot be my disciple."—Luke, xiv. 26; "So likewise, whoever he be of you, that forsaketh not all that he hath, he cannot be my disciple."—Luke, xiv. 33.

Such was the substance of the public teachings of Jesus, after he imbibed the visionary idea of his perpetual rule, either in the then world, or in the new world, which he predicted would speedily come. And all this was demanded by him, solely for the sake of establishing a belief that he was the Messiah predicted by the ancient prophets, to reign over the Jews perpetually upon the earth. The harsh and gloomy feelings of distaste for the world, and of excessive self-abnegation, which Jesus imposed upon himself and his followers in his later days, withdrew him more and more, out of the pale of humanity. It is certain that this idea of Jesus, if only on account of the celibacy and poverty it imposed, could not be carried out in practice. Common sense revolts at such extravagances; to demand the impossible is a mark of weakness and delusion.

We may easily imagine that to Jesus, at this period of his life, everything, which was not the kingdom of God, according to his idea of it, had absolutely disappeared. He was, if we may say so, totally outside of nature; family, friendship, country, had no longer any meaning for him. "Think not," said he, "that I am come to send peace on earth : I came not to send peace, but a sword. I am come to set man at variance against his father, and the daughter against her mother, and the daughter-in-law against her mother-in-law. And a man's foe shall be they of his own household."—Matthew, x. 34, 36 ; Luke, xii. 51, 53. "I am come to send fire on the earth ; and what will I, if it be already kindled?"—Luke, xii. 49.—
"They shall put you out of the synagogues," he continued,

"yea, the time cometh that whosoever killeth you, will think that he doeth God service."—John, xvi. 2.

Sometimes one would have said that his reason was disturbed. He suffered great mental anguish and agitation.—John xii. 27. The great vision of the kingdom of God, which he fancied he was to establish, glistening before his eyes, bewildered him. His disciples at times, thought him mad;—Mark, iii. 21, and following. His enemies declared him to be possessed:—Mark, iii. 22; John, vii. 20; viii. 48. His excessively impassioned temperament carried him incessantly beyond all rational bounds. At this later period he disregarded all human systems; and his work not addressing itself to the reason, that which he most imperiously required was an unquestioning faith—faith in that which time and history have demonstrated to have been visionary;—Matthew, viii. 10; ix. 2, 22, 28, 29; xvii. 19; John, vi. 29, &c. His previous gentleness seemed to have abandoned him; he was sometimes harsh and capricious;—Matthew, xvii. 16; Mark, iii. 15, 18; Luke, viii. 45; ix. 41. His disciples at times, did not understand him, and experienced in his presence a feeling akin to fear.—Mark, iv. 40; v. 15; ix. 31; x. 32. Sometimes his displeasure at the slightest opposition led him to commit acts as inexplicable and absurd as cursing a fig tree because it did not bear fruit out of season;—Mark, xi. 12, 14, 20.

His struggle for the ideal against the real, became insupportable. Contact with the world pained and revolted him. Obstacles irritated him. His ideas concerning himself, as the Son of God, became disturbed, inconsistent, and exaggerated. The fatal law which condemns all impracticable ideas to decay, so soon as an attempt is made to put them into operation, applied to his. But even during the early part of the public ministry of Jesus, and while his mode and manner of portraying the doctrines enjoined on man by natural religion, was in many respects unsurpassed, there was in his teachings a want of consistency, an absence of that harmony which is conspicuous in all things which are unmistakably of God. For while Jesus—the God-Man, as the Church has it—failed to act perfectly his part as a man, he still more signally failed to duly represent God, who, according to Bible record says, "I am the Lord, I change not;" and of whom Balaam says, "God is not a man, that he should lie." The Scriptures do not bear out this claim to unchangeableness and infallibility in relation to Jesus. Several phases of character, or functions were assumed at different times by Jesus, during the few years of his public ministry. Each of these offices or missions was totally inconsistent with the others, as we shall show.

Jesus claimed in the first place, that his mission was to lead or point all men by his teaching, to everlasting happiness beyond the grave; in the second place, he claimed to be the Messiah appointed by God to rule mankind upon this earth, whereon all men were to live forever; thirdly, he claimed to be destined to rule everlastingly, in person and in the flesh, over the whole human race, all of whom were to be righteous and happy, upon a new earth, to be substituted for the present one, which was to be destroyed by fire. Now Jesus' first claim, that his teaching pointed to 'everlasting happiness beyond the grave, is inconsistent with his second claim, which involved that no man, after the kingdom of God was established under him, was to die or pass the grave. His third assumption, which involved the destruction of our present earth, and a continued existence on this side of the grave, is alike inconsistent with his first assumptions, inasmuch as teaching the way to happiness beyond the grave to a people, who were never to pass the grave, would be out of place; and also, inasmuch as he could not possibly rule as the Messiah contemplated on this earth, since the earth was doomed to destruction. Now it is plain that any one of these positions being accepted as true, stamps the others as false. God cannot be false to Himself; he cannot be one manner of Being to-day and another to-morrow. As regards their fitness to the ordinary duties and relations of life and society, it may be noticed further that many of the doctrines of Jesus are irrational and altogether impracticable.

God, according to Moses and the Church, tells us on the authority of Paul's Epistle to Timothy, that "all Scripture is given by inspiration of God," and that, consequently, we must have faith in Moses' announcements. God, we say, put man into Paradise "to dress and keep" the garden of Eden; and this, be it observed, before man had been doomed to labor in the sweat of his brow. But Jesus, after this so-called curse had been affixed upon humanity, inculcated a manner of living entirely at variance with its existence. Men were to take no thought— not undue thought, but no thought whatever—as to their means of subsistence. If smitten on one cheek, they were to turn the other cheek to the smiter. If robbed of their coats, they were to give up their cloaks also. Never gaining or acquiring, they were to give and lend without stint. They were not to pay even funeral rites to the dead, in the urgency of their haste to follow after Jesus. They were, for the same end, to give up their natural affections toward father, mother, wife, and child, implanted in man from the first, and shared in part by the very beasts of the field. As to occupations, livelihood, trade, industry, art, science, learning, the embellishments of life, and the duties of man as a citizen—all these matters are entirely ignored, or are dismissed contemptuously as not worth thought or care.

How full of misery the world would have become, if these injunctions had been obeyed, how starving and utterly forlorn, it is needless to point out. But, without dwelling upon the visionary tendencies of Jesus' code in general, it cannot be inappropriate to remark how slightly in these respects it has bound his followers. The name of Jesus is forever in their mouths; but they have wandered, it must be owned, very far from his teachings. If he varied thrice in his own promulgated views as to his mission and purposes, they by way of a fourth variation have saddled him with the dogma of spiritual salvation through sacrifice of himself. If he preached poverty and self-abnegation, their church has sought power and accumulated wealth, while they as individuals have entered with full ardor and much success upon the multifarious pursuits of man.

Having thus shown, as we conceive, that Jesus—whom the Church adores as perfect God and perfect Man—was neither a worthy representative of God's majestic attributes, nor a fitting type of man under the various relations of life and under the nature which God has stamped upon him, we ask what the conclusion must be. Who shall say that God's representation of Himself throughout the entire universe, and his impress upon broad humanity, are not the true ones under which to live and die?

It is probable that the reported raising of Lazarus from death contributed sensibly to hasten the death of Jesus, as

THE ARREST OF JESUS. 321

is shown in the latter part of the 11th chapter of John's Gospel. The disciples related the fact, with details as to its performance, prepared in expectation of controversy.

The other miracles of Jesus were transitory acts, spontaneously accepted by faith, and exaggerated by popular fame, and were not often referred to after they had once taken place. This raising of Lazarus was an event held to be publicly notorious, and by which it was hoped to silence the Pharisees. The enemies of Jesus were much irritated at all this fame; and, therefore, a council of the chief priests was assembled, and in that council the question was clearly put: "Can Jesus and Judaism exist together?" To raise the question was to resolve it; the high priest could easily pronounce his cruel axiom: "It is expedient that one man should die for the people." The priests saw, in the excitement created by Jesus, the probable overturning of the Temple, the source of their riches and honors.—John, xi. 48. In a general sense, Jesus, if he had succeeded in all he proposed, would have really effected the ruin of the Jewish nation. Hence the men of order, persuaded that it was essential for humanity that the existing belief should not be disturbed, felt themselves bound to prevent the new spirit from extending itself. But never was seen a more striking example of how much such a course of procedure defeats its own object. Left free, Jesus would have exhausted himself in a desperate struggle with the impossible. The unintelligent hate of his enemies, resulting in his persecution and death, contributed to, or was in reality an incident without which he never would have obtained the notoriety that has pertained in relation to him. The death of Jesus being resolved upon,—Matt., xxvi. 15: Mark, xvi. 1, 2: Luke, xxii, 1, 2,—to escape from arrest, he withdrew to an obscure town called Ephraim, or Ephron, in the direction of Bethel, a short day's journey from Jerusalem.—John, xi. 54. It seems that about this time the apprehensions of Jesus that his life was in jeopardy took hold of his disciples. All felt that a very serious danger threatened the Master, and that they were approaching a crisis. At one time Jesus thought of precautions, and spoke of swords. There were two in the company. "It is enough," said he.—Luke, xxii. 36, 38. He did not, however, follow out this idea, seeing clearly that timid provincials would not stand before the armed force of the great powers of Jerusalem. There was, however, some show of resistance on the part of the disciples on the occasion of the arrest of Jesus. One of them—Peter, according to an eye witness: John, xviii. 10,—drew his sword and cut off the ear of one of the servants of the high priest, named Malchus. Jesus restrained this opposition, seeing the impossibility of effectual resistance, especially against authorities who had so much prestige; and he was accordingly captured. It thus appears that instead of Jesus having volunteered to become a sacrifice for sin, according to the Christian theology, he avoided being arrested and crucified to the extent of his ability. Jesus' seeming anticipations of his violent death, whether by crucifixion or otherwise, may well have been the result of his having laid claim to the Messiahship, and not the result of any supernatural foreknowledge, or of any voluntary offering of himself as a ransom for the sins of the world. He was aware, from current events, that whoever set up a claim to the Messiahship put his life in jeopardy; and, being an enthusiast in common with others of his time, he did not hesitate so to risk it. Thus he might naturally predict that it would be the forfeit of his course; and this is the more likely, inasmuch as John was put to death by Herod for having, as is vaguely suggested by Josephus, entered into the politics of the times. This view is further corroborated by the frequent allusions of the Evangelists to Jesus' reasons for moving from place to place. Occasionally the cause assigned is a trivial one, such as the inconvenient pressure of the multitude upon him. Sometimes, also, the movement is recorded as a simple matter of fact. But—until longer escape was impossible—the mention of any danger immediately threatening the life or liberty of Jesus was surely followed by a prudent retreat. John the Baptist was beheaded; "when Jesus heard of it he departed thence by ship into a desert place apart."—Matthew, xiv. 13. The priests plotted against him; "after these things Jesus walked in Galilee; for he would not walk in Jewry, because the Jews sought to kill him."—John, vii. 1. They took up stones to cast at him; "but Jesus hid himself, and went out of the temple, going through the midst of them, and so passed by."—John, vii. 59. "They sought again to take him," says St. John in his 10th chapter, verse 39; and he adds, "but he escaped out of their hands."

Now, although we are told by the Church, and anathematized if we don't believe it, that Jesus volunteered to die upon the cross, we must repeat that the Bible record proves precisely the reverse. If his zeal sustained and bore him onwards until drawn within the fatal circle of events, at least he evaded the penalty so far, and as often as he could; while, even in the closing scene, it is difficult to find any marks of superhuman power. Had it been possible—we speak on his own authority, as handed down to us by his living followers—he would have had the last agony spared him. In immediate anticipation of a cruel death, he prayed with more resignation than courage, Abba Father, all things are possible unto thee; take away this cup from me: nevertheless, not what I will, but what thou wilt.—Mark, xiv. 36. On the cross he uttered the words—inexplicable if we put faith in the Christian theology: "My God, my God, why hast thou forsaken me?"—Mark, xv. 34. It is strange, but not the less true, that many martyrs to the faith of Jesus have shown a holier faith, and a more enduring resolution, than were exhibited by their Master, the Man-God himself. And as there was nothing supremely heroic, assuredly nothing divine, in the spirit in which Jesus encountered death, nor anything uncommon in its manner, crucifixion being an ordinary capital punishment in those days, so was there nothing unique or mysterious in its apparent cause.

The course which the priests had resolved to take against Jesus was quite in conformity with their own established laws. The plan of the enemies of Jesus was to convict him by the testimony of witnesses who had been suborned, and by his own avowals, of blasphemy, and of outrage against the Mosaic religion, to condemn him to death according to law, and then to get the condemnation sanctioned by Pilate.

On the trial of Jesus, the fatal sentence which he had really uttered: "I am able to destroy the temple of God and to build it in three days," was cited by two witnesses. To blaspheme the temple of God was, according to the Jewish law, to blaspheme God Himself. The sentence was predetermined, and they only sought for pretexts. Jesus felt this, and did not undertake a useless defence. In the light of orthodox Judaism, he was truly a blasphemer, a destroyer of the established worship; and the law punished such a criminal with death. With one voice, therefore, the assembly declared him guilty of a capital crime; and Pilate's ratification of the condemnation pronounced by the Sanhedrim was obtained, but not without some reluctance on his part. In his eyes, it is tolerably evident, Jesus was an inoffensive dreamer. But he no doubt feared that too much indulgence shown to a prisoner, to whom was given the title of the "King of the Jews," and who claimed to be the Messiah, might compromise him. He could scarcely have acted otherwise than he did. It was then neither Tiberius nor Pilate that condemned Jesus. It was the old Jewish party. It was the Mosaic Law. Now, it is beyond question that Jesus attacked this worship and aspired to destroy it. The Jews expressed this to Pilate with a truthful simplicity: " We have a law, and by our law he ought to die."

The fate of Jesus was, therefore, the natural fate of a religious reformer, in a cruel age, and among a fanatical people. And it made a very slight, a scarcely perceptible sensation. In this it resembled his life. The life of Jesus was passed entirely in the restricted world in which he was born. During his life he was never heard of in Greek or Roman countries. His name appears only in profane authors of a hundred years later, and then only in an indirect manner, as in Tacitus and Josephus, in connection with seditious movements provoked by his doctrine, or persecutions of which his disciples were the object. The essential work of Jesus was to create around him a circle of disciples whom he inspired with boundless affection. His doctrine was so little dogmatic, that he never thought of writing it or of causing it to be written. Men did not become his disciples, by believing this thing or that thing, but in being attached to his person and in loving him. A few sentences collected from memory and especially the type of character he set forth, and the impression he had left, were what remained of him. Jesus was not a founder of dogmas, or a maker of creeds. His power over the hearts of men consisted in his preaching the religion of the heart and conscience, to which Church theologies and dogmas have since been added and placed in the foreground, while Jesus crucified is the burden of pulpit oratory, to the exclusion of God.

If any one thing is conclusively established in the New Testament, it is that Jesus and his disciples were possessed with the idea of a coming Kingdom of God, changing the whole aspect of the world and its affairs. Their ideas, even Jesus' own ideas, as to what this Kingdom was to be and when it was to come, varied considerably at various periods; but it was ever present to his mind and theirs in some shape, and its proclamation was reiterated over and over again. The Evangelists record how Jesus announced it with a fullness of detail, and a splendor of phrase, that captivates all that is imaginative in human nature. There is to be an abomination of desolation; and the sun is to be darkened, and the moon is to give her light no longer, and the stars are to fall from heaven; and the Son of Man is to come seated on the clouds, and surrounded by angels, with power and great glory, and the Elect are to be gathered together at the sound of a trumpet; and the King is to pass judgment on a multitudinous assemblage from every corner of the earth, calling the righteous into many mansions standing ready for them, and casting the wicked out into everlasting fire prepared for the devil and his angels. The Apostles continue to foretell this coming of the Kingdom; but, warned by the failure of their Master's prediction as to the time of its coming, are more reticent as to particulars, and less distinct in limiting the advent to the lifetime of any person or persons. In saying, however, that the Apostles, so far as we know, were neither expansive nor precise in dealing with this theme, we naturally except St. John. He indeed, in his magnificent rhapsody that bears the august name of "Revelation," may be said to make amends for their short-coming. He is strangely precise, especially in naming three years and a half for the duration of the world as it was, in his curious arithmetical calculation of the one hundred and forty-four thousand chosen ones of the house of Israel, and in his sealing up Satan in the bottomless pit for an exact period of one thousand years—as though the Almighty took pleasure in round numbers, and as though damnation through all eternity was not a prominent feature in the perverted creed that grew out of Jesus' doctrines. On the other hand, how lofty are his imaginings! How marvellous a compound of the grand and the terrific! How they pass in bewildering, yet fascinating, succession before us—the seven mystic candlesticks, and the sea of glass, and the beasts full of eyes before and behind, and the golden vials full of odors, which are the prayers of the Saints, and Death on the pale horse, and the locusts like unto horses prepared for battle, with the hair of women and the faces of men and the tails of scorpions, and the great red dragon, and the angels pouring out the vials of God's distilled wrath, and the great city with its walls of jasper and gates of pearls and foundations of sapphire, chrysolite, topaz, and all kinds of jewels! A magnificent and fantastic poem is all this, we may well allow; but, if asked what connection it has with the practical teaching of Jesus, who condensed religion into two short and simple dogmas, which it is needless to repeat here, we should be compelled to turn to the clergy for an answer. They would tell us, probably, that "all Scripture is given by inspiration of God, and is profitable for doctrine, for reproof, for correction, for instruction in righteousness;" and would bemoan our inability to perceive the force of this remark from the pen of a man who is placed by theologians in the position of a writer reviewing his own works. They might point out, furthermore, how the scholarship and research of learned commentators had proved that certain parts of the apocalyptic vision elucidated and tallied with certain parts of the prophetic visions abounding in the Old Testament. But we confess that our doubts as to the divine inspiration or intrinsic worth of this Revelation would not hereby be greatly diminished, while doubts would be suggested as to studied effort, on the part of St. John to make the old and new correspond.

It is to be observed, also, that not only were Jesus and his immediate followers mistaken as to the manner in which, and the exact time at which, this promised Kingdom was to come—it has never come at all, though it is confidently declared from pulpit to pulpit that not one jot or tittle of Scripture can fail. If, therefore, they were all mistaken on this point, is it not equally clear that theologians must be mistaken in declaring Jesus to be the Messiah? This precludes the idea of his being the Saviour. Jesus lived upon earth; so much we know. But he certainly never sat upon the throne of David; neither did he burn up the world and hold its gathered inhabitants to judgment.

The truth is, this breaking down, this crumbling away, of the Kingdom of God as promised, drives us back to a

THE KINGDOM OF GOD IN THE SOUL. 329

point, to which we have already adverted—in effect, to the Kingdom of God which exists within every human soul. And it was to this, in our belief, that Jesus occasionally referred in his earlier discourses, before his sense of man's need of spiritual affinity with his Maker had been disturbed and then thrown into the back-ground, by his enlarged and yet erroneous ideas concerning his own proper mission—concerning his temporal rule in the first place, and subsequently his new heaven and new earth. This, at least, may be said : it is as true for us as for Jesus' actual hearers, that this inner Kingdom is already established within us, nay, is part of our very nature, though we may fail to comprehend it. It is for us to look to it, that neither tradition, nor superstition, nor an indolent assent to prevailing dogmas, clogs our understanding in this matter. It is for us to determine how soon we shall free ourselves from all that is irrational, and obscure, and fluctuating and contradictory in theology. It is easy for us at any moment and without aid of priest, or temple, or code, or teaching, to recognize as all sufficient that first and only true religion, which was implanted in man before any creeds were concocted, and will survive in him as, one after another, their false claims to divine origin are exposed.

Jesus said unto his disciples, "It is not ye that speak, but the spirit of your Father which speaketh in you."— Matthew, x. 20.

"The words I speak unto you, I speak not of myself: but the Father that dwelleth in me, he doeth the work."— John, xiv. 10.

"For I have not spoken of myself, but the Father which sent me, he gave me a commandment what I should say and what I should speak."—John, xii. 49.

These quotations furnish direct evidence that Jesus places himself precisely on the same footing with his disciples, with regard to God being both their, and his Father; consequently, Jesus and his disciples were alike the sons of God. And when he says that both he and the disciples speak not of themselves, but are only the mouth-piece and instruments of God, to speak His mind, it follows likewise, that Jesus and the disciples stand in the same relation to God, with regard to those traits and functions of character and office, that distinguish each in common, and in which they were all engaged. This will be seen to be the case more especially from the following texts which describe them to be all alike equally endowed by God to work miracles.

Jesus said unto his disciples, "And these signs shall follow them that believe; in my name shall they cast out devils; they shall speak with new tongues." "They shall take up serpents; and if they drink any deadly thing, it shall not hurt them; they shall lay hands on the sick, and they shall recover."—Mark, xvi. 17, 18. If in answer to this it is objected that the difference between the ability of Jesus, and that of his disciples, to heal the sick, and work miracles, is that Jesus and not God, gave power to the latter, the objection is answered by Jesus himself, in the following terms: "The words I speak unto you, I speak not of myself but the Father that dwelleth in me, he doeth the work."—John, xiv. 10.

And in his own case, does he not acknowledge, by thankfulness, that it was his Father, and not himself, who raised Lazarus from the dead. "And Jesus lifted up his eyes and said, Father, I thank thee that thou hast heard me"—John, xi. 41—which shows that the miracle, if miracle it was, was worked by God, and not by Jesus.

And did not Martha, one of those who knew him best, and whom he is said to have loved above all others, both understand, and express her understanding of the matter, by saying that she knew, that whatsoever he were to ask of God, God would give it to him.—John, xi. 22. And does not Jesus' silence on the occasion, prove equivalent to giving assent to her ideas on the subject? The miracle, therefore, if wrought at all, was wrought by God, the Father, in answer to the prayer of Jesus, and not by Jesus himself, in his own strength. This much we grant for the strength of the argument against the divinity of Jesus. The presumption is, however, that no such miracle was ever wrought; but that the whole exhibition was gotten up to strengthen belief in Jesus, for the sake of furthering his interests in relation to his occupying the temporal throne of the Jews.

But again we have shown that the Apostles were equal to Jesus, in all the qualities above enumerated, and equality with God was never claimed for them, how is it then, that these traits in the character of Jesus are cited as proofs of him being co-equal with God the Father? If the answer is, that Jesus on his own, and also on the authority of the prophets, claims himself to have been God, have we not shewn also that such a view as this has been falsified by Jesus himself, where he in various places denies such a claim, either directly or by fair implication. And as to the authority of the Prophets on this subject, is not that set aside by their palpable errors, in connecting Jesus with the expected Messiah, who was to be the temporal ruler, or king of the Jews, which he never was? Jesus neither claimed nor answered to the description given, of the expected Messiah, in the sense put upon it by the Church. Nor could he have been, unless he was co-equal with God, which he disclaims to have been again and again. And if he had claimed to be co-equal with God, he says himself, "If I bear witness of myself, my witness is not true."—John, v. 31.

Peter declares; "Neither is there salvation in any other for there is none other name under heaven given among men, whereby we must be saved."—Acts, iv. 12.

But is Peter a competent witness? As regards his veracity and good character, does he stand sufficiently fair before men to be accredited? Is his testimony of much weight, under these, or any other circumstances? Peter made a false assertion, and at three different times repeated it. He thrice denied that he had any knowledge of Jesus, and more than once, on his oath. His conduct was also highly censurable and dishonest in the transaction wherein he procured, (or speciously lent himself to the procuring,) of very unreasonable sums of money from his converts, by exciting in them the fear of instant death, for their non-compliance with his most exorbitant demands for the support of himself and his associates. (See an account of his conduct in this respect, in another part of this work.)

Why, the unjustifiable doings of Peter so incensed even Jesus himself, that he was constrained to administer to him a rebuke, which for its severity, exceeds anything that Jesus ever uttered to him, or any other of his disciples. "But he turned and said unto Peter, Get thee behind me Satan; thou art an offence unto me; for thou savorest not the things that be of God, but those that be of men."—Matthew, xvi. 23.

Now, in view of such offences as these, are we to be asked to admit his testimony, either in this, or any other case? If he would lie, and cheat, and perjure himself, would he hesitate to do all in his power to advance his own interests by trying to persuade others to believe what he did not believe himself? *We* should say, he would not. He may, however, and probably did, have reference to Jesus being the only Saviour of the Jews from physical bondage, by becoming their King. If he did, his testimony is more reasonable, and therefore more credible; although he was mistaken. This is not the view which Christian theologians take of it. They make it to mean salvation from everlasting torment beyond the grave, for original and actual sin. Peter's probable view of the subject, untrue as it was, is more excusable than that of the theologians, and especially when such texts as the following are taken into consideration: "For I am the Lord thy God, the Holy One of Israel, *thy Saviour:* I gave Egypt for thy ransom, Ethiopia and Seba for thee."—Isaiah, xliii. 3. "I, even I, am the Lord; *and beside me there is no Saviour.*"—Isaiah, xliii. 2. "Tell ye and bring them near; yea, let them take counsel together; who hath declared this from ancient time? who hath told it from that time? have not I the Lord? and there is no God else beside me, a just God *and a Saviour;* there is none beside me."—Isaiah, xlv. 21. "Thou shalt also suck the milk of the Gentiles, and shalt suck the breasts of kings; and thou shalt know that I the Lord am thy Saviour and thy Redeemer, the mighty One of Jacob."—Isaiah, lx. 16. "For therefore, we both labor and suffer reproach, because we trust in the living God, who is the Saviour of all men, specially of those that believe."—1 Timothy, iv. 10.

Can any one attempt, seriously, to maintain the infallibility of the Bible, and the divinity of Jesus with such unmistakable and glaring contradictions as these before his eyes? And these are but the thousandth part of similar contradictions, some not quite perceivable at first glance, but equally apparent and positive, on a critical examination.

All men, by internal and external evidence, combined and coming immediately from God, are brought to the conviction that there is an over-ruling Intelligence—an infinite Mind—which is the author and governor of all things and beings, including man. Man only, however, it is believed, has an innate sense of right and wrong, and of his accountability to God for the proper discharge of his duty. This law of his being is, we say, universal. But, if we go further and say that religion takes in any other object of faith than the one supreme and good God, we are at fault. No such innate or external evidence is furnished to the entire race of men immediately from God, with regard to the so-called supernatural faculties or functions of Jesus. Nor have we any such grounds for believing that he was other than man. God alone—the one God—has the sole power to control all things, and is the only giver of all good things. God alone, therefore, is, and should be, the only object of man's worship. His bounties come to man directly, as they do to the lower animals, and not by mediation. But whether or not these bounties come through one mode or another, this in no way affects man's obligations, nor the worship due from man to God. Neither does multiplying the objects of his worship increase man's disposition to manifest grateful emotions, or to perform good works. And this, for the all sufficient reason that no man, not excepting those who profess to understand it best—the church dignitaries—can comprehend such an anomaly, as that Jesus can be co-equal with God. Is not God infinite; and does He not fill the Universe? What room or occasion, then, can there be for another infinite Being?

There is no end to the mystery which the doctrine of the Trinity involves. It adds mystery to mystery. There is one thing, however, in relation to God which is indispensable to man's welfare; and that is, that he should perceive what his duty is, both to God and man. This, God has made sure that all men shall know, at all events to the extent of their needs, by implanting within their very nature the seeds which must, sooner or later, germinate, and bring forth their legitimate fruits, under the influences which God has spread around them. It would be infinitely better, in our estimation, if man would attend to the manifest instructions of the Almighty, instead of running after false gods—as do those who direct their worship almost exclusively to Jesus. But, admitting that Jesus was sent by God in the capacity claimed by his worshippers, why should religious teachers have Jesus on their lips continually, instead of directing their attention to the Fountain of all that is good and great, who is entitled, above all others to man's most profound devotion? If, also—as is unceasingly preached—God did so love the world as to send his only begotton Son to die here for our sins, why is it that he who was sent is so perseveringly pressed upon the attention in preference to Him who sent? Is the messenger more worthy than the Lord, through whose loving-kindness the messenger was despatched?

But the solution is easy. The sensibilities of the tender-hearted and unsuspecting are readily worked up to a high tension, by over-wrought and over-drawn pictures of the death-scene of Jesus. This is a powerful lever in the hands of the clergy, wherewith to increase the number of their disciples, and, incidentally, their own emoluments. For the same reason, "the blessed Virgin," and the infant Jesus are much dwelt upon, to touch the sympathies of parents, and mothers, and women generally, whose natural affections yearn toward children. God has so constituted us, that our sympathetic organs and corresponding kindliness are peculiarly alive in behalf of a mother and her helpless offspring. And so, even this precious trait in human nature is seized upon by designing priests, and wrought into the means for the acquisition of wealth. If it be not so, why do they not direct, in their church services, glorification and adoration to Jehovah, the Father and instigator of all good emotions and deeds? The Scriptures tell us, that God, the Father, is the giver of all good gifts, and that He is the fountain from whence all our blessings flow. He, therefore, should be the object of our constant praise and adoration; nor is there any lack of material, wherewith to portray God the Father, in a most beautiful and attractive aspect, without resorting to fictions. The most insignificant part of the sober truth that pertains to God's excellence, rightly arranged and brought to view, would present Him in a light so glowing, that the spiritual eye could scarcely withstand its brightness. And if this be so, why attempt to divert the heart's devotion, and the soul's adoration, from the source of all that is good and great, by resorting to false pretences? If the church has a single eye to the glory of God, and the good of men's souls, why does it not teach them to worship God rationally and consistently? If it should be said, however, that there certainly is great benefit to be derived from leading persons to put their faith in religious creeds, even at the expense of an exaggeration or perversion of the truth, the further question then presents itself, as to whether the theologies in which the clergy solicit belief are of themselves true?

One denomination makes eternal life conditional on the ceremony of baptism, and gives the authority of Jesus, if not his command, for this requirement. Another declares with equal confidence that he (Jesus) repudiates all ceremonies, as not being of the essence, or an indispensable part of religion. Baptism may be useful in its way—being performed before witnesses, it stimulates the weak to perseverance in their resolves, and assists them to hold on to their profession with more tenacity than they otherwise might do. Any other act performed before men, with equal solemnity, would answer the same purpose. Water, it is true, is a fitting emblem of purity, but the efficacy, if any there be in baptism, consists, not in the virtue of water being connected with the outward acts; the charm or spell which accompanies it, is the fear of men's remarks in case of backsliding. The effect is analogous to that of the laying on of hands when a temperance pledge is given. Baptism was coupled with belief in Jesus; and was so perseveringly persisted in by the first Apostles and their immediate followers, to prevent the backsliding of any who should subscribe to the pretensions of Jesus to the Messiahship. Incidentally, also, it swelled the number of his followers, and thus might prove the way to his being publicly proclaimed "King of the Jews," and to their enjoyment of the worldly honors, power, and emoluments connected with his ascent of the throne. And so with all church forms and ceremonials, that have at different times been practiced. They are not of the slightest utility, so far as the right appreciation and practice of virtue is concerned—though it may be that ceremonies, enacted before men's eyes, make churches more attractive, and draw larger and more imposing congregations, serving at once to increase the power and influence of the church, and at the same time to fill its coffers.

If the Church's theory is right with regard to God's mode of salvation, no man can possibly comprehend God's justice therein, otherwise than by His placing it within the range of each and every man's free-will to believe or not to believe, that Jesus, the son of Mary, is co-equal with God and the only Saviour of mankind, which it is absurd to say he has done. For if this church doctrine be the proper view of the subject, God's manifest and overwhelming goodness, demands such clear and unmistakable evidence on the side of truth, as to make it palpable to all men, that each and all of them could believe, if they would; and that to neglect or omit to believe, from any cause whatsoever, would entail upon them His eternal displeasure and vengeance. It is evident to all that such is not the case, but that the reverse of this is the fact; because the most overwhelming majority of mankind never heard of Jesus at all. We are aware that the objection or quibble which is put forward in reply to this unanswerable argument is, that those who have not heard of salvation through Jesus, will be judged according to the light they have. But the light which all men have, we insist again, is the religion here advocated; and this is all-sufficient without church theologies, forms, or sacrifices. Nothing but love to God, and kind acts to His creatures, is required of any man as a condition of salvation.

Jesus says, that "from the days of John the Baptist until now, the kingdom of heaven suffereth violence, and the violent take it by force."—Matthew, xi. 12; or as it is in Luke, xvi. 16—"since that time the kingdom of God is preached, and every man presseth into it." Then in answer to the accusation of the Pharisees, that he drives out devils by Beelzebub, he points out that he does it, on the contrary, by the spirit of God, and therefore that the kingdom of heaven is already among them.—Matthew, xii. 28. He says, also—John, xii. 31, "Now is the judgment of this world;" and—Luke, x. 9—"The kingdom of God is come nigh unto you;" and Mark says, i. 14, 15, "Jesus came into Galilee preaching the gospel of the kingdom of God, saying, the time is fulfilled and the kingdom of God is at hand." To the question, again, of the Pharisees, as to when the kingdom of God shall come, he makes answer that it does not come in an external perceptible manner, but it is within them, or already among them.—Luke, xvii. 20, 21. In these passages the kingdom of God, or heaven, is represented as that which is already here present, and has been founded and opened by Jesus during his life on earth, being within and about them to whom he was speaking. Now the Churches say that no man can enter the kingdom of God, until he shall have faith that Jesus voluntarily gave up his life, and shed his blood, for the remission of original sin. But, up to the time of Jesus' speaking, no such occurrence as the shedding of his blood had taken place ; no such faith or belief had been presented to any one for acceptance. These wide discrepancies between the founder and the Church that was built up must, with every reasoning mind, overthrow any faith in Christian theology.

But, it is not the Church alone, that differs with Jesus. He differs with himself, and his disciples differ with him. We have just seen how he represents those around him as having the kingdom of God in and about them, in other words, that God's perfect government was then in operation upon earth. That is, in all conscience, sufficiently definite and explicit, and treats the kingdom, which he looked for, as a fact accomplished. But how does it tally with Jesus' subsequent postponing the kingdom—with his confession, as it were, that after all, it had not absolutely made its appearance? It is in the 12th chapter of John, that Jesus is made to say, "now is the judgment of this world: now shall the prince of this world (Satan) be cast out;" it is in the 14th that he says, "the prince of this world cometh, and hath nothing in me;" and in the 16th, "yea, the time cometh, that whosoever killeth you will think that he doeth God service." This swaying to and fro, this uncertainty as to time and the sequence of events, this attainment and this passing away, this vague advent of good and of evil, the predictions at once minute in some particulars and shadowy in others, this jumble of the past, the present, and the future—all tend to confuse the enquiring mind, and to leave the diligent reader of the New Testament floundering in a strange quagmire of triumphs and tribulations. The Church, indeed, professes to see its way clear, through all difficulties, interpreting one obscure passage literally, and another metaphorically, and another spiritually, and another locally, and another historically. You can never find it at fault, for want of explanation or excuse. But the light that it throws upon the matter is little better than that of a dark lantern. It can be turned on at will, or shut off at convenience. There is another point. When Jesus apparently awoke from the delusion that he had already established God's kingdom on earth, he changed his ground, and connected its coming with his own second advent. But herein the foundation for Christian theology is still weaker. According to the Evangelical accounts, Jesus considered his second Advent so near, that he told his disciples, there were some among those standing round him, who should not taste of death until they had seen the Son of man coming in his kingdom.—Matthew, xvi. 28; that the then living generation should not pass away until this had taken place, *i. e.* until the second Advent of the Son of Man, with all its preparatory and attendant circumstances.—Matthew, xxiv. 34. In particular, he announced that this last great event was to occur immediately after the destruction of Jerusalem, prophesied by him just before.—Matthew, xxiv. 34. In any case, he was greatly mistaken with reference to the date, for not only has that generation passed away, but, for eighteen hundred years, one generation after another has followed its destiny and run out its allotted time, without his predicted second Advent having taken place. Yet all this, from our point of view, does not make the case at all worse.

For, in order to see that the prophecy of a man's return in the clouds is something utterly groundless, we do not require to know that it did not take place at the time predicted. Jesus in prominent passages in Matthew—xxiv. and xxv.—says that after certain lapses and mishaps in the starry constellations, the sign of the Son of Man will appear in the heavens; then, amid the lamentations of all the nations of the earth, the Son of Man will be seen coming on the clouds with power and glory; he will send out his angels with a loud sounding trumpet, in order to gather his elect from all the four winds; and then will he sit upon his throne to judge all men, to doom some to everlasting fire, and welcome others into everlasting life. Such a description resists every attempt to give it a merely symbolical meaning; and as the Christian Church always understood it in the literal meaning of the words, so it was certainly meant by Jesus.

It would appear from all this, that man's destiny, his transcendent bliss, or excruciating torment, for eternity, is irrevocably determined during his probation in the flesh; that this probation results either in extreme happiness or in extreme misery for all time to come; and that there is no lot or state intermediate for man. If this be so, if man's destiny is altogether worked out in this life, it is difficult to see why an eternity should be added to it, since few men live so good a life as to entitle them to an eternity of bliss, and few so bad a life as to deserve an eternity of torment. Moreover, what is to be meted out as the relatively proper state beyond the grave of all the various intermediate grades of merit or demerit, between those who, according to the Church, merit eternal bliss on the one hand, and eternal torment on the other.

If we inquire of the Churches what reliable indication there is on this side of the grave, as to who will be among the blest, and who among the accursed, beyond the grave, we shall receive as many different answers as there are different denominations or sects, all claiming Jesus for their guide. The number of these sects is now so great as to make it difficult to designate them; and they are every day increasing. This leaves us no rational course but to rely, for instruction upon this subject, upon him who, as all mankind acknowledge, cannot deceive or engender delusive hopes—the Creator and Governor of the Universe. The teaching from this source is uniform, and consistent with every day experience. It is that there are none perfectly happy in this life, and none perfectly and irretrievably miserable; that there is every possible intermediate grade between the most happy and the most unhappy; and that the provisions of God to lead all men to a more advanced state of happiness are unceasingly operating, and cannot fail to accomplish the object God designed.

Our experience, on this side of the grave is at total variance with the doctrine that mankind is divided into two classes only; one, being perfectly happy, and the other, perfectly miserable. We cannot believe that our present training by God and its results, and our experience here, should not in a degree foreshadow our state beyond the grave.

With regard to the narratives in the Bible, of occurrences and sayings upon which the Christian Theology of our day claims to be founded, there is little of which, we can say for certain, that it took place; and of all, to which the faith of the Church, especially, attaches itself, the miraculous and supernatural matter, in the fate and destinies of Jesus, it is far more certain that it did not take place. But that the happiness of mankind is to depend upon belief in such things as these is so absurd, that the assertion of the principle does not, at the present day, require refutation.

But, as certainly as men have a common destiny, attainable by all, so a knowledge of the conditions, also, of reaching that object must be given to every man, and that knowledge cannot be an accidental acquaintance with history coming from without, but must be a necessary knowledge attainable by faculties such as every man can find in himself.

APPENDIX.

WE now proceed to attempt a short account of some of the most celebrated of those founders of theology, who were said to be inspired; and of the creeds held, and the moral teachings inculcated, by means of a priesthood or through enacted laws, among the most prominent sects, into which men have been divided. We shall add also a sketch of the views concerning religion, that were entertained by some of the most intellectual persons in ancient times. This account mainly consists of miscellaneous extracts and mostly from the following books. "God in History," by Bunsen; "Essays on the Belief of the Parsees," by Haug; "Life and Teachings of Confucius," by Legge; "Description of the Burmese Empire," by Yandy; the "Koran," translated from the Arabic, by Sale; "Selections from the Koran," by Lane; "Ancient Faiths," by Inman; "Rig Veda, or Hindoo Scriptures," translated from the Sanscrit by Wilson; "History of the Intellectual Development of Europe," by Draper; "History of Civilization in England," by Buckle; "The Ten Tribes of Israel," by Mrs. Simon; "The Dervishes," by Brown; "The Christian Bible;" and "The Talmud." Not only is the historical portion of the several narratives taken from the above named books, but the views and remarks with which they are interspersed are, with slight exceptions, those of the writers of the works in question. The immediate object in compiling this historical account is to show that the point of resemblance, that is common to every denomination or sect—and the only one common to them all—is their teaching love and duty to God and man, or, in other words, natural religion. This suggests the important question, whether this does not comprise the whole of man's religious duty.

The present age is pre-eminently utilitarian. The Koran, the Zend Avesta, the Vedas, the Talmud, are read by the learned and the wise of our times—not with a sole view of refuting them, any more than is the Bible so read. All literature in relation to the doings of man, whether religious, moral or legal, whensoever and wheresoever produced is a part and parcel of humanity. The judicious student seeks to understand the phase of culture, which begot these items of our inheritance—the spirit that moves upon their face—and while that which is dead in them is buried, we rejoice in that which lives in them. Our stores of knowledge are enriched from theirs. We are stirred by their poetry; we are moved to high and holy thoughts when they touch the divine chord in our hearts. The more extended the researches into the history of man, the more reliable are the data, the clearer is the light, upon which and by which to determine the true character of mankind and their relations to God.

The theology and religious precepts promulgated by Zoroaster from 1200 to 1500 years B. C., among the Parsees, have their exponent in a book called Zend Avesta. The Zoroastrian idea of the personality and attributes of the Devil, and of the infernal Kingdom coincide with the Christian idea; as does that of the resurrection of the dead. Zoroaster is represented to have worked miracles; he was called the son of Ormasdes, or God. The Parsees claim that their so-called sacred books were all written by God and given to Zoroaster, as his prophet, to forward them to mankind.

Zoroaster had convened the nobles of the land that he might perform a great public, religious act. Arriving at the head of his disciples, the seers and preachers, he summoned the princes to draw nigh and to choose between faith and superstition.

"Make your choice!" he exclaims; "around man there is a battle waging in the spiritual universe. Even while on earth, he is surrounded by good and evil Spirits. He is endowed with all manner of good gifts and blessings; and his soul is in the hands of the Lord of the Universe, the Creator and governor of the world, the true God. Nevertheless, in this world, Evil has an independent power from the beginning; it must and will be ultimately overcome; but this can only be effected by a sincere breaking with the Evil Power—a personal decision in favor of the Good and True. Choose now blessing or cursing! You cannot serve two masters; and you cannot hold fellowship with lies. One side or the other must yield." The following is also a part of the recorded speech of Zoroaster on this occasion:

ZOROASTRIANISM.

"I will now tell you, who are assembled here, the wise sayings of the most Wise, the praises of the living God. In the beginning there was a pair of twins, two spirits, each of a peculiar activity; these are the good and the base in thought, and word, and deed. Choose one of the two spirits, be good, not base!

"And these two Spirits united, created the first (the material things;) one the reality, the other, non-reality. To the liars, (the worshippers of the devas, *i. e.* base,) existence will become bad, whilst the believer in the true God enjoys prosperity. Of these two spirits you must choose one, either the evil, the originator of the worst actions, or the true holy spirit. You cannot belong to both of them (*i. e.* you cannot be worshippers of the one true God, and of many gods at the same time.) Thus let us be such as help the life of the future. The wise—loving spirits are the greatest supporters of it. The prudent man wishes only to be there where wisdom is at home. He (Ahuramazda) first created through his inborn lustre the multitude of celestial bodies, and through his intellect the good creatures, governed by the inborn good mind.

"When my eyes beheld Thee, the essence of truth, the creator of life, who manifests his life in his works, then I knew Thee to be the primeval spirit, thou Wise, so high in mind as to create the world, and the father of the good mind."

Zoroaster claims to have received instructions from a supreme Being about the highest matters of human speculation. He appears as a prophet before a large assembly of his countrymen to propound to them his new doctrines.

The Magi (or priests) of Persia were at one time split into several sects, one of which was called the Mazda Kyahs, who believed in the transmigration of souls, like the Brahmans, (a doctrine which is altogether strange to the Zend Avesta, the sacred book of the Parsees.) The other sect believed in a revelation made by God to the first man, called Gayomart by the Parsees, corresponding to the Adam of the Bible.

"He therefore who, sacrificing his own selfish interests, devotes himself to the divine will, to goodness, shall receive earthly power, strength, possessions. This earth with her gifts, is the heritage of the good, or is destined to become so. This view pervades all the sayings of Zoroaster.

The Zoroastrian sacred Book furthermore exhibits the following teachings, which will compare advantageously with those of the

Bible. Lying is regarded as the most discreditable thing by them; next to it is the incurring of debt, chiefly for this reason, that the debtor is often compelled to tell lies. Zoroaster acknowledged only one God. "You cannot be worshippers of the one true God, and of many gods at the same time."

"The prudent man wishes only to be there where wisdom is at home.

"Wisdom is the shelter from lies, the annihilation of the destroyer (the evil spirit.) All perfect things are garnered up in the splendid residence of the good mind, the Wise, and the True, who are known as the best beings.

"Therefore, perform ye the commandments which, pronounced by the Wise (God) himself, have been given to mankind; for they are a nuisance and perdition to liars; but prosperity to the believer in the truth; they are the fountain of happiness.

"He first created through his inborn lustre the multitude of celestial bodies, and through his intellect the good creatures, governed by the inborn good mind. Thou living spirit, who art everlasting, makes them (the good creatures) grow.

"Do not listen to the sayings and precepts of the wicked.

"Who are opposed in their thoughts, words and actions to the wicked, and think of the welfare of creation, their efforts will be crowned by success.

"Blessed is he, blessed are all men, to whom the living wise god of his own command should grant those two everlasting powers (wholesomeness and immortality.) For this very good I beseech Thee. (Ahuramazda.) Mayest thou give me happiness, the good true things, and the possession of the good mind!

"I believe Thee to be the best being of all, the source of light for the world. Every body shall choose Thee (believe in thee) as the source of light, Thee, Thee, holiest spirit Mazda! Thou createst all good true things by means of the power of thy good mind at any time, and promisest us (who believe in Thee) a long life.

"I will believe Thee to be the powerful holy (god.) For thou givest with thy hand, filled with helps, good to the pious man, as well as to the impious by means of the warmth of the fire strengthening the good things. From this reason the vigor of the good mind has fallen to my lot.

"Thus I believe in Thee, as the holy God, thou living Wise! Because I beheld Thee to be the primeval cause of life in the creation. For thou hast made (instituted) holy customs, and words, thou hast given a bad fortune (emptiness) to the base, and a good to the good man.

"I believed in Thee, living Wise! in that thou camest with wealth and with the good mind through the actions of which our manners thrive. The everlasting laws, given by thy intellect, nobody may abolish.

"I will be mindful of the truth (to improve all good things) as long as I shall be able. Mayest thou grant me the truth, tell me the best to be done.

"That I will ask Thee, tell me it right, thou living God! By what means are the present things to be supported? That spirit, the holy one, is the guardian of the beings to ward off from them every evil, he is the promoter of all life.

"That I will ask Thee, tell me it right, thou living God! Who was in the beginning the father and creator of truth? Who made the sun and stars the way? Who causes the moon to increase and wane, if not thou? This I wish to know except what I already know.

"That I will ask Thee, tell me it right, thou living God! Who made the lights of good effect and the darkness? Who made the sleep of good effect and the activity. Who made morning, noon and night, reminding always the priest of his duties.

"To become acquainted with these things, I approach Thee, wise, holy spirit! Creator of all beings!

"Tell me good things to perform, the duties which are enjoined by thyself, thou Wise! Which are communicated for the welfare of all beings by the good mind. What good, intended for the increase of life, is to be had: that may come to me.

"Instruct me right in the faith which, being the best of all, may produce the good things, by means of words, and actions. My heart wishes (it is my lively desire,) that I may know Thee, thou Wise!

"To those among you who do not live according to the sayings (of God,) experience may be a help.

"God is endowed with good actions. Not is the being, who creates all, to be deceived.

"God delivered the word, the best to be heard by men. Wholesomeness and immortality are by means of the good mind's actions in the possession of the living Wise.

"By means of his power and his rule the generations gone by subsisted, and also those to come will subsist on him. The sincere man's mind is aspiring to the everlasting immortality.

"Him, whom I desire to worship, him, who knows the truth, him, the living Wise, as the source of the good mind, the good action, and the good word.

"Him will I adore with our good mind, him, who is always propitious to us at day and night; he, the living Wise, who through the sublimity of the good mind protects the truth.

"Thou living God! Tell me the power necessary for holding up the religion.

"What man or what woman performs the best actions, known to Thee, for the benefit of this life, promoting thus the truth and spreading thy rule through the good mind.

"To you I will speak; because you distinguish right from wrong, the truth, contained in the ancient commandments of the living God. I beseech you to assist me.

"Those who, by their base minds, cause mischief and ruin, those who are devoid of all good works and find delight in evil doings only—such men are punished.

"Every one who is truly noble by means of the good inborn mind will be rewarded.

"We praise all good thoughts, all good words, all good deeds, which are and will be (which are being done and which have been done) and we likewise keep clean and pure all that is good.

"We strive to think, to speak, and to do only what of all actions might be best fitted to promote the two lives (that of the body and of the soul.)

"We worship the promotion of all good, all that is very beautiful, shining, immortal, bright, every thing that is good.

"There shall not be overbearance nor low-spiritedness, nor violence, nor deceit. Nor shall there be one of the other signs through which men used to become defiled by the evil spirit."

Zarathustra called into existence a new religious community to be founded on the principle of inviolable faith and truth.

Ahuramazda, as the only Lord, grants blessings to those who worship him with a sincere heart, by speaking always truth, and performing good actions.

A living faith in a moral order of the world can alone explain the influence, which the Zoroastrian religion has now exercised for three thousand years on the populations of Western Asia.

The Zoroastrian system recognizes one God, omnipotent, invisible, without form, the creator, ruler and preserver of the universe, and the last judge. The worship of idols, and indeed of any being except Ormuzd, is held in abomination; but a reverence for fire and the sun is inculcated, as they are emblems of the glory of the Supreme Deity. · It is probably true, however, that the multitude in the course of time have forgotten that discrimination between the symbol and the object of their adoration, which was undoubtedly taught by Zoroaster. To Ormuzd as the source of all good, is opposed Ahriman, the cause of evil. To worship the good spirit and hate the bad, are the two fundamental articles of the Guebre, and Parsee creed. Prayer, obedience, industry, honesty, hospitality, alms-deeds, chastity and truthfulness, are enjoined; and envy, hatred, quarrelling, anger, revenge and polygamy are strictly forbidden. Fasting and celibacy are considered displeasing to Ormuzd.

The Koran of Mohammed is a code of ritual, moral and criminal laws, as well as a rule of faith or theology, and religious duty for a large portion of mankind.

The general religion of the Arabs, before Mohammed, was the Sabian; though there was also great numbers of Christians, Jews, and Magians among the number.

The Sabians believe in one God, and produce many strong arguments for his unity; but they also pay an adoration to the stars, or to the angels, and intelligences which they suppose reside in them, and govern the world under the Supreme Deity. They endeavor to perfect themselves in the four intellectual virtues, and believe that the souls of wicked men will be punished for ages, but will afterwards be received to mercy. Mohammed is said to have been born fifty-three years before the Flight, which happened in the year 622 of the Christian era. His father Abd-Allah was a younger son of Abd-el-Muttalib, the chief of his tribe, and, dying very young and in his father's life-time, left his widow and infant son in very mean circumstances, his whole substance consisting but of five camels and an Abyssinian female slave. Mohammed was instructed in the business of a merchant, which business his uncle followed; and to that end he took him into Syria, when he was but thirteen years of age, and afterwards recommended him to Khadeejeh, a noble and rich widow, for her factor, in whose service he behaved himself so well, that by making him her husband she soon raised him to an equality with the richest in Mekkeh. His age was then five and twenty years, and hers was forty. After fifteen years from the period of his marriage, his age being now forty, he announced for the first time, that he was sent by God to restore the only true and ancient religion which had been professed by Adam, Noah, Abraham, Moses, Jesus, and all the prophets; or, in other words, to destroy the gross idolatry into which the generality of his countrymen had fallen, and by weeding out the corruptions and superstitions which the later Christians and Jews had introduced into religion, to restore it to its original purity, which consisted chiefly in the worship of one God only. Christianity, wherever it was professed, in the time of Mohammed was most grossly corrupted, both in doctrine and in practice. The notion of the divinity of the Virgin Mary appears, from what is said by commentators on the Koran, to have prevailed widely among the Christians of Arabia. Some, also at the Council of Nice, asserted that there were two gods beside the Father; namely, Christ, and the Virgin Mary; and were thence called Mariamites. Others imagined her to be exempt from humanity, and deified. This opinion is justly condemned in the Koran. Other sects there were, of many denominations, within the borders of Arabia, which took refuge there from the proscriptions of the imperial edicts; and several of their tenets the Koran confirmed.

With regard to the Jews, though they were an inconsiderable and despised people in other parts of the world, yet in Arabia, whither many of them fled after the destruction of Jerusalem, they grew very powerful, several tribes and princes embracing their religion. Mohammed at first showed great regard to them, and many of their opinions, doctrines and customs, were sanctioned by the Koran, but that people, agreeably to their wonted obstinacy, were so far from being his proselytes, that they were some of the bitterest enemies he had, waging continual war with him, so that their reduction cost him infinite trouble and danger, and at last his life—a remarkable coincidence as between Mohammed and Christ.

The eloquence of the Koran; the nature of its principal dogmas (which required no one to whom it was preached to renounce altogether his former faith); the general adaptation of its civil and criminal laws to the existing constitution of Arabian society; the political liberty which it conferred upon the mass of its disciples (by making them equal in the eye of the law,) while it limited the power of those in authority (by religious obligations); the smallness of the taxes which it imposed; the simplicity, completeness, and consistency, of its whole code (which was to be observed always according to its spirit rather than its letter); this had an effect to make his teachings acceptable.

Mohammed had certainly the personal qualifications which were necessary for the accomplishment of his undertaking. The Moslem authors are excessive in their commendations of him, and speak much of his religious and moral virtues; as his piety, veracity, justice, liberality, clemency, humility and abstinence. His charity in particular, they say, was so conspicuous, that he had seldom any money in his house, keeping no more for his own use than was just sufficient to maintain his family; and he frequently spared even some part of his own provisions to supply the necessities of the poor; so that before the year's end he had generally little or nothing left. God, says El-Bukháree, offered him the keys of the treasures of the earth, but he would not accept them. The eastern historians also describe him as a man of an excellent judgment, and a happy memory; and these natural parts were improved by a great experience and knowledge of men, and the observations he had made in his travels. They say he was a person of few words, of an equal and cheerful temper, pleasant and familiar in conversation, of inoffensive behaviour towards his friends, and of great condescension towards his inferiors; to all which were joined a comely, agreeable person, and a polite address, which were of no small service in prepossessing those in his favor whom he attempted to persuade.

As to acquired learning (in the common acceptation of the term) it is confessed that he had none at all, having no other education than what was customary in his tribe. This defect was so far from being prejudicial, or putting a stop to his design, that he made the greatest use of it, insisting that the writings which he produced as revelations from God, could not possibly be a forgery of his own; because it was not conceivable that a person who could neither write nor read should be able to compose a book of such excellent doctrine, and in so elegant a style; and thereby obviating an objection that might have carried a great deal of weight. And for this reason his followers, instead of being ashamed of their master's ignorance, glory in it, as an evident proof of his divine mission, and scruple not to call him (as he is indeed called in the Koran itself) the Illiterate Prophet.

Before Mohammed made any attempt abroad, he rightly judged that it was necessary for him to begin by the conversion of his own household. Having therefore conducted his family to a cave in Mount Hera, near Mekkeh, whither he had been accustomed to retire for a month in every year, for the purposes of religious contemplation and worship, he there opened the secret of his mission to his wife Khadeejeh. He acquainted her that the angel Gabriel had just before appeared to him, and informed him that he was appointed the apostle of God; telling her that the angel had previously addressed him, saying, "Recite," whereupon he said, "And what shall I recite?"—to which Gabriel answered, "Recite, [commencing thus,] In the name of thy Lord, who hath created [all creatures]: he hath created man of a little clot of blood. Recite, and thy Lord is the most Bountiful, who hath taught [the art of writing] by the pen: He hath taught man that which he knew not." Khadeejeh received this news with great joy, swearing by Him in whose hand (that is, at whose disposal) was her soul, that she trusted he would be the prophet of his nation? and immediately communicated what she had heard to her cousin Warikah Ibn-Nowfal, who, being a Christian, could write in the Hebrew character, and was tolerably well versed in the Scriptures ; and he as readily came into her opinion, assuring her that the same angel who had formerly appeared unto Moses was now sent to Mohammed. This first overture the Prophet made in the month of Ramadán, in the fortieth year of his age, which he therefore usually called the first of his mission. The next person to whom Mohammed applied was 'Abd-Allah Ibn-Abee-Koháfeh, surnamed Aboo-Bekr, a man of great authority among the tribe of Kureysh, and one whose interest he well knew would be of great service to him, as it soon appeared, for Aboo-Bekr, being gained over, prevailed also on 'Othmán Ibn-'Affán, 'Abd-

MOHAMMEDANISM. 11

Er-Rahmán, Ibn-'Owf, Saad Ibn-Abee-Wakkás, Ez-Zubeyr Ibn-El-'Owwám, and Talhah Ibn-'Obeyd Allah, all principal men in Mekkeh, to follow his example.

These men were the six chief companions, who, with a few more, were converted in the space of three years; at the end of which, Mohammed, having, as he hoped, a sufficient interest to support him, made his mission no longer a secret. He made the following speech:—"I know not a man among the Arabs who hath brought unto his people a more excellent thing than that which I have brought unto you. I have brought unto you happiness in this life and in that which is to come; for God (whose name be exalted!) hath commanded me to call you unto Him."

Mohammed began to preach in public to the people, who heard him with some patience, till he came to upbraid them with the idolatry, obstinacy, and perverseness of themselves and their fathers; which so highly provoked them, that they declared themselves his enemies, and would soon have procured his ruin, had he not been protected by Aboo-Tálib.

Mohammed was not to be intimidated, telling his uncle plainly, that if they set the sun against him on his right hand, and the moon on his left, he would not leave his enterprise: and Aboo-Tálib, seeing him so firmly resolved to proceed, used no further arguments, but promised to stand by him against all his enemies.

The tribe of Kureysh, finding that they could prevail neither by fair words nor menaces, tried what they could do by force and ill-treatment; using Mohammed's followers so very injuriously, that it was not safe for them to continue at Mekkeh any longer. In the sixth year of his mission Mohammed had the pleasure of seeing his party strengthened by the conversion of his uncle Hamzeh, a man of great valor and merit, and of 'Omar Ibn-El-Khattáb, a person highly esteemed, and once a violent opposer of the prophet. As persecution generally advances rather than obstructs the spreading of a religion, El-Islam made great progress among the Arab tribes.

Mohammed was not wanting to himself. He boldly continued to preach to the public assemblies at the pilgrimage; and while doing so at the 'Akabeh (or Mountain road, in the route of the pilgrims from Mekkeh to Mount 'Arafát,) gained six proselytes, inhabitants of Yethrib (afterwards called El-Medeeneh,) of the Jewish tribe of El Khazraj, who, on their return home, failed not to speak much in commendation of their new religion, and exhorted their fellow citizens to embrace the same.

In the same year, which was the next year after the conversion of the six men of Yethrib, twelve men of that city, of whom ten were of the tribe of El-Khazraj, and the other two of that of Ows, came on a pilgrimage, and made a vow of obedience to Mohammed, and which was to this effect, viz: That they should renounce all idolatory: That they should not steal, nor commit fornication, nor kill their children (as the Pagan Arabs used to do when they apprehended that they should not be able to maintain them,) nor forge lies; and that they should obey the prophet in all things that were right. The next year, being the thirteenth of Mohammed's mission, he chose twelve out of their number, who were to have the same authority among them as the twelve apostles of Christ had among his disciples.

Hitherto Mohammed had employed persuasion only to effect his enterprise. So far was he from allowing his followers to use force, that he exhorted them to bear patiently those injuries which were offered them on account of their faith; and when persecuted himself, he chose rather to quit the place of his birth, and retire to El-Medeeneh, than to make any resistance.

But when the opposition of his enemies had become so great as to threaten the lives of himself and his followers, and the latter were sufficiently numerous to take up arms in self-defence, with a fair prospect of success, he proclaimed that God had allowed him and his followers, to defend themselves against the unbelievers.

When Mohammed's party had become sufficiently numerous and powerful to put those laws in execution, by achieving repeated victories over enemies who might easily have overwhelmed them but for want of union, the number of the nominal Muslims was thereby rapidly increased, and the faith of El-Islám indirectly propagated.

Thus was El-Islám established, and idolatry rooted out, in Mohammed's life-time (for he died the next year,) throughout all Arabia, except only El-Yemámeh: where Museylimeh, who set up also for a prophet, as Mohammed's competitor, had a great party, and was not reduced until the the time of the Khaleefeh Aboo Bekr. The Arabs being them united in one faith and under one prince, found themselves in a condition to make those conquests which extended the dominion of the Muslims, and consequently their faith, over so great a part of the world.

The Koran is universally allowed to be written with the utmost elegance and purity of language, in the dialect of the tribe of Kureysh, the most noble and polite of all the Arabs, but with some mixture, though very rarely, of other dialects. It is confessedly the standard of the Arabic tongue, and, as the more orthodox believe, and are taught by the book itself, inimitable by any human pen, and therefore it is insisted on as a permanent miracle, greater than that of raising the dead, and alone sufficient to convince the world of its divine orgin.

To this miracle did Mohammed himself chiefly appeal for the confirmation of his mission, publicly challenging the most eloquent men in Arabia, which was at that time stocked with thousands whose sole study and ambition it was to excel in elegance of style and composition, to produce even a single chapter that might be compared with it.

The style of the Koran is generally beautiful and fluent, but concise, and often obscure; adorned with bold figures after the eastern taste, enlivened with florid and sententious expressions, and in many places, especially where the majesty and attributes of God are described, sublime and magnificent.

The burthen of the teaching of the Koran is the unity of God, and the duty of man to man; it being laid down therein as a fundamental truth, that there never was, and never can be, more than one true religion; for though the particular laws or ceremonies are only temporary, and subject to alteration, yet the substance of it, being eternal truth, is not liable to change, but continues immutably the same.

Other parts of the Koran are taken up in giving necessary laws and directions, in frequent admonitions to moral and divine virtues, and above all, to the worshipping and reverencing of the only true God, and resignation to His will. The following are among its teachings.

The pious is he who believeth in God, and who giveth money to the needy, those who perform their covenant with men in adversity, (or excessive poverty,) and affliction, (or disease,) and done that which is right (according to God's law) they shall have their reward.

Those who do an evil thing shall be punished, but they who have believed, and done good works, these shall be rewarded.

APPENDIX.

These are they who have purchased error in exchange for right direction, and their traffic hath not been profitable: on the contrary, they have incurred loss. And God encompasseth the unbelievers by his knowledge and his powers, so that they cannot escape him.

Those who have believed in God and done righteous works shall be rewarded, the hypocrites shall be punished.

The service of God is as the similitude of a grain that hath produced seven ears, in each ear a hundred grains.

A kind speech, and forgiveness, are better than alms which harm, or reproach, followeth.

Turn away evil by that which is better (as anger by patience, and ignorance by mildness, and evil conduct by forgiveness;) and lo, he between whom and thyself (was) enmity (shall become) as though he were a warm friend: but none is endowed with this disposition except those who have been patient; and none is endowed with it except him who hath great good fortune.

Verily God commandeth justice, and the doing of good, and the giving unto the relation; and He forbiddeth wickedness and iniquity and oppression: He admonisheth you that ye may reflect.

Give the orphans when they come to age their substance, and render them not in exchange bad for good, and devour not their substance, by adding it to your own substance; for this is a great sin.

Those who do evil ignorantly, and then repent speedily; unto them will God be turned: for God is knowing and wise.

Covet not that which God hath bestowed on some of you preferably to others.

The honest women are obedient, careful in the absence of their husbands, for that God preserveth them by committing them to the care and protection of the men, seek not an occasion of quarrel against them, show kindness unto parents, and relations, and orphans, and the poor, and your neighbor. Verily God will not wrong any one, and if it be a good action he will recompense it with a great reward.

God is a sufficient patron; and God is a sufficient helper.

Those who believe and do that which is right, we will bring into gardens watered by rivers, therein shall they remain for ever.

And ye are also allowed to marry free women living chastely with them neither committing fornication, nor taking them for concubines, observe justice when ye appear as witnesses, and let not hatred towards any induce you to do wrong; but act justly, the Lords renders the reward of their works.

Show kindness unto your parents, whether the one of them, or both of them attain to old age with thee, speak respectfully unto them; and submit to behave humbly towards them, out of tender affection.

Give unto him who is of kin to you his due, and also unto the poor and the traveller. And waste not thy substance profusely; let not thy hand be tied up to thy neck; neither open it with an unbounded expansion, lest thou become worthy of reprehension and be reduced to poverty.

Draw not near unto fornication; for it is wickedness, and an evil way.

Meddle not with the substance of the orphan, unless it be to improve it. Perform your covenant. And give full measure, when you measure aught; and weigh with a just balance.

Walk not proudly in the land.

Whosoever resigneth himself unto God, being a worker of righteousness, taketh hold on a strong handle; and unto God belongeth the issue of all things.

Whosoever desireth excellence; unto God doth all excellence belong; unto him ascendeth the good speech; and the righteous work will he exalt.

Those who believe, and put their trust in their Lord; and who avoid heinous and filthy crimes, and when they are angry forgive; and who give alms.

He who forgiveth, and is reconciled unto his enemy, shall receive his reward.

Let not men laugh other men to scorn; who peradventure may be better than themselves; neither let women laugh other women to scorn; who may possibly be better than themselves. Neither defame one another; nor call one another by opprobrious appellations.

Verily the hypocrites are those who act wickedly.

Consume not your wealth among yourselves in vain; nor present it unto judges, that ye may devour part of men's substance unjustly, against your own consciences.

APPENDIX.

BUDDHISM.

The foresight of the great founder of this system was justified by its prodigious, its unparallelled, its enduring success—a success that rested on the assertion of the dogma of the absolute equality of all men, and this in a country that for ages had been oppressed by castes.

Buddhism arose about the tenth century before Christ, its founder being Arddha Chiddi, a native of Capila, near Nepaul, 1000 B. C. The Sanscrit words occuring in Buddhism attest its Hindu orgin. Buddha, itself being Sanscrit for intelligence. After the system had spread widely in India, it was carried by Missionaries into Ceylon, Tartary, Thibet, China, Japan, Burmah, and is now professed by a greater portion of the human race than any other system of theology. Until quite recently, the history of Arddha Chiddi, and the system he taught have, notwithstanding their singular interest, been very imperfectly known in Europe. He was born in affluence, and of a royal family. In his twenty-ninth year he retired from the world, the pleasures of which he had tasted, and of which he had become weary. Leaving his numerous wives, he became a religious mendicant. Profoundly impressed with the vanity of human affairs, he devoted himself to philosophical meditation, by severe self-denial, emancipating himself from all worldly hopes and cares. For the name by which his parents had called him, he substituted that of Gotama, or "he who kills the senses." It is claimed that Gotama was born under the shade of a tree, and that he overcame the love of the world, and the fear of death; under the shade of a tree he preached his first sermon in the shroud, and under the shade of a tree he died.

In four months after he commenced his ministry, he had five disciples; at the close of the year they had increased to twelve hundred. In the twenty-nine centuries that have passed, and since that time they have given rise to sects counting millions of souls, outnumbering the followers of all other religious teachers. The system still seems to retain much of its pristine vigor; yet so much of all the systems of worship as consist of creeds and theologies, gotten up by particular men, are perishable. The religion given by God to all men alone endureth. Gotama died at the advanced age of eighty years; his corpse was burnt eight days subsequently.

But several years before this event, his system must be considered as thoroughly established. It shows how little depends upon the nature of a doctrine, and how much upon effective organization, that Buddhism, the principles of which are far above the reach of popular thought, should have been propagated with so much rapidity, for it made converts by preaching and not, like Mohammedanism, by the sword.

Shortly after Gotama's death, a council of five-hundred ecclesiastics assembled for the purpose of settling the doctrine. A century later, a second council met to regulate the monastic institution. In proclaiming the equality of all men in this life, the Buddhists, as we have seen, came into direct collision with the orthodox creed of India, long carried out into practice in the institution of castes—a collision that was embittered by the abhorrence the Buddhists displayed for any distinction between the clergy and laity.

The fundamental principle of Buddhism is that there is a supreme impelling Power in the universe, a self-existent principle, it rejects inquiry into first causes as being unphilosophical, and considers that phenomena alone can be dealt with by our finite minds.

The Buddhist denies the immediate interposition of any such agency as Providence, maintaining that the system of nature, once arising, must proceed irresistibly according to the laws which brought it into being. To the Brahman priesthood such ideas were particularly obnoxious; they were hostile to any philosophical system founded on the principle that the world is governed by law, for they suspected that its tendency would be to leave them without any mediatory functions, and therefore without any claims on the faithful. Equally does Gotama deny the existence of chance, saying that that which we call chance, is nothing but the effect of an unknown, unvoidable cause.

He will not, however, recognize any vicarious action. Each one must work out for himself his own salvation.

The philosophical ability displayed in the Buddhism creeds is very great; indeed, it may be doubted whether Europe has produced its metaphysical equivalent.

In its early ages, Buddhism had its fables, legends, and miracles Its humble devotees implicitly believed that Mohamaia; the mother of Gotama, an immaculate Virgin, conceived him through a divine influence, and that thus he was of the nature of God and

B

man conjoined; that he stood upon his feet and spoke at the moment of his birth; that at five months of age he sat unsupported in the air: that at the moment of his conversion he was attacked by a legion of demons, and that in his penance-fasting he reduced himself to the allowance of one pepper-pod a day; that he had been incarnate many times before, and that on his ascension through the air to heaven he left his footprints on a mountain in Ceylon which is to be worshipped; that there is a paradise of gems, and flowers, and feasts, and music for the good, and a hell of sulphur, and flames, and torment for the wicked; that it is lawful to resort to the worship of images, that there are spirits, and goblins, and other superhuman forms, that there is a queen of heaven; that the reading of the scriptures is in itself an actual merit; whether its precepts are followed or not; that prayer may be offered by saying a formula by rote, or even by turning the handle of a mill from which invocations written on paper issue forth, that the revealer of Buddhism is to be regarded as the religious head of the world.

He alone who flees to Buddha, who clings to doctrine and the Church—he will understand right purely and clearly the fourfold lofty truth.

The reader cannot fail to mark the resemblance of these ideas to some of those of the Roman Church.

Decorated with these extraneous but popular recommendations, Buddhism has been embraced by four-tenths of the human race. It has a prodigious literature, great temples, and many monuments. Its Monasteries are scattered from the north of Tartary almost to the equinoctial line. In these an education is imparted not unlike that of the European monasteries of the middle ages. It has been estimated that in Tartary one-third of the population are Lamas. There are single convents containing more than two thousand individuals; the wealth the country voluntarily pours into them. Elementary education is more widely diffused than in Europe. It is rare to meet with a person who cannot read. Among the priests there are many who are devout, and as might be expected, many who are impostors. The result is that under the extensive education and information that prevails throughout these countries, the creeds and theologies based upon their early fables, legends, and miracles, are verging into indifference with the masses, as is the case among the educated in Christian countries.

BUDDHISM. 19

The formula under which they live is, "That creeds and theologies are many. The Religion of Brotherhood is one; we are Brothers."

They smile at the credulity of the good-natured Tartars, who believe in the wonders of miracle-workers, for they have miracle-workers, who can perform the most supernatural cures, who can lick red-hot iron, who can cut open their bowels, and, by passing their hand over the wound make themselves whole again, who can raise the dead. In China, these miracles, with all their authentications, have descended to the conjuror, and are performed for the amusement of children.

According to the most credible of the accounts that have come down to us we find in the Founder of the theology of India a character so noble, self-sacrificing, and overflowing with brotherly love, combined at the same time with such sobriety in his mode of action that any idea of either imposture or insanity in his case is utterly inadmissible.

Of the Buddhistic writings that have appeared since the time of Burnouf, either in the original text or in translations, the most important is the text of the oldest Pali book, which is also regarded by all parties among the Buddhists, as the highest authority, the "*Dhamapadam*," or "Footprints of the Law," which is a collection of Aphorisms. These, as well as Westergard's labors, we owe to the praiseworthy encouragement of the Danish Government.

We give the following, selected from THE THREE THOUSAND BUDDHA PROVERBS:

Though a thousand words should range themselves in the empty swell of thy speech.

Far better is one speech full of meaning that shall give one man rest.

Though a thousand words the hymn should number in the empty swell of thy words.

Far better is a single word that shall bring rest to one man.

He who should conquer in battle ten times a hundred thousand were indeed a hero.

But truly a greater hero is he who has but once conquered himself.

To conquer one's self is a greater victory than to gain a battle:

The victory of him who tames himself, who at all times knows how to rule himself.

Neither God nor Gandava, neither Mara nor yet Brahma, can frustrate such a victory, obtained by such a man.

Though one should offer a thousand sacrifices every month, and offer them for a hundred years.

He who for only one moment contemplates himself in utter repose,—that is repose of conscience,—he has performed a better act of devotion than by a hundred years' sacrifices.

And though one should keep the sacred flame alight for a hundred years in a forest.

He who for only one moment contemplates himself in utter repose.

His one act of devotion is better than a hundred years' sacrifices.

Whatever sacrifices the whole world might offer in a year.

Whatever sacrifice any might offer in the hope of reward.

That all is not worth one-quarter so much, as he who cherishes reverence for the virtuous.

He who cherishes reverence in his heart, and ever honors his superiors, to him shall be ever added these four gifts:

Long Life, Beauty, Joy, Power.

He who lives in lust for a hundred years, ever unquiet in his heart.

Much better is a single day of a temperate thoughtful life.

He who lives in folly for a hundred years, ever restless.

Much better is a single day of meditation upon wisdom.

He who lives a hundred years, faint-heartedly, without energy of mind.

Much better is a single day used with firm will and energy.

He who lives a hundred years, not reflecting on the origin and end of life.

Much better is a single day of him who marks its origin and end.

He who lives a hundred years, and does not behold the path to immortality.

Much better is a single day of him who descries that path.

He who lives a hundred years and never discerns the loftiness of the Law.

Much better is a single day of him who beholds the heights of that same.

He who is invincible, whom no one in this world has power to restrain.

Buddha, whose glance explores the Infinite.

Buddha, the Trackless, what track shall lead you to behold him?

He whom no lust can ensnare, whom none can allure to his soul's poison.

The gods themselves envy those who never grow faint and weary of heart.

But rejoice in continual repose, full of remembrance the enlightened one's.

Man's birth is full of trouble, and full of toil is his life also.

Toilsome it is to hearken to true teaching, very toilsome is the beginning of true enlightenment.

Not to do evil, to leave nothing good undone, to keep the course of our thought ever pure.

This is commanded to Buddhas.

The best prayer is patience, ever gentle.

To Buddhas *Nirvana* is the name of that which is alone good.

No tamer of his senses will he become who smites another.

No penitent he who does harm to his neighbor.

To refrain at all times from angry words, and never to do another injury.

To observe temperance in eating and in sleeping on a lonely couch.

To live in profoundest meditation, lo! this is enjoined on the Buddhas.

A shower of wealth will not suffice to our desires; little joy will covetous desires bring thee, but many sorrows, and wise is he who understands this.

Not even revelling with the gods will give joy to a truly wise man.

He who is truly wise, rejoices only in this, that desire is dead within him.

Men who are still enslaved to fear seek many ways of refuge.

They flee to mountain and forest, and resort for shelter to sacred trees.

But that is no sure sanctuary, the highest refuge it never is.

Never will that man be freed from pain who chooses such for his refuge.

He who dutifully honors the men that are of quiet spirit and without fear.

That is verily a good work, that can never be too highly esteemed.

He who has put off sin is called good.

He who leads a silent life.

He who is free from self-love is called a tamer of the senses.

He whose body, words and heart, are altogether without sin; he who holds these three in rein, yea, him do I call good.

He who has discerned the true meaning of the law of piety.

Let him reverence it evermore.

What will jewelled hair profit thee, O fool, or garments set with costly fur?

Unclean hast thou left thy heart, while decking thy outside.

He who hast burst all fetters and trembles before nothing, the unshackled, the truly free, him do I call wise.

The sage whose clear vision beholds high things, discerning the true path and the false path.

Who has climbed to the heights of all things, him do I call a Brahmana.

He who will not punish a beast that is weak, who will not strike or suffer others to strike one that is strong, him do I call a Brahmana.

He who when assailed does not resist, but speaks mildly to his tormentors.

He who grudges nothing to those who grudge him all, him alone I call a Brahmana.

He who has put from him desire and hatred, pride and hypocrisy.

As a grain that flies from the point of an arrow, him do I call a Brahmana.

He whose speech is gentle, truthful, and ever instructive.

He who never utters a harsh word, him only do I call a Brahmana.

He who strives not to obtain aught for himself, who never doubts after he has once perceived the truth, he who has come to know immortality, him alone do I call a Brahmana.

He who is pure as the moon, whose even spirit naught can ruffle, who has quenched all lusts, him do I call a Brahmana.

BUDDHISM. 23

He who has cast behind him all lusts, and wanders harmless abroad.

He who has quenched his lusts, him only do I call a Brahmana.

The Noble one, standing like a stately bull, the Hero, the Seer, free from all lust, the Pure, the Wise, him only do I call a Brahmana.

The whole life and labors of this wonderful man are in perfect harmony. He did not enter into open hostility with the established religion, as regards the ancient rites connected with the worship of fire.

Buddha prescribes to every disciple and follower, certain initial commands, of which four are purely ethical, and the fifth a perfectly general injunction to temperance. Here is the text:—

I. Not to kill that which has life.
II. Not to steal.
III. Not to commit any unchaste act.
IV. Not to lie.
V. To drink no intoxicating liquor.

Only in later times were these expanded into ten, and then into fifteen commandments, by the addition of precepts about externals. That he did not wish to have the third commandment obeyed after the fashion of Origen, is shown by a fine saying forming the twenty-ninth of his forty-two Theses.

"If the spirit, which is the Master, be kept under control, it follows of itself that his servants will also be restrained. What does it avail if the power, but not the wish, to do wrong, be vanquished?"

How strongly he was opposed to bodily austerities is proved by this sentence in his first sermon:

"He who desires to become an object of respect (Arya) must beware of two things, of sinful lusts, and of the bodily austerities of the Brahmans."

Unregenerated, isolated, is every one who remains subject to his desires, whether he be a laymen or an Arya. The oldest comprehensive formula of the Buddhist faith which has been found under an ancient Buddha pyramid in India, on innumerable inscriptions, and which regularly forms the conclusion of the sacred books, and in Ceylon, as well as in Burmah and Thibet, all, even women and children, know by heart, is this:

"The states of all beings which proceed from a cause, the cause thereof has the Blessed One declared; what can heal these states has the Hermit also declared."

What we have translated *States* or *Conditions* is called in Sanscrit, *Dharma*, in Pali, *Dhamma;* and signifies originally Law, Duty; and in a secondary sense, that which exists as a legitimate, necessary consequence of a cause; hence, a condition of being. If we ponder this simple aphorism we see that it involves the "four venerable Truths," which form the substratum, laid by Buddha's own hand, of the later metaphysical erections:—

Existence is suffering (pain.)
Suffering is seen to be the necessary consequence of causes.
To this suffering an end ought to be put.
To this end there is a means, and this also has Buddha taught.

The Sutra of the Forty-two Sayings of Buddha.

There are ten modes in which men may practice virtue, or contrariwise, vice. Of these ten vices, three have reference to the body, four to the speech, three to the mind. The three vices of the body are; murder, theft, and unchastity. Those of speech are; lying, talking nonsense, harsh words, false witness; of the mind; avarice, malice, stupid unbelief in the three precious truths, together with the cherishing of false opinions.

When men have done many wrong things without feeling repentance, the fruit of the evil that they have gradually heaped together in themselves will come to ripeness; just as rivers which are about to discharge themselves into the mighty ocean, and are already deep, spread themselves out wide so that they can with difficulty be crossed. In men who perceive when they have done wrong and then reform, the laws of virtue gather strength, and evil subsides more and more, so that they are able to come to the way of perfectness.

When wicked men would fain do injury to good ones, it is as though they cast forth their spittle against heaven. Heaven cannot be defiled by their spittle, but only themselves. In like manner, when one tries to throw ashes upon another against the wind, and the dust cannot reach the other, but falls back on him who throws it; so is he who shows no honor to the good himself, degraded by the fact that he wished to injure a good man.

In the world there are twenty things which are difficult, viz: it is difficult to confer a gift when one is poor; difficult to learn the way (the true religion of Buddha) when one is rich: difficult to renounce life through the power of the Spirit; difficult to descry the law of the excellent doctrine; difficult to be born again in the region where true Buddhas come into being; difficult to have no desire when one has looked on something pleasant; difficult it is for the powerful not to make use of his power; difficult not to be angry with those who revile us; difficult to set about a work when one has no clear idea of it; difficult to arrive at perfection, even when one has learned much about it; difficult not to despise those who have learnt nothing; difficult to conquer self-seeking pride; difficult to meet with a friend of virtue; difficult to learn the way, when one knows the self-will of one's own heart; difficult to sustain a collision unmoved; difficult to put in practice the means conformable to wisdom; difficult to act in consonance with nature; difficult to attain to equanimity; difficult not to speak of that which has to be done and to be avoided.

What is the highest virtue! To keep one's feet in the way is the highest virtue. What is the chief greatness? To act in accordance with the laws of wisdom is the chief greatness. Who is the chief of the powerful? He who, while he himself is full of toleration, commits no sinful act, men will assuredly honor. Who is pre-eminently enlightened? He who is without spot and pure, has no unrighteous courses, is wholly clean, and who knows in every age, from the beginning of the world till now all that is to be found in all the ten regions, though it be unknown, invisible, quite unnoticed and unheard, without desiring the least thing for himself; such an one is to be called enlightened.

A being whose soul is affected by passion, cannot perceive the way for his blinded eyes. If you throw five different colors into turbid waters, and then stir them up together, the persons who look therein will be unable to discern the reflection of their bodies. Just so, those whose souls are agitated and obscured by passion, are unable to discern the Way. Those, on the contrary, who, full of faith, confess the whole string of their faults, improve their ways and show kindness to the friends of virtue, will discern the Way, just as a reflection becomes visible in water, so soon as it is cleansed from impurities. When the spots of the soul are wholly cleansed away, apprehension discovers whence she has come, and how she has arisen, and toward what fields of Buddha she will travel after death, and at the same time she comes to perceive the virtues of the Way.

When we gaze on the sky and the earth, we ought to reflect that they are not eternal. When we behold the hills and valleys, we ought to remember that they are not eternal. When we see the form and figure of objects increase and expand, we ought to reflect that they are not eternal. If we think thus, we shall soon reach the Way.

Although we attribute being to the elementary components of the body, yet have they nevertheless no real subsistence. For since their being ceases after a short time, and does not endure forever, they are like illusory semblances.

It is with those beings who, impelled by passion, strive after glory, even as it is with the vapor of a smoker. When the vapor of the tobacco is perceived and diffused itself abroad, it cannot continue to subsist after the tobacco is consumed. So will those foolish persons who strive after the vain glory of the world, and do not labor to win the true glory, when they have obtained that which they seek for, be poor and a prey to regrets.

Beauty and wealth are like honey on the edge of a knife. When little boys taste it, they wound their tongue and feel pain.

He who yields himself to passion, is like a fool who takes a candle and walks against the wind. Unless he throw the candle away he will assuredly suffer smart by his hand being burnt. He who suffers himself to be carried away by lust, by anger, or by illusion, is forasmuch as he has not been beforehand enlightened by the Way, like unto those fools who, refusing to throw away their candle, burn their hands and suffer severe pain.

As a tree that has fallen into a river, if when swept by the current it does not touch either shore, if it be not caught up by men, or stopped in its course by good, or evil spirits, if moreover it do not lie in a stagnant pool, and do not decay, may actually come to reach the ocean; even so I tell you, that men who, if they learn the Way, are not befooled by passion, nor seized by perverseness, who do not become unstable, but strive with earnestness, of a truth may attain the Way.

O Shramana! trust not in your own hearts. We must in no wise trust to our own hearts. Exercise watchfulness; do not be ensnared by beauty, else it will bring you sorrow. You must regard an old woman as a mother, those only a little older than yourself as elder sisters, those younger, as younger sisters.

As one must run away with all speed if flame be kindled among dry grass, so must men who would learn the Way, cast far away from them all objects calculated to excite passion.

If a man surrender himself to passion, it brings pain, and pain brings fear. If passion remain far from him, no pain springs up; and if no pain, no fear.

As iron when it has been smelted and purified, gradually wrought and refined by hammering, may be converted into all sorts of vessels, so also will those who are learning the Way, if their mind is gradually freed from all impurity, and if they sedulously exert themselves, no doubt attain to perfect insight. In the contrary case, they earn to themselves vexation; from vexation springs tribulation, and under sharp tribulation they turn back from the Way, thus do they heap sinful actions one upon another.

Both the men who walk in the way, and those who do not so, alike experience sorrow. It is indeed hard to measure how much suffering a being has to undergo from birth to old age, and then in old age from sickness till his death. But if the mind be bewildered through trouble, and have heaped sinful acts upon itself, then tho sufferings that will befall him on account of all that he has done from his birth to his death, cannot be put in words.

O Shramanas! as a laden ox that has fallen into a slough, in spite of all weariness, struggles out to one or the other side without ever thinking of rest, so must a right-minded man labor for nothing but the Way—seeing that the danger arising from the slough of passion is much more urgent—and avert from himself the pain of the cycle, [thus the "cycle" must be in this life.]

Originally Buddhism was simple, ethical, and rational: and hence hostile to mythology, scholasticism, ceremonies, and priestcraft. It was benevolent and humane in the highest degree. It called all men, without any distinction of quality or position, to its fold, opening to all the way of salvation, which it teaches to be attainable by purity of conduct. "There is but one law for all: severe punishment for crime, and great reward for virtue." "My law is one of grace for all; like heaven affording room for men and women, for boys and girls, for rich and poor." "It is difficult to be rich and learn the way." The total number of Buddhists is about 290,000,000.

Right view, right sense, right speech, right action, right position right energy, right memory, and right meditation. "Such is the formula of faith," found upon many monuments, as well as in many books. The essence of Buddhistic morality, is "to eschew every thing bad, to perform every thing good, to tame one's thoughts"—this is the doctrine of Buddha.

All the mythology, sacrifices, penances, hierarchy, scholasticism, mysticism, which we find connected with it, have been super-added in progress of time, in different countries, and under manifold circumstances. A general love of all beings is its nucleus; each animal being our neighbor or possibly relative. To love even our enemies, to offer our lives for animals, to abstain even from defensive warfare, to gain the greatest of victories by conquering oneself, to avoid all vices, to practise of humility and mildness, to be obedient to superiors, to cherish and respect parents, old age, learning, virtuous and holy men, to provide food, shelter, and comfort for men, and animals, to plant trees on the roads, dig wells, &c.—such are the moral duties of Buddhists. No religion is despised by them, religious wars waged against dissenters have never been heard of among them. "Honor your own faith, and do not slander that of others," is a Buddhistic maxim. The persecutions of Christians in Japan, China, Siam, &c., are occasioned by other than religious causes, being commonly reprisals against their intermeddling habits. How different from the history of Christianity.

THE BURMESE.

The following contains the main features of the Theology and religious precepts which have been taught among the Burmese for the last twenty-five hundred years.

The Burmese Empire comprises the tract of territory bounded on the south by the Indian Ocean, on the east by the kingdom of Siam, on the west by Bengal, and on the north by the kingdom of Azen, and the Chinese Empire. It includes not only the kingdom of Ava, but likewise those of Pegu, and Aracan, together with the pretty states of Martaban, Sarvai, Merghi.

According to the sacred books and traditions of the Burmese, four Gods have at different periods appeared in the present world, and have obtained the state of Neban; Chaucasen, Gonagon,

THE BURMESE. 29

Gaspar and Godama. It is claimed by the Burmese Theology that the law of the last mentioned, (to wit, Godama,) is at present obligatory among men. He obtained the privilege of divinity at the age of thirty-five, when he began to promulgate his laws, in which employment he spent forty-five years. Having thus lived to the age of eighty in the practice of every good work, and having conferred salvation on every living creature, he was assumed into the state of Niban. From that time to the year 1763, there have passed two thousand three hundred and six years.

Godama spoke and taught as follows: " I, a God, after having departed out of this world, will preserve my laws and my disciples in it for the space of five thousand years." Having likewise commanded that his statue and relics should be carefully kept, and adored during this period, he thereby gave rise to the custom of adoring them.

The books, which contain the history of Godama, represent him as a king, who having laid aside the ensigns of royalty, withdrew himself into a solitary place, put on the habit of a Talapoin, and gave himself up to the study and practice of virtue.

His merits, united to his present generous abdication, procured for him at the age of thirty, the gift of divine wisdom. This consists in seeing into the thoughts of all living beings, in the foreknowledge of all future events, however distant they may be, in the knowledge of the merits and demerits of all men; in the power of working miracles particularly by causing fire and water to issue from his eyes at the same time, or fire from one eye and water from the other; and finally in a tender love toward all things living. Among other prodigies related of him, we may notice the one said to have happened at his birth; for he was no sooner born than he walked seven paces towards the north, exclaiming; "I am the noblest and greatest among men. This is the last time that I shall be born; never again shall I be conceived in the womb."

During the forty-five years that he spent on earth after becoming a God, he was continually employed in the promulgation of his laws, and it is said that through his preaching, 2,400,000,000 persons obtained the Niban.

Previous to his death, he recommended that his statue and relics should be preserved and adored.

These have hence become objects of veneration to all the Burmese, wherever they are met with; but they are more particularly worshipped, with greater pomp and by greater numbers in the Pagodas. These are pyramidal or conical buildings, made of brick, painted and gilded on the outside.

In these temples there is generally a niche in which is placed the statue of Godama, though in some, both the niche and the statue are wanting. These are the public places of adoration for the Burmese, and are generally set apart from all other buildings, and surrounded by a wall of the same materials as the Pagoda itself.

But the laws of Godama will be observed upon earth for the space of five thousand years, reckoning from the day of his death, five hundred and twenty years before Christ; from which year therefore the Burmese begin their era. Of this period two thousand three hundred and ninety years have already elapsed. As soon as it is at an end, the laws of Godama will cease to be binding, and another God must appear to promulgate a new code for the government of mankind.

The principal duties of the Talapoins, or priests, is the Terà, or preaching to the people; and that in the performance of this duty, they ought to propose as their model the sermons of Godama. The book which contains them is called Sottan, or the rule of life, and is one of the principal works which the Burmese possess.

The following is the best of the, so-claimed, true faith.

Is Godama the only true God in the world?

Yes, Godama is the only true and real God, who knows the laws of the four Sizza, and in whose power it is to raise to the state of Niban.

For a thousand years beforehand, the approaching appearance of a new God was reported; but previous to his coming, six different pretenders, each with five hundred disciples, started up, and gave themselves out for Gods.

Did these false Gods preach and teach any laws?

Yes, but what they taught is false and full of errors.

But when the true God, Godama, appeared, did these false Gods renounce their doctrines?

Some renounced and some did not; and many have remained obstinate to the present day. When Godama saw that many persisted in their errors, he gave a challenge to them all, who could work the greatest miracle under a mango tree. It was accepted, but Godama gained the victory, at which the chief of the Deitti was so vexed, that he threw himself into a river with an earthenware vessel tied about his neck. After the death of their leader many of his disciples abandoned his false doctrines, but others remained obstinate: for it is easy to draw a thorn out of the hand or foot by means of the nails or the *megnac*, but it is very difficult to eradicate false doctrine from the hearts of the Deitti.

But are there no means of doing it?

Yes, it may be done by the doctrine of Godama, and by the lessons of good men; which are like a megnac, of great excellence.

And what are these lessons and doctrines?

First, that all who kill animals or do any thing contrary to the ten commandments, are subject to the punishments allotted to evil deeds. Then that those who give alms and practise the ten good deeds, adore God, the law, and the Talapoins, will enjoy the blessings attached to the performance of good works. Secondly, that these two kinds of works, the good and the bad, and these alone accompany a man through his transmigration in future worlds, in the same way as a shadow follows the body to which it belongs; and that these are the efficient causes of all the good and evil that happen to living beings, in this life or in the next; of high and low birth; of riches and poverty; of transportation to the seats of the Nat, and of condemnation to the state of animals or to hell. These, together with the following, are the revelations made, and the precepts taught by Godama. According to the species of their bad works, the wicked are condemned to punishment. These species are four, according to the Burmese sacred books. One is called grievous, the other three are venial.

To kill one's own mother or father, to kill a priest or Talapoin, to strike or wound any God, as Beodat did who threw a stone against the Godama, and to sow discord among Talapoins, are the five sins that constitute the grievous class; for which the wicked will have to suffer fire and other dreadful torments, in one of the greater hells, the whole duration of a world.

This species of sins is called the first, because it is the first to produce its effect: for although the individual, who has committed one of these five sins, may have done many good deeds, yet he cannot receive the reward, till after this first species is expiated, by his having paid the penalty of that great sin.

After this class come all sins of habit; which although in themselves light, are nevertheless, on account of the evil habit, considered as punishable in the greater hells. The fourth and last species comprises all evil desires, and these are expiated, not in the greater hells but in the minor ones that surround them.

All passionate, quarrelsome, fraudulent and cruel men, all who in their deeds, words or desires, are either dishonest or lascivious, will be cut to pieces after death, in one of the greater hells with instruments of burning iron, and afterwards exposed to the most severe cold; and the parts cut off returning again to their former state, will be a second time cut off, and exposed to the same cold, and in these alternate torments, they will pass five hundred infernal years.

All those who by signs or words insult their relatives or masters, priests, old men, or observers of the law, and all who with nets or snares kill animals, will be condemned to one of the greater hells, there to be tormented upon a fiery bed, by continual lacerations with red-hot wire, and by being sawn with fiery scythes into eight or sixteen pieces, for the course of one thousand infernal years.

Whoever does not assist his fellow creatures, those who, in a state of intoxication commit unlawful and indecent actions, they who dishonor or ill-treat others, will have their bowels burnt up, by a flame entering through their mouths; and this punishment will last four thousand infernal years.

Whoever takes away furtively or by deception, fraud, or open force the property of others, such ministers and judges as receive bribes for deciding suits unjustly, mandarins and generals that desolate the enemy's lands, all who cheat by false scales, weights, or measures, or who in any way appropriate to themselves the goods of others, as well as all who steal or damage things belonging to priests and to Pagodas, etc. all such will be tormented in one of the greater hells, by fire and smoke; which penetrating through the eyes and mouth and all the other inlets of the body, will burn them alive for the course of eight thousand infernal years.

Those who sell wines or poisons, or set fire to villages, cities or woods, in order to destroy animals, those who with poison or arms, or enchantments cause men to perish; all these after death, being hurled headlong from a very high mountain, will be received on the point of a red hot spit, and cut in pieces by the infernal ministers with swords and spears: and this punishment will last sixteen thousand infernal years.

All who honor not their parents, masters and old men; all who drink wine or other inebriating liquors; all who corrupt the waters of lakes or wells, or break up the roads; all dishonest dealers; they who speak bitterly and impatiently, or beat with their hands or with sticks; those who despise the counsel of honest men, and afflict their neighbor; evil-speakers, detractors, the passionate and envious; such as injure others, or torment them by putting them in chains; all who in word, deed, or desire are guilty of evil; lastly, those who afflict the sick with harsh words will be condemned to these minor places of punishment, to be there tortured, in proportion to the heinousness of their offences and evil habits. Besides these hells, there is another, consisting of an immense cauldron, full of melted copper, to ascend and descend which from one surface to the other, requires three thousand years. To this task are condemned the lascivious, that is to say, those who violate the wives, daughters or sons of others; and those who through life despising acts of charity and the observance of holidays, give themselves up to drunkenness and excess. Those equilateral spaces full of very cold water, are also, according to the Burmese books so many hells; to which are condemned all who offend or insult their parents or the observers of the law.

Every one may gain merit or demerit, according to his works, and so pass to a superior or inferior situation.

Rape, highway robbery, murder, and arson are considered the principal capital offences.

False witnesses, who assert anything from passion, and not from love of truth; (and those who affirm what they have neither seen nor heard), are severely punished with death.

Every species of good works, such as alms-deeds, chastity, charity, kindness, diligence, patience, justice, magnanimity, love and moderation, is enjoined, all who adore God and the law, will enjoy the blessings attached to the performance of good works.

Good and bad works accompany a man through future worlds, and are the efficient causes of all the good and evil that happen to living beings in this life, or in the next.

We are forbidden to kill any living thing, to steal; to violate the wives or concubines of another; to tell lies or to deceive; and to use wine, opium, or any intoxicating liquor—also, to covet our neighbor's goods, to envy, and to wish misfortune or death to others.

Whosoever abstains from all these evil deeds will increase in virtue, till, at length, he will obtain the perfect happiness of Niban.

Admit of no unlawful act, even though it be sought to be committed in secret; by the observance of which, a man is preserved from evil-doing.

Searching after the means, by which the hearts of creatures may put off all evil inclinations.

Thee, therefore, do we supplicate, who alone knowest all these things to reveal them to us.

To whom the God replied, know, that to keep far from the company of the ignorant; to be always in the society of the learned; and to give respect and honor to whom they are due; overcoming any inordinate affection; by the choice of a place of abode proper to one's station, and adapted for satisfying all the common wants of life; by having always in store, some merit acquired in a former life; and by ever maintaining in one's own person a prudent carriage; the comprehension of all things that are not evil; the knowledge of the duties of one's state of life; and the observance of piety and modesty in words; these are most excellent means by which we may renounce all wicked actions.

By ministering to one's father and mother proper sustenance, by providing for one's wife and children, by the purity and honesty of every action; by alms-deeds, by the observance of divine precepts; by succoring in their necessities those who are united to us by the ties of kindred; by everything else in which there is no sin; by all these means may we be preserved from evil deeds.

By such a freedom from all faults, that not even the inferior part of the soul manifest any affection for them, by the abstinence from all intoxicating drinks; by the never-failing practice of works of piety; by showing respect to all; by being humble before all; by sobriety; by gratitude to our benefactors; and finally by listening from time to time to the preaching of the word of God; by these means may we overcome our inclinations, and keep ourselves from sin.

The virtue of patience; docility in receiving the admonitions of good men; frequent visits to priests; spiritual conferences on the divine laws; frugality and modesty in our exterior; the observance of the letter of the law; having ever before our eyes the state into which living creatures will pass after death; and finally, the mediation of the happy reposes of the Niban, these are all distinguished precepts for preserving man from wickedness.

That intrepidity and serenity of mind, which good men preserve amid the calamities of life, in abundance and want, in censure and praise, in joy and distress, in popularity and abandonment; the absence of all fear or inquietude of heart; the freedom from the dark mist of concupiscence: these are rare gifts that remove a man far away from all affection to evil.

Imprint well upon your heart the precepts I have just delivered; let them be deeply rooted there, and see to put them in execution, also hospitality to our guests, and to travellers, ministering to the wants of the sick, and in times of scarcity to those of all persons.

But all these are surpassed in merit by the adoration of God and the law.

Godama confirmed all these his precepts, and added that the real adoration of God does not consist in offering him rice, flowers or sandal wood, but in the observance of his laws.

All who aspire to perfection must be careful to avoid the works which do hurt to living creatures; by thus flying away from evil, and ever seeking to acquire merit in this life, as well as in future ones, they will at length attain to the Niban.

The words that do hurt to living creatures, are murder, theft, deceit and adultery.

All those committed by judges, when on account of presents, consanguinity or friendship, they decide unjustly, when through hatred to the party who has reason on his side; they pronounce against him, and finally when through fear or respect of persons, as of mandarins, or rich, or powerful men, they commit injustice. Those offenders also, are here comprised, who do not divide property equally as they ought, through love, fear or hatred.

Besides this, a man must refrain from the things that are called ruinous; which are, the love of intoxicating liquors, the custom of wandering about the streets at unseasonable hours, too great a passion for dancing, games and spectacles, gaming, frequenting vicious company, lastly, slothfulness and negligence in the performance of one's duty.

For from these spring six great evils.

Drunkenness is the cause of loss of goods and reputation, of quarrels, diseases, immodesty of dress, disregard of honor; unseasonable wanderings expose a man to great dangers, and by keeping him from his family, oblige him to leave the chastity of his wife and daughter unprotected; and moreover, his possessions are thus liable to depredations.

A passion for shows draws a man from his occupation, and hinders him from gaining his livelihood.

In gaming, success is followed by intrigues and quarrels; loss, by bitterness and sorrow of heart; as well as dilapidation of fortune; the gamester is incapacitated by law to give testimony.

Finally, frequenting the company of the vicious will lead a man into the houses of women of ill-fame, into drunkenness and gluttony, into deceit and robbery, and all kinds of disorders.

Godama denounced the following: making show of friendship without having its reality, professing a love which they do not feel, giving little, that they may receive much, and being friends to a man only because he is rich, or because they have need of his favor.

Real friends, are those who are such both in adversity and prosperity; those who give good advice on proper occasions, even at the peril of their lives; those who take care of things that belong to him whom they love; those who teach a man what is good, who are delighted in his prosperity, and sorrowful in his misfortunes.

Children are in particular obliged to respect their parents, and to listen to their words and advice.

Parents on the other hand with respect to their children, must keep them far from all wickedness, procure that they always have good companions, they must instruct them, and teach them to give alms, and do other pious works, and when they have arrived at the proper age, be careful to marry them.

The husband should speak to his wife respectfully, should not ill-treat her, should not desert her to live with another woman.

A master should adapt the labors of his slaves to their strength and capacities, should give them their maintenance, should treat them well, but particularly be attentive to them when sick.

Slaves should look to the interests of their masters in their labors, and take nothing but what is allowed them.

We should divide our goods and share them with the poor; for the poor are our companions in the journey to a future life. Alms done by a poor man is of greater merit than of a rich one.

The only faithful companions who will not desert us in the life to come, are our good deeds; and the only good that will continue with us unaltered even to old age, is the observance of the law, for this no thief can take away.

Godama exhorts to lay aside every sentiment of pride; not to let the affections be occupied by this world, not to give ourselves up to the pleasures of sense, but to aspire to Niban alone. Having what is sufficient to satisfy our hunger to-day, we should not think of to-morrow; and that having one coat, we should not wish for another.

He admonishes not to look upon indecent objects, not to listen to lascivious song, not to give way to murmuring, not to exceed in the pleasures of the palate and to restrain the hands from unlawful touches, and to observe modesty in our exterior.

Those who pride themselves in their birth, or in their possessions can never reach to the Niban. All must observe modesty in their five bodily senses; they must not run after feasts and such vanities; they must not make use of any species of vain and idle words; they must not take delight in thinking of anything unlawful; they must extinguish in themselves all evil inclinations; they must not be scrupulous and irresolute in acting; they must, above all things be assiduous in prayer and meditation: they must not seek after magnificence and superfluity; they must fly from sloth, lying, immoderate laughter, vain joy, and play; they must abhor sorcery, and not give credit to dreams; when abused or derided, they must not give way to anger, and when praised, must not be puffed up; they must not envy others their dress; they must not flatter benefactors to draw alms from them, nor preach sermons in which they display their desire of them; they must not admit of any bitterness or acrimony in talking, nor deride, nor despise, nor injure others; they ought to accommodate themselves to the opinions of others not to give occasion for dissension; ought never to consent to any bad thoughts; and he who does consent to them, and take pleasure in them, shows that he has no fear of sinning, and is therefore in a state of sinful cowardice.

But he who does not consent to such thoughts, truly seeks after sanctity.

All are once more recommended to shun vanity, to observe modesty, and to consider that good works are our only hopes and our only true friends, and thus the heart will be fixed in doing all that is good.

He who speaks sweetly and with affability will have many friends; but he whose words are bitter will have few or none.

In judging causes, the testimony of persons respectable by their state in life, and their wisdom, disinterested, and who believe in the merit of good works; ought to be received.

If a husband surprise a man in adultery with his wife, he may lawfully kill him.

The Hindoos.

In the following, will be found the main features of Hindu theology and religious teachings.

The Vedas, which are the Hindu Scriptures, and of which there are four, the Rig, Yagust, Saman, and Atharvan, are asserted to have been revealed by Brahma.

They are based upon an acknowledgment of a universal Spirit pervading all things. Of this God they therefore necessarily acknowledge the unity: "There is in truth but one Deity, the Supreme Spirit, the Lord of the universe, whose work is the universe. The God above all gods, who created the earth, the heavens, the waters."

These scriptures convey the idea that there is a pervading spirit existing every where of the same nature as the soul of man, though differing from it infinitely in degree.

As to the relation between the Supreme Being and man, the soul is a portion or particle of that all-pervading principle, the Universal Intellect or Soul of the World.

The three Vedic divinities, Agni, Indra, and Surga are not to be looked upon as existing independently, for all spirits are comprehended in the Universal Soul. They do not authorize the worship of deified men, nor of images, nor of any visible forms. They admit the adoration of subordinate spirits, as those of the planets. They inculcate universal charity—charity even to an enemy:— "The tree doth not withdraw its shade from the wood-cutter." In the Institutes of Menu, a code of civil and religious law, written about the ninth century before Christ, though like Vedas, betraying a gradual origin, the doctrine of the Divine unity becomes more distinctly mixed up with Pantheistic ideas. They present a description of creation, of the nature of God and the soul, and contain prescribed rules for the duty of man in every station of life, from

THE HINDOOS. 39

the moment of birth to death. Their imperious regulations in all these minute details are a sufficient proof of the great development and paramount power to which the priesthood had now attained; but their morality is discreditable. Their abitrary and all-reaching spirit reminds one of the Papal system; their recommendations to sovereigns, their authorization of immoralities, recall the state of Italian society as reflected in the works of Machiavelli. They hold learning in the most signal esteem, but concede to the prejudices of the illiterate in a worship of the Gods with burnt offerings of clarified butter and libations of the juices of plants. They make a Brahman the chief of all created things.

In their essential principles the Institutes follow the Vedas, though, as must be the case in every system intended for men in the various stages of intellectual progress from the least advanced to the highest, they show a leaning toward popular delusions.

A new ritual, instead of the Vedas, has come into use, these scriptures being the eighteen Puranas, composed between the eighth and sixteenth centuries. They contain theogonies, accounts of the creation, philosophical speculations, fragmentary history, and may be brought to support any sectarian view, having never been intended as one general body, but they are received as incontrovertible authority. In the "Baghavat Gita," the text book of the modern school, the sole essential for salvation is dependence on some particular teacher, which makes up for everything else. The efficacy which is thus ascribed to faith, and the facility with which sin may be expiated by penance, has led to great mental perversion and superstition, which finds its analogy in the Roman Church, and somewhat in all the churches where faith in the Divinity of Christ is held as indispensable to salvation.

Christna or Chrisna, also Vishnu, is one of the most popular of all the Hindoo deities. An immense number of legends are told respecting him, which are not worth recording here, but the following, condensed from the *Anacalypsis* of Godfrey Higgins, will well repay perusal. He is represented as the son of Brahma and Maia, and is usually called "the Saviour," or "the Preserver." He, being a god, became incarnate in the flesh. As soon as he was born, he was saluted by a chorus of devatars or angels. His birth place was Mathurea. He was cradled amongst Shepherds. Soon after his birth he was carried away by night to a remote place for fear of a tyrant, whose destroyer it was foretold he would become, and who ordered all male children to be slain (an episode marked in the sculptures at Elephanta). By the male line he was of Royal descent, though born in a dungeon, which on his arrival he illuminated, whilst the face of his parents shone. Christna spoke as soon as he was born, and comforted his mother. He was preceded by his brother Ram, who helped him to purify the world of monsters and demons. Christna descended into Hades, and returned to Vaicontha. One of his names is "the good shepherd." An Indian prophet, Nared Saphos, or wisdom, visited him, consulted the stars, and pronounced him a celestial being. Christna cured a leper; a woman poured on his head a box of ointment, and he cured her of disease. He was chosen king amongst his fellow cowherds. He washed the feet of Brahmins, and when Brahma stole the sheep and cowboys of his father's farm (Nanda's) Christna made a new set. Christna had a dreadful fight with the serpent Caluga. He was sent to a tutor, whom he astonished with his learning.— Christna was crucified, went into hell, and afterwards into heaven.

Christina and his mother are almost always represented as black. Christna's statue in the temple at Mathura is black, and the temple is built in the form of a cross (Ptolemy calls the place Matura Deorum.) As Vishnu he is painted with a Parthian coronet round his head when crucified. As Wittoba he is painted sometimes with stigmata in his hands, sometimes in his feet, and one of the pictures representing him has a round hole in the side; to his collar hangs a heart, and on his head is a Linga yoni! In another picture he is called Ballaji, and is contending with a seven-headed cobra. His most celebrated temple is at Terputty. The date of Christna's first mystic birth is about six hundred B. C.

Of the deities of the Veda, Agni and Indra, the former comprises the element of *Fire* under three aspects. 1st. As it exists on earth, not only as culinary or religious fire, but in the heat of digestion and of life and the vivifying principle of vegetation; 2d. As it exists in the atmosphere, or mid-heaven, in the form of lightning; and 3d. As it is manifested in the heavens, as light, the sun, the dawn, and the planetary bodies.

The deification of INDRA is more consistent, as he has no incongruous functions to discharge. He is a personification of the phenomena of the firmament, particularly in the capacity of sending down rain. This property is metaphorically described as a conflict with the clouds which are reluctant to part with their

THE HINDOOS. 41

watery stores, until assailed and penetrated by the thunderbolt of Indra.

The SUN, Surya or Savita, occupies a much less conspicuous place in Hindu worship, than we should have anticipated from the visible magnificence of that luminary, and his adoration by neighboring nations.

The sun, like AGNI and INDRA, is the giver of temporal blessing to his worshippers; he is the source of light.

The share of AGNI and INDRA in the production of rain, and their fierce and impetuous nature, are figurative representations of physical phenomena.

The following is contained in the Hindu Sacred Writings.

In the beginning there arose the source of golden light. He was the one born Lord of all that is. He 'stablished the earth and this sky.

He who gives life, He who gives strength; whose command all the bright gods revere; whose shadow is immortality.

He who through his power is the one King of the breathing and awaking world; He who governs all, man and beast; Who is the God to whom we shall offer our worship?

He who by His might looked even over the water-clouds, the clouds which gave strength and lit the sacrifice, He who alone is God above all gods; Who is the God to whom we shall offer our worship?

May He not destroy us—He the creator of the earth; or He the Righteous, who created the heaven; He who also created the bright and mighty waters; Who is the God to whom we shall offer our worship?

All who are wise of heart adore God the Begetter, bringing him offerings of a devout heart with hymn of praise.

The air all around is full of the whispering of the wind, thy breath. Those who are wise, the truthful seers, the ministers of sacrifice, who raise on high the hymn of praise to thee. Even to evil-doers is he merciful; may we all live before thee without sin, faithfully observant of thy eternal laws.

However we break thy laws from day to day, men as we are, O God.

Do not deliver us unto death, nor to the blow of the furious; nor to the anger of the spiteful!

May he, the wise, make our paths straight all our days; may he prolong our lives!

The god, whom the scoffers do not provoke, nor the tormentors of men, nor the plotters of mischief.

Yearning for him, the far seeing, my thoughts move onwards, as kine move to their pastures.

Be pure and pious all, that your way may not go down to the house of death, but that you may enjoy length of days, and abundance of treasures.

As days succeed days, changing seasons, with seasons, lo, give, O Creator, these here to live, that the younger may not leave their parent desolate.

God's coursers bear on high the divine Sun that he may be seen by all (the worlds.)

(At the approach) of the all-illuminating Sun, the constellations depart, with the night.

With that light with which thou, the purifier and defender from evil, lookest upon this creature-bearing world.

Indra abides, humbling the neglecters of holy acts in favor of those who observe them, and punishing those who turn away from his worship, in favor of those who are present (with their praise.)

This adoration is offered to the shedder of rain, the self-resplendent, the possessor of true vigor, the mighty.

Verily, with thy bulk, thou fillest all the firmament: of a truth there is none other such as thou.

May the gods, turning not away, be ever with us for our advancement.

May the benevolent favor of the gods (be ours:) may the bounty of the gods, ever approving of the upright, light upon us; may we obtain the friendship of the gods.

Let us hear gods, with our ears, what is good objects of worship, let us see, with our eyes what is good: let us engage in your praises.

These divinities of the morning have spread light (over the world.)

The deities of the dawn have restored, as of yore, the consciousness of (sentient creatures,) and bright-rayed, have attended upon the glorious sun, bringing every kind of food to the performer of good works.

Ushas cuts off the accumulated (glooms.) The daughter of the sky awaits the glorious sun.

We have crossed over the boundary of darkness. Ushas restores the consciousness (of living beings.) Bright-shining, she smiles, like a flatterer to obtain favor, and lovely in all her radiance, she has swallowed for our delight the darkness.

May he, of whom the excellent measure (of all things,) through strength, eternally and every where cherishes heaven and earth, propitiated by our acts, convey us beyond evil.

Ushas, endowed with truth, let the worker of iniquity depart, for we shall overcome him with our chariot, through thy assistance.

Let words of truth be spoken : let works of wisdom (be performed.)

At thy dawning, (Ushas,) the various birds rise up from their nests, and men who have to earn their bread quit their homes, be glorified by this (my) hymn; graciously disposed towards us, augment (our prosperity;) and may we obtain goddesses, through your favor, a hundred and a thousand fold.

These wonderful (rewards) verily are for those who give (pious) donations: for the donors of (pious) gifts the suns shine in heaven : the givers of (pious) donations attain immortality : the givers of (pious) gifts prolong their (worldly) existence.

May those who propitiate (the gods,) never commit degrading sin : may those who praise the gods and observe holy vows, never experience decay.

Agni, who gives pleasure (to his worshippers,) being pleased (himself,) in like manner as men follow a path that leads to happiness, who is the guardian of all these treasures, has power (to distribute them.)

Agni grants blessings to every (pious) worshipper and opens for him the gates (of heaven.)

Agni is a most amiable friend in human infirmity; the beloved protector of all, he preserves us from the malignity of sin.

Inasmuch as the hero, Indra, rightly judges men by their deeds, therefore do the (pious;) (men) worship him, that by their own strength they may overcome (their foes.)

The timid and anxious (worshipper) praises thee, who art auspicious, for driving (away) thieves; for thou defendest (us) from all beings, (as the reward) of our righteousness ; thou protectest us from the fear of evil spirits, (as the reward) of our righteousness.

APPENDIX.

Whatever individual offers adoration preserve him entirely unharmed from sin; (preserve, from sin the mortal who is sincere in his devotion, who offers worship with praises.

Desirous of happiness, I adore him, whose protection is ever nigh; who is the source of felicity; who, when devoutly worshipped, blends with the thoughts of all (his worshippers:) (though) a deity.

Free from anger, and entitled to ample praise, be ever accessible to us; be our leader in every encounter.

Agni, listen attentively when thou art praised, by us, and repeat (those praises) to the gods who are entitled to worship; to the royal (deities) entitled to worship.

Bestow, Agni, upon our excellent patron a boat ever fitted with oars, (one that may render) our posterity prosperous, and may bear mankind across (the ocean of life) to felicity.

He, the searcher, the accessible, has declared to mortals (the knowledge of) their religious duties.

He who is visible to all, is the parent of that (pious) progeny.

He, who is, as it were, the generator of men as well as of heaven and earth, of whom creation has imbibed life, abides with his glories.

(I ask thee to withhold thy favor) from those who, acknowledging thee not as his lord, is chary of gifts, and from him who rarely praises (the gods.)

He amongst those (who are your followers,) who observes truth, who is considerate, who is commended by the wise.

The purpose of worshipping you, is not the performance, but (even by so much) I may attain to your glory, and there is acquittance (of my duty.)

May I attain his favorite path, in which God-seeking men delight; (the path) in whose exalted station there is a (perpetual) flow of felicity.

I glorify the mighty Heaven and Earth, those two, who, cherishing their worshippers as children

Verily I propitiate, by my invocations, the mind of the benevolent father, and the great and spontaneous (affection) of the mother (of all beings:) The parents, with kindness, have secured, by their excellent protections, the vast and manifold immortality of their progeny.

THE HINDOOS. 45

These, your children, the performers of good works, and of goodly appearance, recognize you as their great parents, through experience of former (kindness) preserve uninterrupted stability in the functions of your progeny, whether stationary or moving, (depending for existence) on none other than you.

Heaven and Earth, are the diffusers of happiness on all, encouragers of truth.

I have beheld the Lord of Men with seven sons; of which delightful and benevolent (deity) who is the object of our invocation.

Who has seen the primeval (being) at the time of his being born?

Ignorant, I enquire of the sages who know (the truth;) not as one knowing (do I enquire,) for the sake of (gaining) knowledge: what is that One alone, who has upheld these six spheres in the form of the unborn.

Let him who knows this (truth) quickly declare it; the mysterious condition of the beautiful ever-moving (sun:) the rays shed (their) milk from his exalted head, investing his form with radiance: they have drunk up the water by the paths (by which they were poured forth.)

The mother (earth,) worships the father, (sun) with holy rites, for the sake of water; but he has anticipated (her wants) in his mind:

Müller says: the idea of revelation, and we mean more particularly book-revelation, is not a modern idea, nor is it an idea peculiar to Christianity.

Though we look for it in vain in the literature of Greece and Rome, we find the literature of India saturated with this idea from beginning to end. In no country we believe, has the theory of revelation been so minutely elaborated as in India.

According to the orthodox views of Indian theologians not a single line of Veda was the work of human authors. The whole Veda is in some way or other the work of the Deity; and even those who received the revelation, or, as they express it, those who saw it, were not supposed to be ordinary mortals, but beings raised above the level of common humanity, and less liable, therefore, to error in the reception of revealed truth. The views entertained of revelation by the orthodox theologians of India are far more minute and elaborate than those of the most extreme advocates of verbal inspiration in Europe. The human element, called "paurusheyatva," in Sanscrit, is driven out of every corner or hiding place; and as the Veda is held to have existed in the mind of the Deity before the beginning of time, every allusion to historical events, of which there are not a few, is explained away with a zeal and ingenuity worthy of a better cause.

The poets of the Veda speak of their hymns as "god-given." One poet says: "O god (Indra) have mercy! Sharpen my mind, like the edge of iron. Whatever I now may utter, longing for thee, do thou accept it; make me possessed of God!" Another utters for the first time the famous hymn, the "Gâyatri," which now for more than three thousand years has been the daily prayer of every Brahman, and is still repeated every morning by millions of pious worshippers: "Let us meditate on the adorable light of the divine Creator: may he rouse our minds." This consciousness of higher influences in those who uttered praise, and thanksgiving, to Him who made us, is the key-note of all religion, whether ancient or modern.

The real history of man is the history of religion—the wonderful ways by which the different families of the human race advanced toward a truer knowledge, and a deeper love of God. This is the foundation that underlies all history: it is the light, the soul, and life of history. Man has but one history, the religious and profane so-called are but one, a man's religion has its best exponent in his every day conduct, good works and love to God being the first and only religion, theologies and creeds being but as chaff.

The whole population of the world, has the same religion of the various theologies and creeds held in the several countries. 31.2 per cent. are Buddhists, 13.4 per cent. are Brahmanists, which together gives 44 per cent. for what may be called living Aryan religions. Of the remaining 56 per cent., 15.7 are Mohammedans, 8.7 per cent. nondescript heathens, 30.7 per cent. Christians, and only 0.3 per cent. Jews.

CONFUCIANISM.

The following contains some of the superstitions, worship, and theology mingled by the priests of China, with the moral teachings of Confucius; together with a short account of his early life and teachings.

Confucius, a great sage, moralist, and teacher, an active advocate of the good, the right, the true, and the practice of love and kind offices between man and man, has been the object of adoration and worship in chapels, specially erected for, and dedicated to the purpose throughout the Chinese Empire, for the last twenty-three centuries. He was born five hundred and fifty-one years before Christ. He was the first born of his mother, who was married when she was quite young to a man much older than herself. Among the legends current connected with his birth, &c., are the following: During the pregnancy of his mother, she dreamed that she was to have a son, and that a four footed beast knelt before her, and cast forth from his mouth a slip or gem, on which was the inscription—"The son of the essence of water shall succeed to the withering Chow and be a throneless King." On the night when the child was born, two dragons came and kept watch on the left and right of the hill, and two spirit ladies appeared in the air, pouring out fragrant odors. As soon as the birth took place, a spring of clear warm water bubbled up from the floor of the cave, which dried up again when the child had been washed in it. The child was born in a designated cave, in obedience to a previous dream. The records which we have of Confucius' early years are very scant. When he was in his third year his father died. It is related of him that as a boy he used to play at the arrangement of sacrificial vessels, and postures of ceremony. Of his schooling, we have no reliable account. He tells us himself at fifteen he bent his mind to learning, but the condition of his family was one of poverty. At the age of twenty he was employed as keeper of the stores of grain. In his twenty-second year he commenced his labors as a public teacher, and at thirty had made great progress in learning and wisdom, gained great and wide-spread fame and was surrounded by disciples. The benefit of his wisdom and counsel was sought after by the high and low, by Princes, Rulers, Students, and enquirers after truth of all classes. So high was the moral tone of all his axioms, and so perfectly in accordance with man's innate perceptions of the right and good were all his teachings, that the many drank them in with the same avidity as they did the early teachings of Christ, before they were adulterated with the theology of the priests.

The number of temples erected to his memory is sixteen hundred and sixty. One of them occupies ten acres of land. The most famous temple in the Empire now rises over the place of the grave on which is inscribed: "The Perfect Sage." On the two festivals in the year sacred to his memory, there are sacrificed some seventy thousand animals of different kinds, and twenty-seven thousand pieces of silk are burned on his altars. Yet his religion is without priests, liturgy, or public worship, except on these two occasions. Kang-he, the second and greatest of the rulers of the present dynasty, in the twenty-third year of his reign, set the example of kneeling thrice, and each time laying his forehead thrice in the dust, before the image of the sage. At first, the worship of Confucius was confined to the country of Loo, but in A. D. 57 it was enacted that sacrifices should be offered to him in the imperial college, and in all the colleges of the principal territorial division throughout the empire.

About A. D. 628 began the custom, which continues to the present day, of erecting temples to him,—separate structures, in connection with all the colleges, or examination-halls, of the country. The sage is not alone in those temples. In a hall behind the principal one occupied by himself, are the tablets—in some cases the images—of several of his ancestors. On the first day of every month, offerings of fruits and vegetables are set forth, and on the fifteenth there is a solemn burning of incense. But twice a year, in the middle months of spring and autumn, when the first "ting" day of the month comes round, the worship of Confucius is performed with peculiar solemnity. At the imperial college the Emperor himself is required to attend in state, and is in fact the principal performer. After all the preliminary arrangements have been made, and the Emperor has twice knelt and six times bowed his head to the earth, the presence of Confucius' spirit is invoked in these words, " Great art thou, O perfect sage! Thy virtue is full; thy doctrine is complete. Among mortal men there has not been thine equal. All kings honor thee. Thy statutes and laws have come gloriously down. Thou art the pattern in this imperial school. Reverently have the sacrificial vessels been set out. Full of awe we sound our drums and bells."

The spirit is supposed now to be present, and the service proceeds through various offerings, when the first of which has been set forth, an officer reads the following, which is the prayer on the occasion: "On this .... month of this .... year, I, A. B., the Emperor, offer a sacrifice to the philosopher K'ung, the ancient Teacher, the perfect Sage, and say,—O Teacher, in virtue equal to Heaven and Earth, whose doctrines embrace the past time and the present, thou didst digest and transmit the six classics, and didst hand down lessons for all generations! Now in this second month of spring (or autumn), in reverent observance of the old statutes, with victims, silks, spirits, and fruits, I carefully offer sacrifice to thee. With thee are associated the philosopher Yen, continuator of thee; the philosopher Ysăng, exhibiter of thy fundamental principles; the philosopher Ysze-sze, transmitter of thee; and the philosopher Măng, second to thee. May'st thou enjoy the offerings!"

I need not go on to enlarge on the homage which the Emperors of China render to Confucius. It could not be more complete. It is worship and not mere homage. He was unreasonably neglected when alive. He is now unreasonably venerated when dead.

At the present day, education is widely diffused throughout China. In no other country is the school-master more abroad, and in all schools it is Confucius who is taught. In many school-rooms, there is a tablet or inscription on the wall, sacred to the sage; and every pupil is required on coming to school on the morning of the first and fifteenth day of every month, to bow before it, the first thing, as an act of worship. Thus, all in China who receive the slightest tincture of learning, do so at the fountain of Confucius. They learn of him, and do homage to him at once.

During his life-time he had three thousand disciples. Hundreds of millions are his disciples now. For two thousand years he has reigned supreme, the undisputed teacher of this most populous land. Confucius is thus, in the empire of China, the one man by whom all possible lessons of social virtue and political wisdom are taught.

Confucius did not trouble himself to account for the origin of man, nor did he pretend to know about his hereafter.

As to creation, and the final destiny of man, we suggest that, the innate consciousness of the totality of the human race is that the soul is immortal, and destined to an eternity of more or less happiness, in proportion as man discharges, under his free-agency, the laws of his maker which have relation to his being, as they are revealed to him.

This is all that God has ever revealed to man on the subject, and it is most unquestionably all that it is well for him to know. If man could know with certainty all that would take place in relation to his future life on earth, it would entirely unfit him for happiness.

Among the things which Confucius taught were "truthfulness, and sincerity," which were celebrated as highly, and demanded as stringently by him, as ever it has been by any Christian moralist. One of Confucius' disciples asked if there was one word which would serve as a rule of practice for all one's life, and was answered, "Is not reciprocity such a word?" What you do not want done to yourself, do not unto others.

The people in China, as elsewhere, believe, what is the beginning and end of all wisdom, that the laws of the moral Order of the world correspond to the universal conscience.

The following declarations of Confucius and others among the Chinese were made five hundred years before Christ.

The last years of the life of Confucius were devoted to editing the Sacred Books, or Kings. As we now have them, they come from him. Authentic records of Chinese history extend back to two thousand three hundred and fifty-seven, B. C. while the Chinese philosophy originated with Fuh-he, who lived about three thousand three hundred and twenty-seven B. C. He it was who substituted writing for the knotted strings which before formed the only means of record. Confucius edited the Yih-King, the Shoo King, the She-King, and the Leke, which constitute the whole of the ancient literature of China which has come down to posterity.

In Shoo-King a personal God is addressed. The oldest books recognize a Divine person: They teach that there is one Supreme Being, who is omnipresent, who sees all things, and has an intelligence which nothing can escape,—that he wishes men to live together in peace and brotherhood. He commands not only right actions, but pure desires and thoughts ; that we should watch all our behavior, and maintain a grave and majestic demeanor, "which is like a palace in which virtue resides," but especially that we should guard the tongue. "For a blemish may be taken out of a diamond by carefully polishing it; but, if your words have the least blemish there is no way to efface that." " Humility is the solid foundation of all the virtues." " To acknowledge one's incapacity is the way to be soon prepared to teach others, for from the moment that a man is no longer full of himself, nor puffed up with empty pride, whatever good he learns in the morning he practises before night." "Heaven penetrates to the bottom of our hearts, like light into a dark chamber. We must conform ourselves to it, till we are like two instruments of music tuned to the same pitch. We must join ourselves with it, like two tablets which appear but one. We must receive its gifts the very moment its hand is open to bestow. Our irregular passions shut up the door of our souls against God."

"Man has received his nature from Heaven. Conduct in accordance with that nature, constitutes what is right and true,— is a pursuing of the proper path. The cultivation or regulation of that path is what is called instruction.

"Man has received from Heaven a moral nature by which he is constituted a law to himself, over this nature man requires to exercise a jealous watchfulness; and as he possesses it, absolutely and relatively, in perfection, or attains to such possession of it, he becomes invested with highest dignity and power.

"The way of the superior man reaches far and wide, and yet is secret, the path of duty is to be pursued everywhere and at all times while yet the secret spring and rule of it is near at hand, in the Heaven-conferred nature, the individual consciousness, with which no stranger can intermeddle.

" When one cultivates to the utmost the moral principles of his nature, and exercises them on the principle of reciprocity, he is not far from the path. What you do not like when done to yourself, do not do to others: serve my father as I would require my son to serve me: serve my elder brother as I would require my younger brother to serve me: set the example in behaving to a friend as I would require him to behave to me.

" Be earnest in practising the ordinary virtues, and careful in speaking about them; if in his practice he has anything defective, the superior man dares not but exert himself, and if in his words he has any excess, he dares not allow himself such license; have respect to his actions, and his actions have respect to his words; is it not just an entire sincerity which marks the superior man?

" The duties of universal application," those between husband and wife, father and son, elder and younger brother, and friends.

The sincere or perfect man, is he who satisfies completely all the requirements of duty in the various relations of society, and in the exercise of government. " There is government when the prince is prince, and the minister is minister, when the father is father, and the son is son."

There is a sufficient foundation in nature for government in the several relations of society, and if those be maintained and developed according to their relative significancy, it is sure to obtain. This was a first principle in the political ethics of Confucius.

The moment the ruler ceases to be a minister of God for good and does not administer a government that is beneficial to the people, he forfeits the title by which he holds the throne, and perseverance in oppression will surely lead to his overthrow.

"Recompense injury with justice, and recompense kindness with kindness. He who recompenses injury with kindness is a man who is careful of his person. Filial piety and fraternal submission! are they not the root of all benevolent actions?" "Fine words and an insinuating appearance are seldom associated with true virtue."

The philosopher said, "I daily examine myself on three points: whether, in transacting business for others, I may not have been faithful;—whether, in intercourse with friends, I may not have been sincere."

"A youth, when at home, should be filial, and abroad, respectful to his elders. He should overflow in love to all, and cultivate the friendship of the good."

"Hold faithfulness and sincerity as first principles.

"When you have faults, do not fear to abandon them."

Tsze-kung said, "what do you pronounce concerning the poor man who yet does not flatter, and the rich man who is not proud?" The Master replied, "they will do; but they are not equal to him, who, though poor, is yet cheerful, and to him, who, though rich, loves the rules of propriety."

"He who exercises government by means of his virtue, may be compared to the north polar star, which keeps its place and all the stars turn towards it." In the Book of Poetry are three hundred pieces, but the design of them all may be embraced in *that* one sentence—' Have no depraved thoughts.'

The duties of filial piety must be performed with a cheerful countenance.

The Duke Gae asked, saying, "What should be done in order to secure the submission of the people." Confucius replied, "advance the upright and set aside the crooked, then the people will submit. Advance the crooked and set aside the upright, then the people will not submit.".

Ke K'ang asked how to cause the people to reverence *their ruler*, to be faithful to him, and to urge themselves to virtue. The Master said, " Let him preside over them with gravity ; then they will reverence him. Let him be filial and kind to all ; then they will be faithful to him. Let him advance the good and teach the incompetent ;—then they will eagerly seek to be virtuous."

The Master said, " I do not know how a man without truthfulness is to get on. How can a large carriage be made to go without the cross-bar for yoking the oxen to, or a small carriage without the arrangement for yoking the horses ?"

The Master said, " For a man to sacrifice to a spirit which does not belong to him is flattery.

" To see what is right and not to do it, is want of courage.

" He who offends against Heaven has none to whom he can pray.

" If the will be set on virtue, there will be no practice of wickedness.

" Riches and honors are what men desire. If it cannot be obtained in the proper way, they should not be held. Poverty and meanness are what men dislike. If it cannot be avoided in the proper way, they should be endured.

" The superior man does not, even for the space of a single meal act contrary to virtue. In moments of haste, he cleaves to it. In seasons of danger he cleaves to it.

" If a man in the morning hear the right way, he may die in the evening without regret.

" *A man should say*, I am not concerned that I have no place— I am concerned how I may fit myself for one. I am not concerned that I am not known,—I seek to be worthy to be known." " My doctrine is that of an all-pervading unity."

" Be true to the principles of our nature and the benevolent exercise of them to others.

" When we see men of worth, we should think of equalling them ; when we see men of a contrary character, we should turn inwards and examine ourselves.

" The cautious seldom err.

" The superior man wishes to be slow in his words and earnest in his conduct.

"Virtue is not left to stand alone. He who practises it will have neighbors."

The Master said, "I have not seen a firm and unbending man." Some one replied, "There is Shin Ch'ang." "Ch'ang," said the Master, "is under the influence of his lusts, how can he be firm and unbending?"

The Master said of Tsze-ch'an that he had four of the characteristics of a superior man :—in his conduct of himself, he was humble; in serving his superiors, he was respectful; in nourishing the people, he was kind; in ordering the people, he was just.

"In regard to the aged, give them rest; in regard to friends, show them sincerity; in regard to the young, treat them tenderly."

The Duke Gae asked which of the disciples love to learn. Confucius replied to him, there was Yen Hwuy; He loved to learn. He did not transfer his anger; he did not repeat a fault. Unfornately, his appointed time was short and he died; and now there is not such another. I have not yet heard of any one who loves to learn as he did.

"They who know the truth are not equal to those who love it, and they who love it are not equal to those who find delight in it."

Fan Ch'e asked what constituted wisdom. The Master said, "To give one's-self earnestly to the duties due to men. The man of virtue makes the difficulty to be overcome his first business, and success only a subsequent consideration."

"The wise are active; the virtuous are tranquil. The wise are joyful; the virtuous are long-lived.

"The superior man, extensively studying all learning, and keeping himself under the restraint of the rules of propriety, may thus likewise not overstep what is right.

"Perfect is the virtue which is according to the Constant Mean!

"The man of perfect virtue, wishing to be established himself, seeks also to establish others; wishing to be enlarged himself, he seeks also to enlarge others.

"To be able to judge of others by what is nigh in ourselves;— this may be called the art of virtue."

The Master said, "The leaving virtue without proper cultivation; the not thoroughly discussing what is learned; not being able to move towards righteousness of which a knowledge is gained; and not being able to change what is not good :—these are the things which occasion me solicitude.

"Let the will be set on the path of duty.

"Let every attainment in what is good be firmly grasped.

"Let perfect virtue be accorded with.

"Let relaxation and enjoyment be found in the polite arts.

The Master said, "With coarse rice to eat, with water to drink, and my bended arm for a pillow;—I have still joy in the midst of these things. Riches and honors acquired by unrighteousness are to me as a floating cloud.

"Do you think, my disciples, that I have any concealments? I conceal nothing from you. Could I see a man possessed of constancy, that would satisfy me.

"Having not and yet affecting to have, empty and yet affecting to be full, straitened and yet affecting to be at ease:—it is difficult with such characteristics to have constancy.

"Hearing much and selecting what is good and following it, seeing much and keeping it in memory:—this is the second style of knowledge.

"Is virtue a thing remote? I wish to be virtuous, and lo! virtue is at hand."

The Master said, "The sage and the man of perfect virtue:— how dare I rank myself with them? It may simply be said of me, that I strive to become such without satiety, and teach others without weariness.

"When those who are in high stations perform well all their duties to their relations, the people are aroused to virtue.

"There are three principles of conduct which the man of high rank should consider specially important:—that in his deportment and manner he keep from violence and heedlessness; that in regulating his countenance he keep near to sincerity; and that in his words and tones he keep far from lowness and impropriety.

"It is by the Odes that the mind is aroused.

"It is by the Rules of propriety that the character is established.

"It is from Music that the finish is received."

The Master said, "It is not easy to find a man who has learned for three years without coming to the good.

"With sincere faith he unites the love of learning; holding firm to death, he is perfecting the excellence of his course.

"Learn as if you could not reach your object, and were always fearing also lest you should lose it."

There were four things from which the Master was entirely free. He had no foregone conclusions, no arbitrary predeterminations, no obstinacy, and no egotism.

"The prosecution of learning may be compared to what may happen in raising a mound. It may be compared to throwing down the earth on the level ground. Though but one basketful is thrown at a time, the advancing with it is my own going forward.

"Hold faithfulness and sincerity as first principles.

' The commander of the forces of a large State may be carried off, but the will of even a common man cannot be taken from him.

"The wise are free from perplexities; the virtuous from anxiety; and the bold from fear.

"A great minister, is one who serves his prince according to what is right, and when he finds he cannot do so, retires.

"Look not at what is contrary to propriety; listen not to what is contrary to propriety; speak not what is contrary to propriety; make no movement which is contrary to propriety."

Chung-kung asked about perfect virtue. The Master said, "It is when you go abroad, to behave to every one as if you were receiving a great guest; not to do to others as you would not wish done to yourself; to have no murmuring against you in the country, and none in the family.

"Be cautious and slow in speech.

"When a mans feels the difficulty of doing, can he be other than cautious and slow in speaking?

"When internal examination discovers nothing wrong, what is there to be anxious about, what is there to fear?

"He with whom neither slander that gradually soaks into the mind, nor statements that startle like a wound in the flesh, are successful, may be called intelligent, indeed, may be called farseeing.

"Hold faithfulness and sincerity as first principles, and be moving continually to what is right;—this is the way to exalt one's virtue.

"The art of governing is to keep its affairs before the mind without weariness, and to practise them with undeviating consistency.

CONFUCIANISM.

"The superior man seeks to perfect the admirable qualities of men.

"To govern, means to rectify. If you lead on the people with correctness, who will not dare to be correct?

"The man of distinction is solid and straightforward, and loves righteousness.

"To assail one's own wickedness and not assail that of others;—this is the way to correct cherished evil. For a morning's anger to disregard one's own life, and involve that of one's parents;—is not this a case of delusion?"

Fan Ch'e asked about benevolence. The Master said, "It is to love all men.

"Employ the upright and put aside all the crooked;—in this way, the crooked can be made to be upright.

"Faithfully admonish your friend, and kindly try to lead him.

"When punishments are not properly awarded, the people do not know how to move hand or foot.

"If he cannot rectify himself, what has he to do with rectifying others?

"In the management of business, to be reverently attentive; in intercourse with others, to be strictly sincere.

"The ardent will advance and lay hold of truth; the cautiously-decided, will keep themselves from what is wrong.

"The superior man is affable, but not adulatory; the mean is adulatory, but not affable.

"The superior man has a dignified ease without pride. The mean man has pride without a dignified ease.

"The firm, the enduring, the simple, and the modest, are near to virtue.

"He who speaks without modesty will find it difficult to make his words good.

"The way of the superior man is three-fold. Virtuous, he is free from anxieties; wise, he is free from perplexities; bold, he is free from fear.

"What do you say concerning the principle that injury should be recompensed with kindness?"

The Master said, "With what then will you recompense kindness?

"Recompense injury with justice, and recompense kindness with kindness.

"If a man take no thought about what is distant, he will find sorrow near at hand.

"The superior man in everything considers righteousness to be essential. He performs it according to the rules of propriety. He brings it forth in humility. He completes it with sincerity.

"What the superior man seeks, is in himself. What the mean man seeks, is in others.

"Is there one word which may serve as a rule of practice for all one's life?" The Master said, "Is not Reciprocity such a word? What you do not want done to yourself, do not do to others.

"Specious words confound virtue. Want of forbearance in small matters confounds great plans.

"To have faults and not to reform them,—this indeed, should be pronounced having faults.

"By nature, men are nearly alike; by practice, they get to be wide apart.

"If you are grave, you will not be treated with disrespect. If you are generous, you will win all. If you are sincere, people will repose trust in you. If you are earnest, you will accomplish much. If you are kind, this will enable you to employ the services of others.

"Without recognizing the ordinances of Heaven, it is impossible to be a superior man.

"The illustrious virtue is the virtuous nature which man derives from Heaven.

"The cultivation of the person is the prime, radical thing required from all.

"Let there be daily renovation. What truly is within will be manifested without.

"Riches adorn a house, and virtue adorns the person. The cultivation of the person depends on the rectifying of the mind. The regulation of one's family depends on the cultivation of his person.

"There are few men in the world who love, and at the same time know the bad qualities of the object of their love, or who hate, and yet know the excellences of the object of their hatred.

"Act as if you were watching over an infant. If a mother is really anxious about it, though she may not hit exactly the wants of her infant, she will not be far from doing so."

"From the loving example of one family, a whole State becomes loving, and from its courtesies, the whole State becomes courteous.

"The ruler must himself be possessed of the good qualities, and then he may require them in the people. When the ruler as a father, a son, and a brother, is a model, then the people imitate him.

"When the sovereign behaves to his aged, as the aged should be behaved to, the people becomes filial; when the sovereign behaves to his elders, as elders should be behaved to, the people learn brotherly submission; when the sovereign treats compassionately the young and helpless, the people do the same. Thus the ruler has a principle with which, as a measuring square, he may regulate his conduct. The ruler's words going forth contrary to right, will come back to him in the same way, and wealth, gotten by improper ways, will take its departure by the same.

"To love those whom men hate, and to hate those whom men love; this is to outrage the natural feeling of man.

"Let there be activity in the production, and economy in the expenditure. Then the wealth will always be sufficient.

"What Heaven has conferred is called THE NATURE; an accordance with this nature is called THE PATH of duty; the regulation of path is called INSTRUCTION.

"While there are no stirrings of pleasure, anger, sorrow, or joy, the mind may be said to be in the state of Equilibrium. When those feelings have been stirred and they act in their due degree, there ensues what may be called the state of Harmony. This Equilibrium is the great root from which grow all the human actings in the world, and this Harmony is the universal path which they all should pursue.

"Let the states of equilibrium and harmony exist in perfection, and a happy order will prevail throughout heaven and earth, and all things will be nourished and flourish.

"To show forbearance and gentleness in teaching others, and not to revenge unreasonable conduct.

"When men try to pursue a course, which is far from the indications of consciousness, this course cannot be considered THE PATH.

"In hewing an axe-handle, the pattern is not far off. We grasp one axe-handle to hew the other, and yet, if we look askance from the one to the other, we may consider them as apart.

"When one cultivates to the utmost the principles of his nature, and exercises them on the principle of reciprocity, he is not far from the path.

"The superior man can find himself in no situation in which he is not himself.

"Happy union with wife and children is like the music of lutes and harps. When there is concord among brethren, the harmony is delightful and enduring.

"How abundantly do spiritual beings display the powers that belong to them.

"We look for them, but do not see them; we listen to, but do not hear them; yet they enter into all things, and there is nothing without them, like overflowing water, they seem to be over the heads, and on the right and left of their worshippers."

It is said in the Book of Poetry. "The approaches of the spirits you cannot surmise; and can you treat them with indifference?

"Such is the manifestness of what is minute! Such is the impossibility of repressing the outgoings of sincerity.

"He who is greatly virtuous will be sure to receive the appointment of Heaven.

"The administration of government lies in getting proper men. Such men are to be got by means of the ruler's own character. That character is to be cultivated by his treading in the ways of duty. And the treading those ways of duty is to be cultivated by the cherishing of benevolence.

"Benevolence is the characteristic element of humanity. Righteousness is the accordance of actions with what is right.

"If principles of conduct have been previously determined, the practice of them will be inexhaustible.

"Sincerity is the way of Heaven. The attainment of sincerity is the way of men. To this attainment there are requisite the extensive study of what is good, accurate inquiry about it, careful reflection on it, the clear discrimination of it, and the earnest practice of it.

"Let a man proceed in this way, and, though dull, he will surely become intelligent; though weak, he will surely become strong. It is only he who is possessed of the most complete sincerity that can give full development to his nature.

"He who cultivates to the utmost the shoots of goodness in him. From those he can attain to the possession of sincerity. This sincerity becomes apparent. From being apparent it becomes manifest. From being manifest it becomes brilliant. Brilliant it affects others. Affecting others they are changed by it. Changed by it they are transformed.

"Heaven and Earth are without any doubleness, and so they produce things in a manner that is unfathomable.

"What needs no display is virtue.

"Learn the past and you will know the future.

"Grieve not that men know not you, grieve that you know not men.

"The essence of knowledge is, having it, to apply it; not having it, to confess your ignorance.

"Worship as though the Deity were present.

"If my mind is not engaged in my worship, it is as though I worshipped not."

MEXICO AND PERU.

The social condition of Mexico and Peru, at the time of the discovery of America, demonstrates what is claimed in the introduction of this work, that similar usages make their appearance spontaneously in the progress of civilization of different countries, showing how little they depend on accident, how closely they are connected with the nature and organization, and therefore with the necessities of man. From important ideas and great institutions down to the most trifling incidents of domestic life, so striking is the parallel between the American aborigines and Europeans that with difficulty do we divest ourselves of the impression that there must have been some intercommunication. Each was, however, pursuing an isolated and spontaneous progress; and yet how closely does the picture of life in the New World answer to that in the Old! The monarch of Mexico lived in pomp; wore a golden crown resplendent with gems; was aided in his duties by a privy council; the great lords held their lands of him by the obligation of military service. In him resided the legislative power, yet he was subject to the laws of the realm. The judges held their office independently of him, and were not liable to removal by him. The laws were reduced to writing, which though only a system of hieroglyphics, served its purpose so well that the Spaniards, were obliged to admit its validity in their courts, and to found a professorship for perpetuating a knowledge of it. Marriage was regarded as an important social engagement. Divorces were granted with difficulty.

In the human hives of Europe, Asia, and America, the bees were marshalled in the same way and were instinctively building their combs alike.

The religious state, that is true religion, is a reflection of that of Europe, and Asia! as also their theology. Their worship was mixed up with imposing ceremonial. The common people had a mythology of many gods, but the higher classes were strictly Unitarian, acknowledging one Almighty, invisible Creator. Of the popular deities, the god of war was the chief. With sedulous zeal, the clergy engrossed the duty of public education, thereby keeping society in their grasp.

The condition of astronomy in Mexico is illustrated, as it is in Egypt, by the calendar. At the conquest, the Mexican calendar was in a better condition than the Spanish. They had sun-dials for determining the hour, and also instruments for the solstices and the equinoxes. They had ascertained the globular form of the earth and the obliquity of the ecliptic. Their agriculture was superior to that of Europe ; there was nothing in the Old World to compare with the menageries and botanical gardens.

They employed a currency of gold dust, pieces of tin, and bags of cacao. In their domestic economy though polygamy was permitted, it was in practice, confined to the wealthy. The women did not work abroad, but occupied themselves in spinning, embroidering, feather-work, music. Ablution was resorted to both before and after meals ; perfumes were used at the toilet. The Mexicans gave to Europe tobacco, snuff, the turkey, chocolate, cochineal. Like us, they had in their entertainments solid dishes, with suitable condiments, gravies, sauces and desserts of pastries, confections, fruits, both fresh and preserved. They had chafing-dishes of silver or gold. Like us, they knew the use of intoxicating drinks; like us, they not unfrequently took them to excess; like us, they heightened their festivities with dancing and music. They had theatrical and pantomimic shows. At Tezcuco there was a council of music, which, moreover, exercised a censorship on philosophical works, as those of astronomy and history. In that city, North American civilization reached its height. The king's palace was a wonderful work of art. It was said that two hundred thousand men were employed in its construction.

The prevailing religious feeling is expressed by the sentiments of one of the kings, many of whom had prided themselves in their

MEXICO AND PERU. 63

poetical skill: "Let us," he says, "aspire to that heaven where all is eternal, and where corruption never comes." He taught his children not to confide in idols, but only to conform to the outward worship of them in deference to public opinion.

To the preceding description of the social condition of Mexico we shall add a similar brief account of that of Peru, for the conclusions to be drawn from a comparison of the spontaneous process of civilization in these two countries with the process in Europe, is of importance to the attainment of a just idea of the development of mankind. The most competent authorities declare that the Mexicans and Peruvians were ignorant of each other's existence.

The state of Peruvian civilization is at once demonstrated when it is said that these mountain slopes had become a garden, immense terraces having been constructed wherever required, and irrigation on a grander scale than that of Egypt carried on by gigantic canals and aqueducts. Advantage was taken of the different mean annual temperatures at different altitudes to pursue the cultivation of various products, for difference in height topographically answers to difference in latitude geographically; and thus, in a narrow space, the Peruvians had every variety of temperature, from that corresponding to the hottest portions of Southern Europe to that of Lapland. In the mountains of Peru, as has been graphically said, man sees "all the stars of the heavens and all the families of plants." On plateaus at a great elevation above the sea there were villages and even cities. Thus the plain upon which Quito stands, under the equator, is nearly ten thousand feet high. So great was their industry that the Peruvians had gardens and orchards above the clouds; and on ranges still higher flocks of lamas, in regions bordering on the limit of perpetual snow.

Through the entire length of the empire two great military roads were built; one on the plateau, the other on the shore. The former, for nearly two thousand miles, crossed sierras covered with snow, was thrown over ravines, or went through tunnels in the rocks.

The public couriers, as in Mexico, could make, if necessary, two hundred miles a day. Of these roads, Humboldt says that they were among the most useful and most stupendous ever executed by the hand of man.

In Cuzco, the metropolis, was the imperial residence of the Inca and the Temple of the Sun. It contained edifices which excited the amazement of the Spanish.

APPENDIX.

The Peruvian religion ostensibly consisted of a worship of the Sun, but the higher classes, had already become emancipated from such a material association, and recognized the existence of one almighty, invisible God. They expected the resurrection of the body and the continuance of the soul in a future life.

To the Supreme Being but one temple was dedicated. It was in a sacred valley, to which pilgrimages were made.

Besides the sun, the visible god, other celestial bodies were worshipped in a subordinate way.

As to the people, nowhere else in the whole world was such an extraordinary policy of supervision practised.

They were divided into groups of ten, fifty, one hundred, five hundred, one thousand, ten thousand, and over the last an Inca noble was placed. Through this system a rigid centralization was ensured, the Inca being the pivot upon which all the national affairs turned. It was an absolutism worthy of the admiration of many existing European nations.

The Inca, at once emperor and pope, was enabled, in that double capacity, to exert a rigorous partriarchal rule over his people, who were treated like children, not suffered to be oppressed. Industry was encouraged ; for, with a worldly wisdom which no other nation presents, labor was here acknowledged not as a means, but also as an end. It was the boast of the system that every one lived exempt from social suffering,—that all enjoyed competence.

In their extraordinary provisions for agriculture, the national pursuit, the skill of the Peruvians is well seen.

A rapid elevation from the sea-level to the heights of the mountains gave them, in a small compass, every variety of climate, and they availed themselves of it. They terraced the mountainsides, filling the terraces with rich earth. They excavated pits in the sand, surrounded them with adobe walls, and filled them with manured soil. On the low level they cultivated bananas and cassava; on the terraces above, maize and quinoa; still higher, tobacco; and above that, the potato. From a comparatively limited surface, they raised great crops by judiciously using manures, employing for that purpose fish, and especially guano. Their example has led to the use of the latter substance for a like purpose in our own times in Europe. The whole civilized world has followed them in the cultivation of the potato.

We have dwelt at some length on the domestic history of Mexico
and Peru because it is intimately connected with one of the
philosophical principles which it is the object of this book to teach,
viz: that human progress takes place under an unvarying law,
and therefore in a definite way. The trivial incidents mentioned
in the preceding paragraphs may perhaps have seemed insignificant and wearisome, but it is their very commonness, their very
familiarity, that gives them, when rightly considered a surprising
interest. There is nothing in these minute details but what we
find to be perfectly natural from the European point of view.
They might be, for that matter, instead of reminiscences of the
spontaneous evolution of a people shut out from the rest of the
world by impassable oceans, a relation of the progress of some
European or Asiatic nation. The man of America proceeded
forward in his course of civilization as did the man of the Old
World, devising the same institutions, guided by the same intentions, constrained by the same desires. From the great features of
his social system down to the little details of his domestic life, there
is a sameness with what was done in Asia, Africa, Europe. But
similar results imply a similar cause. What, then is there possessed
in common by the Chinese, the Hindoo, the Egyptian, the European,
the Americans? Simply nothing but the sameness of the endowments which constitute human nature—God working through Man
to produce his will and pleasure. The same instincts, intuitions,
incentives, and common sense guides men all over the world. Man
in his social progress, the free-will of which he so prides himself, in
his individual capacity gives way, or is so modified by the action
and influence of others and the domination of general laws, as that
God's exact purpose in creating man shall be attained; notwithstanding, that individual man (short-sighted as he is) has partial
control over his destiny.

The free agency of the individual is so restrained by instincts,
intuitions, and other influences, that none can hopelessly stray
from the path assigned to him. To each individual bee, the career
is open; he may taste of this flower and avoid that; he may bo
industrious in the garden, or idle away his time in the air; but the
history of one hive is the history of another hive; there will be a
predestined organization—the queen, the drones, the workers.
In the midst of a thousand unforeseen, uncalculated, variable acts,
a definite result, with unerring certainty, emerges; the combs are

built in a pre-ordained way, and filled with honey at last. At the time of the conquest the moral man in Peru was fully equal to the Europeans, and we will add, the intellectual man also. Nor in Spain, or even in all Europe, was there to be found a political system carried out into the practical details of actual life, and expressed in great public works as its outward, visible, and enduring sign, which could at all compare with that of Peru.

Manco Capac is generally spoken of by historians as having introduced the worship of the sun; this mistake seems to have arisen from the title of the GREAT LIGHT, by which many branches of the Indian people characterized the Creator, and this is perfectly scriptural, as we are taught to consider the sun as a symbol or representation of that Great moral Light and Life, which is emphatically called the "Sun of Righteousness." The sun is illustrative of the Divine power and Godhead, as well as are all the other works of the Creator; the term Great Light, and its symbol the sun, seem to have been considered by historians a synonyme; and therefore they have erroneously charged the Incas with the worship of the sun, instead of the great moral Light by whom as men, and as a community, they were greatly enlightened.

The following were among the regulations for governing the people; there were judges in small controversies. Idleness was punished with stripes. Each colony had a supreme judge. Theft, murders, and adultery were punished chiefly by death, in order not to leave a bad man more incensed or necessitated to commit new crimes.

These laws had so good an effect, that sometimes a year passed without one execution. * * * "After a long and revered reign, at the approach of the last period of life, Mango Capac called together all his children and grand-children; he told them he was going to repose himself with his Father. To his eldest son he left his empire, and advised and charged them all to continue in the paths of reason and virtue, which he had taught them, until they followed him on the same journey, and that this was the only course by which they could prove themselves the children of the GREAT LIGHT, and as such be honored and respected. He commanded his successor, whose name was Sinchi Roca, to govern his people with justice, mercy, piety, clemency, and care of the poor; and that when he should go to rest, &c., he should give the same instructions and exhortations to his successor."

Inca Roca erected schools for the education of the princes; it was a saying of this Inca, that, "If there be anything in this lower world which we might adore, it is a wise and virtuous man, who surpasses all other objects in dignity: but how can we pay Divine honors to one who is born in tears, who is in a daily state of change, who arrived but as yesterday, and who is not exempt from death—perhaps to-morrow." Ibid. ch. 2. p.75.

Pacha Cutec (the reformer) made many new laws and regulations; he was severely just, and was esteemed a wise monarch. The following were some of his apophthegms:—

"He who envies the wise and good, is like the wasp which sucks poison from the finest flowers."

"Drunkenness and anger admit of reformation, but folly is incurable."

"He who kills another unlawfully condemns himself to death."

"A noble and generous heart is known by the patience with which it supports adversity."

"How ridiculous is he who is not able to count by quipos, and yet pretends to number the stars."

The Inca Yupanqui was, by universal consent, surnamed the charitable! His son Tupac Yupanqui preserved the conquests of his virtuous predecessors; he "governed his empire with wisdom and mildness." The emperor at length, feeling the approach of death, gave orders that his children "should come into his presence to hear his last injunctions." He recommended them by living in peace and justice, to prove themselves the true children of the Supreme Light.

Among other maxims of this Inca, he said,—"Avarice and ambition like other Passions have no bounds of moderation: the first unfits a man for the government of his own family, or for any public employment; the second renders the understanding not susceptible of the counsels of the wise and virtuous."

"In the kingdom of Acolhuan, the judicial power was divided amongst seven principal cities. The judges remained in their tribunals from sun-rise until sun-set. Their meals were brought to them, that they might not be taken off from their employment by the concerns of their families, nor have any excuse for being corrupted. They were assigned possessions, and also laborers to cultivate their fields. Those possessions belonged to their office, and could not be inherited by their sons. Every Mexican month (twenty days) an assembly of Judges was held before the king, in order to determine all cases then undecided. If very intricate and perplexed, they were, if not then decided; reserved for the grand solemn general assembly, which was held every eighty days, and was called the conference of the eighty; at which all cases were finally disposed of, and punishment pronounced on the guilty.

He who at market altered the measures established by law, was guilty of felony, and was severely punished.

A murderer forfeited his own life for his crime, even although the person murdered was a slave.

"In the legislature of Acolhuan, if a nobleman was intoxicated to the losing of his senses, he was thrown into a river or lake; if a plebian, for the first offence, he lost his liberty, for the second, his life. And when the legislator was asked why the law was more severe upon nobles than others, he answered that the crime of drunkenness was less pardonable in them, as they were bound in duty to set a good example.

Hardwick says: There is reason to believe that some of these advances towards civilization in Mexico should be dated from a very high antiquity, especially in Yucatan. That Mexicans had borrowed largely from the Mayan builders, who already, in the dawn of history, erected towns and palaces and pyramid temples, rivalling those of Egypt in area and magnificence; her creed, her laws, her ritual, and administrative principles, had all assumed a very definite and distinctive character.

The wild man of America expresses a belief in some Great Spirit, (Mr. Schoolcraft says this doctrine is at the base of their religion. Mr. Prescott says "that the rude tribes inhabiting the vast American continent had attained to the sublime conception of one Great Spirit, the Creator of the universe,") manifesting itself, not only, as the root and basis of all being, but in the light of a beneficent Creator.

The Mexican name for God is teo-tl. The Mexicans beheld in him the being "by whom we live," "omnipresent, that knoweth all thoughts and giveth all gifts," "without whom man is as nothing," "invisible, incorporeal, one God of perfect perfection and purity," "under whose wings we find repose and a sure defence." This Being also had been worshipped by some elevated spirits, without image, sacrifice or temple. He was called the "Cause of causes," and the "Father of all things."

THE TALMUD. 69

In the address of the Mexican high-priest, the language runs as follows: "We entreat that those who die in war may be graciously received by thee, our Father."
The Mexicans conceive the proper home of the divine Being to be in the heavens: he is declared to be impalpable as "night and air."

THE TALMUD.

Among the ancient literature of the Hebrews was the Talmud, containing the laws and compilations of expositions of duties imposed upon the people by scripture, by traditions, by authority of their doctors, or by custom. The history of the time over which the composition of the Talmud ranges is about one thousand years, and its origin is co-eval with the return from the Babylonish captivity.

"Six hundred and thirteen injunctions" (says the Talmud) "was Moses instructed to give the people. David reduced them all to eleven in the fifteenth Psalm: "Lord who shall abide in thy tabernacle? Who shall dwell in thy holy hill? He that walketh uprightly, and worketh righteousness, and speaketh the truth in his heart. He that backbiteh not with his tongue, nor doeth evil to his neighbor, nor taketh up a reproach against his neighbor. In whose eyes a vile person is contemned ; but he honoreth them that fear the Lord. He that sweareth to his own hurt, and changeth not. He that putteth not out his money to usury, nor taketh a reward against the innocent. He that doeth these things shall never be moved."

The prophet Isaiah reduced them to six—xxxiii 15.—"He that walketh righteously and speaketh uprightly, he that despiseth the gain of oppressions, that shaketh his hands from holding of bribes, that stoppeth his ears from the hearing of blood, and shutteth his eyes from seeing evil; He shall dwell on high: his place of defence shall be the munitions of rocks: bread shall be given him; his waters shall be sure."

The prophet Micah reduced them to three,—vi. 8.—"What doth the Lord require of thee but to do justly, love mercy and walk humbly with thy God?"

Isaiah once more reduced them to two,—lvi. 1.—"Keep ye judgment and do justice."

APPENDIX.

Amos reduced them all to one,—v. 4.—"Seek me and ye shall live."

But lest it might be supposed from this that God could be found in the fulfilment of his whole law only, Habakkuk said,—ii. 4.—"The just shall live by faith."

As God is pure, so the soul is pure. This purity is specially dwelt upon in contradistinction to the theory of hereditary sin, which is denied.

There is no everlasting damnation according to the Talmud. There is only a temporary punishment even for the worst sinners. No human being is excluded from the world to come. The punishment of the wicked is not specified, as indeed all the descriptions of the next world are left vague, yet with regard to Paradise, the idea of something inconceivably glorious is conveyed at every step.

The "philosophy of religion" will be best comprehended by some of those "small coins," the popular and pithy sayings, gnomes, proverbs,—and the rest,—which, even better than street songs, characterize a time. We have thought it preferable to give them at random as we found them, instead of building up from them a system of "Ethics" or "Duties of the Heart." We have naturally preferred the better and more characteristic ones that came in our way.

"Be thou the cursed, not he who curses. Be of them that are persecuted, not of them that persecute. Look at Scripture: there is not a single bird more persecuted than the dove; yet God has chosen her to be offered up on His altar. The bull is hunted by the lion, the sheep by the wolf, the goat by the tiger. And God said, "Bring me a sacrifice, not from them that persecute, but from them that are persecuted." "Has God pleasure in the meat and blood of sacrifices?" asks the prophet. No; He has not so much ordained as permitted them. It is for yourselves, he says, not for me that you offer. Even when the gates of prayer are shut in heaven, those of tears are open. When the righteous dies it is the earth that loses. The aim and end of all wisdom is good works. The dying benediction of a sage to his disciples was: I pray for you that the fear of heaven may be as strong upon you as the fear of man. You avoid sin before the face of the latter: avoid it before the face of the All-seeing. "If your God hates idolatry, why does He not destroy it?" a heathen asked. And they answered him: Behold, they worship the sun, the moon, the stars; would you have Him destroy this beautiful world for the sake of the foolish? If your God is a "friend of the poor," asked another, "why does He not support them?" Their case, a sage answered, is left in our hands, that we may thereby acquire merits. But what a merit it is! the other replied; suppose I am angry with one of my slaves, and forbid him food and drink, and some one goes and gives it him furtively, shall I be much pleased? Not so, the other replied. Suppose you are wroth with your only son and imprison him without food, and some good man has pity on the child, and saves him from the pangs of hunger, would you be so very angry with the man? And we, if we are called servants of God are also called His children. He who has more learning than good works, is like a tree with many branches but few roots, which the first wind throws on its face; whilst he whose works are greater than his knowledge is like a tree with many roots and fewer branches, but which all the winds of heaven cannot uproot.

Love your wife like yourself, honor her more than yourself. Whosoever lives unmarried, lives without joy, without comfort, without blessing. Descend a step in choosing a wife. If thy wife is small, bend down to her and whisper into her ear. He who forsakes the love of his youth, God's altar weeps for him. He who sees his wife die before him, has, as it were, been present at the destruction of the sanctuary itself—around him the world grows dark. It is woman alone through whom God's blessings are vouchsafed to a house. She teaches the children, speeds the husband to the place of worship, and instruction, welcomes him when he returns, keeps the house godly and·pure, and God's blessings rest upon all these things. The birds in the air even despise the miser. He who gives charity in secret is greater than Moses himself. Honor the sons of the poor, it is they who bring science into splendor. Let the honor of thy neighbor be to thee like thine own. Hospitality is an important part of Divine worship. There are three crowns: of the law, the priesthood, the kingship; but the crown of a good name is greater than them all.

How can you escape sin? Think of three things: whence thou comest, whither thou goest, and to whom thou wilt have to account for all thy deeds; even to the King of Kings, the All-Holy, praised be He. Four shall not enter Paradise; the scoffer, the liar, the hypocrite, and the slanderer—There is a great difference between him who is ashamed before his own self, and him who is only ashamed before others. It is a good sign in man to be capable of being ashamed. One contrition in man's heart is better than many flagellations. He who walks daily over his estates finds a little coin each time. He who humiliates himself will be lifted up; he who raises himself up will be humiliated. Whosoever runs after greatness, greatness runs away from him, he who runs from greatness, greatness follows him. He who curbs his wrath, his sins will be forgiven. Whosoever does not persecute them that persecute him, whosoever takes an offence in silence, he who does good because of love, he who is cheerful under his sufferings—they are the friends of God, and of them the Scripture says, "And they shall shine forth as does the sun at noonday." Pride is like idolatry. Commit a sin twice and you will think it perfectly allowable. When the end of a man is come, everybody lords it over him. The day is short, and the work is great; but the laborers are idle, though the reward be great and the master of the work presses. It is not incumbent upon thee to complete the work; but thou must not therefore cease from it. If thou hast worked much, great shall be thy reward; for the master who employed thee is faithful in his payment. But know that the true reward is not of this world. "Have a care in legal decisions, send forth many disciples, and make a fence around the law." "On three things stands the world; on law, on worship, and on charity."

"Of all things, the most hated were idleness and asceticism, piety and learning themselves only received their proper estimation when joined to healthy bodily work. It is well to add a trade to your studies; you will then be free from sin."

Before leaving this period of Mishnic development, we have yet to speak of one or two things. This period is the one in which Christianity arose; and it may be as well to touch here upon the relation between Christianity and the Talmud. The New Testament, written as Lightfoot has it, "among Jews, by Jews, for Jews," cannot but speak the language of the time, both as to form and broadly speaking, as to contents. There are many more vital points of contact between the New Testament and the Talmud than divine seem fully to realize, for such terms as "Redemption," "Baptism," "Grace," "Faith," "Salvation," "Regeneration," "Son of Man," "Son of God," "Kingdom of Heaven," were not, as we are apt to think, invented by Christianity, but were household words of Talmudical Judaism. No less loud and bitter in the Talmud are the protests against "lip-serving," against "making the law a burden to the people," against "laws that hang on hairs," against "Priests and Pharisees." The fundamental mysteries of the new Faith are matters totally apart; but the Ethics in both are, in their broad outlines, identical. That grand dictum, "Do unto others as thou wouldst be done by," is quoted by Hillel, the President, at whose death, Jesus was ten years of age, not as anything new, but as an old and well-known dictum "that comprised the whole Law." "Thou shalt love thy neighbor as thyself," is a precept of the Old Testament, as Christ himself taught his disciples. The "Law" as we have seen and shall further see, was developed, to a marvellously, and perhaps, oppressively minute pitch. "The faith of the heart"—was a thing that stood much higher with the Pharisees than this outward law. It was a thing, they said, not to be commanded by any ordinance; yet was greater than all.

. About thirty years (B. C.) Hillel became President. Of his meekness, his piety, his benevolence, the Talmudical records are full. A few of his sayings will characterize him better than any sketch of ours could do. "Be a disciple of Aaron, a friend of peace, a promoter of peace, a friend of all men, and draw them near unto the law." "Do not believe in thyself till the day of thy death."

"Do not judge thy neighbor until thou hast stood in his place." "Whosoever does not increase in knowledge decreases." One day a heathen went to Shammai the head of the rival academy, and asked him mockingly to convert him to the law while he stood on one leg. The irate master turned him from the door. He then went to Hillel, who received him kindly, and gave him that reply— since so widely propagated. "Do not unto another what thou wouldst not have another do unto thee. This is the whole Law, the rest is mere commentary."

EGYPTIAN HISTORY.

It is ascertained to a certainty by the reading of hieroglyphics on the monuments of Egypt, that as long as five thousand years ago, Egypt was an old country, and the wild barbarian state "when wild in woods the noble savage ran," appears as remote from that period as from the present.

Art, luxury, even the vices of wealth and power are apparent, but of the so-called state of nature nothing is to be seen. The carliest king of all Egypt must have ascended the throne about B. C. 3643, and the paintings in the tombs at Ben Hassan must date at least B. C. 2800; giving them at his time an actual antiquity very little short of five thousand years: for they bear the names of that far-famed king of the twelfth dynasty, whose extraordinary stature, extensive conquests, and long reign are recorded by Manethon and Herodotus. His name is variously written by the different transcribers: in some it is Sesostris, in others Sesonchosis, and in the monuments, Sesortesen.

It was at one of the most brilliant periods of the Egyptian monarchy, therefore, that we have the elaborate representation of social life which these tombs afford: and this brilliant period was apparently anterior by many centuries to the birth even of Abraham.

At this epoch, five thousand years ago, the Egyptians were skilled in the art of glass-blowing; the smelting and working of metals, weaving, pottery, brick making, boat building, rope making, preparing leather, making wine from the grape, writing, painting, sculpture; they had saws for the carpenter, sickles for the reaper, scythes for the cutter of stubble, chisels for the sculptor: their buildings were supported by columns; they had gardens elaborately laid out, boats covered like a gondola to protect the passengers from the rays of the sun; the rich enjoyed field sports in their preserves, which were stocked with wild animals by the labor of slaves; ladies had their social meetings, where they were entertained by flute players and admired or criticised each other's dress; guests came to feasts in chariots drawn by caparisoned horses, and were entertained by tumblers and dancing girls, dressed in transparent robes, for the manufacture of which Egypt was always famous.

From the above enumeration of what we are wont to term the arts of civilization, we might fancy ourselves introduced to the dominions of a Hindoo prince of our own times. No! It is the picture of an age of the world when primeval barbarism has been supposed to have prevailed.

Trace back the Egyptians from the age of the great Sesortesen toward that of the founder of the sole monarchy, and what do we find? Pyramids, obelisks, gigantic statues, temples; all the evidences of wealth and power. Writing materials are depicted on the monuments of the fourth dynasty. The age of barbarism like the rainbow, recedes at the attempt to follow it.

EGYPTIAN HISTORY. 75

The priests, here, as in all other countries, were a favored class segregated from the rest by their learning and their riches, no less than by their privilege of caste; despising this ignorance of the lower orders, devised ceremonies to amuse, rather than to enlighten them; and thus perpetuated and even increased this ignorance. All that we are told of the mysteries, the secret doctrines &c., which the Greeks affirm to have been introduced from Egyyt, comfirms this; the religion of the heart, which ought to have expressed itself in the simple prayer or thanksgiving which formed the first worship of man, was exchanged for a set of ceremonies so complicated, that the complete knowledge of them became an art requiring long instruction; the truth was hid under a vein which common eyes were unable to see through; and the sacerdotal caste arrogated consequence to itself for knowing what it had itself originally concealed.

There is a tendency in mankind to keep that a secret which is profitable; and it is seldom that any priesthood, existing as a corporate body, has entirely escaped the dangerous influence of the spirit of caste. NOTE.—It is to this probably, that most of the corruptions of Christ's teaching have been owing. Man is discouraged by the priests from believing that the approach to his Maker is easy, or his laws simple as nature itself; they are taught to despise the plain short order "Wash and be clean." Hence the gorgeousness of ceremonial worship.

In the paintings of Beni-Hassan, though the act of prayer, and the offering of incense are often represented, no figure of the deity to whom this service was dedicated, is given. At a later period both paintings and sculpture abound with representations of strangely misformed deities, which are receiving the homage of their worshippers. Yet in the midst of all this, the books of the priesthood (for such we must imagine the ceremonial ritual of which so many fragments are still existing) tell of a judgment after death, according to the actions performed during life; of the immortality of the soul; and of its re-union with the body.

We have no positive knowledge of the state of man in other countries at the early period to which the monuments of Egypt carry us back; but India, China, and Persia, claim for themselves a civilization as ancient, and there is no reason why a state of things which we find certainly proved in one country, should not have extended to others. Indeed, if we may be allowed to reason from analogy, it is much more probable that other nations should have reached to something near the same point, than that Egypt should have stood alone. China has been so much a sealed book, hitherto, that we can say little as to its antiquities, or even as to its present habits; but there is much in modern Hindostan which reminds us of the state of manners depicted in the tombs of the ancient Egyptians.

Within a short time the opinions here advanced, have received a farther corroboration from the disinterment of sculptures from the palaces, or temples of the ancient Assyrian empire; which mark a state of civilization very similar to that of Egypt. We find there a monarch sumptuously apparelled and attended; horses harnessed to chariots; swords elaborately ornamented on the hilt; dresses embroidered and fringed; and a style of sculpture greatly resembling that of ancient Egypt.

" The centre of the consciousness which the Egyptains possessed of God's agency in our history is the Osiris worship, the oldest, and most sacred portion of their religion—Osiris is the Lord, the God and father of each individual soul, the judge of men, who passes sentence strictly according to the right and wrong, rewarding goodness and punishing crime.—The judgment held upon the souls of the dead is nothing else than the reflection of that general theory of the universe according to which the good prevails, on earth in the midst of conflict, while evil annihilates itself, promoting the good against its own will—It involves the recognition that there is a solution of the enigma of existence which is not to be found in the term of a single life on earth, and yet which we are compelled to seek after, in order to explain this life—All guilt must be expiated—but the final issue, although reached only after the lapse of unnumbered ages, will be the triumph of the good, the general reconciliation, and a life in God will be the eternal heritage of the soul—This thought pervades all the records we possess respecting the trial held upon the deceased in Egypt—This special mystery of the Egyptian religion implies a faith in the two great fundamental laws of all religious consciousness—the unity of the human reason in the conscience, and the indestructibility of personal identity—All mankind are judged by Osiris according to one standard"—The foregoing are among the religious views held by the Egyptians three thousand years B. C.

STOICISM.

Dugal Stewart says, "The Stoics were a large sect, and of its members so many have been celebrated, that a separate work would be needed to chronicle them all. From Zeno, the founder, down to Brutus and Marcus Antonius, the sect embraces many Greek and Roman worthies, and not a few solemn pretenders. Some of these we would willingly introduce; but we are forced to confine ourselves to one type; and the one we select is Zeno."

He was born at Citium, a small city in the island of Cyprus, of Phœnician origin, but inhabited by Greeks. The date of his birth is uncertain, probably about three hundred and fifty years B. C. His father was a merchant, in which trade he himself engaged, until his father, after a voyage to Athens, brought home some works of Socratic philosophers; these Zeno studied with eagerness and rapture, and determined his vocation.

When about thirty, he undertook a voyage, both of interest and pleasure, to Athens, the great mart both for trade and philosophy. Shipwrecked on the coast, he lost the whole of his valuable cargo of Phœnician purple: and thus, reduced to poverty, he willingly embraced the doctrine of the Cynics, whose ostentatious display of poverty had captivated many minds.

The gross manners of the Cynics, so far removed from true simplicity, and their speculative incapacity, soon caused him to seek a master elsewhere.

As a man, Zeno appears deserving of the highest respect. So honored and respected was he by the Athenians, that they entrusted to him the keys of the citadel; and when he died they erected to his memory a statue of brass.

Zeno the stoic had a Roman spirit; and this is the reason why so many noble Romans became his disciples: he had deciphered the wants of their spiritual nature.

Alarmed at the scepticism which seemed inevitably following speculations of a metaphysical kind, Zeno, like Epicurus, fixed his thoughts principally upon morals. His philosophy boasted of being eminently practical, and connected with the daily practices of life. But, for this purpose, the philosopher must not regard pleasure so much as virtue: nor does virtue consist in a life of contemplation, but in a life of activity.

Zeno taught as follows: Not to regard pleasure so much as virtue: nor does virtue consist in a life of contemplation and speculation, but in a life of activity; for what is virtue? Virtue is manhood. And what are the attributes of man? Are they not obviously the attributes of an active, as well as of a speculative being? and can that be virtue which excludes or neglects man's activity? Man was not made for speculation only; wisdom is not his only pursuit. Man was not made for enjoyment only; he was made also to do somewhat, and to be somewhat.

If the universe be subject to a general law, every part of that universe must also be duly subordinate to it. The consequence is clear; there is but one formula for morals, and that is, "Live harmoniously with nature," both individual and universal nature.

The Stoics placed the supreme good in rectitude of conduct, without any regard to the event. They taught that nature pointed out to us certain objects of choice and of rejection, and amongst these some to be more chosen and avoided than others: and that virtue consisted in choosing and rejecting objects according to their intrinsic value.

"The Stoics, in the character of their virtuous man, included rational desire, aversion, and exultation, included love and parental affection, friendship, and a general benevolence to all mankind."

Nor did they exclude wealth from among the objects of choice. The Stoic Hecato, in his Treatise of Offices quoted by Cicero, tells us, "That a wise man, while he abstains from doing anything contrary to the customs, laws, and institutions of his country, ought to attend to his own fortune. For we do not desire to be rich for ourselves only, but for our children, relations, and friends, and especially for the commonwealth, inasmuch as the riches of individuals are the wealth of a State."

By the Stoics, virtue was supposed to consist in the affectionate performance of every good office towards their fellow-creatures, and in full resignation to Providence for everything independent of their own choice.

"The Stoic enlisted himself as a willing instrument in the hands of God for the good of his fellow-creatures. For himself, the cares and attentions which this object required were his pleasures, and the continued exertion of a beneficent affection, his welfare and his prosperity."

Upon the whole, it cannot be disputed, that its leading doctrines are agreeable to the purest principles of morality and religion.

Indeed, they all terminate in one maxim: That we should not make the attainment of things external an ultimate object, but place the business of life in doing our duty, and leave the care of our happiness to him who made us.

It was the precepts of this school which rendered the supreme power in the hands of Marcus Aurelius a blessing to the human race; and which secured the private happiness, and elevated the minds of Helvidius and Thrasea under a tyranny by which their country was oppressed.

Classical Antiquity.

In ancient Rome the political institutions, and therefore, civil liberty, were the organs of religious consciousness.

Now, if we take both these series of development as a whole, we shall readily convince ourselves, that in some particular branches history shows nothing elsewhere equal in splendor to the phenomena presented by the religious consciousness of classical antiquity. This holds good, more especially, of its manifestations in public life. In this field, freedom forms a constant unit. And where else do we find so high a level attained by the community at large, combined with that public spirit and readiness to make sacrifices for the common wealth of a beloved and free fatherland, which ever betokens a high grade of culture; as among Greeks and Romans? Where so organic an unfolding, elaboration, and permanent fruitage of art and poetry? Where so finished a form of historical and philosophical composition?

And the social, no less than the public life of this ancient world, is much more thoroughly inter-penetrated with the sense of divine sanction than is that of our modern world.

The comparison of the parallel phenomena presented by Aryan Christendom and classical antiquity, must leave a depressing impression on the impartial observer.

The Romans had no hereditary sacred code, relating to spiritual and moral things, similar to those of the Hebrews, or even such as the Greeks possessed in that early period we have in view. Nor, again, had the Romans any prophets, either in the same sense as the Hebrews, or such as the Greeks were familiar with.

The Romans were not mere warriors and conquerors. They had their wise law-givers, who made efficient regulations, and adhered to them, from Servius Tullius onwards; courageous Statesmen, and upright Judges.

Cicero.

Cicero, who lived B. C., 106, says: that, "Law properly understood, is no other than right reason, agreeing with nature, spread abroad among men, ever consistent with itself, eternal, whose office is to summon to duty by its commands, to deter from vice by its prohibitions,—which, however, to the good never commands or forbids in vain, never influences the wicked, either by commanding or forbidding. In contradiction to this law, nothing can be laid down, nor does it admit of partial or entire repeal. Nor can we be released from this law either by vote of the Senate, or decree of the people. Nor does it require any commentator, or interpreter besides itself. Nor will there be one law at Athens, and another at Rome, one now, and another hereafter: but one eternal, immutable law will both embrace all nations and at all times. And there will be one common Master, as it were, and Ruler of all, namely, God, the great Originator, Expositor, Enactor of this Law; which law, whoever will not obey, will be flying from himself, and having treated with contempt his nature, will, in that very fact, pay the greatest penalty, even if he shall have escaped other punishments, as they are commonly considered.

All men acknowledge that which we are led by nature to suppose, namely, that there are Gods.

Surely the mighty power of the Infinite Being is most worthy of our great and earnest contemplation.

Ignorance is inconsistent with the nature of the Gods, and imbecility with their majesty.

Is he worthy to be called man, who attributes to chance, not to an intelligent cause, the constant motions of the heavens, the regular courses of the stars, the agreeable proportion and connection of all things, conducted with so much reason, that our intellect itself is unable to estimate it rightly. When we see machines move artificially, as a sphere, a clock, or the like, do we doubt whether they are the production of reason? And when we behold the heavens moving with a prodigious celerity, and causing an annual succession of the different seasons of the year, which vivify and preserve all things, can we doubt that the world is directed by a reason most excellent and divine?

Among men there is no nation so savage and ferocious as not to admit the necessity of believing in a God. From whence we conclude that every man must recognize a Deity.

The law of virtue is the same in God and man.

What nation is there, which has not a regard for kindness, benignity, and gratitude? What nation is there, in which arrogance, cruelty, and unthankfulness are not reprobated and detested?

There is no expiation for the crimes and impieties of men. The guilty, therefore, must pay the penalty, and bear the punishment; not so much those punishments inflicted by courts of justice, which were not always in being, do not exist at present in many places, and even where established, are frequently biased and partial,— but those of conscience; while the furies pursue them, not with burning torches as the poets feign, but with remorse of conscience, and the tortures arising from guilt.

Pindar.

Pindar, the Theban, a Greek Poet, born about B. C. 520, had extraordinary honors paid to him during his life, and after his decease. His odes and religious hymns were chanted in the temples of Greece before the most crowded assemblies, and on the most solemn occasions. The priestess of Apollo at Delphi declared that it was the will of that divinity that Pindar should receive half of the first fruits offered at his shrine. The Athenians erected a statue of brass in honor of him.

Pindar speaks of the divine load-stars of this earthly life, virtue, piety, and reason, which ponder on the seriousness of life, and pious reverence for moderation. In no case does he refer man to omens and dreams and auguries.

The Hellenes possessed no sacred historical records, and therefore, escaped, the dangers of deducing intellectual dogmas of belief from historical traditions or symbolical legends and fables.

Pindar proclaimed, that in human destinies a divine law rules, and this is the same law which the wise and pious man discovers in his own bosom.

There exists an Order of the World: it is a Moral Order. It subsists not only for the brief earthly existence of the soul, for it is of a divine nature; but already here below it regulates human destinies with a divine authority.

Again, he declares that, human things have their origin and subsistence by virtue of the divine element which resides in them.

The self-seeking principle in individuals or states.

F

Pindar preached this doctrine, not after the fashion of an Orphic theologian : he set it before all men's eyes in the events and experiences of actual life. If any one expects to escape the notice of the Deity in doing aught, he errs.

As many as have steadfastness, to keep their soul altogether from unjust actions, accomplish their way on the path of Zeus.

Hateful is deceitful speech, meditating guile, ill report that maketh mischief. May I never have this character, Father Zeus, but may I hold to the guileless paths of life.

As to what shall befall us, no sure presage attends men, whereby they may foreknow the decrees of Providence.

Hope binds the frame of man with strong enchantment.

The bitterest end awaits the pleasure that is contrary to right.

PLATO.

Plato first established himself at Athens as a lecturer about 386 B. C.

Plato says that, in order to be happy, a man must be at once wise, brave, temperate, just.

He does not indeed lay his main stress on the retribution and punishments which follow injustice, because he represents injustice as being in itself a state of misery, to the unjust agent: nor upon the rewards attached to justice, because he represents justice itself as a state of intrinsic happiness to the just agent.

The just man will be well-esteemed and well-treated by men ; he will also be favored and protected by the Gods, both in this life and after this life. The unjust man, on the contrary, will be ill-esteemed and ill-treated by men; he will be disapproved and punished by the Gods, both while he lives, and after his death. Perhaps for a time the just man may seem to be hardly dealt with and miserable—the unjust man to be prosperous and popular—but in the end, all this will be reversed.

Man is happy or miserable, in and through himself, or essentially; whether he be known to Gods and men or not—whatever may be the sentiment entertained of him by others.

Plato declares that it is impracticable and impious to attempt to appease the displeasure, or to conciliate the favor of the Gods by means of prayer and sacrifice.

He accounts it a greater crime to believe in indulgent and persuadeable Gods, than not to believe in any Gods at all.

Every one loves, desires, or aspires to happiness: this is the fundamental or primordial law of human nature, beyond which we cannot push enquiry. Good, or good things, are nothing else but the means to happiness: accordingly every man, loving happiness, loves good also, and desires not only full acquisition, but perpetual possession of good.

EPICURUS.

Epicurus, a Greek Philosopher, 280 B. C., in his letter to Menœcus gives his Code of Morals, and mode of life, at some length, which are as follows: "No one," he says, "ought to think himself too young or too old for philosophic contemplation: since it is the great business of man to consider what is requisite to the living well: happily as regards himself, and worthily as regards his relations to society. And in the first place as a needful constituent of this knowledge, we must take care that, believing God to be an immortal and perfectly happy Being, we attribute nothing to Him that is inconsistent with these attributes." Seneca reproached Epicurus with reverencing God only as a parent, to be honored and worshipped for His excellence, without thinking of any gain to be obtained by so doing.

"The wise man," continues Epicurus, "will not consider the loss of life an evil, but as food is chosen for its quality, rather than its quantity, so he will endeavor to make his life pleasant rather than long. It is needful to satisfy our physical wants in a certain degree, both for the sake of living in comfort, and in order to keep the body tranquil, so as to leave the mind free from disturbance; for our endeavor should be to avoid suffering and perturbation: since pleasure is the great object of life. But it is not every kind of pleasure that will be sought by a wise man; for luxurious feasts are not needful to him who by temperance and exercise has made his bread and water sweet to his taste; therefore when I speak of pleasure as the summum bonum ; I do not mean licentious pleasures; for he only enjoys a truly happy life, who examines his desires by the light of sober reason, and determines which ought to be qualified, which repressed. In short, no man can live happily who does not live wisely and justly, and no man can live wisely and justly without being happy, for virtue and happiness cannot be separated. Nay, were it possible, it would be better to live wisely and to be unhappy, than to be irrational and fortunate. One who acts on these principles lives among men as if he were already a god; he has nothing about him that resembles the brute animal, but though a man, he lives among the immortals."

SOCRATES.

Socrates, who taught 430 years B. C., remarks, that honorable things are good things, and that every one without exception desires good. On this point all men are alike; the distinctive features of virtue must then consist in the power of acquiring good things, such as health, wealth, money, power, dignities, &c. But the acquisition of these things is not virtuous, unless it be made consistently with justice and moderation.

Socrates recommends virtue on the ground of its remunerative consequences to the agent, in the shape of wealth and other good things. He, as well as Xenophon, agree in the same doctrine: presenting virtue as laborious and troublesome in itself, but as being fully requited by its remunerative consequences in the form of esteem and honor, to the attainment of which it is indispensable.

When I have learnt, says Socrates, which are my worst and which are my best points, I shall evidently be in a condition to cultivate and pursue the latter, and resolutely to avoid the former.

My mission from the Gods, says Socrates, is to dispel the false persuasion of knowledge, to cross-examine men into a painful conviction of their own ignorance, and to create in them a lively impulse towards knowledge and virtue.

Justice, which is good both in itself, and by reason of its consequences, I rank among the noblest qualities.

The just man should act with a view to good.

The just man is happy, and the unjust miserable.

Socrates maintains, that justice is good, per se, ensuring the happiness of the agent by its direct and intrinsic effects on the mind: whatever its ulterior consequences may be. He maintains indeed that these ulterior consequences are also good: but that they do not constitute the paramount benefit; or the main recommendation of justice: that the good of Justice, per se, is much greater.

The fundamental principle (Socrates affirms) to which cities or communities owe their origin, is, existence or wants and necessities in all men. No single man is sufficient for himself: every one is in want of many things, and is therefore compelled to seek communion or partnership with neighbors and auxiliaries. Reciprocal dealings begin : each gives to others, and receives from others, under the persuasion that it is better for him to do so.

In regard to religion, the raising of temples, arrangement of sacrifices, &c., we know nothing about these matters. We must examine it, and see where we can find Justice and Injustice.

Justice is in the mind what health is in the body, when the parts are so arranged as to control, and be controlled pursuant to the dictates of nature. Injustice is in the mind what disease is in the body, when the parts are so arranged as to control, and be controlled contrary to the dictates of nature ; virtue is thus health, beauty, good condition of the mind : vice is the disease, ugliness, weakness of the mind.

It is profitable to a man to be just, and to do justice, per se, even though he be not known as just either by Gods or men, and may thus be debarred from the consequences which would ensue if he were known. It is unprofitable to him to be unjust, even though he can continue to escape detection and punishment. As health is the greatest good, and sickness the greatest evil of the body : so Justice is the greatest good, and Injustice the greatest evil of the mind.

Socrates says, that the Gods are good, and therefore cannot be the cause of anything except good. The Gods must be announced as causes of all the good which exists. No poetical tale can be tolerated which represents the Gods as assuming the forms of different persons, and going about to deceive men into false beliefs.

A perfectly reasonable man will account death no great evil.

If a man passes his life pleasurable until its close, it may be said that he has lived well : at least, provided he lives taking pleasure in fine or honorable things.

To do wrong is worse than to suffer wrong, as well as more disgraceful.

If a man be punished for wrong doing, he suffers what is just, and the punisher does what is just.

We ought to do—continues Socrates—what is pleasing for the sake of what is good : not vice versa. But every thing becomes good by possessing its appropriate virtue or regulation. The regulation appropriate to the mind is, to be temperate. The temperate man will do what is just—his duty towards men : and what is holy—his duty towards the Gods. He will be just and holy. He will therefore also be courageous : for he will seek only such pleasures as duty permits, and he will endure all such pains as duty requires. Being thus temperate, just, brave, holy, he will be a perfectly good man, doing well and honorably throughout. The man who does well, will be happy : the man who does ill, and is wicked, will be miserable.

Every thing has its own fixed and determinate essence, not relative to us nor varying according to our will and pleasure, but existing, per se, as nature has arranged. All agencies, either by one thing upon other things, or by other things upon it, are in like manner determined by nature, independent of our will and choice.

XENOPHANES.

Xenophanes maintained that there was but one God, identical with, or a personification of the whole Uranus. "The whole Kosmos, or the whole God, sees, hears, and thinks." The divine nature, he said, did not admit of the conception of separate persons, one governing the other, or of want and imperfection in any way.

HERAKLEITUS.

Herakleitus says, "Every man, individually considered, was irrational: reason belonged only to the universal or to the whole, with which the mind of each living man was in conjunction, renewing itself by perpetual absorption, inspiration or inhalation, transition, and impressions through the senses."

PROTAGORAS.

Protagoras asserts that no good citizen can be without a sense of justice, and of shame.

GRECIAN HISTORY.

Orpheus, a Thracian, visited Egypt and brought from thence the doctrines with which he afterwards corrupted the simple religion of Greece, The doctrine he taught was that of One, Self-existent God, the Maker of all things, who is present to us in all His works; but this great truth was disguised under a mass of fables.

Orpheus taught that the One Supreme Deity was the source of all, and that tutelary gods of air, fire, earth, &c., were in fact only emanations of his power made manifest to men by visible and tangible objects. But when the Most High was no longer to be approached by the vulgar, the especial manifestations was soon

SACRED BOOK OF THE MEXICANS. 87

individualized, and a polytheism, which probably the first introducers of this mysterious doctrine, never contemplated, was built upon it.

The mysterious doctrine of Orpheus, which gave tangibility and distinctness to the notions of the Deity, soon struck the imaginations of the poet. Homer and Hesiod took it up and finished the individualizing process by giving names and forms to the various sub-deities of the different powers of nature. Yet these were for a long time, only the poetical version of the old belief: the one Supreme God still held the reins, and Destiny was looked up to as the ruler of these sub-gods no less than of men.

SACRED BOOK OF THE MEXICANS.

We gather the following from Müller: A book called "Popol Vuh," and pretending to be the original text of the sacred writings of the Indians of Central America. The "Popol Vuh" is a literary composition in the true sense of the word. It contains the mythology and history of the civilized races of Central America, and comes before us with credentials that will bear the test of critical inquiry.

"Popol Vuh" means the book of the people, and referred to the traditional literature in which all that was known about the early history of the nation, their religion and ceremonies, was handed down from age to age. We find material for studying their character, for analyzing their religion and mythology, for comparing their principles of morality, their views of virtue, beauty, and heroism, to those of other races of mankind. This is the charm, the real and lasting charm, of such works as that presented to us for the first time in a trustworthy translation by the Abbé Brasseur de Bourbourg. There are some coincidences between the Old Testament and the Quiché MS. which are certainly startling. Yet even if a Christian influence has to be admitted, much remains in these American traditions which is so different from anything else in the national literatures of other countries, that we may safely treat it as the genuine growth of the intellectual soil of America.

EXTRACTS FROM "POPOL VUH."

The Quiche MS. begins with an account of the creation, the Quichés believed that there was a time when all that exists in heaven and earth was made. All was then in suspense, all was calm and silent; all was immovable, all peaceful, and the vast space of the heavens was empty. There was no man, no animal, no shore, no trees; heaven alone existed. The face of the earth was not to be seen; there was only the still expanse of the sea and the heaven above. Divine beings were on the waters like a growing light. Their voice was heard as they meditated and consulted, and when the dawn arose, man appeared. Then the waters were commanded to retire; the earth was established, that she might bear fruit, and that the light of day might shine on heaven and earth.

"For, they said, we shall receive neither glory nor honor from all we have created until there is a human being—a being endowed with reason. 'Earth' they said, and in a moment the earth was formed. Like a vapor it rose into being, mountains appeared from the waters like lobsters, and the great mountains were made.— Thus was the creation of the earth, when it was fashioned by those who are the Heart of heaven, the Heart of the earth; for thus were they called who first gave fertility to them, heaven and earth being still inert and suspended in the midst of the waters."

Then follows the creation of the brute world, and the disappointment of the gods when they commanded the animals to tell their names, and to honor those who had created them. Then the gods said to the animals:

"You will be changed, because you cannot speak. We have changed your speech. You shall have your food and your dens in the woods and crags; for our glory is not perfect, and you do not invoke us. There will be beings still that can salute us; we shall make them capable of obeying. Do your task; as to your flesh, it will be broken by the tooth."

Then follows the creation of man. His flesh was made of earth— terre glaise.—But man was without cohesion or power, inert and aqueous; he could not turn his head, his sight was dim, and though he had the gift of speech, he had no intellect. He was soon consumed again in the water.

And the gods consulted a second time how to create beings that should adore them, and after some magic ceremonies, men were made of wood, and they multiplied. But they had no heart, no intellect, no recollection of their Creator; they did not lift up their heads to their Maker, and they withered away and were swallowed up by the waters.

SACRED BOOK OF THE MEXICANS. 89

Then follows a third creation, man being made of a tree called "tzité," woman of the marrow of a reed called "sibac." They, too, did neither think or speak before him who had made them, and they were likewise swept away by the waters and destroyed. The whole nature—animals, trees, and stones—turned against men to revenge the wrongs they had suffered at their hands, and the only remnant of that early race is to found in small monkeys which still live in the forests.

Three attempts, as we saw, had been made and had failed. We now hear again that before the beginning of dawn, and before the sun and moon had risen, man had been made, and that nourishment was provided for him which was to supply his blood, namely, yellow and white maize. Four men are mentioned as the real ancestors of the human race, or rather of the race of the Quichés. They were neither begotten by the gods, nor born of woman, but their creation was a wonder wrought by the Creator. They could reason and speak, their sight was unlimited, and they knew all things at once. When they had rendered thanks to their Creator for their existence, the gods were frightened, and they breathed a cloud over the eyes of men that they might see a certain distance only, and not be like the gods themselves. Then while the four men were asleep, the gods gave them beautiful wives, and these became the mothers of all tribes, great and small. These tribes, both white and black, lived and spread in the East. They did not yet worship the gods, but only turned their faces up to heaven, hardly knowing what they were meant to do here below. Their features were sweet, so was their language, and their intellect was strong.

A legend which is current among the Thlinkithians, who are one of the four principal races inhabiting Russian America, is as follows: They believe in a general flood or deluge, and that men saved themselves in a large floating building. When the waters fell, the building was wrecked on a rock, and by its own weight burst into two pieces. Hence arose the difference of languages. The Thlinkithians with their language remained on one side; on the other side were all the other races of the earth.

Neither the Esthonian nor the Thlinkithian legend, however, offers any striking points of coincidence with the Mosaic accounts. The analogies, therefore, as well as the discrepancies, between the ninth chapter of Genesis and the chapter here tranlated from the Quiché MS. require special attention.

BELIEFS OF THE AMERICAN INDIANS.

Müller says, "the Greenlander believes that when a man dies his soul travels to Torngarsuk, the land where reigns perpetual summer, all sunshine and no night; where there is good water, and birds, and fish, seals, and reindeer without end, that are to be caught without trouble, or are found cooking alive in a huge kettle. But the journey to this land is difficult; the souls have to slide five days or more down a precipice, all stained with the blood of those who have gone down before. And it is especially grievous for the poor souls, when the journey must be made in winter or in tempest, for then a soul may come to harm, or suffer the other death, as they call it.

The native tribes of the lower end of South America believe in two great powers of good and evil, but likewise in a number of inferior deities. These are supposed to have been the creators and ancestors of different families, and hence when an Indian dies his soul goes to live with the deity who presides over his particular family. These deities have each their separate habitations in vast caverns under the earth, and thither the departed repair to enjoy the happiness of being eternally drunk.

Messrs. Lewis and Clarke give the following account of the belief in a future state entertained by another American tribe, the Mandans:

"Their belief in a future state is connected with this tradition of their origin: The whole nation resided in one large village under ground near a subterraneous lake. A grape-vine extended its roots down to their habitation and gave them a view of the light. Some of the most adventurous climbed up the vine, and were delighted with the sight of the earth, which they found covered with buffalo, and rich with every kind of fruit. Returning with the grapes they had gathered, their countrymen were so pleased with the taste of them that the whole nation resolved to leave their dull residence for the charms of the upper region. Men, women, and children ascended by means of the vine, but when about half the nation had reached the surface of the earth, a corpulent woman who was clambering up the vine, broke it with her weight, and closed upon herself and the rest of the nation the light of the sun. Those who

BELIEF OF NEW HOLLANDERS—ICELANDERS. 91

were left on earth made a village below where we saw the vine villages; and when the Mandans die they expect to return to the original seats of their forefathers, the good reaching the ancient village by means of the lake, which the burden of the sins of the wicked will not enable them to cross."

Catlin's account of the Choctaw belief in a future state is equally curious. They hold that the spirit lives after death, and that it has a great distance to travel towards the west; that it has to cross a dreadful, deep, and rapid stream, over which, from hill to hill, there lies a long, slippery pine log, with the bark peeled off. Over this the dead have to pass before they reach the delightful hunting-grounds. The good walk on safely, though six people from the other side throw stones at them; but the wicked, trying to dodge the stones, slip off the log and fall thousands of feet into the water which is dashing over the rocks.

BELIEF OF THE NEW HOLLANDERS.

The New Hollanders, according to Mr. Oldfield, believe that all who are good men and have been properly buried, enter heaven after death. Heaven, which is the abode of the two good divinities, is represented as a delightful place, where there is abundance of game and food, never any excess of heat or cold, rain or drought, no malign spirits, no sickness or death; but plenty of rioting, singing, and dancing for evermore. They also believe in an evil spirit who dwells in the nethermost regions, and, strange to say, they represent him with horns and a tail.

OF THE ICELANDERS.

The following traditions in relation to creation are contained in the book Edda, the sacred book of the Icelanders.

"'Twas the morning of time,
When yet naught was,
Nor sand nor sea were there,
Nor cooling streams;
Earth was not formed,
Nor heaven above;
A yawning gap there was,
And grass nowhere."

In the "Edda," man is said to have been created out of an ash-tree, and God is portrayed as follows: "Who is first and eldest of all gods?" He is called "Allfadir,"—the Father of All, the Great Father—in our tongue. He lives from all ages, and rules over his realm and sways all things, great and small. He made heaven and earth, and the sky, and all that belongs to them; and he made man, and gave him a soul that shall live and never perish, though the body rot to mould, or burn to ashes. All men that are right-minded shall live, and be with him in a place called "Vingolf:" but wicked ones fare to Hell and thence into Niflhell, that is, beneath in the ninth world.

CHRISTIAN THEOLOGY NO RESTRAINT.

We have heretofore remarked that all motives to virtue have their only foundation in, and all good works proceed from, the moral faculties—that is the conscience, and the instincts originally given to man; and that the evil-doings of man find their only check or restraint in this reflex of God in man. There is no restraint found in the Christian theology, or elsewhere, not found in every man's conscience: while on the other hand, history shows us that Christianity has been the most powerful of all agents in stifling the voice of conscience, and in bringing horrors and calamities upon mankind. The assertion may seem a startling one, but its truth can scarcely be denied by the reader, who follows us through the dismal record of great crimes committed by people supposed to be specially chosen of God and enjoying his immediate supervision, by others taking the Old Testament as their guide, and by others still, whose iniquities and atrocities were perpetrated in the name of Jesus. We propose to glance successively, at the bloody contentions of the early Church; at the crimes and corruptions of the Church during the Middle Ages; at the Crusades; at the persecutions of the Jews by the Christians; at the sacrifice of human life in the so-called holy wars waged by Christians for theological opinions alone; at the persecution of the Protestants by the Catholics; at the massacre of St. Bartholomew, under a king, one of whose titles was, the "Most Christian;" at the cruel course of Spain in overrunning and despoiling Mexico and Peru.

Let us commence with the

CONTENTIONS OF THE EARLY CHURCH.

From the Trinitarian controversy which began in the reign of Constantine—about A. D. 323—we may date the introduction of

CONTENTIONS OF THE EARLY CHURCH. 93

rigorous articles of belief, which required the submissive assent of the mind to every word and letter of an established creed, and which raised the slightest heresy of opinions into a more fatal offence against God, and a more odious crime in the estimation of man, than the worst moral delinquency or the most flagrant deviation from the spirit of Christianity.

Such was the question which led to all the evils of human strife,—hatred, persecution, bloodshed.

The distribution of the superior dignities of the Church became an object of fatal ambition and strife. The streets of Alexandria and of Constantinople were deluged with blood by the partisans of rival bishops.

In the latter, an officer of high distinction, sent by the Emperor to quell the tumult, was slain, and his body treated with the utmost indignity by the infuriated populace.

The triumph of the Catholics in Egypt was accompanied by every variety of plunder, murder, sacrilege and outrage, and Arius himself was probably poisoned by Catholic hands. The followers of St. Cyril of Alexandria, who were chiefly monks, filled their city with riot and bloodshed, wounded the prefect Orestes, dragged the pure and gifted Hypatia into one of their churches, murdered her, tore the flesh from her bones with sharp shells, and having stripped her body naked, flung the mangled remains into the flames. In Ephesus, during the contest between St. Cyril and the Nestorians, the cathedral itself was the theatre of a fierce and bloody conflict. Constantinople, on the occasion of the deposition of St. Chrysostom, was for several days in a condition of absolute anarchy. After the Council of Chalcedon, Jerusalem and Alexandria were again convulsed, and the Bishop of the latter city was murdered in his baptistry. Athanasius stand out as the prominent character of the period in the history of Christianity. That history is one long controversy, the life of Athanasius, one unwearied and incessant strife. It is neither the serene course of a being elevated by his religion above the cares and tumults of ordinary life, nor the restless activity of one perpetually employed in a conflict with the ignorance, vice, and misery of an unconverted people. Yet even now (so completely has this polemic spirit become incorporated with Christianity) the memory of Athanasius is regarded by many wise and good men with reverence, which in Catholic countries, is actual adoration, in Protestant approaches towards it.

A council was held at Tyre, in which Athanasius was deposed and Gregory appointed in his stead. Scenes of savage conflict ensued, the churches were taken as it were by storm; the priests of the Athanasian party were treated with the utmost indignity; virgins scourged; every atrocity perpetuated by unbridled multitudes, embittered by every shade of religious faction. Athanasius returned for a time to Alexandria, but was again deposed.

The Arians exacted ample vengeance for their long period of depression, houses were plundered, monasteries burned; tombs broken open, to search for concealed Athanasians, or for the prelate himself, who still eluded their pursuit, bishops were insulted; virgins scourged: the soldiery encouraged to break up every meeting of the Catholics by violence, and even by inhuman tortures. The duke Sebastian, at the head of three thousand troops, charged a meeting of the Athanasian Christians. No barbarity was too revolting; they are said to have employed instruments of torture to compel them to Christian unity with the Arians; females were scourged with the prickly branches of the palm tree.

Persecution was universal—persecution by every means of violence and cruelty; the only question was, in whose hands was the power to persecute. Bloodshed, murder, treachery, assassination, even during the public worship of God—these were the frightful means by which each party strove to maintain its opinions, and to defeat its adversary. The most unaggressive and unobtrusive forms of Paganism were persecuted with the same ferocity.

To offer a sacrifice was to commit a capital offence,—and yet the offering of Jesus as a sacrifice for man's sin, is claimed as the foundation of Christian Theology.—To hang up a simple chaplet was to incur the forfeiture of an estate.

Contrast with this, the policy of the Pagan emperor, Julian, thus described by his favorite orator:

"He thought that neither fire, nor sword, could change the faith of mankind: the heart disowns the hand which is compelled by terror to sacrifice. Persecutions only make hypocrites who are unbelievers throughout life, or martyrs honored after death." He strictly prohibited the putting to death the Galileans—his favorite appellation of the Christians,—as worthy rather of compassion than of hatred. Julian revoked the sentence of banishment pronounced against Arians, Apollinarians, and Donatists. He determined, it is said, to expose them to a sort of public exhibition of intellectual gladiatorship. He summoned the advocates of the several sects to dispute in his presence, and presided with mock solemnity over their debates. His own voice was drowned in the clamor, till at length, as though to contrast them, to their disadvantage, with the wild barbarian warriors with whom he had been engaged. "Hear me," exclaimed the emperor: "The Franks and the Alemanni have heard me." "No wild beasts," he said, "Are so savage and intractable as Christian sectaries."

During the reign of Anastasius, two hundred Eastern monks, headed by Severus, were permitted to land in Constantinople; they here found an honorable reception. Other monks of the opposite faction swarmed from Palestine. The two black cowled armies watched each other for some months, working in secret on their respective partisans.

At last there was a wild, fierce fray, the presence of the Emperor lost its awe; he could not maintain the peace. The Bishop Macedonius took the lead. Men, women, children, poured out from all quarters; the monks, at the head of the raging multitude, echoed their religious war cries.

Throughout Asiatic Christendom it was the same wild struggle. Bishops were deposed quietly; or where resistance was made, the two factions fighting in the streets, in the churches: cities, even the holiest places ran with Christian blood.—*Milman's History of Christianity.*

LATER CRIMES OF THE CHURCH.

In A. D. 498, the feuds of the Roman clergy, broke out on the customary occasion of the election of a new Pope. Each party elected their Pope. The two factions encountered with the fiercest hostility; the clergy, the senate, and the populace were divided; the streets of the Christian city ran with blood. The contest was decided by Theodoric, the Gothic king of Italy. But not long after, the sanguinary tumults between the two factions broke out with greater fury: priests were slain, monasteries fired, and even sacred virgins treated with the utmost indignity.

With the power of the clergy increased both those other sources of influence, pomp and wealth.

Distinctions in station and in authority naturally lead to distinctions in manners, and those adventitious circumstances of dress and habits, which designate different ranks. The ministering functionaries multiplied, with the rapidly increasing variety and pomp.

At the festival of a martyr, the day closed with an open banquet, in which all the worshippers were invited to partake. As the evening drew on, the solemn and religious thoughts gave way to other emotions, the wine flowed freely, and the healths of the martyrs were pledged, not unfrequently to complete inebriety. Dances were admitted, pantomimic spectacles were exhibited, the festivals were prolonged till late in the evening, or to midnight, so that other criminal irregularities profaned, if not the sacred edifice, its immediate neighborhood.

A demoniac accused the Bishop Fortunatus of refusing him the rights of hospitality; a poor peasant receives the possessed into his house, and is punished for this inferential disrespect to the Bishop, by seeing his child cast into the fire and burnt before his eyes. A poor fellow with a monkey and cymbals is struck dead for unintentionally interrupting a Bishop Boniface in prayer.

In A. D. 726, the emperor Leo issued an edict, commanding the total destruction of all images, and the white-washing the walls of the churches. The thronging multitude, saw with horror, the officer mount the ladder. The women seized the ladder, threw down the officer, and beat him to death with clubs. The emperor sent an armed guard to suppress the tumult; a frightful massacre took place. The pious were punished with mutilations, scourgings, exile, confiscation: the schools of learning were closed, a magnificent library burned to the ground.

At the accession of Constantine Copronymus, two religious parties divided the empire. A battle took place near Ancira, fought with all the ferocity of civil and religious war. The historian expresses his horror that, among Christians, fathers should thus be engaged in the slaughter of their children, brothers of brothers.

Charlemagne was prodigal of grants of land to churches and monasteries. But these estates were not always obtained from the pious generosity of the king or the nobles. The stewards of the poor were the spoilers of the poor. They compelled the poor free man, to sell his property, or forced him to serve in the army, and that on permanent or continual duty, and so to leave his land either without owner, with all the chances that he might not return, or to commit it to the custody of those who remained at home in

LATER CRIMES OF THE CHURCH. 97

quiet and seized every opportunity of entering into possession. No Naboth's vineyard escaped their watchful avarice.

The payment of tithe originated in the following manner: Pepin had commanded the payment of tithe for the celebration of peculiar litanies during a period of famine. Charlemagne made it a law of the empire: he enacted it in its most strict and comprehensive form, as investing the clergy in a right to the tenth of the substance, and of the labor alike of freeman and the serf. The collection of tithe was regulated by compulsory statutes; the clergy took note of all who paid or refused to pay; the contumacious were three times summoned, if still obstinate, excluded from the church; if they still refused to pay, they were fined over and above the whole tithe, six solidi; if further contumacious, the recusant's house was shut up; if he attempted to enter it, he was cast into prison. This tithe was by no means a spontaneous votive offering of the whole Christian people—it was a tax imposed by Imperial authority, enforced by Imperial power. It had caused one, if not more than one sanguinary insurrection among the Saxons. It was submitted to in other parts of the empire, not without strong reluctance.

In A. D. 974, during the pontificate of Benedict VI., Bonifazio, a Cardinal Deacon, seized the unsuspecting Pope, and cast him into a dungeon, where shortly after he was strangled. Bonifazio assumed the papacy; but he had miscalculated the strength of his faction, in one month he was forced to fly from the city. Yet he fled not with so much haste, but that he carried off all the treasures, even the sacred vessels from the church of St. Peter.

Suddenly the fugitive Bonifazio, re-appeared in Rome, seized the Pope, imprisoned him in the Castle of St. Angelo, of which important fortress he had become master, and there put him to death by starvation or by poison. He exposed the body to the view of the people, who dared not murmur, he seated himself, as it seems, unresisted, in the papal chair, but soon after died. The people revenged themselves for their own base acquiescence in his usurpation, by cowardly insults on his dead body; by dragging it through the streets.

For twelve years Benedict IX. ruled in Rome, in the words of one of his successors, Victor III. leading a life so shameful, so foul and execrable, that he shuddered to describe it. He ruled like a captain of banditti, rather than a prelate. Adulteries, homicides,

G

perpetrated by his own hand, passed unnoticed, unrevenged. He became deeply enamored of his cousin. The father refused his daughter, unless the Pope would surrender the papacy.

He actually sold the papacy to an arch-Presbyter, named John.

There were at one time three Popes, by themselves, or by their factions, engaged in deadly feud. They laid aside, or taught each other to despise, their spiritual arms; they encountered with the carnal weapons of ordinary warfare.—*Milman's History of Latin Christianity.*

For ten dreary years,—A. D. 1198,—with but short intervals of truce, Germany was abandoned to all the horrors of civil war. The repeated protestations of Innocent, that he was not the cause of these fatal discords, betray the fact that he was accused of the guilt; and that he had to wrestle with his own conscience to acquit himself of the charge. It was a war, not of decisive battles, but of marauding, desolation, havoc, plunder, wasting of harvests, ravaging open and defenceless countries; war waged by Prelate against Prelate, by Prince against Prince; wild Bohemians and bandit soldiers of every race were roving through every province. Throughout the land there was no law: the high roads were impassable on account of robbers; traffic cut off, except on the great rivers from Cologne down the Rhine, from Ratisbon down the Danube; nothing was spared, nothing sacred, church or cloister. Some monasteries were utterly impoverished, some destroyed. The ferocities of war grew into brutalities; the clergy and sacred persons, were the victims and perpetrators. The wretched nun, who, it is said, was stripped naked, anointed with honey, rolled in feathers, and then set on a horse with her face to the tail, and paraded through the streets, was no doubt only recorded because her fate was somewhat more horrible then that of many of her sisters. The Abbot of St. Gall seized six of the principal burghers of Arbon, and cut off their feet, in revenge for one of his servants who had suffered the like mutilation for lopping wood in their forests.

. In these times—A. D. 1200—began the persecutions of the so-called Heretics; for men were beginning to weary of the narrow and complicated theology of the Church, and to believe only that which they found in their own hearts. Fires were kindled and heretics burned, in Oxford, in Rheims, in Arras, in Besançon, in Cologne, in Trèves, in Vezelay. In this latter stately monastery,

LATER CRIMES OF THE CHURCH. 99

the Archbishops of Lyons and Narbonne, the Bishops of Nevers and Laon, and many abbots and great theologians, sat in solemn judgment on some, it should seem poor ignorant men, called Publicans. They denied all but God, they absolutely rejected all the Sacraments, infant baptism, the Eucharist, the sign of the cross, holywater, the efficacy of tithes, and oblations, marriages, monkhood, the power and functions of the priesthood. Appeal was made to the whole assembly: "What shall be done with them?' "Let them be burned! Let them be burned!" And burned they were, to the number of seven, in the valley of Ecouan.

In the market place of Milan were raised, here a cross, there blazing pyre. The Heretics were brought forth, commanded to throw themselves before the cross, confess their sins, accept the Catholic faith, or to plunge into the flames, a few knelt before the cross; the greater number covered their faces, rushed into the fire and were consumed. In Cologne also, heretics were thrown into the flames.

But in the twelfth century, Heresy became rampant, bold, undisguised. The desperate Church was compelled to resort to the irrefragable argument of the sword and the stake. Woe to the prince or to the magistrate, who refused to be the executioner of the stern law.

In many places, the people were delighted at seeing a priest keep a mistress, that the married women might be safe from his seductions. What humiliating scenes did the house of a priest in those days present! The wretched man supported the women and the children she had borne him, with the tithes and offerings. His conscience was troubled: he blushed in the presence of the people, before his domestics, and before God. The mother fearing to come to want if the priest should die, made provision against it beforehand, and robbed her own house. Her honor was lost. Her children were ever a living accusation against her. Despised by all, they plunged into quarrels and debauchery. Such was the family of the priest!

If we go higher in the hierarchical order, we find the corruption not less great. The dignitaries of the Church preferred the tumult of camps to the hymns of the altar. To be able, lance in hand, to reduce his neighbors to obedience was one of the chief qualifications of a bishop. Everywhere, the bishops were continually at war with their towns. The citizens demanded liberty, the bishops required implicit obedience. If the latter gained the victory, they punished the revolters by sacrificing numerous victims to their vengeance.

And what a spectacle was presented by the pontifical throne in the times immediately preceding the Reformation! Rome, it must be acknowledged, had seldom witnessed so much infamy. Rodrigo Borgia, after having lived with a Roman lady, had continued the same illicit connection with one of her daughters, named Rosa Vanozza, by whom he had five children. He was a cardinal and archbishop, living at Rome with Vanozza and other women, visiting the churches and the hospitals, when the death of Innocent VII. created a vacancy in the pontifical chair. He succeeded in obtaining it by bribing each cardinal at a stipulated price.

On the day of his coronation, his son Cæsar, a youth of ferocious and dissolute manners, was created archbishop of Valencia and bishop of Pampeluna. He next celebrated in the Vatican, the marraige of his daughter Lucretia, by festivities, at which his mistress, Julia Bella, was present; and which were enlivened by licentious plays and songs. "All the clergy," says an historian, "kept mistresses, and all the convents of the capital were houses of ill-fame."

Thus had the clergy brought not only themselves, but their faith into disrepute. Well might Luther exclaim: The ecclesiastical order is opposed to God and to his glory. The people know it well; and this is but too plainly shown by the many songs, by proverbs and jokes against the priests, that are current among the commonalty, and all those caricatures of monks and priests on every wall, and even on the playing cards. Every one feels a loathing on seeing or hearing a priest in the distance. The evil had spread through all ranks: the corruption of manners corresponded with the corruption of faith.

"We Italians" says Machiavelli, "are indebted principally to the Church and the priests for having become impious and immoral."

A great agitation prevailed at that time, A. D. 1517, among the German people. The Church had opened a vast market upon earth. From the crowds of purchasers, and the shouts and jokes of the sellers, it might have been called a fair, but a fair conducted by monks. The merchandise that they were extolling, and which they offered at a reduced price, was, said they, "the salvation of souls." Tetzel a monk, who played the chief part at these sales, delivered the following sermon: "Indulgences" said he, "are the most precious and the most noble of God's gifts.

"Come, and I will give you letters, all properly sealed, by which even the sins that you intend to commit may be pardoned."

"There is no sin so great, that an indulgence cannot remit."

"But more than this," said he, "indulgences avail not only for the living, but the dead. For that repentance is not even necessary."

"Priest! noble! merchant! wife! youth! maiden! do you not hear your parents and your other friends who are dead, and who cry from the bottom of the abyss: We are suffering horrible torments! a trifling alms would deliver us; you can give it, and you will not!"

"At the very instant," continued Tetzel, "that the money rattles at the bottom of the chest, the soul escapes from purgatory and flies, liberated, to heaven."

For particular sins, there was a particular tax. For polygamy, it was six ducats; for sacrilege and perjury, nine ducats; for murder, eight ducats; for witchcraft, two ducats.

In a letter given at Rome, under the seal of the Fisherman, in November, 1517, Leo requires of his commissary of indulgences 147 gold ducats, to purchase a manuscript of the thirty-third book of Livy. Of all the uses to which he applied the money of the Germans, this was undoubtedly the best. Yet it was a strange thing to deliver souls from purgatory to procure the means of purchasing a manuscript of the history of the Roman wars.

A married schoolmaster, desiring to enter holy orders, obtained his wife's consent with this view, and they separated. The new priest, finding it impossible to observe his vow of celibacy, and unwilling to wound his wife's feelings, quitted the place where she lived, and went into the see of Constance, where he formed a criminal connection. His wife heard of this and followed him. The poor priest had compassion on her, and dismissing the woman who had usurped her rights, took his lawful spouse into his house. The procurator-fiscal immediately drew up a complaint; the vicar-general was in a ferment; the councillors of the consistory deliberated . . . . . and ordered the curate either to forsake his wife or his benefice. The poor wife left her husband's house in tears, and her rival re-entered it in triumph. The Church declared itself satisfied, and from that time the adulterous priest was left undisturbed.—*Milman's Latin Christianity.*

THE CRUSADES.

In the spring of 1096, a large body of the lower orders, under the lead of Peter the Hermit, and under the guidance of a goose and a goat, began to march across Germany. They were compelled to divide, and the smaller party, led by a Burgundian knight, Walter the Penniless, going in advance, was annihilated in Bulgaria. The larger party suffered severely, and was guilty of great atrocities; but Peter brought the bulk of it to Constantinople, where he was joined by Walter. They were landed in Asia, where they were nearly all destroyed by the Turks, Peter having left them.

A third division, consisting of Germans, was led by a monk named Godeschal, and was massacred in Hungary. A fourth, estimated at two hundred thousand, and composed of various peoples, was led by some nobles, from Germany, but it was destroyed by the Hungarians, after having perpetrated terrible outrages.

The siege of Jerusalem during the first crusade was closed with an assault, and a massacre of almost unequalled atrocity. No barbarian, no infidel, no Saracen, ever perpetrated such wanton and cold-blooded atrocities of cruelty, as the wearers of the Cross of Christ—who, it is said, had fallen on their knees and burst into a pious hymn at the first sight of the Holy City—on the capture of that city. Murder was mercy, rape tenderness, simple plunder the mere assertion of the conqueror's right. Children were seized by the legs, some of them plucked from their mother's breasts and dashed against the walls, or whirled from the battlements. Others were obliged to leap from the walls; some tortured, roasted by slow fires. They ripped up prisoners, to see if they had swallowed gold. Of seventy thousand Saracens there was not left enough to bury the dead; poor Christians were hired to perform the office. Every one surprised in the temple was slaughtered, till the reek from the dead bodies drove away the slayers. The Jews were burned alive in their synagogue. Even the day after, all who had taken refuge on the roofs were hewn to pieces.

At the surrender of Acre, during the third Crusade, the crusaders, in violation of their word, butchered five thousand Musselmen who had been left in their hands as hostages.

Bootless carnage, distinguished the crusades from almost all other wars; the unseemly spectacle of crimes, cruelties, unbridled licentiousness, strife, jealousies, and treacheries too often prevailed in the Christian camp.

To all who embarked in the crusades, the Pope promised, on their sincere repentance, the remission of all their sins, and eternal life in the great day of retribution. Those who were unable to proceed in person, might obtain the same remission in proportion to the bounty of their offerings.

The Crusaders advanced to the siege of Constantinople, a Christian city, in the name of Christ.

Nicetas, himself an eye-witness and sufferer in these scenes, contrasts the discipline and and self-denial of the Mohammedans, who under Saladin, stormed Jerusalem, with the rapacity, the lust, the cruelty of the Christian conquerors of Constantinople. They spared neither religion, nor age, nor sex; they practiced fornications, incests, adulteries, in the sight of men; abandoned matrons and virgins dedicated to God, to the lewdness of grooms. Many rushed at once to the churches and monasteries. In the church of Santa Sophia, the silver was rent off from the magnificent pulpit: the table of oblation, admired for its precious material and exquisite workmanship, broken to pieces. Mules and horses were led into the churches to carry off the ponderous vessels; if they slipped down on the smooth floor, they were forced to rise up by lash and spur, so that their blood flowed on the pavement.

A prostitute mounted the Patriach's throne, and screamed out a disgusting song, accompanied with the most offensive gestures.

Instead of the chants, the aisles rung with wild shouts of revelry or indecent oaths and imprecations.

But, according to the theory of the Church, the erring believer was as declared an enemy to God, as the Pagan or the Islamite: in one respect more inexcusable and odious, as obstinately resisting or repudiating the truth. The heretic appeared to the severely orthodox Christian, as worse than the unbeliever, he was a revolted subject; not a foreign enemy. Civil wars are always the most ferocious. Excommunication from the Christian Church implied outlawry from Christian society; the heretic forfeited not only all dignities, rights, privileges, immunities, even all property, all protection by law: he was to be pursued, taken, despoiled, put to death, either by the ordinary course of justice—the temporal authority was bound to execute, even to blood, the sentence of the ecclesiastical court,—or if he dared to resist by any means whatever, however peaceful, he was an insurgent, against whom the whole of Christendom might, or rather was bound at the summons of the spiritual power to declare war; his estates, even his dominions, if a sovereign, were not merely liable to forfeiture, but the Church assumed the power of awarding the forfeiture, as it might seem best to her wisdom.

The army which should execute the mandate of the Church was the army of the Church, and the banner of that army was the Cross of Christ. So began Crusades, not on the contested borders of Christendom, not in Mohammedan or heathen lands, in Palestine, on the shores of the Nile, among the Livonian forests or the sands of the Baltic, but in the very bosom of Christendom; not among the implacable partisans of an antagonistic creed, but among those who still called themselves by the name of Christians.—*Milman's History of Latin Christianity.*

The Persecution of the Jews.

When the horde of fanatics under the command of Peter the Hermit, was assembled near the city of Treves, a murmur rapidly spread through the camp, that while they were advancing to recover the sepulchre of their Redeemer from the Infidels, they were leaving behind worse unbelievers, the murderers of the Lord. In the words of Jewish tradition, no doubt generally faithful in its record of their calamities, "the abominable Germans and French rose up against them,—people of a fierce countenance, that had no respect to the persons of the old, neither have they mercy upon the young; and they said, 'Let us be revenged for our Messiah upon the Jews that are among us, and let us destroy them from being a nation, that the name of Israel may be had no more in remembrance; then will we go to the East.'" With one impulse the Crusaders rushed to the city, and began a relentless pillage, violation, and massacre of every Jew they could find. In this horrible day men were seen to slay their own children, to save them from the worse usage of these savages. Women, having deliberately tied stones round themselves that they might sink, plunged from the bridge, to save their honor and escape baptism. Their husbands had rather send them to the bosom of Abraham than leave them to the mercy, or rather the lustful cruelties of the Christians. The rest fled to the bishop's palace as a place of refuge. They were received by the bishop, Engelbert, with these words:—" Wretches, your

THE PERSECUTION OF THE JEWS. 105

sins have come upon you; ye who have blasphemed the Son of God and calumniated his Mother. This is the cause of your present miseries,—this, if ye persist in your obduracy, will destroy your body and soul forever." The same bloody scenes were repeated in Metz, in Spiers, in Worms, in Mayence, in Cologne. The locust band passed on; everywhere the tracks of the Crusaders were deeply marked with Jewish blood. A troop under Count Emico, offered the same horrid sacrifices to the God of Mercy, in the cities on the Maine and the Danube, even as far as Hungary.

There was at Seville a fierce popular preacher, Ferdinand Martinez, Archdeacon of Ecija. During the reign of John I., his inflammatory harangues against the obstinacy and the usury and the wealth of the Jews, had excited the populace. The Jewries were attacked; and a general pillage, violation, and massacre took place of men and women, old and young. Fire and sword raged unresisted through these quarters of the city. The streets of noble Seville ran with blood, and the wild voice of the Archdeacon in the pulpit rose over all, and kept up the madness. Four thousand Jews perished in the massacre.

The terrible example of their impunity the fame of the blood which they had shed without rebuke, the wealth which they had acquired without restitution, spread throughout the kingdom. Hardly more than a year had passed, when in one day—August 8—the populace rose in Cordova, in Valencia, in Toledo, in Burgos. Each of these cities, says a Spanish author, was another Troy: All the horrors of a town taken by storm were suffered by the Jewries: plunder, rape, massacre, conflagration.

In 1492 appeared the fatal edict commanding all unbaptized Jews to quit the realm of Spain in four months.

For three centuries their fathers had dwelt in this delightful country, which they had fertilized with their industry, enriched with their commerce, adorned with their learning. Yet there were few examples of weakness or apostasy; the whole race,—variously calculated at 166,000, 300,000, 650,000, or 800,000,—in a lofty spirit of self-devotion—we envy not that mind which cannot appreciate its real greatness,—determined to abandon all rather than desert the religion of their fathers. They left the homes of their youth, the scenes of their early associations, the sacred graves of their ancestors, the more recent tombs of their own friends and relatives. They left the synagogues in which they had so long worshipped their God; the schools where those wise men had taught who had thrown a lustre which shone, even through the darkness of the age, upon the Hebrew name. They were allowed four months to prepare for this everlasting exile. The unbaptized Jew found in the kingdom after that period was condemned to death. The persecutor could not even trust the hostile feeling of his bigoted subjects to execute his purpose, a statute was thought necessary, prohibiting any Christian from harboring a Jew after that period. Many were sold for slaves; Christendom swarmed with them. The wealthier were permitted to carry away their movables, excepting gold and silver, for which they were to accept letters of change or any merchandise not prohibited. Their property they might sell; but the market was soon glutted, and the cold-hearted purchasers waited till the last instant, to wring from their distress the hardest terms. A contemporary author states that he saw Jews give a house for an ass, and a vineyard for a small quantity of cloth or linen. Yet many of them concealed their gold and jewels in their clothes and saddles; some swallowed them, in hopes thus at least to elude the scrutiny of the officers. The Jews consider this calamity almost as dreadful as the taking and ruin of Jerusalem. For whither to fly? And where to find a more hospitable shore? Incidents, which make the blood run cold, are related of the miseries which they suffered. Some of those from Aragon found their way into Navarre; others to the sea-shore, where they set sail for Italy, or the coast of Morocco; others crossed the frontier into Portugal. "Many of the former were cast away, or sunk," says a Jewish writer, "like lead, into the ocean." On board the ship which was conveying a great number to Africa, the plague broke out. The captain ascribed the infection to his circumcised passengers, and set them all on shore, on a desert coast, without provisions. They dispersed: one, a father, saw his beautiful wife perish before his eyes—fainted himself with exhaustion—and, waking, beheld his two children dead by his side.

In Portugal the king named a day for all Jews to quit the kingdom, and appointed certain ports for their embarkation. Before that time he issued another secret order to seize all children under fourteen years of age, to tear them from the arms, the bosoms of their parents, and dispersed them through the kingdom, to be baptized and brought up as Christians. The secret transpired, and lest they should conceal their children, it was instantly put in execution. Great God of Mercy, this was in the name of Christianity! Frantic mothers threw their children into the wells and rivers,—they destroyed them with their own hands. One mother threw herself at the feet of the king as he was riding to church. She had already lost six children ; she implored that her youngest might be spared to her. The courtiers repelled her with scorn and ill-usage. The king told them to let her go, "the poor bitch deprived of her whelps!"—*Milman's History of Christianity.*

ALBIGENSIAN WAR.

Never in the history of man were the great eternal principles of justice, the faith of treaties, common humanity, so trampled under foot as in the Albigensian war. Never was war waged in which ambition, the consciousness of strength, rapacity, implacable hatred, and pitiless cruelty, played a greater part. And throughout the war it cannot be disguised that it was not merely the army of the Church, but the Church itself in arms. Papal legates and the greatest prelates headed the host, and mingled in all the horrors of the battle and the siege. In no instance did they interfere to arrest the massacre, in some cases they urged it on. "Slay all, God will know his own," was the boasted saying of Abbot Arnold, Legate of the Pope, before Beziers. Arnold was the Captain-General of the army.' Hardly one of the great prelates of France stood aloof.

In A. D., 1207, the army appeared before Beziers, which, in the strength of its walls and the courage of its inhabitants, ventured on bold defiance. The Bishop Reginald of Montpellier demanded the surrender of all whom he might designate as heretics. On their refusal of these terms, the city was stormed. A general massacre followed; neither age nor sex were spared; even priests fell in the remorseless carnage. In the Church of St. Mary Magdalene were killed seven thousand by the defenders of the sanctity of the Church. The account of the slain is variously estimated from twenty thousand even up to fifty thousand. The city was set on fire, even the Cathedral perished in the flames. The law of conquest was put in force. The lands of a heretic were as the lands of a Saracen.

The barbarity at Lavour passed all precedent, even in this fearful war. A general massacre was permitted; men, women, children were cut to pieces, till there remained nothing to kill except some of the garrison, and others reserved for a more cruel fate. Four hundred were burned in one great pile, which made a wonderful blaze, and caused universal rejoicing in the camp. Aymeric of Montreal, the commander, was brought, with eighty nobles—Lavour seems to have been thought a safe place of refuge—before De Montfort. He ordered them all to be hanged; the overloaded gibbets broke down; they were hewn in pieces. Giralda, the Lady of Lavour, was thrown into a well, and huge stones rolled down upon her. The Bishops preached in vain to five hundred heretics, but converted not one; sixty, however, they burned with great joy.

In 1487, Innocent VIII., the father of the Romans, issued a bull against the Waldenses. "To arms" said the pontiff, "and trample these heretics under foot as venomous serpents."

At the approach of the Legate, followed by an army of eighteen thousand men, and a number of volunteers who wished to share the spoils of the Waldenses, the latter abandoned their houses and took refuge in the mountains, caverns, and clefts of the rocks, as the birds flee for shelter when the storm begins to lower. Not a valley, nor a wood, nor a rock escaped their persecutors; everywhere in this part of the Alps, and particularly on the Italian side, these poor disciples of Christ were hunted down like beasts of prey. At last the Pope's satellites were worn out; their strength was exhausted, their feet could no longer scale the steep retreats of the "heretics," and their arms refused to strike.

The Reformation had made considerable progress among the people of the Netherlands during the reign of Charles V., and Philip, soon after his accession, undertook to root out entirely the new doctrines, and to restore the exclusive supremacy of the Roman Catholic Church.

An insurrection of the Protestants, breaking out in Flanders, August 14, 1566, Philip determined to resort to the most severe measures to suppress Protestantism, and accordingly the cruel duke of Alva, a soldier of great reputation, was sent to the Netherlands in 1567, with a powerful army of Spanish veterans; and for six years the country suffered under a tyranny which, for extent and ferocity, has few parallels in history.

After the execution of Huss—A. D. 1415—the Hussite war broke out in all its fury. Of all wars, none was so horribly remorseless, ostentatiously cruel as this—a war of races, of languages, and of religion. It was a strife of revenge, of reprisal, of extermination, considered to be the holiest of duties. On one side no faith was to be kept, no mercy shown to heretics: to cut off the spreading plague by any means was paramount to all principles of law or gospel. On the other, vengeance was to be wreaked on the enemies of God's people, and therefore the enemies of God ; to root out idolatry was the mission of the Bohemians; mortal sin was to be cut off with the righteous sword; and the whole priesthood, all monks, friars, nuns, were so utterly depraved, according to their sweeping condemnation, that it was only to fulfill the Divine commandment to extirpate the irreclaimable Order. These terrible theories were relentlessly carried into more terrible practice. Kuttenburg, the second city in the realm, the rival of Prague, Catholic and German as Prague was, Hussite and Bohemian, burned, beheaded, hanged all who would not retract their opinions. They bought the prisoners taken in war for a few groschens a head—five times as much for a preacher as for a common man—and executed them without trial, without mercy. They are charged with having put to death sixteen hundred men. The Hussites, wherever they could, perpetrated horrible reprisals; for so many of their brethren as were burned, they hanged as many monks or friars.—*Milman's History of Latin Christianity.*

THE PERSECUTION OF THE HERETICS.

After the Albigensian Crusade, when the open war was at an end, the Church still pursued her exterminating warfare against her still rebellious subjects. The inquisition continued its silent, but not less inhuman, hardly less destructive crusade.

That tribunal, with all its peculiar statutes, its jurisdiction, its tremendous agency, was founded during this period. Its statutes framed after the successful termination of the war, in order absolutely to extirpate every lingering vestige of heresy, form the code of persecution, which not merely aimed at suppressing all public teaching, but the more secret freedom of thought. It was a system which penetrated into the innermost sanctuary of domestic life; and made delation not only a merit and a duty, but an obligation also, enforced by tremendous penalties.

The court sat in profound secresy; no advocate might appear before the tribunal, no witness was confronted with the accused: who were the informers, what the charges, except the vague charge of heresy, no one knew. The suspected heretic was first summoned to declare, on oath, that he would speak the truth, the whole truth, of all persons whatsoever, living or dead, like himself, under the suspicion of heresy. If he refused, he was cast into a dungeon—a dungeon the darkest in those dreary ages—the most dismal, the most profound, the most noisome. No falsehood was too false, no craft too crafty, no trick too base for this calm, systematic moral torture, which was to wring further confession against himself, denunciation against others. It was the deliberate object to break the spirit. The prisoner was told that there were witnesses, undeniable witnesses against him; if convicted by such witnesses, his death was inevitable. In the meantime his food was to be slowly diminished till body and soul were prostrate. He was then to be left in darkness, solitude and silence. Then were to come one or two of the faithful, dexterous men, who were to speak in gentle words of interest and sympathy: "Fear not to confess that you have had dealings with those men, the teachers of heresy, because they seemed to you men of holiness and virtue; wiser than you have been deceived." These dexterous men were to speak of the Bible, of the Gospels, of the Epistles of St. Paul, to talk the very language, the scriptural language of the heretic. "These foxes," it was said, "can only be unearthed by fox-like cunning." But if all this art failed, then came terror, and the goading to despair. "Die you must—bethink you of your soul." Upon which, if the desperate man said, "If I must die, I will die in the true faith of the Gospel,'—he had made his confession: justice claimed her victim.

The Inquisition had three penalties: for those who recanted, penance in the severest forms which the Church might enact; for those not absolutely convicted, perpetual imprisonment: for the obstinate or relapsed, death,—death at the stake. Such was the procedure, of which the instructions may now be read in their very words. Two inquisitors were appointed in every city, but the Bishops needed no excitement to their eager zeal, no remonstrance against mistimed mercy to the heretics. At the Council of Narbonne, was issued a decree, that there were not prisons vast enough to contain those who deserved imprisonment for life.

A division of the Franciscans, calling themselves spirituals, were loud in their denunciations of the corruptions of the Church. John XXII. was too sagacious not to foresee the peril; too arrogantly convinced, and too jealous, of his supreme spiritual authority not to resent; too merciless not to extirpate by the most cruel means these slowly-working enemies. Soon after his accession, Bull followed Bull equally damnatory. The Inquisition was committed to Michael di Cesena, still the faithful subject of the Pope, and to seven others. Twenty-five monks were convicted, and sentenced first to degradation, then to perpetual imprisonment. They were brought to the stake and burned at Marseilles. They were condemned for the heresy of denying the Papal authority.

The prisons of Narbonne and of Carcassonne were crowded with those who were spared the last penalty. Among these was the friar Deliciosus of Montpellier, a Franciscan, who had boldly withstood the Inquisition, and was immured for life in a dungeon. He it was who declared that if St. Peter and St. Paul should return to earth, the Inquisition would lay hands on them, as damnable heretics. At Toulouse the public sermons of the Inquisition took place at intervals, and these sermons were rarely unaccompanied by proofs of their inefficacy. Men who would not be argued into belief must be burned. The corollary of a Christian sermon was a holocaust at the stake.

In England a Statute was necessary to legalize the burning of heretics. The judgment was passed in the Ecclesiastical court or that of the Inquisition. The Statute bears the ill-omened appellation, "for the burning of heretics." The preamble was directed in the most comprehensive terms against the new preachers. These preachings, schools, books, were strictly inhibited. The Bishop of the diocese was empowered to arrest all persons accused or suspected of these acts, to imprison them, to bring them to trial in his court. "If he shall refuse to abjure such doctrines, or having abjured, relapse, sentence is to be recorded: a writ issued to the sheriff of the county, the mayor or bailiff of the nearest borough, who is to take order that on a high place in public, before the face of the people he be burned."

Nor was this Statute an idle menace; the Primate and the Bishops hastened to make examples under its terrible provisions.

And, when later than this, Luther struck at the root of Roman Catholicism, though the power of the church was on the wane, persecution was again resorted to.—*Milman's History of Latin Christianity.*

Fanaticism grew fiercer every day; evangelical ministers were expelled from their churches; magistrates were banished; and at times the most horrible punishments were inflicted. In Wurtemburg, an inquisitor named Reichler caused the Lutherans, and above all the preachers, to be hanged upon trees. Barbarous ruffians were found, who unfeelingly nailed the pastors by their tongues to a post; so that these unhappy victims, tearing themselves violently from the wood to which they were fastened, were horribly mutilated in attempting to recover their liberty, and thus deprived of that gift which they had long used to proclaim the Gospel.

At Landsburg nine persons were consigned to the flames, and at Munich twenty-nine were thrown into the water.

Leclerc, one of the French reformers, was sentenced to be burnt alive, and taken out to the place of execution. Here a fearful scene awaited him. The cruelty of his persecutors had been contriving all that could render his punishment more horrible. Near the scaffold men were heating pincers that were to serve as the instruments of their rage. Leclerc, firm and calm, heard unmoved the wild yells of the monks and people. They began by cutting off his right hand; then taking up the burning pincers, they tore off his nose; after this, they lacerated his arms, and when they had thus mangled them in several places, they concluded by burning his breasts. After these tortures Leclerc was burnt by a slow fire, in conformity with his sentence.

It has been estimated that the number of persons burned alive under Torquemada, the first grand inquisitor, amounted to 8,800, those under Deza, to 1,664, and those under Cardinal Ximenez to 2,536.

The Massacre of St. Bartholomew.

The massacre of St. Bartholomew, was planned by the infamous Catharine de Medici, to take place at the celebration of the marriage of Henry of Navarre and Marguerite de Valois, with the object of exterminating the nobles and gentry of the Huguenot party, while plunged in the festivities of that joyous occasion. The city gates were shut and guarded, and all the Catholic inhabitants were ordered to illuminate their houses, both as a distinguishing mark, and as a means of giving sufficient light, by which to carry on the work of destruction. Orders were also dispatched to the royal governors of the principal cities of all the provinces to commence the same massacre at the same hour, and, although, in some instances, the humanity of the officers led them to disobey their orders, the instructions were too generally followed. Coligni was run through the body, in spite of the resistance of some of his household, and thrown out of the window at the feet of the duke of Guise, who sat on horseback, coolly awaiting the performance of the dreadful deed, and when the bloody corpse was flung before his charger's hoofs on the pavement, dismounted and wiped the clotted gore from the victim's features, with his handkerchief, in order to assure himself that there had been no mistake ; when the fatal tocsin rang from the church of St. Germain, the horrid slaughter began on the instant, and was deliberately prosecuted during several days, both in the capital and the large provincial towns. Neither sex nor age was spared !

THE SPANIARDS IN MEXICO.

The Spaniards entered Mexico with the sole intention of conquest. Setting aside the question of *right*, in this intention, we will speak only of their manner of conducting this conquest.

While occupying the city of Cholula, Cortés, fearing some treachery on the part of the Indians, determined to make an example of them that would strike the whole nation with terror. Large numbers of the Indians being gathered in a square of the city, the fatal signal, the discharge of an arquebuse, was given. In an instant every musket and cross-bow was levelled at the unfortunate Cholulans in the court-yard, and a frightful volley poured into them as they stood crowded together, like a herd of deer in the centre. They were taken by surprise, and made scarcely any resistance to the Spaniards, who followed up the discharge of their pieces by rushing on them with their swords; and, as the half-naked bodies of the natives afforded no protection, they hewed them down with as much ease as the reaper mows down the ripe corn in harvest time. Some endeavored to scale the walls, but only afforded a surer mark to the arquebusiers and archers. Others threw themselves into the gateways, but were received on the long pikes of the soldiers who guarded them. Some few had better luck in hiding themselves under the heaps of slain with which the ground was soon loaded.

While this work of death was going on, the countrymen of the slaughtered Indians, drawn together by the noise of the massacre, had commenced a furious assault on the Spaniards from without.

But Cortés had placed his battery of heavy guns in a position that commanded the avenues, and swept off the files of the assailants as they rushed on. In the intervals between the discharges, which, in the imperfect state of the science in that day, were much longer than in ours, he forced back the press by charging with the horse into the midst. The steeds, the guns, the weapons of the Spaniards were all new to the Cholulans. Notwithstanding the novelty of the terrific spectacle, the flash of fire-arms mingling with the deafening roar of the artillery, as its thunders reverberated among the buildings, the despairing Indians pushed on to take the places of their fallen comrades. At last, forced to give way, they flung themselves into the wooden turrets that crowned the temple, and poured down stones, javelins and burning arrows on the Spaniards, as they climbed the great staircase, which, by a flight of one hundred and twenty steps, scaled the face of the pyramid. But the fiery shower fell harmless on the steel bonnets of the *Christians*, while they availed themselves of the burning shafts to set fire to the wooden citadel, which was speedily wrapt in flames.

All was now confusion and uproar in the fair city, which had so lately reposed in security and peace. The groans of the dying, the frantic supplications of the vanquished for mercy, were mingled with the loud battle-cries of the Spaniards as they rode down their enemy. The tumult was still further swelled by the incessant rattle of musketry, and the crash of falling timbers, which sent up a volume of flame that outshone the ruddy light of morning, making altogether a hideous confusion of sights and sounds, that converted the Holy City into a Pandemonium. As resistance slackened, the victors broke into the houses and sacred places, plundering them of whatever valuables they contained, plate, jewels, which were found in some quantity, wearing apparel, and provisions. Cortés, in his letter to Charles the Fifth, admits three thousand slain, most accounts say six, and some swell the amount yet higher.

It was common for the Aztecs to celebrate an annual festival in May, in honor of their patron war-god. The Spaniards gave their consent to this feast, on condition that they should come without weapons. They assembled accordingly on the day appointed, to the number of six hundred, at the smallest computation.

Alvarado and his soldiers attended as spectators, some of them taking their station at the gates, as if by chance, and others mingling in the crowd. They were all armed, a circumstance, which, as it was usual, excited no attention. The Aztecs were soon engrossed by the exciting movement of the dance, accompanied by their religious chant, and wild, discordant minstrelsy. While thus occupied, Alvarado and his men, at a concerted signal, rushed with drawn swords on their victims. Unprotected by armor or weapons of any kind, they were hewn down without resistance by their assailants, who, in their bloody work, says a contemporary, showed no touch of pity or compunction. Some fled to the gates, but were caught on the long pikes of the soldiers. Others, who attempted to scale the Coatepantli, or Wall of Serpents, as it was called, which surrounded the area, shared the like fate, or were cut to pieces, or shot by the ruthless soldiery. The pavement, says a writer of the age, ran with streams of blood, like water in a heavy shower. Not an Aztec, of all that gay company, was left alive! It was repeating the dreadful scene of Cholula, with the disgraceful addition, that the Spaniards, not content with slaughtering their victims, rifled them of the precious ornaments on their persons! On this sad day fell the flower of the Aztec nobility. Not a family of note, but had mourning and desolation brought within its walls.

And now, with all allowance for the ferocity of the age and the laxity of its principles, it must be admitted that these are passages which every Spaniard, who cherishes the fame of his countrymen, would be glad to see expunged from history; passages not to be vindicated on the score of self-defence, or of necessity of any kind, and which must forever leave a dark spot on the annals of the Conquest. And yet, taken as a whole, the invasion was conducted on principles less revolting to humanity, than most, perhaps than any, of the other conquests of the Castilian crown in the New World.—*Prescott.*

The Spaniards in Peru.

Soon after the Spaniards entered Peru, the Inca consented to visit them, and to come unarmed. He entered Caxamalca at the head of a large number of his people, and was received in one of the squares of the city by Pizarro's chaplain, who, after explaining the Christian belief, and dwelling particularly on the Pope's authority over all nations, concluded with beseeching the Peruvian monarch to abjure the errors of his own faith, and embrace that of the Christians now proffered to him, the only one by which he could hope for salvation; and, furthermore, to acknowledge himself a tributary of the Emperor Charles the Fifth, who, in that event, would aid and protect him as his loyal vassal.

The eyes of the Indian monarch flashed fire, and his dark brow grew darker as he replied,—"I will be no man's tributary. I am greater than any prince upon earth. Your emperor may be a great prince; I do not doubt it when I see that he has sent his subjects so far across the waters; and I am willing to hold him as a brother. As for the Pope, of whom you speak, he must be crazy to talk of giving away countries which do not belong to him. For my faith," he continued, "I will not change it. Your own God, as you say, was put to death by the very men whom he created. But mine," he concluded, pointing to his Deity,—then, sinking in glory behind the mountains,—"my God still lives in the heavens, and looks down on his children."

Pizarro saw that the hour had come. He waved a white scarf in the air, the appointed signal. The fatal gun was fired from the fortress. Then, springing into the square, the Spanish captain and his followers shouted the old war-cry of "St. Jago and at them." It was answered by the battle-cry of every Spaniard in the city, as, rushing from the avenues of the great halls in which they were concealed, they poured into the plaza, horse and foot, each in his own dark column, and threw themselves into the midst of the Indian crowd. The latter, taken by surprise, stunned by the report of artillery and muskets, the echoes of which reverberated like thunder from the surrounding buildings, and blinded by the smoke which rolled in sulphureous volumes along the square, were seized with a panic. They knew not whither to fly for refuge from the coming ruin. Nobles and commoners,—all were trampled down under the fierce charge of the cavalry, who dealt their blows, right and left, without sparing, while their swords, flashing through the thick gloom, carried dismay into the hearts of the wretched natives, who now, for the first time, saw the horse and his rider in all their terrors. They made no resistance,—as, indeed, they had no weapons with which to make it. Every avenue to escape was closed, for the entrance to the square was choked up with the dead bodies of men who had perished in vain efforts to fly; and, such was the agony of the survivors under the terrible pressure of their assailants, that a large body of Indians, by their convulsive struggles, burst through the wall of stone and dried clay which formed part of the boundary of the plaza! It fell, leaving an opening of more than a hundred paces, through which multitudes now found their way into the country, still hotly pursued by the cavalry, who, leaping the fallen rubbish, hung on the rear of the fugitives, striking them down in all directions.

Meanwhile the fight, or rather the massacre, continued hot round the Inca, whose person was the great object of the assault. His faithful nobles, rallying about him, threw themselves in the way of the assailants, and strove by tearing them from their saddles, or, at least, by offering their own bosoms as a mark for their vengeance, to shield their beloved master. Thus they continued to force back the cavaliers, clinging to their horses with dying grasp, and, as one was cut down, another taking the place of his fallen comrade with a loyalty truly affecting.

The Indian monarch, stunned and bewildered, saw his faithful subjects falling round him without fully comprehending his situation. The litter on which he rode heaved to and fro, as the mighty press swayed backwards and forwards; and he gazed on the overwhelming ruin, like some forlorn mariner, who, tossed about in his bark by the furious elements, sees the lightning's flash and hears the thunder bursting around him with the consciousness that he can do nothing to avert his fate. At length, weary with the work of destruction, the Spaniards, as the shades of evening grew deeper, felt afraid that the royal prize might, after all, elude them; and some of the cavaliers made a desperate attempt to end the affray at once by taking Atahuallpa's life. But Pizarro, who was nearest his person, called out with stentorian voice, "Let no one, who values his life, strike at the Inca;" and, stretching out his arm to shield him, received a wound on the hand from one of his own men,—the only wound received by a Spaniard in the action.

The number of slain is reported, as usual, with great discrepancy. Pizarro's Secretary says two thousand natives fell. A descendant of the Incas swells the number to ten thousand.

It was not long before Atahuallpa discovered, amidst all the show of religious zeal in his conquerors, a lurking appetite more potent, in most of their bosoms, than either religion or ambition. This was the love of gold. He determined to avail himself of it to procure his own freedom.

In the hope, therefore, to effect his purpose, by appealing to the avarice of his keepers, he one day told Pizarro, that if he would set him free, he would engage to cover the floor of the apartment on which they stood with gold. Those present listened with an incredulous smile; and as the Inca received no answer, he said with some emphasis, that "he would not merely cover the floor, but would fill the room with gold as high as he could reach;" and, standing on tiptoe, he stretched out his hand against the wall. Although this ransom was paid, the Spaniards on some frivolous accusation, sentenced him to death. When the sentence was communicated to the Inca, he exclaimed, "What have I done, or my children, that I should meet such a fate? And from your hands, too," said he, addressing Pizarro, "you, who have met with friendship and kindness from my people, with whom I have shared my treasures, who have received nothing but benefits from my hands!" In the most piteous tones, he then implored that his life might be spared, promising any guaranty that might be required for the safety of every Spaniard in the army, promising double the ransom he had already paid, if time were only given him to obtain it.

Finding, however, that he had no power to turn his conqueror from his purpose, he recovered his habitual self-possession, and from that moment submitted himself to his fate with the courage of an Indian warrior.

Civilization and Theology.

Many of these cruelties were committed by those who prided themselves on being in the head and front of the civilization, which is claimed to have sprung from the teaching and influence of Christian theology, but which, in fact, has sprung up in these our times—as it has, in other times, in Egyptian, Grecian, Roman and South American communities, under the advantages afforded by the accumulation of wealth which goes, hand in hand, with mental culture and the development of the arts and sciences, each fostering and forwarding the other. The discovery of the art of printing has been of immense service in increasing and perpetuating civilization in later days, by diffusing and retaining knowledge for the benefit of each succeeding generation, and by bringing mind into collision with mind.

Printing and Civilization.

But the inventor of the printing press was denounced by the Christian theologians of his day, as being in league with the devil, inasmuch as copies of the Bible could be produced by means of printing, with a celerity, and in quantities, never before heard or dreamed of—thus leading the way to the discovery of the cheat which the theologians were practising on the masses. Now, however, the Church authorities seize upon the evident and rapid advance in intellectual culture and knowledge in Christian countries, as compared with others, and claim that this is due entirely to the promulgation of Christianity ; where, as it is due entirely to the circumstance that the printing press was invented and put into operation in a Christian country, in despite of the theologians who denounced it. That the dark side of human nature here presented, is the exception and not the general rule, even in Christian countries, we freely admit. It is one of the objects of this work to maintain that the good, the true, and the kind in the human nature largely predominate, notwithstanding the habit of the clergy of representing unregenerate man—that is, all not within the pale of, and paying tithes to the church—as utterly corrupt and having no good in them. This habit of dilating so continually on the darker side of human nature amounts to a gross and palpable libel on the species. Theologians, habitually measuring character by its aberrations, and estimating strong and passionate natures by their failings, rather than by their virtues—which largely predominate, have fallen into a signal injustice. And this is the more inexcusable, inasmuch as in their own sacred volume, the Psalms of David are a conspicuous proof how a noble, tender, and passionate nature could survive, even in an adulterer and a murderer.

Now, from whatever cause this persistent course of the Christian Theologians, in representing man in his natural state as altogether under the empire of evil, proceeds—whether from love of denomination, interest, or other causes—nothing can be more certain than that excellence and not vice is prominent and distinctive in human nature in its most primitive state.

The more the intellectual faculties are cultivated and lend their aid to the moral perceptions, and kindly promptings of the heart, the more rapid is the advance in the pursuit of the good, the right, and the virtuous. But good greatly preponderates over evil, even in the incipient stages of human society. Benevolence is more common than cruelty. The sight of suffering produces pity, rather than joy. Gratitude, not ingratitude, is the normal result of a conferred benefit. The sympathies of man naturally follow heroism and goodness. In fine, virtue and not vice—love, and not hate, predominate in human nature; while vice itself is usually but an exaggeration or distortion of tendencies that are in their own nature perfectly innocent.

We have herein presented to notice some of the great crimes known to history, that have been committed by the inhabitants of Christian countries, who are understood to have had the benefit of the teachings of the Church. And we would remind those who attempt to build up Church interests, and prove its beneficial effects upon man, by contrasting the moral conduct of Christian nations with that of Heathen, that—when fairly made—Christians lose rather than gain by the comparison. As to attributing the advanced state of mental culture and civilization to the influence of the Church, instead of the art of printing, the cause of truth will be served by calling attention to certain doings of the Church here given, before the printing press came into use.

LIST OF BOOKS CONSULTED,

AND FROM WHICH EXTRACTS HAVE BEEN MADE.

"Essays on the Language, Writings and Religion of the Parsees," by Martin Haug.
"Ancient Faiths Embodied in Ancient Names," by Thomas Inman, M. D.
"Sangermano's Burmese Empire," by Tandy.
"The Rig-Veda Sanhita," Translated by Wilson and Cowell.
Legge's "Life and Teachings of Confucius."
Grote's "Plato."
"The Ten Tribes of Israel, and Mexican Antiquities," by Mrs. Simon.
"The Koran," by George Sale.
"A Voice from the Ganges."
"The Dervishes," by J. P. Brown.
"A Brief View of Greek Philosophy," by a Pariah.
"Philosophical Theories, and Philosophical Experience," by a Pariah.
The Works of Thomas Hobbes; Dugald Stewart; John Stuart Mill; Lord Macaulay; Dr. Channing; Theodore Parker; Humboldt; J. G. Fichte; and George Combe.
"The Bridgewater Treatises," by Drs. Chalmers, Whewell and others.
Bishop Colenso on the Pentateuch.
Bunsen's "God in History."
Buckle's "History of Civilization in England."
Lecky's "History of European Morals, from Augustus to Charlemagne."
Renan's "Life of Jesus."
"New Life of Jesus," by Strauss.
"The Divine Government," by Southwood Smith.
"Fellowes' Religion of the Universe."
"The Universal Church."
"Maurice's "Religions of the World."

McCausland's "Adam and the Adamites."
"Vestiges of the Natural History of Creation."
Prescott's "Conquest of Mexico;" and "of Peru."
"Essays and Reviews."
Draper's "Intellectual Development of Europe."
Mansel's "Bampton Lectures."
Froude's "Short Studies on Great Subjects.'
"Ecce Homo."
"Force and Matter," by Louis Büchner.
Lewes' "History of Philosophy."
"The State of Man before Christianity."
S. W. Hall's "Law of Impersonation."
"Discussion of the Unity, Duality and Trinity of the Godhead."
Bernard's "Cambridge Free Thoughts."
Quarterly Review on "The Talmud."
F. W. Newman's "Phases of Faith."
"What is Truth?"
Coupland's "Incentives to the Higher Life.
Leigh Hunt's "Religion of the Heart."
"The Creed of Christendom," by W. R. Greg.
"The Method of the Divine Government, by Dr. McCosh.
"Pindar," and "Cicero," in Bohn's Classical Library.
"Indigenous Races of the Earth."
Milman's "History of the Jews;" "of Christianity;" and "of Latin Christianity."
"Chips from a German Workshop," by Max Muller.
D'Aubigné's "History of the Reformation."
"Christ, and other Masters," by Archdeacon Hardwick.
Appleton's Cyclopœdia.

INDEX.

	PAGE.
PREFACE	iii
INTRODUCTORY	v

Some pretend to inspiration	1
Signs and Creeds at variance	3
Jews but little known	5
Jesus' protest only partial	7
Councils assume infallible power	9
Massacre of the Innocents	11
Ancient legends	13
Incredible statements of the Old Testament	15
Jesus tempted of the Devil	20
Divinity of Jesus not believed	21
Mythology of the Virgin Mary	23
Influence of the Printing Press	25
Progress of the Sciences	27
Infidelity no reproach	29
The Christian Heaven	31
Science undermining Theology	33
A Protest against Theologies	35
God all-powerful	37
The Teachings of the Book of Nature	39
Labor, Pain and Death, not evils	41
Man's wonderful organization	45
Instances of Instinct	47
Recuperative Powers of Nature	51
Church Method of Salvation	53
God's Method of Salvation	55
Prayer	57
Fasting injurious	59
God's Laws all-sufficient	61
None destined to endless misery	63

INDEX.

	PAGE.
Moral Evil	65
Prayer the effect of ignorance	67
The God of Moses	71
Priestcraft	73
Influence of the True Religion	75
God's care for man	77
Man's intellect expanding	79
Eternal happiness	81
The Clergy shall accept truth	83
Moral Instincts	85
It guides us unperceived	87
Good Works	89
True Basis of Religion	91
Early History of Man	93
Study of other Theologies	95
Innate promptings of the heart	97
The Devil	99
Punishment not retrospective	101
Happiness of this Life	103
Man's trust in God	105
Pain—a blessing	107
Man's individuality hereafter	109
Limited free agency	111
God's laws unchangeable	113
Supposed Saviours	115
Jesus' Second Coming	119
Man's craving for truth	121
Yearning of the human soul	123
The Trinity	125
God's Laws	127
Moral Laws	129
Conscience	131
Man's confidence in Nature	135
The Moral Law	137
Science the ally of Religion	143
Providential interference	145
Erroneous Ideas of Heaven	147
Attributes of God	149
God in Nature	151
The Divine Character	153

INDEX.

	PAGE.
No remission of penalty	155
Introduction to Bible Criticism	157
Vagueness of Prophecies	159
Supernatural inspiration incredible	161
Failure of precise predictions	163
Different Parables	165
Erroneous deductions	167
Christianity not original	171
Simplicity of True Religion	173
Christ's real teachings	175
God's evil passions	177
God likened to man corporeally	181
Blind reliance on Scripture	183
Compounding for sin	185
Adam's doom not spiritual	187
The story of the Fall of Man	189
Its inconsistencies	191
Bible account of the Fall of Man	193
Man's original condition	197
Instant change in animal life	199
Death indispensable	201
The food of animals	203
Beautiful Laws of Nature	205
God's original laws unchanged	207
Origin of the Human Race	209
Eternal Life is to be earthly	211
Salvation not spiritual	213
The World—Past, Present and Future	217
Christ's pretended Miracles	219
Some Miracles explained	221
Different Miracles	225
Jewish Tests of the Messiahship	227
The Throne of David	231
Jesus' progressive ideas	233
He becomes imperious	235
Object of Christ and Apostles	237
Priesthood naturally incensed	241
Christian Sacrifice absurd	243
Jesus repudiates it	245
The Old Testament on Sacrifice	247

INDEX.

	PAGE.
The New Testament on Sacrifice	249
Christ denounces it	253
Obscurity of the Bible	257
Sectarian recrimination the result	259
Jesus did not claim Divinity	261
His opinion of himself	263
Miracles—the means of Proof of his Divinity	265
Texts in favor of One God only	267
Further proofs	271
Jesus' idea of his Mission	275
No warrant for this idea	277
Texts disproving Jesus' Divinity	279
Jesus' teaching	281
Jesus never claimed Divinity	283
Ingenuity of the Priests	285
Character of Jesus' Precepts	287
Ananias and Sapphira	293
Rational explanations of their death	295
Threat of Eternal Punishment	297
Jesus not a Saviour	299
The Spirit of Man restless	301
Belief in Jesus	303
Jesus as a Teacher	305
No good results from the belief in the Divinity of Jesus	309
Working of Miracles	313
Jesus' teaching impracticable	315
Jesus' code visionary	319
The Arrest of Jesus	321
His Crucifixion	323
Jesus' character	325
The Prophecies in Revelations	327
The Kingdom of God in the Soul	329
The Apostles equal to Jesus	331
God the Only Saviour	333
Worship of Jesus	335
Ceremonies of the Churches	337
Jesus' teaching not uniform	339
Jesus' Second Advent	341
Salvation for all	343

APPENDIX.

	PAGE.
Zoroastrianism	1
Mohammedanism	7
Buddhism	16
The Burmese	28
The Hindoos	38
Confucianism	46
Mexico and Peru	61
The Talmud	69
Egyptian History	73
Stoicism	77
Classical Antiquity	79
Cicero	80
Pindar	81
Plato	82
Epicurus	83
Socrates	84
Xenophanes	86
Herakleitus	86
Protagorus	86
Grecian History	86
Sacred Book of the Mexicans	87
Extracts from "Popol Vuh"	87
Beliefs of the American Indians	90
Belief of the New Hollanders	91
Belief of the Icelanders	91
Christian Theology no restraint	92
Contentions of the Early Church	92
Later Crimes of the Church	95
The Crusades	102
The Persecution of the Jews	104
Albigensian War	107
Persecution of the Heretics	109
The Massacre of St. Bartholomew	112
The Spaniards in Mexico	113
The Spaniards in Peru	115
Civilization and Theology	118
Printing and Civilization	118
LIST OF BOOKS CONSULTED	121

www.ingramcontent.com/pod-product-compliance
Lightning Source LLC
Chambersburg PA
CBHW020835020526
44114CB00040B/796